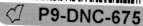 P9-DNC-675

Essentials

of **PSYCHOLOGICAL ASSESSMENT** *Series*

Every ~~~~~~~~~~~~~~ **rpret,**
and s

BF 698.8 .M5 N53 2001   Nichols, David S.

Essentials of MMPI-2 assessment.

I'd like t
ESSEN

- ❏ WAIS-III Assessment / 28295-2 / $34.95
- ❏ CAS Assessment / 29015-7 / $34.95
- ❏ Millon Inventories Assessment / 29798-4 / $34.95
- ❏ Forensic Psychological Assessment / 33186-4 / $34.95
- ❏ Bayley Scales of Infant Development-II Assessment / 32651-8 / $34.95
- ❏ Myers-Briggs Type Indicator® Assessment / 33239-9 / $34.95
- ❏ WISC-III and WPPSI-R Assessment / 34501-6 / $34.95
- ❏ Career Interest Assessment / 35365-5 / $34.95
- ❏ Rorschach Assessment / 33146-5 / $34.95
- ❏ Cognitive Assessment with KAIT and Other Kaufman Measures 38317-1 / $34.95
- ❏ MMPI-2™ Assessment / 34533-4 / $34.95
- ❏ Nonverbal Assessment / 38318-X / $34.95
- ❏ Cross-Battery Assessment / 38264-7 / $34.95
- ❏ NEPSY Assessment / 32690-9 / $34.95

Please send this order form with your payment (credit card or check) to:

JOHN WILEY & SONS, INC., Attn: J. Knott, 10th Floor
605 Third Avenue, New York, N.Y. 10158-0012

Name _____

Affiliation _____

Address _____

City/State/Zip _____

Phone ———————————— E-mail ————————————

❏ Would you like to be added to our e-mailing list?

Credit Card: ❏ MasterCard   ❏ Visa   ❏ American Express
(All orders subject to credit approval)

Card Number _____

Exp. Date ———————— Signature ————————————

TO ORDER BY PHONE, CALL 1-800-225-5945   WILEY
Refer to promo code #1-4081

To order online: www.wiley.com/essentials

Essentials of Psychological Assessment Series

Series Editors, Alan S. Kaufman and Nadeen L. Kaufman

Essentials

of MMPI-2™ Assessment

David S. Nichols

John Wiley & Sons, Inc.

NEW YORK · CHICHESTER · WEINHEIM · BRISBANE · SINGAPORE · TORONTO

This publication is designed to provide accurate and authoritative information in regard to the subject matter covered. It is sold with the understanding that the publisher is not engaged in rendering professional services. If legal, accounting, medical, psychological or any other expert assistance is required, the services of a competent professional person should be sought.

Designations used by companies to distinguish their products are often claimed as trademarks. In all instances where John Wiley & Sons, Inc. is aware of a claim, the product names appear in initial capital or all capital letters. Readers, however, should contact the appropriate companies for more complete information regarding trademarks and registration.

Library of Congress Cataloging-in-Publication Data:

Nichols, David S.

    Essentials of MMPI-2 assessment / David S. Nichols.

       p. cm. — (Essentials of psychological assessment series)

    ISBN 0-471-34533-4 (pbk. : alk. paper)

      1. Minnesota Multiphasic Personality Inventory.   I. Title: Essentials of Minnesota Multiphasic Personality Inventory-Two assessment. II. Title. III. Series.

BF698.8.M5 N53 2001

155.2'83—dc21

00-047991

DEDICATION

To the memory of my father,

Ambrose R. Nichols, Jr.

1914–2000

Curious, gracious, good, and lovely.

And who, on the eve of his last year observed,

"But, I'm not Y2K compliant."

He was the best of men.

CONTENTS

SERIES PREFACE

In the *Essentials of Psychological Assessment* series, our goal is to provide the reader with books that will deliver key practical information in the most efficient and accessible style. The series features instruments in a variety of domains, such as cognition, personality, education, and neuropsychology. For the experienced clinician, books in the series offer a concise, yet thorough way to master utilization of the continuously evolving supply of new and revised instruments, as well as a convenient method for keeping up to date on the tried-and-true measures. The novice will find here a prioritized assembly of all the information and techniques that must be at one's fingertips to begin the complicated process of individual psychological diagnosis.

Wherever feasible, visual shortcuts to highlight key points are utilized alongside systematic, step-by-step guidelines. Chapters are focused and succinct. Topics are targeted for an easy understanding of the essentials of administration, scoring, interpretation, and clinical application. Theory and research are continually woven into the fabric of each book, but always to enhance clinical inference, never to sidetrack or overwhelm. We have long been advocates of "intelligent" testing—the notion that a profile of test scores is meaningless unless it is brought to life by the clinical observations and astute detective work of knowledgeable examiners. Test profiles must be used to make a difference in the child's or adult's life, or why bother to test? We want this series to help our readers become the best intelligent testers they can be.

In *Essentials of MMPI-2™ Assessment,* the author presents a range of basic information that will enable the student and beginning test user to understand a complete range of MMPI-2 scales, the relationships among them, and a broad range of test patterns. This text also provides a level of depth suitable for experienced clinicians, as a reference and source of mnemonics that will support the routine tasks of personality assessment, diagnosis, and treatment planning. The text blends recent and past MMPI and MMPI-2 research findings with almost 60 years of clinical lore, and the author's 30 years of direct experience using the test with a very wide range of psychiatric patients and clinical problems. Its goal is to enable the examiner to approach the task of MMPI-2 interpretation with a sound appreciation of its limits and complexities, but also with a secure confidence that he or she can successfully apply the MMPI-2 in the service of understanding patients, guiding their care, and helping them toward better and more fulfilling lives.

Alan S. Kaufman, PhD, and Nadeen L. Kaufman, EdD, Series Editors
Yale University School of Medicine

One

HISTORY AND DEVELOPMENT

The road that led to the development of the Minnesota Multiphasic Personality Inventory (MMPI) was circuitous, its course passing by a number of notable psychometric failures, and one surprising success, in the area of occupational psychology. The achievement of Starke Rosecrans Hathaway, a physiological psychologist, and J. Charnley McKinley, a neuropsychiatrist, rested on 30 years of experience with self-report questionnaires created to discern personality features. The need to evaluate the fitness of military personnel to serve in the Armed Forces during World War I was a major stimulus to the development of personality questionnaires. The best-known of these was the Woodworth Personal Data Sheet (1920), which incorporated its author's *Psychoneurotic Tendencies,* a scale developed 3 years earlier in an effort to assess the vulnerability of military personnel to "shell shock," "battle fatigue," or other emotional instability. The test was a qualified success, presumably, in part, because prospective soldiers who feared combat or otherwise considered themselves on check were more than willing to acknowledge their attitudes on the test (Hathaway, 1965).

The *Psychoneurotic Tendencies* scale was adapted as one of the scales of the Bernreuter Personality Inventory (1933), which was to become hugely popular despite telling research failures that appeared almost immediately following its publication. Landis and Katz (1934) found, for example, that its scale for neuroticism was unable to discriminate neurotics from psychotics. Moreover, some of the scale's items were endorsed by members of a normal sample more frequently than by neurotics. The Achilles' heel of the Bernreuter lay in the strategy of its construction. The composition of the test items was guided by rational considerations applied to textbooks or case histories on the assumption that neurotics, for example, would respond to the items as expert opinion suggested they should. The work of Landis and Katz (1934) and others served to show that neurotics, among others, could be somewhat perverse in this regard.

The Humm-Wadsworth Temperament Scale (1935) was the first personality questionnaire to use the actual responses of psychiatric patients to determine the direction in which items should be scored and their suitability for scale development. It was also the first inventory to attempt to model a specific theory of personality, that of psychiatrist Aaron Rosanoff. The Humm-Wadsworth contained 318 items and provided scores for seven scales: *Normal, Hysteroid, Manic, Depressive, Autistic, Paranoid,* and *Epileptoid.* The item assignments for each scale were based on the difference between the item's frequency of endorsement among a group of patients judged high on the trait, and a comparison group of normals. For whatever reason, the test didn't catch on in clinical settings, but it became popular for use in industry (Goldberg, 1971). The method of contrasted groups was not discovered by Humm and Wadsworth. It had been known since at least the early 1920s and had been used to conspicuous advantage by E. K. Strong in the development of the Strong Vocational Interest Blank (SVIB; 1927). Strong had built his interest inventory by requiring that the items on his scales discriminate between occupational groups (e.g., lawyers) and "men-in-general."

As Hathaway began to develop the MMPI, he was aware of the criticisms of the Bernreuter and of the rational approach to inventory construction in general. He also knew both of the methods used to develop the SVIB, and of the success of this inventory in practice. Finally, Hathaway knew of the Humm-Wadsworth, which figured in his first publication in the field of clinical psychology (1939), and from which he borrowed about a quarter of his MMPI items.

It might be supposed that the method of contrasted groups appealed only to Hathaway's scientific scruples, but this is far from the case. Hathaway was a tinkerer, an inventor, a builder of gadgetry and apparatus. He was by temperament a thoroughgoing pragmatist with a deep distrust of theory and an abiding belief in practical experience. The method of contrasted groups provided Hathaway a practical means of avoiding theory and sidestepping rational or intuitive guidance in the selection of the items for the MMPI clinical scales. Hathaway did not pretend to know how different kinds of patients would respond to his items. The method of contrasted groups allowed him a satisfactory way of finding out: It allowed him to ask them.

There was another advantage to this method that was not wasted on Hathaway. He knew that the previous rationally developed inventories had failed at least in part because their developers' attention had wandered from the central question of *validity*. By relying on the method of contrasted groups, Hathaway required items to surmount a validity hurdle from the beginning: Each item had to demonstrate construct relevant variance by concretely discriminating between groups. This was no guarantee that the item would survive subsequent challenges to its validity. For example, it could fail on cross-validation to discriminate the same group of criterion cases from a different group of normal controls; or a similar but separately constituted group of criterion cases from the same group of normal controls; or in comparisons in which both the criterion cases and normal controls involved previously untested subjects. The advantage of the method was that the items exposed to such subsequent challenges had achieved at least some initial, concrete, discriminative advantage, a claim no rationally derived item could make.

Hathaway intended the MMPI to achieve a "sampling of behavior of significance to the psychiatrist," and it was this aim that determined the range of clinical scales to be developed for the inventory. From an initial pool of more than 1,000 items drawn from psychiatric textbooks, guides for the mental status examination, and previously published tests, Hathaway and McKinley winnowed the pool to 504 items divided into twenty-five content areas. These included items related to general medical and neurological symptoms, political and social attitudes, affective and cognitive symptoms, and fears and obsessions; items implicating family, educational, and occupational experience; and a set of items to reveal an overly virtuous self-presentation on the inventory. An additional 55 items thought to be related to masculinity-femininity were later added, and 9 items were subsequently deleted to achieve the final pool of 550 items.

The item format chosen was the first-person declarative sentence, written with simplified wording based on contemporary word-frequency tables. Brevity, clarity, and simplicity were occasionally given precedence over grammatical precision. Common English slang and idioms were used but esoteric or specialized language was avoided. Responses were limited to *True, False,* or *Cannot Say.*

The group of normals selected to contrast with the pathological criterion groups were 724 University of Minnesota hospital and outpatient clinic visitors between the ages of 16 and 65 (hereafter referred to as the "Minnesota Normals"). Each affirmed that he or she was not currently under a physician's care for the treatment of any illness. The demographics of this group of normals corresponded well to 1930 census values for Minnesota regarding age, sex, and marital status (Colligan, Osborne, Swenson, & Offord, 1983). According to Dahlstrom, Welsh, and Dahlstrom (1972, p. 8), "In 1940, such a Minnesota normal adult was about 35 years old, was married, lived in a small town or rural area, had eight years of general schooling, and worked at a skilled or semi-skilled trade (or was married to a man with such an occupational level)."

First published in 1942, the MMPI was an immediate success. By the end of April 1943, 230 copies had been sold for use in clinics, correctional facilities, corporations, and universities, generating enough revenue to more than cover the costs of initial publication. The Psychological Corporation, which had turned down the test when it was first submitted, became its licensed distributor in 1943, by which time the ninth and last of the clinical scales, *Hypomania* (*Ma*), was ready to be included in the revised *Manual* (Hathaway & McKinley, 1943) and test materials. A manual supplement introducing a booklet form of the test as an alternative to the original box form was published in 1946. This supplement also introduced the *K* scale—which thereafter took its place next to *F* on the standard profile form—as well as the practice of adding fractions of *K* to suppress some of the scale score variances related to response style. The MMPI arrived in its final form in the 1951 *Manual* with the addition of the *Social Introversion* scale (*Si*), the last of the standard clinical scales. Rapid Reference 1.1 summarizes the MMPI-2 Standard Validity and Clinical scales.

The success of the MMPI was measured not only by its sales and distribution, but also by the amount of research interest it attracted. By the mid-1950s, the MMPI literature had accumulated 700 references, and by 1965 this number had expanded to more than 2,000. In the next decade, the latter number would triple. Over time, the success of the MMPI in the United States drew the interest of psychologists and psychiatrists from countries around the world, eventually culminating in scores of translations for use in dozens of countries.

The passage of time also exposed weaknesses in the test. Some that were present from the beginning had been allowed to go uncorrected; others became evident only gradually, with the accumulation of research, the march of cultural and demographic changes within the United States, and the introduction of

≡ Rapid Reference 1.1

Summary of Standard MMPI-2 Validity and Clinical Scales

Validity Scales

L   *Lie.* Assesses naive attempts to place oneself in a morally and culturally favorable light by denying moral imperfections.

F   *Infrequency.* Assesses the tendency to claim highly unusual attitudes and behaviors as a function of severe psychopathology; a subject's seeking to place himself or herself in an unfavorable light; or a subject's difficulties completing the inventory (e.g., reading problems or random or careless responding).

K   *Correction.* Assesses the tendency to control and limit the disclosure of distress, discomfort, and problems relating to others. Fractions of K are added as a correction to Scales *1, 4, 7, 8,* and *9* to discourage false negative/false positive scores on these scales.

Clinical Scales

1. *Hypochondriasis (Hs).* Measures the tendency to manifest physical symptoms as an expression of emotional discomfort, to be preoccupied with one's health, and to reject nonmedical (i.e., psychological) explanations for such symptoms.

2. *Depression (D).* Measures aspects of symptomatic depression: dysphoria, distress, pessimism, low morale, inhibition, intropunitiveness, physical discomfort and vegetative symptoms, and problems in thinking.

3. *Hysteria (Hy).* Measures the tendency to develop physical symptoms under stress, to experience pain, and to deny social friction or discord with others.

4. *Psychopathic Deviate (Pd).* Measures alienation, social disinhibition, and the tendency to come into conflict with family, authorities, and others through rebellion, exploitation, misconduct, poorly developed conscience, and the lack of internalized moral standards.

5. *Masculinity-Femininity (Mf).* Measures broad patterns of interests, activities, attitudes, and sentiments that tend to follow gender stereotypes.

6. *Paranoia (Pa).* Measures personal/moral rigidity, interpersonal sensitivity, resentment, and ideas of being misunderstood, mistreated, persecuted, or controlled by others, and the tendency to construe the actions, intentions, and motives of others as unfair, degrading, or hostile.

(continued)

7. *Psychasthenia (Pt)*. Measures the tendency to express stresses through tension, anxiety, apprehensiveness, worry, phobias, obsessions, rumination, compulsions, and fears of losing control, with willful and inflexible efforts to control such symptoms.

8. *Schizophrenia (Sc)*. Measures severe alienation, self-contempt, apathy, cognitive disruption, inertia, feelings of unreality, alien impulses, and motor and sensory impairment.

9. *Hypomania (Ma)*. Measures a rapid and energetic personal tempo, hyperarousal, hyperactivity, stimulation-seeking, euphoria, imperviousness, undercontrol, and rebellious impulses (high scores), versus lethargy, slowness, submissiveness, vulnerability, scrupulousness, and occasionally, depression (low scores).

10. *Social Introversion (Si)*. Measures introversion, shyness, social anxiety, social timidity and awkwardness, and social avoidance (high scores), versus extroversion, outgoingness, social comfort and skill, social intrepidity, and social stimulation-seeking (low scores).

previously unforeseen applications. The chief chronic inadequacy of the MMPI stemmed from Hathaway's need to base his test norms on the original sample of 724 normals that had served as the primary nonpathological reference group for the development of the eight *basic* clinical scales (i.e., Scales *1, 2, 3, 4, 6, 7, 8,* and *9*); these basic clinical scales, plus Scales *5* and *0,* comprise the *standard* clinical scales of the MMPI/MMPI-2. The repeated use of these subjects as contrasts for Hathaway's pathological criterion groups deprived those groups, in a statistical sense, of their "normal" levels of abnormality. Hathaway and McKinley wanted to collect data from a large additional sample of normal subjects on which a proper set of norms could be based, but were prevented from doing so by a lack of funds. They therefore had to make do with their tainted sample for the purpose of establishing the MMPI norms. The inadequacy of these original norms was later made strikingly clear (Colligan et al., 1983; Pancoast & Archer, 1989), as the results of research conducted around the country repeatedly found the scores of newly collected normal samples to hover around *T*-55. There were other reasons for newly collected normals to score higher than Hathaway's normals. For the most part, the newer subjects were not excluded from samples because they were under a doctor's care at the time of testing, as Hathaway's subjects had been. Another factor was the tendency for later test administrators to discourage the use of the *Cannot Say (?)* response category, thereby increasing the number of responses that could contribute to scale elevations (the original normals had not been discouraged from leaving items unmarked). Perhaps anticipating this consequence of the hypernormal bias of the original normative sample, Hathaway set the optimal boundary for distinguishing nonpathological from pathological elevations at a T-score of 70, two standard deviations from the mean. The wisdom of this choice will become evident later when we discuss the MMPI-2.

In the postwar period, and with the passage of the GI Bill, the average educational attainment of the U.S. population began to rise sharply. The original Minnesota Normals had averaged an eighth-grade level of education; by 1970, the average years of education had soared to 12 and college enrollment levels were swelling. The population was also becoming more ethnically and culturally diverse, and more women were entering the labor force. With the passage of time, the colloquial language of some of the items had become dated and was at risk of becoming obscure, such as references to "sleeping powders," "streetcars," and "drop-the-handkerchief." Other items contained grammatical errors that were overdue for correction, and still others contained references to cultural activities that had become less familiar. With the expansion of the MMPI beyond the hospital and clinic to applications in employment screening and the forensic arena came increasing complaints about sexist wording and items dealing with religious matters, eliminatory functioning, and sexual adjustment that were deemed to be intrusive or offensive. A number of areas of item content were thought to be underrepresented in an instrument that had already begun to be more frequently applied to the assessment of substance abuse, suicide risk, and treatment planning. During the 1970s it became increasingly clear that the time for restandardizing the MMPI had come. The copyright holder, the University of Minnesota Press, appointed a committee to undertake this work.

RESTANDARDIZATION LEADING TO THE MMPI-2

In preparation for the restandardization, the committee developed a new form of the MMPI, *MMPI-AX*, containing all of the original MMPI items, less 16 items that repeated earlier items on the original MMPI, plus 154 newly written items. Subjects between the ages of 18 and 84 were recruited by newspaper ads and solicited using directories and mailing lists from Minnesota (21.6% of total sample), North Carolina (18.8%), Ohio (17.3%), Pennsylvania (11.7%), Virginia

(9.7%), California (9.4%), and Washington (8.3%). Subsamples of Native Americans from a federal reservation in Washington state (2.2%) and military personnel on active duty from several US bases (0.92%) completed the restandardization sample. Unlike the Minnesota Normals, restandardization subjects were not disqualified for being under the care of a physician or mental health professional. Subjects were paid and were required to provide basic demographic data on sex, age, ethnicity, attained education, marital status, and income, and to complete a Recent Life Events Survey (*LES;* Holmes & Rahe, 1967), in addition to completing the MMPI-AX. A small proportion of the sample (111 women and 82 men) was retested an average of eight and a half days later to provide preliminary data on temporal stability. Marital couples or unmarried partners (832 women, 823 men) sharing a household for at least one year completed the Spanier Dyadic Adjustment Scale (Spanier, 1976) and provided ratings on their spouses or partners using a modified form of the Katz Adjustment Scales (Katz, 1968). The final restandardization sample of 2,600 (1,462 women, 1,138 men) remained from a larger sample of about 2,900 subjects, with the data from about 300 subjects removed because of omitted demographic or *LES* information, excessive (> 39) item omissions on the MMPI-AX, or excessively (> 19) deviant scores on the *F* scale or on an experimental scale that was devised to detect highly deviant responding on the second half of the test.

The restandardization sample was made to conform as closely as possible to 1980 census data, excluding geographic distribution. In terms of marital status, income distribution, and ethnic diversity this goal was largely met, but with some underrepresentation of Hispanics and Asian Americans. There was also some underrepresentation of subjects at the extremes of the age distribution, particularly for younger (< 20) men and older (> 70) women. However, the sample grossly exceeded census estimates for educational level and occupational status. Schinka and LaLone (1997) drew a subsample of 1,000 subjects from the restandardization sample stratified in accordance with census projections and 1995 educational statistics for age, gender, ethnicity, and educational attainment. They found that differences on the standard validity and clinical scales, the content scales, and the supplementary scales between the full restandardization sample and the census-matched subsample were virtually nonexistent. Thus, there do not appear to be large sources of systematic bias in the restandardization sample that would lead to significant errors of measurement or interpretation in most situations. This does not mean that the MMPI-2 can be assumed to be free of biasing factors in all situations. Mere correspondence to census values cannot guarantee that the MMPI-2 will provide a reliable normative standard against which the profiles of atypical samples can be interpreted. For example, the profiles of poor, inner-city African Americans, Native Americans in most parts of the United States, itinerant Hispanic laborers, or even homeless or geographically isolated Caucasians may deviate significantly from the restandardization norms in ways that may lead to overpathologizing or underpathologizing the interpretations derived from them.

The restandardization of the MMPI consumed almost a decade, ending when the MMPI-2 was published (Butcher, Dahlstrom, Graham, Tellegen, & Kaemmer, 1989). Rapid Reference 1.2 provides publication information.

≡ Rapid Reference 1.2

Minnesota Multiphasic Personality Inventory–2 (MMPI-2)

Authors: Starke R. Hathaway, PhD, and J. Charnley McKinley, MD. Restandardized by James N. Butcher, PhD, W. Grant Dahlstrom, PhD, John R. Graham, PhD, Auke Tellegen, PhD, and Beverly Kaemmer

Publication date: 1989

Copyright holder: University of Minnesota Press

What the test measures: Psychopathology and normal/abnormal personality functioning

Age range: 18 years and above

Administration time: 1–2 hours

Qualifications of examiners: Graduate-level training in psychodiagnostic assessment. Purchase of MMPI materials requires an "A Level" qualification (licensed mental health professionals).

Publisher and distributor: National Computer Systems (NCS)
5605 Green Circle Drive
Minnetonka, MN 55343
Phone: (800) 627-7271

Products and services: Manual, test materials, and scoring and/or interpretation services, including on-site scoring, are available from NCS. Alternate computer scoring, with or without interpretation, is available from Caldwell Report, 1545 Sawtelle Boulevard, Los Angeles, CA 90025, phone (310) 478-3133.

SIMILARITIES AND DIFFERENCES BETWEEN THE MMPI AND MMPI-2

Apart from the deletion of a few items that previous test-takers had identified as objectionable (mostly items with religious, sexual, bowel, or bladder content), from scales F (four items), Hs (one), D (three), Mf (four), and Si (one), the standard validity and clinical scales of the MMPI are unchanged in the MMPI-2, assuring substantial continuity with the research and clinical literature built up over the previous half-century. The revised instrument contains 567 items, of which none are repeated within the instrument, versus the MMPI's 566 items, of which 16 were repeated. One hundred seven of the MMPI-2 items are new; 90 were dropped from the original item pool. With very few exceptions, any scale developed for the MMPI can be adapted for use with the MMPI-2. The most common exceptions are scales with religious item content, because 16 of these items were among those dropped from the MMPI-2. Sixty-eight of the items retained from the MMPI were rewritten to correct grammar, eliminate sexist language, or reduce ambiguity. None of the changes materially affected the performance of these items (Ben-Porath & Butcher, 1989). The scale level factor structure of the MMPI-2 is essentially identical to that of the MMPI.

The Harris-Lingoes subscales for six of the eight basic scales were essentially unchanged for the MMPI-2, although the subscales for Scale 4 (Pd), which had originally included some items not on Pd itself, no longer include these items. The 13 Wiggins content scales for the MMPI have been replaced by 15 MMPI-2 content scales. The Koss-Butcher and Lachar-Wrobel critical items were retained, with augmentation of two of the Koss-Butcher item sets (those dealing with depression/suicide and alcohol abuse) by some of the new MMPI-2 items. Several new scales have been developed for the MMPI-2, including five validity or response-style indicators, three subscales for Scale 0 (Si) to replace the six Serkownek (1975) subscales, two gender-role scales, two posttraumatic stress disorder (PTSD) scales, two alcohol/substance abuse scales (with a revision of the MacAndrew addiction scale), seven Martin-Finn subscales for Scale 5 (Mf) to replace the earlier six Serkownek Mf subscales, a marital distress scale, and five scales to assess abnormal personality. All of these scales will be discussed in detail in later chapters.

Scores for all of the scales of the MMPI were transformed onto the *T* distribution to enable comparison between scales with different numbers of items and with different means and variances. The standard linear *T*-score formula did not permit a direct comparison of percentile ranks because each scale had its own characteristic skewness and kurtosis. The restandardization committee adjusted the distributional characteristics of the basic clinical and content scales to permit *T*-scores to be represented as percentile equivalents.

The new uniform *T*-score distributions were designed by first creating a composite distribution for each scale set, then mapping each scale in each set (basic and content) onto its own composite distribution (Tellegen & Ben-Porath, 1992). In this way, percentile-rank uniformity among scales could be achieved without distortion of the characteristic positive skew of these scales.

Finally, unlike the original normals, the restandardization subjects were actively discouraged from leaving items unmarked, so that their average *Cannot Say (?)* score was lower than that of the Minnesota Normals, thereby reducing the distorting influence of omitted items on MMPI-2 mean scale scores. Hathaway had set a fifth-grade reading level as the minimum competency for taking the MMPI; subsequent research on reading skills showed that the difficulty of many of the items was well beyond this level of reading competency. As a result of studies of the difficulty of the MMPI-2 items carried out as a part of the restandardization, the authors set an eighth-grade level of reading proficiency as the minimum for the MMPI-2.

ESSENTIAL REFERENCES FOR THE MMPI-2

The *MMPI-2: Manual for Administration and Scoring* (Butcher, Dahlstrom, Graham, Tellegen, & Kaemmer, 1989) is the most basic reference, containing the publisher's guidelines for use and extensive psychometric information about the test. Many important references on the test, including the original articles on

DON'T FORGET

The expression *basic* clinical scales refers to the scales developed using hospitalized patient criterion groups, Scales 1–4 and 6–9. The *standard* clinical scales are Scales 1–0; that is, the basic clinical scales and Scales 5 and 0.

scale development, are collected in *Basic Sources on the MMPI-2* (Butcher, 2000). Among several guides and manuals for the MMPI-2, the most comprehensive are *The MMPI-2: An Interpretive Manual* (Greene, 2000) and *Psychological Assessment with the MMPI-2* (Friedman, Lewak, Nichols, & Webb, 2001).

🪶 TEST YOURSELF 🪶

I. The primary developer of the MMPI, Starke Hathaway, was a

   (a) clinical psychologist.

   (b) physiological psychologist.

   (c) social psychologist.

   (d) psychoanalyst.

2. The test whose purpose and development were most similar to those of the MMPI was

   (a) the Woodworth Personal Data Sheet.

   (b) the Bernreuter Personality Inventory.

   (c) the Humm-Wadsworth Temperament Scale.

   (d) the Strong Vocational Interest Blank.

3. The method of contrasted groups used in the development of the MMPI was the invention of Hathaway and McKinley. True or False?

4. The success of the MMPI following its initial publication was virtually immediate. True or False?

5. The last of the original 13 validity and clinical scales to be added to the MMPI was

   (a) Scale *K*.

   (b) Scale *5 (Mf)*.

   (c) Scale *9 (Ma)*.

   (d) Scale *0 (Si)*.

6. The MMPI-2 restandardization sample tended to match 1980 census values for

   (a) marital status but not educational level.

   (b) educational level but not income distribution.

   (c) income distribution but not marital status.

   (d) educational level but not ethnic diversity.

   (e) b and d.

7. Uniform *T*-scores were designed to correct for the characteristic positive skew of the basic clinical scales. True or False?

Answers: I. b; 2. c; 3. False; 4. True; 5. d; 6. a; 7. False

Two

ADMINISTRATION

The MMPI-2 is intended for use with adults ages 18 and older. For adolescents, a separate form of the MMPI, the *MMPI-A,* is generally preferred in order to take advantage of the norms available for this age group. In some instances, depending on the clinical questions to be addressed, the MMPI-2 may be administered to certain late adolescents if reading comprehension levels are adequate, with the understanding that such use falls outside the normal guidelines advocated by the publisher and outside the adult test norms. For example, late adolescents who are emancipated (whether employed or in school) and living outside the parental home may have more in common with young adults than with adolescent peers. Readers should consult the MMPI-2 *Manual* for the copyright holder's recommendations on administration and scoring.

ESTABLISHING RAPPORT AND ENGENDERING MOTIVATION

Establishing suitable rapport is an outcome of the total context of testing, of which the relationship between patient and clinician is only a part. Because of the test's self-report format, most patients view the MMPI-2 as an opportunity to communicate with the clinician. To the extent that good rapport between patient and clinician can be established prior to testing, the interest of the patient in candidly communicating his or her feelings and attitudes is likely to converge with the clinician's interest in a reliable and valid appraisal of the patient's personality functioning. Each aspect of the test situation stands to enhance or degrade rapport and thus to influence the patient's motivation to follow the test instructions and to produce results that are accurate, informative, and useful to both parties.

CAUTION

The clinician must strive to provide an environment for administration that is conducive to a favorable testing outcome.

HOW TO ADMINISTER THE MMPI-2

The paper-and-pencil format of the MMPI-2 may create an impression of greater simplicity of administration than is warranted. The MMPI-2 answer sheet contains a standard set of instructions that the clinician must review with the patient. These instructions provide the patient with clear but minimal guidance for responding to the test items; they do not, and are not intended to, influence motivational set—that is, the group of testing-related attitudes and experiences the examinee brings to the inventory. Chapter 5 will discuss in greater detail how the production of valid and reliable findings from the MMPI-2 is highly dependent on the examinee's willingness to become involved in the task in a manner that engages him or her as a stakeholder in the outcome of the accuracy of the assessment. Rapid Reference 2.1 presents a flexible set of steps for administering the MMPI-2.

═Rapid Reference 2.1

Steps for Administering the MMPI-2

- Obtaining informed consent
- Describing the clinician's ethical obligations to the examinee*
- Appealing for questions (the clinician may invite questions at any step, as may be indicated)*
- Making explicit the clinician's relationship to any third parties (e.g., court, patient's psychotherapist, etc.) to clarify the clinician's obligations to persons or agencies other than the examinee
- Providing a practical overview of the assessment, including location(s), date(s), and time(s) for testing and report preparation, access to the report, and arrangements for feedback and fees
- Introduction of the MMPI-2
- Assessment of sensory and motor barriers to completing the MMPI-2
- Assessment of reading comprehension
- The test session
- Post-test review

*Optional

Obtaining Informed Consent

The clinician must inform the patient of the advantages and disadvantages of cooperating with the assessment, including how the information derived will be used, and

with whom and for what purposes it may be shared. Where possible, the clinician should describe the conditions under which the test results may influence decisions about the patient's treatment or disposition, and which specific decisions may be so influenced.

Clinician's Obligations to the Examinee

Clinicians may also wish to describe their ethical and professional obligations to the patient with regard to the confidentiality and security of test results as well as to privilege, particularly when these issues may have a bearing on informed consent, or when the results are likely to be a factor in a present or anticipated legal proceeding.

Appeals for Questions

Next, clinicians should encourage patients to raise any questions about the purposes of the assessment. Such questions should be answered fully, and clinicians should invite patients to ask any others they may have throughout the assessment process.

Clinician's Relationship to Third Parties

Although not always possible, it is desirable that the relationship between clinician and patient be one in which the former is the agent of the latter. When this is not possible, clinicians should indicate clearly the extent to which they are able to act in the patient's interest, including the limits to such action. For example, in assessments undertaken under forensic auspices, such as in child custody or "aid and assist" evaluations, the clinician may be acting as an agent of a protective services agency or the court, rather than for the patient. Clinicians are obligated to be explicit about such relationships and their consequences, just as they must remain personally and professionally impartial in their analyses of test data produced in evaluations.

Providing an Overview of the Assessment

The examinee should be provided a broad overview of the practical aspects of the assessment, including: its steps and overall duration; the location(s) where testing and feedback will occur; scheduling arrangements for testing; the amount of time required to complete testing; the time required to score and interpret the test results and prepare the written report; who will have access to the report; the scheduling arrangements for feedback to the examinee about the results of testing; who will provide the feedback; who is responsible for the clinician's fee; and billing arrangements. If the assessment clinician is providing service in cooperation with the patient's primary therapist, the patient must be informed of the limits of the assessor's service. Recently Finn (1995) developed a sophisticated model for "therapeutic assessment" that specifically engages patients in the assessment process by eliciting questions to which they would like the test results to speak, and arranges for the assessment to be structured in a way that maximizes its therapeutic benefits.

Introducing the MMPI-2

The patient should be briefly introduced to the MMPI-2: its history, purposes, and popularity for understanding the kinds of problems for which the patient is in (or seeking to be in) treatment. This introduction should include its scientific development, its current uses, and the confidence placed in its results by clinicians of widely differing experience, training, and theoretical backgrounds. The purpose here is to increase patients' confidence that their time is being used wisely; that the test is a respected diagnostic aid; that its construction was guided by scientific principles; that they will be taking a test that millions of others have taken before; that the results of the MMPI-2 have helped to guide clinicians in the direction of more rapid (and economical) understanding of patient problems and the selection of more effective treatment procedures; that the test has helped patients around the world to understand themselves and their problems better; and that this better understanding has often led to greater insight and confidence regarding their eventual resolution and recovery.

Assessing Barriers to Completing the MMPI-2

The clinician must assess the presence and impact of any sensory or motor barriers to the accurate completion of the MMPI-2, including decreased visual acuity or motor control, restlessness, tremor, and similar factors that may affect performance. Reading glasses or other corrective lenses should be worn if needed. If the patient is prescribed a hearing aid it should be worn if an audiotaped administration (discussed shortly in "Alternative Test Settings") is contemplated. Clinicians should also be alert to acute states such as alcohol intoxication that may affect the assessment. In such cases, testing may have to be reconsidered or postponed until the conditions likely to interfere with an accurate test protocol can be resolved.

> **C A U T I O N**
>
> Although most conventional psychiatric symptoms will not unduly disrupt MMPI-2 performance, certain organic conditions and toxic states, such as alcohol intoxication or withdrawal, may severely distort the test findings.

Assessing Reading Comprehension

The clinician must also assess the patient's ability to read and understand the MMPI-2 items. An adequate level of reading proficiency cannot be assumed solely on the basis of grades completed in school. If this information is not already known, it may be gathered unobtrusively from registration information forms and so forth. Although the *Manual* recommends an eighth-grade reading level, many of the items on Scale *9 (Ma)* require a ninth-grade level of reading comprehension. In assessing reading comprehension it is helpful to have more detailed information about the patient's educational background (e.g., grades, favorite subjects) and current reading habits. Assessing comprehension by such informal means is less likely to cause the patient embarrassment. In some cases it will be necessary to assess reading comprehension directly by means of a standardized reading or achievement test, or by having the patient read and explain sample items at several levels of difficulty. In addition, some patients may have special difficulty with items made double-negative by the *False* response (e.g., I do not always . . .), and the clinician may wish to assess the patient's comprehension of items of this specific type. Samples both of

≡Rapid Reference 2.2

Test Items for Reading Comprehension

Low Difficulty Items (Grade Levels 2–6)
Items 8, 14, 20, 51, and 91

Average Difficulty Items (Grades 7–9)
Items 122, 297, and 106

High Difficulty Items (Grades 10–11)
Items 263 and 425

Double Negatives
Items 114, 226, and 445

items varying in difficulty from easiest to most difficult and of some double-negative items are presented in Rapid Reference 2.2. The clinician may reemphasize to the patient that the MMPI-2 results must be both valid and reliable if they are to be of maximum benefit to the patient.

Clinicians should use extra caution when they discover problems with reading comprehension. Because the written instructions have been found to be more difficult than the test items themselves (Dahlstrom, Archer, Hopkins, Jackson, & Dahlstrom, 1994), the instructions may require more thorough explanation and review when uncertainties regarding reading comprehension remain.

The Test Session

Providing Demographic Information

At the time the instructions are read and discussed with the patient, the identifying and demographic information on the answer sheet may be completed.

Exhortation to Answer All Items

The clinician should encourage the patient to respond to all of the items, even those that don't appear to apply to them. He or she may reassure the patient that marking such items will not distort the test results, but rather will increase the likelihood of an accurate and useful test protocol.

The 370-Item Abbreviated Form

The examiner can obtain complete scores for the standard validity and clinical scales, the Wiener and Harmon *Subtle* and *Obvious* subscales, the Harris-Lingoes and Scale *0* subscales, and Keane's *Post-Traumatic Stress Disorder* scale *(PK)* from the first 370 items of the inventory. Although the abbreviated format is not recommended because it prevents access to reliable scores on the content, supplementary, and other scales, on some occasions the patient may be unable or unwilling to provide a complete set of item responses. In these cases, responses to items 1 to 370 can provide useful clinical information.

The Physical Setting for Testing

The test-administration setting will also convey the importance the clinician attaches to the accurate completion of the MMPI-2. Signs that the clinician has considered the patient's comfort and convenience in creating a physical space conducive to completing the MMPI-2 can enhance both the patient's confidence in the assessment process and the rapport between patient and clinician. The testing area should be clean, adequately insulated for comfortable temperature and sound, and free of distractions. The typical patient will feel most at ease in a chair positioned at a table or desk. The writing surface should be ample, free of clutter, and well-lit. A few extra sharpened pencils should be provided, along with access to water or other beverage if the patient desires. He or she should be shown where the toilet facilities are if needed, and where to find the clinician or a designee to answer questions or assist with word definitions. Such definitions may be given on request but should come from a standard dictionary. Some patients will request definitions for indefinite quantifiers such as "at times," "frequently," "many," "most," "much," "often," or "usually"; in such cases, the clinician should avoid giving a definition and instead indicate that the patient's own interpretation of the expression is what matters. For example, a once-a-week occurrence may be viewed as frequent by some patients, whereas others may view a twice-a-week occurrence as infrequent. Except in the case of group administration, the clinician or designee should be readily accessible without being physically present in the immediate testing area to avoid distracting the patient and influencing the test results.

Alternative Test Settings

The ideal conditions for testing described previously, however desirable, cannot always be provided; however, both research and clinical experience have shown that the MMPI-2 is robust across a wide array of variations in administration. Group-administration formats that allow for the simultaneous testing of several patients are acceptable, provided that enough distance separates examinees to guarantee privacy and discourage interaction. Such formats require closer supervision, however. For patients with inadequate reading comprehension or subnormal intelligence (i.e., IQ < 80–85), an audiotape recorded format is available; standard equipment needed is a recorder with a volume control and pause button that the patient operates. This format requires closer supervision to assist with rewinding and relocating particular items and ensuring that the patient maintains correspondence between the item numbers on the tape and those on the answer sheet. A final format for administering the MMPI-2 is the computer, using software that presents instructions and test items on a monitor for responses entered via keyboard. Computer administration has the advantages of shorter administration times, fewer item omissions, and immediate scoring once the inventory has been completed. Although switching formats (e.g., audiotape to booklet, booklet to computer, etc.) once testing has begun may be inconvenient for the administrator, the publisher does not prohibit doing so. The MMPI-2 need not be administered by the clinician who will provide test feedback or the written report—with adequate training and supervision, psychometricians or clerical/secretarial staff can handle all of the routine administration tasks.

Administration Time

The amount of time required to complete the MMPI-2 is 1 to 2 hours for most people, but some will require much more time and occasionally even multiple sittings. Among psychiatric inpatients, testing times in the 3- to 4-hour range are common, if not routine. Timeliness in completing the inventory should always be secondary to accuracy. Especially with highly disturbed patients, frequent rest breaks and even dividing the test session across successive days may be needed to get the most useful results. Patients' emotional states and attitudes are always in a state of flux, and it cannot be assumed that a test result that has taken a week to produce will be the same as one that might have been produced within a couple of hours. Nevertheless, it is almost always preferable to be flexible about allowing as much time as necessary to obtain a valid protocol, not least for the reason that such flexibility conveys the clinician's interest in test results that accurately reflect the patient's symptoms and situation.

Test Security

It is important that during MMPI-2 administration the clinician maintains control over access to the test materials and to the examinee while testing is in progress. Test materials should not leave the oversight of the test administrator, and interaction with persons other than the test administrator is to be strongly discouraged during the test session.

Post-Test Review

At the conclusion of administration, the clinician may invite the patient to report any reactions to the experience of testing, and should again offer the opportunity to ask questions. The answer sheet may be examined at this point for any unmarked or double-marked items *(Cannot Say[?])* and the patient given a final appeal to respond to them.

 TEST YOURSELF

1. **The guidelines for administration offered by the test publisher support the use of the MMPI-2 for adolescents under age 18, provided that they are emancipated.** True or False?

2. **The MMPI-2 is typically viewed by the examinee as an opportunity to**
   (a) have his or her problems accurately diagnosed.
   (b) communicate with the clinician.
   (c) search for any and all potential problems.
   (d) help the examinee understand himself or herself.
   (e) qualify for insurance coverage.

3. **Which characteristics of the MMPI-2 may be discussed with examinees prior to testing?**
   (a) Its history and uses
   (b) The names of the validity scales but not of the clinical scales
   (c) Its popularity
   (d) a and b
   (e) a and c

4. **As long as the instructions are read and understood, the examinee's level of rapport with the clinician is unimportant for valid assessment with the MMPI-2.** True or False?

5. **The examinee's level of reading comprehension need never be assessed using formal reading tests.** True or False?

6. **The examinee should be encouraged to respond to all of the test items, even those that don't seem to apply to him or her.** True or False?

7. **The use of the 370-item abbreviated form of the MMPI-2 will limit the results to scores on only the 13 original validity and clinical scales.** True or False?

(continued)

8. **The MMPI-2 is robust under a wide variety of variations in administration.** True or False?

9. **The recommendations of the publisher require that once the examinee has commenced testing under one format of administration—whether booklet, audiotape, or computer—the test must be completed under these conditions, even if the examinee wishes to switch to another format.** True or False?

10. **Administration time for the MMPI-2 may not exceed 4 hours and the test must be completed in a single sitting.** True or False?

11. **Provided that the examinee is trustworthy and rapport with the clinician is good, the MMPI-2 may be sent home with the examinee for completion, but must be returned promptly to the clinician.** True or False?

Answers: 1. False; 2. b; 3. e; 4. False; 5. True; 6. True; 7. False; 8. True; 9. False; 10. False; 11. False

Three

SCORING

One of the strengths of structured personality inventories like the MMPI-2 is their objective scoring. At no stage of scoring is human judgment required to derive or tabulate scores. The scoring of the MMPI-2 is a completely mechanical process of counting the items endorsed for each scale and converting the raw scores thus derived to T-scores. The T-distribution is a fixed standardized distribution having the properties of a mean of 50 and a standard deviation of 10. The transformation of scale scores onto the T-distribution renders the examinee's performances on the numerous MMPI-2 scales comparable, despite their differing means, variances, and numbers of items. The scoring process for the MMPI-2 requires a fixed sequence of steps, which are given in Rapid Reference 3.1.

SCORING METHODS

Because the scoring format is entirely objective, the scoring procedures for the MMPI-2 can be fully automated via computer. Computer scoring services are available from National Computer Systems (NCS) and from Caldwell Report (see Rapid Reference 1.2). NCS also provides special equipment and answer sheets that enable scanning as a means of data input for computer scoring.

If preferred, hand-scoring materials are also available from NCS, enabling raw scores to be taken from the answer sheet using a template for each scale (including separate templates for Scale 5 for each gender), then transferred, corrected, and plotted onto standard profiles of T-scores for each gender. Given the large number of routinely scored scales, hand-scoring the MMPI-2 is not only more cumbersome and time consuming than computer scoring, it is also subject to errors of counting, transcription, correction, plotting, and profiling. For these reasons, most clinicians strongly prefer computer scoring.

⟰Rapid Reference 3.1

Steps for Scoring the MMPI-2

1. Identify the number of item omissions (unmarked and double-marked items) to derive the *Cannot Say (?)* score.
2. Derive raw scores for the other scales.
3. Select profile forms appropriate to the patient's gender.
4. Place the identifying information on the profile form in the spaces provided.
5. Transcribe raw scores, including the *(?)* score, to the appropriate spaces on the profile forms.
6. Transcribe fractions of *K* from the "Fractions of *K*" table on the clinical scale profile form onto the spaces provided below the raw scale scores for those scales receiving this correction.
7. Add these corrections to the raw scores of these scales.
8. Convert all raw scores to *T*-scores.
9. Plot profiles of *T*-scores for the scales.
10. Print the MMPI-2 profile code.
11. Prepare a list of Critical Items.*

*Critical Items are not discussed in this book. The reader is referred to the *Manual* and the texts by Friedman, Lewak, Nichols, and Webb (2001) and Greene (2000).

However, because computer scoring is available for only a fixed number of scales approved by the copyright holder, many users create and apply special scoring templates to score scales that have not yet been approved, or that the copyright holder has abandoned. A number of such scales are discussed in Chapters 5, 6, and 7, and the reader is referred to Friedman et al., (2001) or Greene (2000) for the items and norms for these scales.

Because of the order of placement of the items in the test booklet and answer sheet, complete scores for the standard validity and clinical scales, including the Harris-Lingoes subscales and the Wiener and Harmon *Subtle* and *Obvious* subscales, can be obtained from the first 370 items of the test. For this abbreviated version, the use of hand-scoring materials is more feasible. Although the 370-item option is convenient for salvaging important test data when this number of items has been marked but the patient fails to complete the full answer sheet, whether through fatigue, waning cooperation, or mishap, it is generally to be discouraged. This option severely limits the assessment of the consistency of the patient's responses and therefore protocol validity, and of the major areas of item content endorsed on the inventory, thereby imposing significant limitations on interpretation.

CODING THE PROFILE

After the *T*-scores have been plotted on the main MMPI-2 profile form, the profile can be represented in the form of a numerical code by recording the scale numbers (i.e., 1 for Scale *1*) in descending order of elevation,

═══*Rapid Reference 3.2*

Elevation Criteria and Symbols for Coding the MMPI-2 Profile

T-score Range	Symbol
>119	**** (or !!)
110–119	*** (or !)
100–109	**
90–99	*
80–89	"
70–79	'
65–69	+
60–64	-
50–59	/
40–49	:
30–39	#
<30	to the right of #

followed by the punctuation of this series of numerals by symbols indicating ranges of elevation. The same procedure is followed separately to indicate the pattern of scores on the three validity scales *L, F,* and *K.* The coding criteria and elevation symbols are given in Rapid Reference 3.2. Scores falling within a single *T*-score of one another are underlined and scales with identical *T*-scores are coded in numerical order. An example of a coded profile is

Scale	L	F	K	1	2	3	4	5	6	7	8	9	0
Number				*Hs*	*D*	*Hy*	*Pd*	*Mf*	*Pa*	*Pt*	*Sc*	*Ma*	*Si*
T-Score	48	76	54	56	96	57	69	38	79	70	81	62	71

Code: 2*8"6 <u>07</u>'4+9-<u>31</u>/:5# *F*'+-*K/L*:

The profile code is the preferred medium of description among clinicians using the MMPI-2, as it provides an economical and efficient means for conveying the primary features of profile patterns: shape, elevation, and scatter (variation between scale scores). Both the research literature of the MMPI/MMPI-2 and guides and manuals for the clinical use of the MMPI-2 use the high points of the profile code (in this case *2-8* or *2-8-6*) to designate the outstanding features of the profile as a basis for establishing the similarity of profile patterns for the purpose of research or clinical description. As such, the profile code provides a convenient entree for the clinical interpretation of MMPI-2 profiles, as we will see in Chapter 4.

 TEST YOURSELF

1. **The standard score distribution used to represent most MMPI-2 scores is called the**
   (a) uniform distribution.
   (b) composite distribution.
   (c) *T*-distribution.
   (d) scale distribution.
   (e) test distribution.

2. **For a profile coded 37"40'65+2-91/8: K'F-/L: which of the following are true?**
   (a) 6 is in the clinical range.
   (b) 4 is greater than 80*T*.
   (c) 3 and 7 are equal.
   (d) *F* is greater than 5.
   (e) 6 is greater than *F*.
   (f) 8 and *L* are equal.
   (g) 2 is equal to or greater than 65*T*.
   (h) 3 and 7 are greater than *K*.
   (i) 5 and 2 are equivalent.
   (j) 8 and *L* are equivalent.
   (k) 9 exceeds 40*T*.

Answers: 1. c; 2. a, e, h, i, k

Four

INTRODUCTION TO INTERPRETATION

Interpreting the MMPI-2 is a complex skill that requires extensive practice and experience to be accomplished efficiently. No single approach will yield satisfactory results in all cases. All approaches, however, require the user's familiarity with the standard validity and clinical scales and their components, item content, and correlational and factorial interrelationships. In addition, interpretation of the standard scales is often significantly amplified and qualified by scores on myriad other scales, including the MMPI-2 content scales and their components, and many supplementary scales that have been developed to address specific questions.

TEST-TAKING ATTITUDE

The origin of the referral, the purpose of testing, the consequences of the results, the way they will be used and the people who will be privy to them, and other factors play a role in the approach the patient takes to the test. To be widely useful, a personality inventory must be robust to vagaries in patients' perceptions and motivations related to the test-taking situation. The means for assessing test-taking attitude are discussed in Chapter 5.

FACTOR STRUCTURE

One quick and reliable way to obtain an overview of a set of MMPI-2 test results is to evaluate the patient's performance in relation to the major structural characteristics of the test. Repeated analyses of the factor structure of the MMPI/MMPI-2 have found from 10 to 20 item-level factors but only 2 to 5 scale-level factors; only the first two scale-level factors have been shown to be relatively stable across populations. These have been variously named, but typically

DON'T FORGET

The first stage in the interpretive process is assessing the extent to which the obtained set of test scores provides an adequate basis for describing the patient's characteristic symptoms, attitudes, and behavior pattern.

include a major dimension of general maladjustment or subjective distress (the *First Factor*), and a second dimension of emotional-behavioral control (the *Second Factor*). The kinds of secondary factors extracted from scale-level analyses vary considerably by population, but typically include dimensions related to gender-role interests or identification, somatic complaints, introversion-extroversion, and occasionally psychoticism. In some studies, the Second Factor (control) and the introversion-extroversion factor appear to fuse. Rapid Reference 4.1 provides a graphic representation of the MMPI-2 scale-level factor structure with markers for the two major factors.

Item-level factor analyses typically reveal these same dimensions; subdimensions of scale-level factors that distinguish among different kinds of distress (e.g., anxiety, depression, fears/phobias, and psychoticism, in the case of the first scale-level factor); dimensions related to control; and a few others. Item-level factors tend strongly to aggregate items based on the similarity of their manifest content.

≋Rapid Reference 4.1

Markers for the MMPI-2 Scale-Level Factor Structure (First and Second Factors Only)

First Factor

A, 7 (raw), PS, WRK, Mt, PK, DEP, ANX, 8 (raw), etc.

Overcontrol	Second Factor	Undercontrol
R, GF, S5, Re, D2		DIS, ASP2, Pd2, MAC-R, AGG

An initial appraisal of a patient's test performance should consider his or her standing in relation to the two major dimensions of the MMPI-2. One of the first questions to address is, *What is the level of distress?* Because most mental disorders are by their very nature associated with emotional/psychological discomfort and distress, it is not surprising that the major source of variance in the MMPI-2, the First Factor, reflects this dimension. Welsh's *A (Anxiety)* is generally considered to be the best marker for this factor. It does not matter whether the specific form of psychological distress is anxious, depressed, fearful, or psychotic; each of these states tends to partake of elements of discomfort that are common to all, and the First Factor *(A)* is the most convenient way to gauge the strength of this common, or generalized, source of subjective distress.

The First Factor is a unipolar dimension, reflecting very severe distress, not excluding the extreme ranges of panic, desperation, and feelings of disintegration and psychotic disorganization seen in severe psychopathology at the high end, and the absence (or denial) of general maladjustment and emotional discomfort at the low end. This factor is pervasive in the MMPI/MMPI-2 as would be expected in any omnibus instrument designed to assess abnormal personality and general psychopathology. Among the standard validity and clinical scales, Scales *F, 7,* and *8* obtain high positive loadings on this factor, and *K* obtains a moderate-to-high negative loading. Among the supplementary and content scales, high positive loadings are found for *Mt, PK, PS, ANX, OBS, DEP, LSE, WRK,* and *TRT,* and high negative loadings for *Es* and *GM.*

The second question to ask is, *What is the patient's overall level of emotional and behavioral control, and are these levels different from each other?* The Second Factor is a bipolar dimension of emotional-behavioral control reflecting the generalized inhibition of psychopathological expressions at the high end and the facilitation of such expressions at the low end. Although this factor has traditionally been marked by Welsh's *R (Repression),* Nichols and Greene (1995) have argued that there are grounds for considering *R* the primary marker for the emotional aspects of this dimension, but that *DIS (Disconstraint;* Harkness, McNulty, & Ben-Porath, 1995) more effectively measures the behavioral aspects. These two scales are negatively correlated at .46. Among the standard validity and clinical scales, the *R* aspect of the control dimension is best marked by Scales *L, 2,* and *3* (positively), and Scale *9* (negatively). Among the supplementary and content scales, high positive loadings are found for *Re, O-H,* and *LPE* (posi-

DON'T FORGET

1. To determine quickly the patient's overall level of general maladjustment and subjective **distress,** refer to Welsh's A.
2. To determine quickly the patient's overall level of **control,** refer to Welsh's R (emotional control) and to Harkness, McNulty, and Ben-Porath's DIS (behavioral control).

tively), and *MAC-R, APS, ASP,* and *AGG* (negatively). For the aspect of this dimension marked by *DIS,* the corresponding scales with the highest loadings are Scales *L* (negatively) and *9* (positively); *MAC-R, AAS, APS, ASP,* and *AGG* (positively); and *Re, O-H,* and *GF* (negatively).

Patient performance on these dimensions affords an overall context into which the interpreter may place more specific and delimited information from the other MMPI-2 scores and patterns. For example, if a patient tests as highly distressed (high *A*), it is helpful to know whether this distress is accompanied by emotional and behavioral controls that will make it possible for the patient to participate (however reluctantly) in treatment (high *R,* low *DIS*), or will likely disrupt treatment (low *R,* high *DIS*). Conversely, when indications of distress and discomfort are low (low *A*), it is helpful to know whether the patient is trying to "keep a lid" on symptoms (high *R,* low *DIS*), or whether the patient's problems are largely confined to disinhibition and acting out (low *R,* high *DIS*).

PATTERN VERSUS CONTENT APPROACHES TO INTERPRETATION

The most consistent tradition in the history of the MMPI/MMPI-2 has been the concern with the empirical relationships among scores and patterns of scores. Not surprisingly, considering the largely atheoretical environment within which the MMPI was developed, an elevation on a particular scale has not been taken as a diagnostic sign that the high scorer belongs to the population of patients of which the original criterion group was a sample. For example, it is not assumed that a patient with a high score on Scale *1* is a hypochondriac, even though that was how the members of the criterion group for Scale *1* were diagnosed. Rather, it is believed that the external correlates that have been demonstrated in subsequent research to be associated empirically with high scores on Scale *1* will aid in clinically describing high Scale *1* scorers, and that these elements of description will help the clinician make reliable, valid predictions about such patients' diagnoses, future behaviors, and responses to various kinds of treatment.

Before enough clinical and research experience with the test had accumulated to demonstrate otherwise, it was anticipated that the elevation on a single scale would "point the way" to diagnosis and treatment. Soon, however, the commonalities among different kinds of psychopathologies and the overlap of items between scales caused by these likenesses made it clear that profiles with a single scale elevation (a *spike*) were relatively rare, and that multi-peaked profiles would be the rule. Shared features of abnormal mental states (e.g., distress) would be translated into shared variances among the scales. Within a few years, it had become standard practice to describe profiles using their highest two or three scales (see the discussion of coding in Chapter 3). These scales, termed the profile's *code,* proved an efficient medium of exchange among clinicians using the test, and set the stage for the collection of empirical correlates for common code patterns. For example, by 1950 the profile showing peak scores on Scales *4* and *9* was known to occur frequently among Caucasian and African-American penitentiary inmates, manic patients, and psychopaths, but rare among disorders having anxiety as a significant manifestation. In the 1960s and 1970s several large-scale investigations into the empirical correlates of common code types were published (Gilberstadt & Duker, 1965; Gynther, Altman, & Sletten, 1973; Marks & Seeman, 1963), laying the groundwork for most subsequent interpretive practice. This research has recently been extended to the MMPI-2 (Graham, Ben-Porath, & McNulty, 1999).

For the first 25 years of the MMPI, the importance of test-item content was obscured by the empirical method of item selection, especially by Meehl's (1945) vigorous defense of this strategy. One implication of this strategy—one that tended to be overstated in practice—was that the patient's self-report, as manifested in his/her responses to the test items, was an unreliable guide to personality description. As a result, the consideration of or reference to responses to individual items was thought to be at variance with acceptable standards of clinical practice, even though the content-based subscales devised by Harris and Lingoes (1955, 1968) for six of the eight basic MMPI scales had been widely accepted. The status of item content began to change with the publication of the 13 Wiggins (1966) content scales, which he had developed by applying fairly rigorous statistical procedures to Hathaway's 26 original content categories to maximize their internal consistency and independence. Within 10 years of their publication, considerable evidence had accumulated demonstrating their generalizability across populations, their concurrent validity, and the consistency of their interpretive implications with inferences based on the analysis of code types. The success of the Wiggins scales inspired the development of the MMPI-2 content scales (Butcher, Graham, Williams, & Ben-Porath, 1990), which are discussed individually in Chapter 7.

Content scales provide a vantage point from which the clinician can assess the patient's approach to the major content dimensions of the MMPI-2 item pool. Their items are not limited to those selected by Hathaway's empirical methods for inclusion on the standard clinical scales. In some cases the items contained in the content and basic scale versions of similarly named scales coincide closely (such as Scale *1* and *HEA [Health Concerns]*; Scale *0* and *SOD [Social Discomfort]*), but more often they do not (such as Scale *2* and *DEP [Depression]*; Scale *8* and *BIZ [Bizarre Mentation]*). The relative independence of the content and standard clinical scales corresponds with the relative independence of the examinee's self-perception and how he or she is typically seen by others. This difference corresponds to Leary's (1956, 1957) distinction between what he calls *Level I*, that of public communication, emphasizing the surface characteristics of personality and symptoms and their interpersonal impact—the person's social stimulus value—and *Level II*, that of conscious self-description, emphasizing how the person sees his or her world and self—the person's phenomenological field. Leary viewed the MMPI clinical scales as measures of Level I phenomena: "the interpersonal pressure exerted on the clinician by the patient's symptoms" (1957, p. 78). As substantive dimensions of self-report, the MMPI-2 content scales, and item content generally, correspond to Leary's Level II.

Although clinical scale– and content scale–derived personality descriptions typically coincide, they often are sufficiently different that comparing the patient's performance from these two vantage points can yield insights and predictive advantages that are unavailable when examining either set of scales alone. For example, a patient may elevate Scale *7*, a measure of distress and psychological discomfort, but the particular symptomatic form this discomfort will take is often readily apparent in the relative elevations among the *ANX (Anxiety), FRS (Fears), OBS (Obsessiveness), DEP (Depression),* and *LSE (Low Self-Esteem)* content scales. Conversely, a patient may elevate *DEP,* a measure of dysphoria, guilt, apathy, pessimism, and self-criticism, without concurrently elevating Scale *2,* which also gives some emphasis to the vegetative symptoms and the inhibition commonly seen in depressive syndromes. Thus, information derived from item content may reinforce that provided by the clinical scales, but it may also elaborate, supplement, and refine inferences based on clinical scales and code types.

The clinical and content scales may at times suggest opposing interpretive hypotheses. For example, an elevation on Scale *8* may appear to be contradicted by a lower than average score on *BIZ (Bizarre Mentation),* suggesting alienation and impaired thinking and motivation, and perhaps vulnerability to psychosis, but without currently active psychoticism. Conversely, high *BIZ* and low Scale *8* may suggest a transient and more readily reversible psychotic condition than is characteristic of schizophrenia. In the case of unusual profiles or profiles having features that are ambiguous or that might suggest classification under different code types, the content scales often provide indispensable guidance for a more accurate interpretation of the clinical profile. MMPI-2 interpretation is likely to yield the most satisfactory results when both sets of scales are allowed to contribute, with each set serving as a check upon the other.

Recently, Greene and Nichols (1995; Nichols & Greene, 1995) developed the MMPI-2 Structural Summary, a way of organizing all of the MMPI-2 scales on the basis of their item content. In this schema, all MMPI-2 scales are organized into the format outlined in Rapid Reference 4.2.

≡Rapid Reference 4.2

An Outline of the MMPI-2 Structural Summary

Test-Taking Attitudes

1. Omissions
2. Consistency
3. Accuracy
   a. Self-Unfavorable
   b. Self-Favorable

Factor Scales

1. First Factor Scales
2. Second Factor Scales
   a. Emotional Overcontrol
   b. Behavioral Overcontrol

Moods

1. Depression
   a. Depressed Mood/Dysphoria
   b. Depressed Ideation/Attitudes
   c. Mental Insufficiency
   d. Vegetative Signs
2. Anhedonia
3. Elation
4. Anxiety
5. Guilt
6. Fears
7. Emotional Alienation (Hopelessness)
8. Anger/Hostility
9. Denial of Anger/Hostility

Cognitions

1. Unconventional Thought Processes
2. Psychotic Thought Processes
3. Grandiosity
4. Paranoid Thought Processes
5. Obsessions/Ruminations

6. Cynicism
7. Memory, Attention, Concentration
8. Defense Mechanisms
   a. Repression
   b. Denial
   c. Somatization
   d. Rationalization/Intellectualization
   e. Externalization
   f. Projection
   g. Acting Out
   h. Fantasy

Interpersonal Relations

1. Extraversion/Introversion
   a. Extraversion
   b. Introversion
2. Social Alienation
3. Self-Alienation
4. Masculinity/Femininity
5. Family Alienation
6. Delinquency/Antisocial Practices
7. Authority Conflict/Antisocial Attitudes
8. Passive/Aggressive Struggles
9. Passivity/Submissiveness
10. Dependency
11. Dominance/Assertiveness
12. Narcissism

Other Problem Areas

1. Substance Abuse
2. Suicidal Ideation
3. Sleep Disturbance
4. Sexual Difficulties

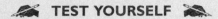 **TEST YOURSELF**

1. The First Factor of the MMPI-2 refers to

(a) emotional control.

(b) general maladjustment.

(c) behavioral control.

(d) subjective distress.

(e) a and b.

(f) b and d.

2. The First Factor in some MMPI-2 factor analytic studies is more "psychotic" than in other studies. True or False?

3. The Second Factor in some MMPI-2 factor analytic studies may not be clearly distinguishable from introversion-extraversion. True or False?

4. The Second Factor represents a unipolar general dimension of

(a) behavioral control.

(b) general maladjustment.

(c) emotional control.

(d) subjective distress.

(e) a and c.

(f) none of the above.

5. Regardless of whether MMPI-2 scales or MMPI-2 items are factor analyzed, the number of factors extracted is about the same. True or False?

Answers: 1. f; 2. True; 3. True; 4. e; 5. False

Five

Hathaway was among the first to recognize that the suitability of personality inventory data for personality description and clinical prediction depended heavily on the patient's ability and willingness to cooperate with the assessment process and to respond to the test items in a way consistent with his or her "true" self-appraisal. He did not consider it necessary that patients respond to each item in a factually accurate manner. It is generally sufficient that the responses to items be reasonably coherent and in accord with patients' own views of themselves.

One feature of the MMPI/MMPI-2 that has influenced its usefulness with both clinical and nonclinical populations is its array of scales and indices for evaluating the examinee's test-taking attitude(s). All self-report measures are susceptible to a variety of willful or self-deceptive manipulations and distortions. Nichols and Greene (1997) have identified seven dimensions along which deceptive test-taking influences may vary, as well as the strategies examinees may employ on the MMPI-2 to achieve these influences. A means to identify, describe, and measure such influences is essential if accurate inferences about behavior, symptoms, problems, and attitudes are to be drawn from test results. These seven dimensions are listed in Rapid Reference 5.1, and are discussed further in Chapter 9.

The initial and crucial steps in evaluating MMPI-2 results establish the interpretability of the individual's test protocol. The scales described in this section enable the interpreter to determine (a) when an answer sheet is eligible for scoring ("Is the test administration complete?"); (b) when scores appear to reflect a cognizant interaction between the examinee and the MMPI-2 items ("Are the responses to the test items consistent?"); and (c) the examinee's pattern of attitudes toward completing the MMPI-2, the elements, origins, and possible motives of these attitudes, and the potential distortions they may have introduced into test findings ("Is the examinee's self-portrayal accurate?").

DETERMINING COMPLETENESS

The first step involves determining whether a sufficient number of item responses have been provided. The patient has been instructed to provide responses to all of the items, and excessive deviation from this instruction will attenuate scale scores to such an extent that scoring is unjustified. The *Cannot Say (?)* score is the sum of items for which the examinee has not provided responses (unanswered/unmarked items) and the number of items for which both *True* and *False* alternatives have been endorsed (double-marked items). Although a large number of omitted items suppress raw scores, the reversal of scoring on Scale *5* for women tends to inflate their *T*-scores when *Cannot Say (?)* is high.

There is no hard and fast rule on the permissible number of item omissions, but a conventional upper limit has been set at 30. In the 370-item abbreviated form of the MMPI-2, the corresponding number is 20. If the patient has not been unduly selective in concentrating item omissions within particular areas of item content, this number may in rare cases be exceeded without precluding useful interpretation; however, as the number of omitted items reaches or exceeds 100, effects on scale scores, their order (profile code), and the average elevation of the scales within a given group (e.g., content scales) can be dramatic. However, *Cannot Say (?)* scores below 30 can also have important effects on scores, especially when omissions are concentrated in one or only a few content domains. For example, when concentrated in content areas that are represented by relatively few items—such as anger, indecision, or substance abuse—even relatively small numbers of omitted items can dramatically suppress the scores of those scales in which such content is proportionately high relative to total scale length. Even when the content of omitted items is heterogeneous, omis-

≡*Rapid Reference 5.1*

Dimensions of Deceptive Test-Taking Strategies

1. Inconsistency versus inaccuracy
2. Dissimulation versus simulation
3. Generic versus specific deception
4. Crude versus sophisticated deception
5. Intentional versus nonintentional deception
6. Self-deception versus impression management
7. Selectivity versus inclusiveness

CAUTION

Whenever *Cannot Say (?)* is greater than 5, (a) examine the content of the omitted items, (b) note where in the sequence of items they are occurring (e.g., first half versus second half), (c) note the percentage of items for which responses were provided on each scale, and (d) review omitted items with the examinee at the time test feedback is given.

sions may affect the relations among scale scores, and hence the order of high points and the profile code. For these reasons, whenever *Cannot Say (?)* exceeds 5 or so, it is almost always worthwhile to examine (a) the content of omitted items, in order to discern themes and possible areas of conflict that may have given rise to them; (b) where in the sequence of items the omissions are occurring, especially whether they are occurring among the first 370 items and may thus be affecting scores on the standard validity and clinical scales, or are mostly falling after this point and are affecting content and supplementary scale scores; and (c) the percentage of items for which responses have been provided on each scale. Query the examinee directly for possible reasons for omissions when test feedback is given.

Factors leading to unmarked or double-marked items include failure to understand instructions (i.e., that all items are to be marked); general intellectual deficits; problems with reading comprehension (which may lower scores on Scale *9*); ambiguity or semantic confusion, such that the patient feels unable to decide among response alternatives; content that the examinee may find offensive; and suspiciousness and resistance to self-disclosure.

ANALYZING CONSISTENCY

MMPI-2 interpretation rests on the assumption that the examinee has, in general, responded to semantically similar items in similar ways (Nichols and Greene, 1995). The second step in the assessment of protocol validity is to determine whether the patient read the items with sufficient care and understanding to render the responses meaningful as elements of self-report. A series of item responses must show an adequate level of consistency for interpretive efforts to proceed. When such a level of consistency cannot be met, attempts to interpret the MMPI-2 must be abandoned and the protocol discarded. Rapid Reference 5.2 contains a useful summary description of the consistency scales that are discussed in depth in the following sections.

≡ Rapid Reference 5.2

The Consistency Scales

VRIN

Overlap: *VRIN* contains five *True-True* and five *False-False* item pairs that overlap with *TRIN*.

Relations with Other Scales: Scores on *VRIN, TRIN, F, F_B*, and *F_p* are all highly sensitive to approaches to completing the MMPI-2 in which item responses are determined by factors other than the content of the items. The most direct confirmation of *VRIN* scores, whether high or low, is the score on *TRIN*. Because *VRIN* and *TRIN* are essentially uncorrelated, when both scales are elevated above *T-65*, it is very likely that the test items have been endorsed inconsistently. When *VRIN* is elevated but *TRIN* is within normal limits, elevations on *F, F_B*, and *F_p* tend to confirm a pattern of carelessness, exaggeration, or noncooperation in responding to the items, and would therefore recommend against proceeding with interpretation. When *F, F_B*, and *F_p* are elevated and *VRIN* is low, carelessness in responding to the items can be ruled out, leaving *F, F_B*, and *F_p* to be interpreted more confidently in terms of psychopathology, exaggeration of symptoms, or malingering.

TRIN

Overlap: See *VRIN*.
Relations with Other Scales: See *VRIN*.

Variable Response Consistency Scale (*VRIN*)

General

VRIN is composed of 67 pairs of items (97 total items; 49 unique pairs) selected on the basis of their statistical associations and semantic similarities.

Consider a pair of items, one asserting that sleep is restful and refreshing, and another asserting that sleep is fitful and disturbed. One would anticipate that affirming both items as *True* is a statistically rare occurrence relative to the other response alternatives: one *True* and the other *False,* or both *False* (i.e., indicating

> **DON'T FORGET**
>
> When *Cannot Say (?)* exceeds 5, it may be helpful to determine on which scales the omissions occurred, to examine the content of the omitted items, and to query the examinee about reasons for the omissions.

sleep that is neither especially restful nor especially disturbed). Of the 67 *VRIN* pairs, 18 are scored symmetrically, 17 either *True-False* or *False-True* and 1 either *True-True* or *False-False;* and 31 are scored asymmetrically, 4 *True-True,* 13 *True-False,* 10 *False-True,* and 4 *False-False.* Reasons for elevated scores on *VRIN* include severe personality disturbances, such as psychosis manifested by disrupted attention and concentration, confusion, uncertainty, and indecision. Elevations on *VRIN* are also commonly caused by carelessness in completing the inventory, lack of cooperation by the examinee such that items are endorsed without regard to their content, difficulties with reading, lapses in motivation, and accidental misalignments between booklet and answer sheet such that item numbers no longer coincide. *VRIN* elevations cannot rule out symptom exaggeration, because some examinees may seek to convey impairment by deliberately responding inconsistently to the test items. The endorsement of semantically inconsistent item pairs may occur at any point, and the clinician may wish to place greater or lesser confidence in the interpretation of various scales and patterns, depending upon where inconsistent responding is concentrated. For example, because 15 of the *VRIN* item pairs occur after item 370, a high *VRIN* score based upon inconsistent responses to these pairs would enable confident interpretation of the standard validity and clinical scales, whereas interpretation of the content scales would require caution or should be avoided altogether. Because the scoring of *VRIN* depends upon the configural relations among its constituent item pairs, this scale is more liable to errors when hand-scoring is used. It is therefore especially important to double-check hand-scored *VRIN* scores for accuracy.

Interpretation

A completely random pattern of item endorsement yields a raw score of 16.75 on *VRIN,* against a mean score of about 5 for the restandardization sample. The MMPI-2 *Manual* recommends a cut-off score of 13. In general, scores below 8 are acceptable. As scores rise to 11 or so, the probability that random elements have entered the response process increases. At these levels it can be difficult to discern whether such random elements are due to carelessness or to a compromised mental state characterized by confusion and uncertainty. For scores in a range of 8–16, it may be helpful to determine if (and where) the inconsistently endorsed *VRIN* item pairs are concentrated, and especially on which side of item 370 the endorsements occur.

Errors in judgment about consistency are most common for scores in the range of 11–16, with many inconsistent protocols erroneously judged to be consistent and many consistent protocols erroneously judged to be inconsistent. Scores in a range of 8–11 should be of particular concern when it can be shown that most of the inconsistent item pairs come from one specific part of the protocol (e.g., first half or second half) rather than being randomly distributed throughout it. Scores on $TRIN$, F, F_B, and F_P should be consulted. Scores in the range of 8–11 are also achieved when there is a relatively extreme imbalance in the proportion of *True*

DON'T FORGET

Reasons for elevated scores on *VRIN* include severe personality disturbance, carelessness in completing the inventory, lack of cooperation by the examinee, difficulties with reading, lapses in motivation, accidental misalignments between booklet and answer sheet, and symptom exaggeration or malingering.

CAUTION

VRIN (and *TRIN*) cannot be used to rule out exaggeration or malingering, because some examinees may seek to convey impairment by intentionally marking items inconsistently.

to *False* responses, and such scores carry an increased risk of being erroneously judged consistent. Scores on *TRIN* are especially informative when *VRIN* scores are in a range of 7–12. As scores approach 16, the level of inconsistency in item responses is such that interpretation is very likely to be compromised unless scores among *TRIN*, F, F_B, and F_P are especially favorable. Scores in the 12–16 range suggest a lack of cooperation in completing the MMPI-2, psychotic disruption, or both. Protocols with *VRIN* scores greater than 16 should be discarded.

True Response Consistency Scale (TRIN)

General

TRIN is composed of 23 pairs of items (40 total items; 20 unique pairs), 14 of which are scorable when both response alternatives are endorsed *True*, and 9 of which are scorable when both response alternatives are endorsed *False*. Like the *VRIN* item pairs, the items in the *TRIN* pairs were selected on the basis of their statistical associations and semantic similarities. Reasons for elevated *TRIN* scores are largely the same as those for elevations of *VRIN* scores. However, unlike *VRIN, TRIN* is sensitive to the acquiescence response style (and its opposite)—that is, the tendency to mark items *True* (or *False*) without regard to item content. As with *VRIN*, elevations are achieved by endorsing items inconsistently, but *TRIN* is primarily useful in exposing inconsistent responding in the specific context of an acquiescent *(yeasaying)* or nonacquiescent *(naysaying)* response style. These response styles are most readily identified by marked deviations in the percentage of items endorsed *True* or *False*, with defensive protocols tending to show a low percentage of items endorsed *True* (and a high percentage of items endorsed *False*), and exaggerated protocols showing the opposite pattern. Such patterns of *True* or *False* percent may or may not be associated with inconsistent responding (i.e., high *TRIN* scores), except when the percentage of items marked *True* or *False* becomes extreme (approaches 90%). The *TRIN* score is obtained by summing the 14 item pairs marked *True*, subtracting the sum of the nine item pairs marked *False*, and then adding 9 points (a constant). The addition of this constant prevents negative scores (i.e., scores below *T*-50). Raw scores between 10 and 19 reflect a bias toward *True* responding, whereas raw scores between 0 and 9 reflect a bias toward *False* responding. Both biases result in elevated *T*-scores on *TRIN*. As with *VRIN*, the scoring of *TRIN* depends upon the configural relations among its constituent item pairs and is complicated by the need to subtract the *True*-keyed pairs endorsed from the *False*-keyed pairs endorsed and to add the constant. The *TRIN* scale thus is also liable to errors in scoring when manual procedures are used. Hand-scored TRIN values should always be double-checked for accuracy.

Interpretation

The mean raw score for the restandardization sample was about 9, which corresponds to a *T*-score of 50. *TRIN* raw scores of 8–10 are unremarkable. Raw *TRIN* scores below 6 or greater than 12 (corresponding to *T*-scores of 78–79) should be considered sufficiently inconsistent to make retesting advisable. Raw scores of 6 and 7, and of 11 and 12, are of uncertain significance. When *TRIN* exceeds *VRIN* and *True* percent is low (~25%), raw scores of 6–7 suggest an indiscriminate preference for *False*-marking or naysaying, and retesting may be warranted. Similarly, when *TRIN* exceeds *VRIN* and *True* percent is high (~60%), raw scores of 11–12 suggest an acquiescent or yeasaying response style and may also warrant retesting. In all other cases, such moderate elevations on *TRIN* may be allowed unless *VRIN* exceeds *TRIN*, in which case the interpretation of the *VRIN* score should supercede the interpretation of *TRIN*.

CAUTION

VRIN and *TRIN* scores are especially liable to errors when hand-scoring is used.

The |F – F_B| Index

General

The *F* and *F Back* (F_B) scales are both composed of infrequently endorsed items. Because the items of the *F* scale occur mostly among the first 300 test items and those of F_B occur mostly among the 267 remaining items, the *absolute* difference between the raw scores on these scales provides a rough measure of the consistency of performance on the front and back portions of the test, and tends to confirm indications of inconsistency from other scales, such as *VRIN* and *TRIN*. The performance of this measure is enhanced when combined with *VRIN* ($VRIN + |F - F_B|$) or with its constituent scales ($F + F_B + |F - F_B|$). These indices are especially helpful in deciding whether a protocol has reached an excessive level of response inconsistency when scores on *VRIN* are equivocal. Further information on the characteristics and uses of these indices is contained in Greene (2000).

ANALYZING ACCURACY

Once it has been determined that the MMPI-2 protocol has achieved a satisfactory level of response consistency, the next issue to be addressed is the accuracy of the examinee's self-report. Examinees may respond to the test items consistently, but their self-representations in responding to the test items may or may not be true and accurate. At the simplest level, examinees may exaggerate distress, symptoms, and negative personal attributes; conversely, they may minimize or deny such features. Moreover, such exaggeration or minimization may be inadvertent—a function of self-deception or self-misunderstanding. It may also be a function of naivete, subnormal intel-

DON'T FORGET

The use of hand-scoring procedures makes it necessary to double-check scores on *VRIN* and *TRIN* because these may be especially prone to errors in scoring.

ligence, or the result of difficulties in reading comprehension, or it may be deliberately self-serving or an attempt to mislead the examiner and bias the results, frustrating the purposes of the assessment. It should be understood that the terms *overreporting* and *underreporting* reflect points along a dimension; each response style will shade into a middle range of this dimension that reflects an accurate self-description. The issue of accuracy is not necessarily related closely to the presence or absence of psychopathology. For example, the clear presence of exaggeration or minimization of pathological symptoms and traits, considered in isolation, may not imply the presence or absence of genuine psychopathology. Both overreporting and underreporting may be undertaken from a range of mental states, some of which are well within the normal range, and others of which reflect severe mental disorder.

Three of the scales described in this section, F, F_B, and F_P, are all sensitive to overreporting. All are based on the premise that endorsing items that others endorse only rarely is, given sufficient numbers of such endorsements, likely to reflect exaggeration of psychopathology. A fourth scale, *Dissimulation (Ds)*, reflects common misconceptions by normals of the way mentally disordered individuals are likely to describe themselves. A final measure, the Gough (1950) *Dissimulation Index (F – K)*, combines one scale that is mostly sensitive to overreporting with another that is sensitive to both overreporting and underreporting.

OVERREPORTING SCALES

The *F (Infrequency)* Scale

General

The items of the F scale were selected on the basis of their endorsement by 10% or fewer of the original Minnesota Normals (not the restandardization sample). Half of these items occur among the first 180 items of the test, and all are contained within the first 361 items. Because the examinee places himself or herself in a small minority with each endorsement of an F item, the endorsement of many such items places the examinee in a very small statistical minority of test-takers. In this sense, elevations on F can indicate deviance or unconventionality. The higher the elevation, the more extreme and visible such deviance tends to be, provided that the elevation has not been achieved

≋ Rapid Reference 5.3

Summary Descriptive Features of *F*

Number of Items: 60

True/False Balance: 41/19

Overlap: Scales 8, with which F shares 15 items, and 6, with which it shares 9 items. F also shares 14 items with *Infrequency Psychopathology (F$_p$)* and 10 items with *BIZ (Bizarre Mentation)*.

Content: About one-third of the items reflect paranoid ideation or psychotic processes. Other groups of 8 to 12 items each reflect schizoid apathy and underinvolvement, cynicism and antisocial attitudes, family enmity, and somatic symptoms.

Relations with Other Scales: F is correlated to the extent of ~.80 or greater with most overreporting scales and indices. The F scale tends to accelerate most of the clinical scales, especially Scales 8, 7, 6, and 4, and may therefore contribute significantly to the elevation of the profile as a whole. Elevations on F also tend to drive up the content scales, especially *BIZ, DEP, TRT, WRK,* and *LSE.*

---

by an intentional effort to exaggerate or malinger psychopathology, and provided that reading problems can be ruled out. In most cases, *F* elevations that occur in general clinical settings should be interpreted in terms of distress and severity of psychopathology. In forensic settings, where the base rates and incentives for deliberate exaggeration and malingering may be considerably higher, the latter motives must be taken into account more regularly. (See Rapid Reference 5.3 for a summary description of *F*.)

Interpretation

The *F* scale is highly variable in its item content but emphasizes psychoticism. *F* is sensitive to both symptom exaggeration and severe psychopathology in the form of psychosis or major personality disturbance. Elevations on *F* may occur for the following reasons: (a) severe psychopathology, especially of psychotic type; (b) problems in completing the inventory, such as difficulties in reading comprehension, confusion due to active psychotic disruption, or a random or careless pattern of responding to the test items; (c) the exaggeration of psychopathology out of a sense of fear, panic, distress, or as a cry for help; or (d) malingering. Identifying the reasons for elevated *F* scores in individual cases is complicated. Probable or actual problems in completing the inventory can usually be identified by evaluating reading comprehension prior to testing (see Chapter 2), or, where these can be ruled out, by elevations on the inconsistency scales *VRIN, TRIN,* or both. When the elevation on F is a result of severe psychopathology, it should exceed the elevation on F_p, and the elevation on the latter scale should not exceed *T*-75. When high F scores are the result of distress or panic, the elevation on F should be exceeded by the elevation on F_B. In instances of willful exaggeration or malingering, elevations on F will be accompanied by similar elevations on F_p, and such motives are especially suggested when $F_p > F$.

T-scores between 60 and 80 are considered moderate and reflect levels of distress and disturbance common in outpatient and inpatient psychiatric populations. Examining the items endorsed can aid in interpretation because items may be drawn from specific content areas (e.g., paranoid ideation, somatic symptoms, family enmity, etc.). *T*-scores between 80 and 100 are the most difficult to interpret. Accurate interpretation at these levels requires reference to other scales such as *VRIN, TRIN, F_B,* and F_p. At *T*-90, arguably the best single cutting score for F, either exaggeration or severe psychopathology may be indicated. F scores exceeding *T*-90 should be ruled the result of exaggeration rather than psychopathology when F_p exceeds *T*-75. Use considerable caution when interpreting F scores greater than *T*-100. *T*-scores greater than 110 approach a region that is commonly reached when the test items have been endorsed randomly; these scores are rarely seen in valid profiles. In most such cases, scores on *VRIN* and/or *TRIN, F_B,* and F_p will all be elevated in ranges characteristic of inconsistent responding. The few valid cases generally reflect either severe exaggeration or malingering, in which case F_B and F_p will also be highly elevated, or very severe psychopathology, in which case *VRIN* and *TRIN* are at acceptable levels and the pattern $F > F_B > F_p$ is most commonly seen.

Low Scores

Scores below *T*-50 are infrequent in clinical populations but do often occur in civil forensic contexts such as child custody evaluations and employment screening. In general, low scores suggest conventionality, if not overconventionality, when unaccompanied by elevations on scales such as L and K. When F is low but L, K, or both are elevated in clinical populations, an effort to deny distress, alienation, and abnormality is usually suggested. Among normals, this pattern reflects overconventionality and the minimization or denial of problems.

The F Back (F_B) Scale

General

The F_B scale consists of 40 items that members of the MMPI-2 restandardization sample endorsed infrequently, and was intended to serve the same function for items falling on the last half of the test as that served by the F scale for items on the first half. Almost half of the F_B items occur among the final 100 items on the test, and all occur after item number 280. Although the scale is variable in content, it has a substantially different emphasis than does the F scale. The sharp differences in the item content of the two scales confounds the developers' intent that F_B function in a way fully analogous to that of F. That is, whereas both scales are sensitive to overreporting, substantial elevations on F are often achieved on the basis of psychotic mentation, but substantial elevations on F_B are often achieved on the basis of severe affective upheaval. (See Rapid Reference 5.4 for a summary description of F_B.)

Interpretation

The differences in content between F and F_B lead to problems interpreting F_B. For example, in some cases an elevated F_B score when F is in an acceptable range signifies that the examinee chose to simulate mood disturbance and suicidal ideation rather than psychoticism, whereas in others this pattern of elevation reflects actual panic anxiety or depressive symptoms. Exaggeration or malingering can be safely interpreted only when *both* F and F_B are elevated beyond acceptable limits. The elevation guidelines for F, including low scores, are generally applicable to the interpretation of F_B scores, bearing in mind the differences in the content of the two scales. Use caution when interpreting F_B scores greater than T-95. Interpreting scores below T-75 is often aided by examining the specific items endorsed, as these may be concentrated within a specific area of concern such as panic/fear, suicidal ideation, or alcohol abuse. The different content emphases between F and F_B create a special dilemma

≡Rapid Reference 5.4

Summary Descriptive Features of F_B

Number of Items: 40

True/False Balance: 37/3

Overlap: Scale 8, with which F_B shares 10 items (4 appear on Sc2, and three on Sc1). F_B also shares 7 items each with the *Infrequency Psychopathology* (F_p) scale and the *Fears (FRS)* content scale, and 6 items with the *Depression (DEP)* content scale.

Content: The largest subset of items reflects panic/fear (9 items), with smaller subsets reflecting depression and low self-esteem (8 items), suicide/self-harm (4 items), alcohol abuse (4 items), and family estrangement (3 items). Only three items reflect psychotic processes.

Relations with Other Scales: F_B is correlated to the extent of ~.80 with most overreporting scales and indices. Like F, it tends to accelerate most of the clinical scales, especially Scales 8, 7, 6, and 4, and thus may contribute significantly to the elevation of the profile as a whole. Elevations on F_B also tend to drive up virtually all of the content scales, especially *DEP, TRT, WRK,* and *LSE.*

when F_B scores are elevated but F scores are not. As a rule of thumb, such scores are generally acceptable if the scores on at least two of the four content scales—*DEP, LSE, WRK,* and *TRT*—exceed the score on *BIZ,* or if the scores on *ANX* and *FRS* exceed that on *BIZ.* When these conditions cannot be met, F_B can be interpreted to reflect exaggeration of problems or a lack of care in completing the second half of the MMPI-2. In this case the content scales and other scales that draw most of their items from this half of the test should be interpreted with caution, if at all.

The F_p (Infrequency Psychopathology) Scale

General

Whereas the F and F_B scales were developed by evaluating the frequency of item responses among normals, F_p was developed and cross-validated within a sample of psychiatric inpatients, and again with the MMPI-2 restandardization sample. To qualify for inclusion on F_p, items could not be endorsed by more than 20% of either the patient or normal groups. The manner in which F_p was

≋Rapid Reference 5.5

Summary Descriptive Features of F_p

Number of Items: 27

True/False Balance: 18/9

Overlap: The F scale, with which the F_p shares 14 items, and 7 items with Scales 8 (3 on $Sc1$). Four items overlap L (51F, 77F, 93F, 102F).

Content: The content of F_p is heterogeneous with two exceptions: Two subsets of items reflect persecutory ideation (four items [162, 216, 228, 336], three of which are on $BIZ1$) and severe family enmity (90F, 192F, 276F, 478).

Relations with Other Scales: F_p is highly correlated with F and F_B (~.70), and moderately correlated with $F - K$, Scale 8, BIZ, and PSY (~.60).

developed exerted some control for psychopathology. As evidence of this, the correlations between F_p and the basic and content scales are less than two-thirds the magnitude of those between F and these scales. Although this reduction in variance attributable to psychopathology is less than may be desired, it is sufficient to make F_p the most sensitive and specific measure of overreporting on the MMPI-2. Similar to F and, to a lesser extent, F_B, F_p retains some sensitivity to psychoticism. Nor is it free of other problems. Its overlap with L can produce F_p scores well above T-65 for protocols in which all four of the overlapping items are endorsed. Misleading elevations may also be produced by endorsing the family enmity items contained within F_p, even though no other items on F_p have been endorsed. Thus, endorsing a few items from each of the largest areas of content within F_p is sufficient to yield very high scale elevations. For example, a raw score of 5 obtained on the basis of responding to two of the persecutory items and three of the family enmity items (or vice versa) yields a T-score of 77 for men and 81 for women. (See Rapid Reference 5.5 for a summary description of F_p.)

CAUTION

Endorsing a few items from each of the largest areas of content within F_p is sufficient to yield very high scale elevations. When the content of the endorsed items falls into only one or two content domains, F_p generally should not be interpreted as indicating overreporting unless scales F and F_B are concurrently elevated, and $F - K$ is high.

CAUTION

F_p may achieve spurious elevations by high scores on L; Pd1, Sc1, and FAM; BIZ1; or a combination of these. When L or many among Pd1, Sc1, FAM, and BIZ1 are elevated concurrently with F_p, check the items endorsed on F_p to be sure they are sufficiently heterogeneous.

Interpretation

Interpreting F_p is complicated by its inclusion of relatively dense areas of specific pathological content. Interpreting relatively low scores (e.g., below T-75) as ruling out overreporting is likely to be much more reliable than interpreting higher scores as indicating underreporting, unless the latter are extremely high (e.g., greater than 100). Scores between 75 and 100 are best interpreted with reference to the range of content among the items of F_p that have been endorsed. When the items manifest a wide range of content, overreporting is indicated. When the content of the endorsed items falls into only one or two content domains, F_p generally should not be interpreted as indicating overreporting unless scales F and F_B are concurrently elevated, and $F - K$ is high.

The Ds (Gough Dissimulation) Scale

General

Gough (1954) developed Ds by comparing the responses of a group of neurotic patients with those of college students and mental health professionals who had been instructed to respond as if they suffered from a neurosis. The items differentiating the neurotics from those attempting to simulate neurosis were obviously abnormal in character but difficult to place in terms of any specific clinical picture. The level of psychopathology implied in these items is generally mild to moderate rather than blatant, severe, overwhelming, or grossly deviant, as is the case with the items of F, F_B, and F_p. Ds performs unusually well in the detection of overreporting (cf. Greene, 2000). Among the overreporting scales discussed in this section, Ds is uniquely sensitive to instances of exaggeration or malingering in which examinees do *not* wish to appear psychotically disabled. This response style may be more common in settings of employment and civil forensic contexts involving claims of disability based on stress and injury than in criminal forensic contexts. Given its method of construction, Ds may be more sensitive to negative impression management—that is, to deliberate efforts to fake bad—than are other over-

≡ *Rapid Reference 5.6*

Summary Descriptive Features of *Ds*

Number of Items: 58

True/False Balance: 48/10

Overlap: The *Ds* scale shares 19 items with 8 (8 on *Sc1*), 11 with *F*, 10 with *PK*, 9 with *PS*, and 8 items each with *HEA* and *FAM*. In contrast with the other overreporting scales, it shares no items with *BIZ*, and only two with *PSY*.

Content: The content of *Ds* is quite heterogeneous but emphasizes general demoralization, instability, health concerns, incompetence, disability, and relatively severe alienation from others. Few of its items reflect severe depressive and psychotic symptoms.

Relations with Other Scales: Scores on *Ds* are raised by elevations on Scale 8 and virtually all other measures of general maladjustment and subjective distress, including *PK*, *PS*, Scale 7, and *A*, with which *Ds* is correlated in the .85–.90 range. *Ds* correlates with *F* − *K* at .90.

reporting scales. (See *Mp* and *Sd* on pages 72–75; see Rapid Reference 5.6 for a summary description of *Ds*.)

Interpretation

Unlike those of *F*, *F$_B$*, and *F$_p$*, the items of *Ds* are commonly endorsed by both patients and examinees wishing to overreport psychopathology. The difference is that examinees who exaggerate symptoms tend to endorse these items as much as three or four times more often than patients do. As a result, scores between about *T*-55 and *T*-80 are generally unremarkable. Scores between *T*-80 and *T*-90 are equivocal, and scores exceeding *T*-90 suggest exaggeration or deliberate malingering. Scores below the range *T*-80 to *T*-100 do not rule out malingering, as some examinees seeking to malinger may respond selectively to items of grossly pathological content such as those found on *F*, *F$_B$*, and *F$_p$*, while overlooking items that patients endorse more frequently. More typically, however, malingerers tend to endorse items at all levels of severity.

It is possible that extreme elevations on *F*, *F$_B$*, *F$_p$*, or a combination of these when *Ds* scores are only moderately elevated are more strongly associated with extreme and deliberate overreporting (malingering), and that patterns in which these four scales are concurrently elevated are also frequently obtained by patients with actual psychopathology who are exaggerating their symptoms and distress. Research has yet to confirm this speculation, however. Extreme elevations on Ds that are not accompanied by similar elevations on F and F_p (scores on F_B are equivocal in this context) suggest an effort to exaggerate selectively or to malinger nonpsychotic disability in order to bolster claims of stress or injury.

Low Scores

Among psychiatric patients, scores below T-55 suggest that the examinee has been highly selective and discriminating in responding to the test items in an effort to achieve a clear and accurate portrayal of problems and symptoms. Caldwell (1988) has pointed out that such scores may accompany an unusually good fit between the patient and the clinical profile when the latter shows a clear pattern of elevations. Scores below T-45 suggest unusual freedom from symptoms and attitudes consistent with mental disorder and may raise the question of undue guardedness in responding to the items.

The Gough F – K Index

General

The $F - K$ Index is the difference between the *raw* scores on the F and K scales. Positive values for the index are associated with overreporting, and negative values are associated with underreporting. Gough (1947, 1950) developed the index by comparing the F and K values for patients with those for mental health professionals who'd been instructed to simulate neurotic and psychotic performances on the MMPI. The index discriminates between the profiles of patients and those of nonpatients attempting to simulate or exaggerate psychopathology, but the cutting scores for best separating actual from simulated profiles have varied widely among studies and samples. Rothke, Friedman, Dahlstrom, Greene, Arredondo, and Mann (1994) reported data on the distributional characteristics of several patient and nonpatient samples on $F - K$. In both research and practice, the $F - K$ Index has performed much better at detecting overreporting than underreporting. $F - K$ is highly correlated with F (~.90) among psychiatric patients, and some studies have shown it to be slightly less effective in identifying exaggeration and malingering than the F scale alone.

Interpretation

Among psychiatric patients, attempts to exaggerate psychopathology typically result in $F - K$ Index values of +20 to +25, with values in a range of +15 to +20 being equivocal, depending on the patient's clinical status. Values in the latter range are not uncommon among patients who are disorganized or who are seeking to dramatize their distress and discomfort. Values exceeding +25 point to exaggeration. Values in a range of −11 to −16 can indicate an overly favorable self-presentation emphasizing freedom from symptoms and distress; values of −16 to −20 suggest such a bias. In psychiatric populations, these values tend to be associated with a lack of insight, fear of evaluation, or the pursuit of a specific goal (e.g., discharge from the hospital). $F - K$ values less than −20 represent a highly defensive response set. In many cases such extreme values will indicate the catastrophic lack of insight characteristic of psychosis, especially paranoid conditions.

True Percent (T%)

General

Because most of the nonsomatic items on the MMPI-2 are scorable when endorsed in the *True* direction, the proportion of items bearing *True* responses affords a rough guide to the patient's attitude in completing the MMPI-2. A typical range of values for this index is 30–40% *True*. Higher values tend to be strongly associated with elevations on F and Scales *6, 8,* and *9.* Very low values (i.e., high *False%*) for this index are associated with elevations on *L, F, K, 1, 2, 3, 4* and *8.*

Interpretation

Values for *True* percent (or $T\%$) are of clinical interest only at extremes of less than 25% or more than 60% in psychiatric populations. High values reflect the acquiescence response set, which, if indiscriminate, is accompanied by high scores on *TRIN.* Because a bias toward endorsing items *True* suggests a crude approach to exaggerating symptoms, scores on $F, F_B, F_p,$ and Ds are usually extremely high and should be checked. The only clinical group that tends to produce high values on $T\%$ without extremely high scores on $F, F_B, F_p,$ and Ds with any consistency are bipolar manics. Clinical groups often producing unusually low values on this index are among the somatization disorders. Interpreting protocols with $T\%$ values exceeding 70 or less than 15 is discouraged, as these are almost always the result of a deviant response style, and the resulting profiles are so distorted as to provide a misleading basis for personality description.

UNDERREPORTING SCALES

The scales discussed in this section fall into two main groups: those that are sensitive to a form of favorable self-presentation that is inadvertent, self-deceptive, or both; and those that are sensitive to the deliberate and self-conscious effort to minimize or deny psychopathology. This division follows the research of Paulhus (1984, 1986), who proposed a two-factor model of social-desirability responding that distinguished between what he called "self-deception" and "impression management" (other-deception). Paulhus's findings replicated those of Wiggins (1964) and have themselves been replicated (1988) and later discussed (1997) by Nichols and Greene. The three self-deception scales described in this section are K; *Superlative Self-Presentation* (S; Butcher & Han, 1995); and *Socioeconomic Status* (Ss; Nelson, 1952). The three impression management scales discussed are L; *Positive Malingering* (Mp; Cofer, Chance, & Judson, 1949); and *Social Desirability* (Sd; Wiggins, 1959).

The *L (Lie)* Scale

General

L is one of the impression management scales. It was rationally developed from items adapted from Hartshorne and May's *Studies in Deceit* (1928). The L scale items do not implicate lying as such; they merely deny minor and widespread failings of character and observance that carry little or no social opprobrium because such flaws are so widespread in Anglo-American culture that to deny such failings may be considered naive if not obtuse. Those not denying such failings (i.e., those who claim the corresponding virtues) are typically outside the cultural mainstream. They are able to appreciate the virtues embodied in the items, but fail to understand that people are not expected to claim them. Among such cultural "outsiders" are members of the clergy, who may feel expected to adhere to an unusually high standard of conscientiousness and moral propriety; immigrants and subcultural groups (e.g., the Hopi) who are not yet acculturated to Anglo-American norms; and people of limited intellectual sophistication who may not have full cognitive or contextual access to those norms. Apart from these groups are individuals within the larger culture, including patients, who will construe the context of assessment as one in which their moral standing, even their moral worth, may come under review, and are threatened by this. Some individuals approach the test with a broad set to deny not only minor failings but also symptoms, discomfort, interpersonal difficulties, "negative" traits and attitudes, and the like, whereas others candidly reveal problems and symptoms but remain narrowly guarded about admitting to what they fear may be viewed as moral shortcomings. Members of both groups may thus obtain elevated L scores based upon fears that the assessment results may inspire negative moral judgments about them. Both groups also tend to manifest suppressed clinical scale scores, with the former group showing greater suppression than the latter group. Among the impression management scales, L is the weakest and most readily manipulated. The items are transparently virtuous and easily avoided. Most normals and patients tend to avoid endorsing the L items, with normals averaging only 3.5 items and patients only slightly more.

Scores are negatively correlated with education, intelligence, and cultural sophistication, and bright, well-educated, and acculturated examinees tend to obtain low scores, even when motivation to underreport is high. (See Rapid Reference 5.7 for a summary description of L.)

Interpretation

Because L scores are influenced by education, intelligence, and general sophistication, interpretive ranges are approximations. At any given elevation above average, L scores are more remarkable when obtained from intelligent and well-educated examinees. The motives leading to elevations on L are numerous but tend to divide into two overlapping

---

≡*Rapid Reference 5.7*

Summary Descriptive Features of L

Number of Items: 15
True/False Balance: 0/15
Overlap: The L scale shares seven items with Sd and six with Mp.
Content: The content of L is obvious, the items referring to evident but infrequent and therefore improbable virtues such as always telling the truth. The items are phrased in a way that a *False* response denies moral imperfections.
Relations with Other Scales: L is moderately correlated with the other impression management scales, Mp (.65) and Sd (.54).

classes: apprehensions about how the examinee's responses will be received (that is, motives based on fear), and impression management, in which misleading or deceiving the clinician is the primary motive. Referring to scores on *Mp* and *Sd* helps to distinguish between these two groups, because these scales are more sensitive to impression management than is *L*. Scores greater than *T*-65 on *Mp* or *Sd* strongly suggest that impression management, rather than fear, is the motive for high *L* scores.

Scores above *T*-65 to *T*-70 suggest naivete or rigidity in moral outlook and a sense of constraint in self-presentation that is designed to forestall negative moral judgment, even though the examinee may exhibit significant problems, especially health concerns and dysphoria. Such patients are generally unsophisticated, significantly lacking in insight, and often severely lacking in awareness of how they are perceived by others (i.e., of their stimulus value). Their self-concept may also be unrealistic. Their efforts to project an image of moral virtue and self-control tend to be unsuccessful and may even backfire. Others may see them not as virtuous but as self-centered, predictable, unoriginal, stereotyped in their thinking, narrow in their interests, and naive or inflexible in their outlook. They are also seen as slow to adapt to unfamiliar ideas and situations, and are consequently vulnerable to stress, especially interpersonal stress. In psychiatric settings, patients with somatization disorders not infrequently have *L* scores in this range, with concurrent elevations on Scales *1, 2,* and *3* and combinations thereof (e.g., *3-1, 2-3,* etc.), as do some manics (with Scale *9* elevated) and patients manifesting paranoid syndromes. Among the latter, *L* may be elevated in isolation. Extremely high scores (> *T*-80) indicate rigid and broad-based denial, and typically result in the suppression of most if not all of the clinical scales. Such scores also result from a bias toward *False* responding (low *T%*). At these levels, the profile is usually distorted and interpretation of the clinical and other scales is likely to be compromised.

Scores above *T*-65 are often viewed as an effort to appear virtuous primarily for purposes of impression management. Such scores are especially common in child custody evaluations, where scores in the range of *T*-60 to *T*-65 are routine. Similar scores are seen in employment screening, especially for positions that do not require college education. Elevations in a moderate range (*T*-55 to *T*-65) reflect a pattern of traits and motives similar to those characteristic of higher scores, but in attenuated form. That is, scorers in this range may show a pattern of conformity, conventionality, and inflexibility, but to a milder degree not likely to distort the clinical scale profile unduly. Scores at the lower end of this range are also obtained by relatively sophisticated examinees who, while not necessarily seeking to mislead, may wish to polish their image to achieve a more favorable impression.

Low Scores

Scores below T-45 reflect candor about revealing minor faults and failings, but this may or may not translate into a frank and open response to other content areas. In general, low scorers are seen as independent, self-possessed, and untroubled—if not relaxed and self-confident—about how others perceive them, and occasionally as going out of their way to ostentatiously present themselves "warts and all."

The K Scale

General

The K scale was the last of the original validity scales to be constructed and functions primarily as one of the self-deception scales, although it is also susceptible to impression management. It was developed to fill the need for a scale to reduce the number of false negatives occurring when the patient produces a profile within normal limits (WNL) although hospitalized and manifesting significant psychopathology. Meehl and Hathaway (1946/1980) compared the item responses of 50 (25 male and 25 female) adult inpatients with behavior disorders (i.e., very few patients with neuroses or psychoses) who produced WNL profiles *and* elevations on L of at least T-60, with the normal contrast sample used in the development of the basic clinical scales. Separate analyses were conducted by gender, resulting in a preliminary scale (called L_6) of 22 items keyed in the self-favorable direction. Further investigation of L_6 indicated that it reduced both false positive and false negative cases but was insufficiently sensitive to severe depression and schizophrenia. In order to correct for this, eight items were identified that, first, showed no tendency to change in their endorsement frequency in groups of male psychology students under instructions to overreport ($n = 54$) or underreport ($n = 53$) psychopathology, but that, second, did discriminate between the depression and schizophrenia criterion groups and the normal contrast sample. When added to L_6 and keyed in the direction of the depressives and schizophrenics, these items appeared to increase the sensitivity of the resulting scale, since known as K. The items of the K scale (both the L_6 and the correction items) are more subtle than those found on L, making them much less susceptible to conscious efforts to over- or understate psychopathology.

The items of L_6, like most of the MMPI/MMPI-2 items, are sensitive to both psychopathology and response style. The addition of the eight correction items, keyed in the pathological direction (i.e., in the direction opposite to the trend of the items of L_6), neutralized some of the psychopathology variance in the final scale, leaving K a relatively purified measure of test-taking attitude, with high scores indicating a bias toward underreporting and low scores reflecting the contrasting bias (overreporting). After completing K, McKinley, Hathaway, and Meehl (1948/1980) developed weights for those of the basic scales of the MMPI for which some fraction of K, when added to basic scale raw scores, appeared to increase the discrimination between a sample of 200 normals (100 men, 100 women) and groups of varying numbers (36–101) of new inpatient test cases, with each group judged to bear important similarities to the original criterion cases used in developing the basic scales. These investigators found that the differentiation of the distributions of test cases from those of the comparison normals could be maximized for five of the scales— *1, 4, 7, 8,* and *9*—by adding K weights of .5, .4, 1.0, 1.0, and .2, respectively. Increased separation between distributions of normals and the test cases for scales *2, 3,* and *6* by adding various fractions of K could not be demonstrated. However, the authors observed that "there seems to be some indication that the optimal amount of K for a given clinical scale is inversely related to the proportion of 'subtle' items the scale already contains" (p. 138). This is an important insight. As noted earlier, the K scale is subtle and therefore relatively resistant to deliberate efforts to manipulate its score. It thus may function as a common pool of items that, when appended in appropriate amounts to scales composed of excessively obvious items (i.e., those scales most susceptible to over- and underreporting), serves to compensate for this weakness. In effect, the intent of the K-correction is to lend subtlety to scales with a shortage of subtle items, and in amounts that reflect the extent of that shortage. There has been little research validating the original K weights, and it is likely that shifts in item response patterns in the intervening 50 years since they were devised are sufficient to have rendered these weights no longer optimal. There is even some question that the response patterns to items of K may have shifted to a point that K may no longer separate normals from clinical groups as satisfactorily as it did a half-century ago. Thus revising or constructing a new K scale and establishing contemporary weights are important future tasks. However, the scale's basic logic and its function as a correction to suppress the effects of over- and underreporting among patients in psychiatric settings remain compelling. Whether the *K*-correction remains justified in other settings (e.g., in employment screening, in civil and criminal forensic contexts, in general medical hospitals, or even among mental health consumers with relatively minor patterns of maladjustment or situationally determined crises) is uncertain and, on current evidence, doubtful.

K is one of the self-deception scales. It is responsive primarily to relatively stable and deeply ingrained self-attitudes rather than to the kinds of situational incentives that may lead to calculated attempts to over- or underreport psychopathology. The *K* scale is not insensitive to this influence, however. Caldwell (June 25, 1999, personal communication) has argued that *K* may be decomposed into three primary sources of variance: socioeconomic status (a source highlighted by Meehl and Hathaway in 1946), impression management, and emotional constriction. Using *Ss* as the marker for socioeconomic status, *Mp* and *Sd* as markers for impression management, and *R* as the marker for emotional constriction, Caldwell organizes the correlations of these scales with *K* and with each other according to the matrix in Figure 5.1.

The scales Caldwell identifies as marking his three sources of variance for *K*

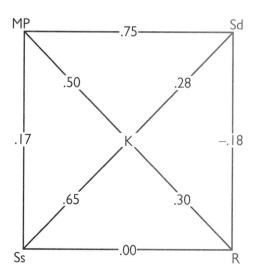

Figure 5.1. Caldwell's Matrix of Scale Correlations with K.

≡ Rapid Reference 5.8

Summary Descriptive Features of *K*

Number of Items: 30

True/False Balance: 1/29

Overlap: The *K* scale shares 10 items with *S* (five with *S1*), nine with *Hy-S*, seven with *Pd-S*, six with *D* (five on *D-S*), four each with *Hy2*, *Ma-S* and *Ma3*, and *Mp*. Overlapping items scored in reverse include eight with *Si* (four on *Si3*), and five with *CYN* (four on *CYN1*).

Content: The content of *K* is subtle and includes themes of negative and unstable emotionality (e.g., hostility), interpersonal difficulties, cynicism and mistrust, introversion, and other problems in adaptation, all of which are denied.

Relations with Other Scales: *K* is highly correlated with *S* (.88), *F − K* (−.86), *Si3* (−.85), and *Hy-S* (.82); with all of the First Factor scales (*A*, Scale *7*, *PK*, *PS*, *Mt*, *ANX*, *OBS*, *TRT*, *WRK*, and *NEN*, all in the −.70 to −.80 range); and with many of the anger, hostility, and cynicism scales (e.g., *CYN*, *ANG*, and *TPA*, also in the −.70 to −.80 range). It is moderately correlated with broadly positive trait markers such as *Ss*, *Do*, *Re*, *GM*, and *Es*, in a range of .60 to .65. Given their association with the First Factor, *K* scores will have a strong influence on those scales whose content reflects distress and negative emotionality.

are remarkably uncorrelated with each other, with the exception of *Mp* × *Sd* (= .75). The next highest correlation is between *Sd* and *R* at −.18. The correlations between *R* and *Ss* (.00), *Ss* and *Mp* (.17), *Mp* and *R* (.03), and *Ss* and *Sd* (.05) are so low as to indicate that Caldwell's proposed three sources of variation for *K* scores are essentially independent. (See Rapid Reference 5.8 for a summary description of *K*.)

Interpretation

Interpreting *K* is complex, encompassing its influence when considered both in isolation and as a correction to five of the basic scales. The empirical correlates of the *K*-corrected basic scales may vary in proportion to the contribution of the *K*-correction to the total raw score. For example, a patient who achieves a total raw score of 36 on Scale *8*, on the basis of 24 raw Scale *8* items and 12 *K* items, is likely to be described in substantially different terms from another patient who obtains the same total raw score, but on the basis of 24 *K* items and only 12 Scale *8* items, especially when deliberate overreporting in the former case and underreporting in the latter case can be ruled out. All other things being equal, a relatively high proportion of K items in relation to the total raw score suggests better overall adaptation, better control over symptomatic expressions, better-preserved social and interpersonal skills, better prognosis for psychotherapy, and lesser disability than when the proportion of K items in relation to the total raw score is low. Even among the scales receiving smaller K corrections, notably Scales 4 and 9, the amount of K that is added to the raw score is often associated with the content of the clinical scale items endorsed. When K is high, scores on these scales are likely to reflect a preponderance of subtle items ($Pd - S$, especially $Pd3$; $Ma - S$, especially $Ma3$), whereas low K scores suggest that more of the obvious items from these scales have been endorsed. These differences can and often should influence interpretation because the empirical correlates for these scales when K is high are likely to reflect relatively mild and less socially disruptive features of personality, such as extroversion, social fearlessness, and "cool," whereas low K scores are likely to be associated with more severe and disruptive personological, or symptomatic features, or both.

Following Caldwell, the interpretation of K should be informed by the scores on Ss, Mp, Sd, and R. It is also useful to compare K routinely with scores on Barron's (1953) *Ego Strength (Es)* scale. The two scales are moderately correlated ($\sim$.60) but share only one item. The differences between their respective constructions and purposes have important clinical implications. K is predominantly subjective, measuring primarily the tendency to present the self in self-favorable (versus self-negative) terms. *Es*, on the other hand, was developed on the basis of an objective adjustment criterion, success in psychotherapy, and has subsequently been found to correlate with various measures of stress tolerance (see description of *Es* in Chapter 7), and therefore provides a helpful point of reference against which to judge K scores. As a rule of thumb, when K exceeds *Es* by 10 T-scores or more, the patient's subjectively reported level of adjustment is likely to be overstated and to exceed that reported by observers. Conversely,

> ## DON'T FORGET
>
> A relatively high proportion of K items in relation to the total raw score suggests better overall adaptation, better control over symptomatic expressions, better-preserved social and interpersonal skills, better prognosis for psychotherapy, and lesser disability than when the proportion of K items in relation to the total raw score is low.

when the elevation on Es exceeds that on K by a similar or greater amount, patients are likely to see themselves as less adequate, more disabled, or both, relative to the way in which others objectively observe the patient's functioning. When the elevation on these two scales is approximately equal, observers will likely confirm the patient's subjective report of level of coping and adjustment.

In most cases, K elevations will be determined by non-deliberate, self-favorable biases (self-deception) rather than by intentional and calculated self-serving efforts to deceive the clinician and frustrate the purposes of the assessment (impression management). K elevations between T-55 and T-65 suggest moderate self-favorableness and are generally achieved by giving oneself the benefit of the doubt. Such patients often see themselves as well adjusted and as sufficiently able to cope with the difficulties they face that they feel little or no need to call attention to them.

When scores on Ss are in a similar range or higher, F exceeds L, M_p, and S_d are at or below T-55, and the patient has at least some college, scores in this range of K are usually associated with positive attributes (e.g., independence, self-control, effectiveness/efficiency, self-confidence, resourcefulness, constructive relations with others, and good social skills and self-esteem). On the other hand, when Ss is below T-50 and scores on M_p or S_d reach or exceed T-60 (especially if L exceeds F with fewer than 12 years of education), K scores in this range are more likely to reflect a highly selective self-description in which only socially acceptable problems and symptoms (e.g., pain) are admitted, but distress, problems, and conflicts viewed as less socially acceptable are minimized or denied outright. Interpreting scores in this range can be aided by comparing the elevations on the *Obvious* and *Subtle* scales for *2, 3, 4, 6,* and *9.* In most cases, the *Subtle* will exceed the *Obvious* subscale, but in some, the *Obvious* subscale may exceed its *Subtle* counterpart, affording the clinician a focus for interpretive emphasis.

K scores greater than T-65 suggest a level of underreporting sufficient to distort the profile to the point of compromised reliability for personality description and clinical prediction. At these levels, self-reported adjustment may be unrealistic and reflect a need to deny problems, and weaknesses, and to present an image of adequacy and self-control inconsistent with—if not directly contradicted by—other clinical information. Scores in this range usually reflect a strong bias against obvious item content, especially when F is in an average or low range, but they tend to stimulate elevation on most if not all of the

Subtle subscales. Reference to L, Ss, S, M_p, and S_d should be made to clarify the meaning and shape the interpretation of scores in this range. In addition to clarifying the motivational basis for K scores in this range, examining the pattern of scores on L, Ss, M_p, and S_d may reveal much about the patient's level of insight. Insight is likely to be better preserved when scores on M_p, S_d, or both exceed those for L and Ss. Conversely, when L exceeds Ss and M_p, especially if S_d exceeds K (see subsequent discussion of S_d), insight is likely to be narrow if not impaired. The *Obvious* and *Subtle* subscales may be checked for the presence and consistency of the expected *Subtle*-greater-than-*Obvious* pattern; scales for which this expectation is not confirmed (i.e., *Obvious* subscale more elevated than *Subtle*) may be given greater emphasis in the interpretation of the profile. $T\%$ should be checked to rule out an extreme *False* bias.

Low Scores

K scores in the T-35 to T-45 range suggest either overreporting or limited resources for coping with the stresses and demands of daily life, or both. When overreporting can be ruled out (i.e., scores on F, F_B, F_P, Ds, and $F - K$ are within acceptable ranges), the patient is likely to be seen as highly self-critical, pessimistic, dissatisfied, cynical, irritable, unstable, helpless, and poorly defended, and frequently as manifesting psychotic signs and symptoms (e.g., hallucinations, delusions, disordered thinking, behavioral disorganization). Such examinees typically are socially unskilled, awkward, or inept, and may inspire aggression or exploitation in others. Although they may have diagnostic insight (i.e., they may be able to admit psychological/psychiatric problems), they generally lack insight into their own or others' motives. Patients of higher socioeconomic status (SES) may have levels of distress and disability considerably greater than those among undereducated and lower SES patients who score similarly on K. Reference to Ss is also helpful; patients for whom Ss exceeds K tend to function more poorly and at a greater level of suffering than patients for whom K exceeds Ss (the more common pattern). Occasionally, patients in psychotic crises will score in this range or even lower, dramatizing catastrophic distress, panic, and a sense of impending disorganization. If not already hospitalized, such patients usually require hospitalization in order to stabilize, and may show fairly dramatic upward shifts in K upon retesting.

K scores of T-35 and below usually indicate overreporting, and it is unusual for F, F_B, F_P, Ds, and $F - K$ values to be within acceptable ranges when K is so low. These levels of K are associated with highly pathological-appearing profiles with multiple scale peaks, extreme positive slope, and an inadequate fit between profile and patient, even when F, F_B, F_P, Ds, and $F - K$ values are not extreme. $T\%$ should be checked to rule out an extreme *True* bias.

The S (Superlative Self-Presentation) Scale

General

Primarily a self-deception scale but one that, like K, is influenced by the presence of impression management, S was developed to assess "the presentation of self in a superlative manner" (Butcher & Han, 1995, p. 25). The item responses of 274 male airline-pilot applicants were contrasted with those of the 1,138 men in the restandardization sample. Items were selected for the final scale if their endorsement frequencies differed significantly (.001) between the two groups and if the items contributed to the scale's internal consistency. (See Rapid Reference 5.9a for a summary description of S.) Five subscales were derived by a factor analysis of the 50 items and all but one of them (number 184) appear on one of the subscales. These subscales are described in Rapid Reference 5.9b.

The extremely high correlation between S and K indicates that S, like K, is saturated with the First Factor. Both scales are negatively correlated with all of the MMPI-2 content scales, but the magnitude of these correlations is consistently slightly higher for S. The S items also appear to possess higher social-desirability ratings than those of K (Dahlstrom, Welsh, & Dahlstrom, 1975, Appendix B) for the thirty-nine S and thirty K items for which such ratings are available. These considerations suggest that S is likely to suppress content scale scores and the endorsement of obvious items in general. It is uncertain whether S possesses the same degree of independence of psychopathology as K, but it does appear that it is at least as sensitive to self-favorable versus self-unfavorable test-taking attitudes (Greene, 2000). S has performed very well in studies that compare the ability of different underreporting scales to discriminate MMPI-2s completed under instructions to fake good from one completed under standard instructions; in at least two such studies (Baer, Wetter, Nichols, Greene, & Berry, 1995; Bagby, Nicholson, Buis, Radovanovic, & Fidler, 1999), S and Sd (described later) demonstrated clear incremental validity over L and K. Such a pattern of performance in the research to date suggests that S is the best of the self-deception scales.

≡ Rapid Reference 5.9a

Summary Descriptive Features of *S*

Number of Items: 50

True/False Balance: 6/44

Overlap: The S scale shares 10 items with K (5 on S1, 3 on S2, and 1 each on S3 and S4), 6 with Mp (4 on S2), and 5 with Hy − S (all on Hy2). Overlapping items scored in reverse include 14 with CYN (9 on CYN1; 5 on CYN2), 12 with the Cook-Medley Hostility (Ho) scale (10 on S1), 6 each with Mt, ASP (all on ASP1) and TPA (4 on TPA1), 5 each with ANG (all on ANG2) and WRK.

Content: The content of the items on S is less subtle and more socially desirable than for items on K, emphasizing the denial of misanthropic attitudes, cynicism, mistrust, irritability, hypersensitivity, anxiety, internal conflict or dissonance, and the assertion of a benevolent belief in the virtue, honor, and nobility of others, contentment with one's situation in life, an even temper, composure, and conformity/conventionality.

Relations with Other Scales: S is highly correlated with K (.88), Si3 (−.84), NEN (−.84), F − K (−.86), with all of the First Factor scales (A, Scale 7, PK, PS, Mt, ANX, OBS, TRT, WRK; all in the −.70 to −.80 range), and with many of the anger, hostility, and cynicism scales (e.g., CYN, ANG, TPA, also in the −.70 to −.80 range). It is moderately correlated with broadly positive trait markers such as Ss, Do, Re, GM, and Es, in a range of .60 to .65. Given its association with the First Factor, S scores will have a strong influence on scales the content of which reflect cynicism, distress, and negative emotionality.

Despite the supportive and promising research findings on *S*, a number of questions can be raised about its origins and applications. Apart from the scale's having been constructed using all-male samples, and thus its likely greater sensitivity to underreporting and self-deception in men than in women, there is reason for concern about the meaning and interpretation of *S* even among men. The criterion pilot applicants may have approached the MMPI-2 in several different ways: some claiming extraordinary adjustment, others claiming unusual freedom from common weaknesses, and still others with superior adjustment marking items to reflect their adjustment without overstating it. It is also likely that some applicants, harboring no conscious desire to slant their test results in a favorable direction, did so inadvertently, whereas others very actively, deliberately tried to create a favorable impression on the prospective employer. In short, the *S* criterion group was likely com-

≡ Rapid Reference 5.9b

Subscales for *S**

S1 (Belief in Human Goodness—15 items): All but one of these items appear on *CYN*, and are proportionally divided between *CYN1* and *CYN2* but scored in reverse. Scores over T-60 reflect the examinee's belief that others are honest, fair, and reasonable, and that the examinee's ideas and motives are readily understood and respectfully treated by others, including those who may be supervising him or her. With some examinees, especially those of lower socioeconomic status, scores in this range suggest a naive if not obtuse confidence in others' virtue and trustworthiness. Conversely, low scores (< T-40) reflect a cynical and mistrustful, if not hostile, view of others and their motives.

S2 (Serenity—13 items): These items deny worries, fears, concerns, and inner conflicts, and suggest a placid and tranquil psychic world. High scorers (> T-60) report that they take a peaceful, confident, and unhurried approach to living. Low scorers (< T-40) report a great deal of internal conflict and turbulence, with worries, indecision, a lack of self-confidence, and a sense of being rushed.

S3 (Contentment with Life—8 items): These items deny dissatisfaction with one's basic life circumstances. High scorers (> T-60) report virtually complete contentment with family, work, and finances; low scorers (< T-40) express a tense or strained discontent in these areas.

S4 (Patience/Denial of Irritability and Anger—8 items): High scorers (> T-60) report that they do not become angry, irritable, or impatient with others, even when provoked. Low scorers (< T-40) admit to anger, impatience, and retaliatory motives.

S5 (Denial of Moral Flaws—5 items): Four of these items overlap *GF*. High scorers (> T-60) deny unusual sex practices, temptations to be dishonest, using alcohol and marijuana, and having guilty secrets. Such scores suggest an avoidance of risk-taking. Low scorers (< T-40) admit these items and may show a low threshold for risk-taking.

*Nonoverlapping

posed of several subgroups of unknown size and uncertain influence in determining the ultimate composition of the *S* scale. Moreover, this criterion group was atypical in many ways—all were four-year college graduates, and virtually all were Caucasian, successful, in good health, and of higher SES. It is thus appropriate to use caution in interpreting the *S* scores of women, ethnic minorities, and individuals of lower SES.

Interpretation

As with K, interpretation of S is complex. Its relation to SES is at least as strong as that of K, considering the origins of the criterion sample and that the correlations between both Ss and S, and Ss and K are identical at 0.65. The interpretation of S may be strengthened by viewing its scores within the context of scores on L, Ss, M_p, and S_d when S scores are high, on F, F_B, F_P, Ds, and $F - K$ when S scores are low, and in relation to Es, regardless of whether the score on S is high or low, using the same guidelines given for interpreting K scores. Scores on S tend to exert considerably greater upward pressure on K and Mp than on L or Sd, such that it is not uncommon to find K, S, and Mp elevated simultaneously. In such cases, interpretive weight should be given to Sd, with scores greater than T-60 tending to support an impression management interpretation of Mp, but scores less than T-55—especially less than T-50—indicating the possibility that Mp may have been spuriously elevated by variance shared with S and K. The latter would not contradict or compromise a self-deception interpretation for S and K.

Interpreting high and low S scores is aided by scores on the S subscales. Although it is difficult for scores on S to reach T-65 without drawing item endorsements from at least four of the five S subscales, it is worthwhile to evaluate the contribution of each of the subscales to the total S score, and to shade its interpretation accordingly. Bear in mind, however, that high or low scores on $S1$ and $S5$ may be strongly or completely determined by scores on CYN and GF, respectively.

Elevations in a range of T-60 to T-70 suggest an overly favorable self-presentation as a result of naive self-attitudes, limited insight and self-awareness, or apprehensions about how the test results will be viewed and used. At these levels, deliberate attempts to mislead are uncommon but readily identified by elevations on M_p and S_d, especially when $S_d > M_p$. As with K, Ss may be an important moderator of S scores. When both S and Ss are elevated, and especially when Ss is higher, the examinee's self-description in terms of S and its subscales is likely to resemble closely the descriptions given by others, including those who know the examinee well (Butcher & Han, 1995), and thus should be interpreted conservatively.

Elevations exceeding T-70 indicate underreporting to the degree that the clinical profile is distorted and content scale scores are markedly suppressed. In such cases, focus on response style. Although typically reflecting self-deception and insightlessness, scores at this level may also reflect impression management (refer to scores on M_p and S_d). $T\%$ should be checked to rule out an extreme *False* bias.

Low Scores

Scores below T-45 reflect a degree of distress and behavioral disturbance that may result from either psychopathology or overreporting. When overreporting can be ruled out on the basis of scores for F, F_B, F_p, Ds, and $F - K$, the examinee is likely characterized as interpersonally abrasive, cynical, and hostile, as well as anxious, indecisive, preoccupied, and defeatist.

The Ss (Socioeconomic Status) Scale

General

Observing that mental health providers (a group of typically high social status) could misconstrue such behaviors as wife-beating, heavy drinking, improvident spending habits, siding with and covering for children vis-à-vis school authorities, and changing residence without notice to avoid creditors (although all common if not normative among some segments of the lower-lower class) as psychopathic, Nelson (1952) sought to investigate the relationship between psychopathology and SES. He rated the years of education and the occupational levels (as determined by a seven-step scale of occupational status categories) of an initial pool of 710 male Veterans Administration (VA) patients (Warner, Meeker, & Eells, 1949). The item responses of 41 patients with 13 or more years of education and occupations within the two highest-status categories (e.g., engineer, manager) were compared with those of 43 patients with 8 or fewer years of education and occupations within the two lowest-status categories (e.g., laborer, dishwasher). The items separating these groups at the .01 level or less were selected for Ss. Nelson (1952) found highly significant correlations for education (.47), occupational level (.45), and intelligence (.41) in new samples of patients; Ss was unrelated to age in either the original or the new samples.

Ss shares considerable variance with K and S, correlating with both at about .65 despite sharing only a single item with K and only two with S. Both the strength of these correlations and the content of the scale raise the question of whether subtle defensiveness determines high Ss scores. However, individuals of high SES do enjoy a degree of protection from stressors, sources of instability, and threats to their survival and well-being unavailable to those at the lowest SES levels. Thus high SES individuals are likely to benefit from such status through better reputations; more stable and reliable social support systems, including better access to services of all kinds; better financial resources, including higher incomes, more savings, and better credit histories, and therefore greater access to credit; greater discretion in how money is spent; greater access to information; and more leisure to assess the nature and sources of difficulty and to plan and implement measures for its alleviation. Moreover, individuals of higher SES tend to possess higher intelligence, knowledge, skills, and abilities, attributes that were helpful in attaining those higher SES levels in the first place, than those who fail to attain such status. These advantages confer benefits of two kinds: (a) considerable flexibility and a wider range of alternatives to cope with hardships of most kinds, including interpersonal conflict, situational difficulties (e.g., automobile breakdowns), and economic reverses; and (b) insulation from stresses, problems, and maladjustment, including their experienced severity and their potential for creating more widespread disruptions in the individual's relationships and circumstances. These advantages tend to translate into higher thresholds for feelings of inadequacy and insecurity, developing symptoms of maladjustment and psychopathology, and for expressing feelings of distress over problems even when the distress is experienced internally.

This latter point deserves elaboration: One consideration involved in marking an MMPI-2 item in the pathological or symptomatic direction is the examinee's subjective estimate of his or her own coping capacity in relation to the symptom or problem. Is the problem sufficiently disabling that it needs to be called to the attention of the clinician through responses to the test items, or can it be managed without assistance? Such judgments may at times be unrealistically (i.e., self-deceptively) optimistic. However, when they *do* reflect individual coping capacity realistically, the examinee's not acknowledging problems that he or she feels are manageable without help can actually advance the goals of assessment, keeping it focused on areas where help is genuinely needed. That is, test results are most informative to both clinician and patient when they take a selective rather than an exhaustive approach to revealing symptoms and problems. Such an approach also makes the patient an agent in the treatment process, unlike an approach that dumps an exhaustive catalogue of every conceivable problem and difficulty into the clinician's lap to be sorted out. The relationships among Ss, Es, K, and S are informative in this connection. The correlation between Ss and Es is .83, almost as high as that between K and S (.88). However, the correlations between Es and K, and between Es and S, are .61 and .64, respectively. As noted earlier, privileged SES confers significant advantages in coping with adversity, be it psychological, interpersonal, or material. Hence, the very high correlation with Es (a scale demonstrated to be sensitive to stress tolerance and to physiologically organized responses to stress) suggests that, although Ss may not be free of variance related to self-deception, such variance is probably secondary to both actual and realistically perceived coping capacity. If so, the interpretive implications of Ss, as distinct from those of (for example) S, would seem largely positive, especially when Ss clearly exceeds S. Ss appears to be largely free of variance related to impression management ($Ss \times Mp = .17$; $Ss \times Sd = .05$). A significant limitation of Ss is its lack of "top," with raw scores being exhausted out at about T-75. (See Rapid Reference 5.10 for a summary description of Ss.)

Interpretation

In general, elevations on Ss reflect a self-portrayal of alertness, concern about one's physical appearance and social presentation, maturity, tolerance, sophistication, discretion, a candid recognition of fallibility, moral flexibility, and freedom from incapacitating (especially psychotic) symptoms. It is helpful to routinely review scores on Ss in relation to K, S, Es, Mp, and Sd.

Elevations of T-60 and above suggest SES-related coping advantages and a self-presentation the favorable aspects of which are likely both sincere and warranted. At these levels, provided that scores for Mp and Sd are average to low and that Ss exceeds S, the interpretation of K should be benign (i.e., without implications of defensiveness or self-deception). When both Ss and S are elevated to this extent *and* S exceeds Ss, the interpretation of K should reflect both high coping capacity and a self-deceptive, defensive style. At substantially higher elevations of Ss (T-70) the denial of symptoms and complaints suggests a self-deceptive pattern of response; in such cases, both K and S are likely to be strongly elevated.

Low Scores

Scores below T-30 to T-40 are consistent with a lower SES and its often concomitant experiences and disadvantages, including poverty and economic instability; clumsy, harsh, insensitive, neglectful, or inconsistent parenting;

≣Rapid Reference 5.10

Summary Descriptive Features of *Ss*

Number of Items: 73

True/False Balance: 13/60

Overlap: *Ss* shares 11 items with *Es*, 7 with *GM*, and 6 with *GF*, but only 1 item with *K*, 2 with *S*, and none with either *Mp* or *Sd*. It negatively overlaps Scale 8 (12 items, 6 on *Sc5* and 4 on *Sc1*), Scale 6 (9 items, 6 on *Pa1*), *F* (9 items), *PS* (9 items), *Ds* (8 items), *HEA* (8 items, 4 on *HEA2*), *PK* (7 items), *BIZ* (7 items, 3 on *BIZ2*), Scale 4 (6 items, 4 on *Pd-O* and 4 on *Pd4*), F_B (6 items), *FRS* (6 items, 3 on *FRS2*), *CYN* (6 items), Scale 9 (5 items), *PSY* (5 items), and *Mt* (4 items).

Content: The content of *Ss* is wide ranging, with denial of somatic complaints and sleep difficulties, persecutory ideation and psychotic thinking, cynicism and suspiciousness, phobias and obsessive-compulsive traits, problems with memory and cognition, dysphoric mood, passivity, moral rigidity, introversion, impulsiveness, and nonintellectual interests and occupations that depend largely on physical (vs. mental) activity.

Relations with Other Scales: *Ss* is highly correlated with *Es* (.83), and moderately correlated with *Do* (.72), *GM* (.67), *S* (.65), and *K* (.65). It has strong negative correlations with Scale 8 (−.83), *PS* (−.81), *PK* (−.81), *Ds* (−.80), F_B (−.78), *PSY* (−.78), Scale 7 (−.77), *F* (−.77), *HEA* (−.77), Scale 1 (−.76), and *BIZ* (−.76). This pattern of relationships indicates that self-sufficiency and stress tolerance (*Es*) and self-deception (*S*) can raise *Ss* scores, and that psychoticism (Scale 8, *PSY*, *BIZ*), broad maladjustment and subjective distress (*PS*, *PK*), and symptom exaggeration and malingering (*F*, F_B) can suppress *Ss* scores.

exposure to acrimonious domestic disputes and to drunkenness, crime, and violence in the family, neighborhood, or both; inadequate health care; limited or nonexistent educational support and achievement; poor and unstable social supports and supports for self-esteem; and so on. In the absence of such factors, low scores reflect impaired self-esteem, especially in the areas of efficacy and competence. *T*-scores between 0 and 30 constitute a range of variable interpretive significance. At the upper end of this range, interpretation emphasizing lower SES attitudes and experiences (including a history of acute and chronic stresses, or a generally negative or degraded self-concept) is appropriate for most patients, and overreporting is not suggested. At the lower end of this range, the overreporting of psychopathology becomes increasingly tenable as a focus for interpretation, and marked elevations (> *T*-90) on *F* and/or *Ds* are to be expected. *T%* should be checked to rule out a *True* response bias. A final hypothesis of relevance for some patients is that low scores may reflect both the psychotic, especially schizophrenic, illness and the economic disadvantage and decline (downward drift) noted in the families of schizophrenics.

The *Mp* (Positive Malingering) Scale

General

Cofer et al. (1949) had 81 college sophomore men and women complete the MMPI under three conditions: The negative malingering (NM) group was instructed to create an impression of emotional disturbance to avoid induction into the Army. The positive malingering (PM) group was instructed to create the best possible impression to be attractive to recruiters for a highly desirable Naval midshipman training program. Each of these groups also completed the MMPI under standard instructions in counterbalanced order. A third (control) group completed the MMPI twice under standard instructions to control for regression toward the mean often observed when personality tests are administered a second time. The items selected for *Mp* were those for which endorsement frequency did not change in either the NM or control groups, but did change in the PM group.

Most of the *Mp* items are reminiscent of *L* items, as they also refer to minor flaws and shortcomings most people find easy to admit but may deny when seeking to create a highly favorable impression. Although the inclusion of the masculine interest items is understandable given the wartime (Korea) atmosphere that inspired the instructional sets for the NM and PM conditions, their retention introduces a possible gender bias for *Mp*; the mean for women is about 1.33 raw score points lower than that for men. This may reduce the sensitivity of *Mp* to impression management among women. On the other hand, these items may increase the sensitivity of *Mp* for certain employment screening applications (e.g., police), as Caldwell (1988) has suggested. (See Rapid Reference 5.11 for a summary description of *Mp*.)

Interpretation

Elevations on *Mp* are best considered in relation to scores on *L, K, S, Ss,* and *Sd*. Scores on *L* may raise *Mp* scores because of their overlap and thematic sim-

≡ *Rapid Reference 5.11*

Summary Descriptive Features of *Mp*

Number of Items: 26

True/False Balance: 11/15

Overlap: *Mp* shares 13 items with *Sd*, 6 items each with *L* and *S* (4 on *S2*). Five items each overlap with Scale *5-Male* and *GF*, but are scored in reverse.

Content: *Mp* items are subtle and cover a wide variety of content, including the denial of minor and common worries or of lapses in honesty or conscientiousness; the assertion of high self-confidence and a potential for leadership; freedom from doubts, fears, angry impulses, and internal struggles; and unusual circumspection about sexuality. Several items claim masculine interests (military service, hunting, auto racing).

Relations with Other Scales: *Mp* is correlated highly with *Sd* (.75) and moderately with *L* (.65), *S* (.56), and *Ma3* (.47). It is negatively correlated with *Mf2* (−.66), *APS* (−.59), *NEN* (−.58), *A* (−.57), *ANX* (−.56), Scale 7 (−.55), *WRK* (−.55), *Mt* (−.55), *OBS* (−.54), *Pd5* (−.52), *PS* (−.51), *DEP* (−.50), *LSE* (−.50), *LSE1* (−.50), *PK* (−.50), and *MDS* (−.50).

ilarity. Occasionally, when *L* and *Mp* are jointly elevated and *L* is greater than *Mp*, the examinee's understatement of psychopathology may be more naive than deliberate, growing out of a fear of moral judgment rather than a conscious attempt to deceive the clinician and frustrate the assessment. In such cases, *Ss* is generally below *T*-50.

Mp scores at or above *T*-60 suggest an intention to present oneself unrealistically in terms of adjustment and freedom from commonplace human flaws and temptations, especially when accompanied by equal or greater elevations on *L* and/or *Sd*. As *Mp* scores reach *T*-65, especially when *Sd* is of equal or greater elevation, or when both exceed *K*, impression management is strongly suggested and interpretation should proceed with caution.

Wiggins *Sd* (Social Desirability) Scale

General

Wiggins (1959) compared the item responses of 55 male and 85 female Stanford undergraduates, who had completed the MMPI under standard instructions, with those of 72 men and 106 women who had been instructed to answer each item according to what they thought "people in general" would consider the more socially desirable response, given "the general values of American culture." The data for men and women were analyzed separately, and the items separating the desirability and control administrations at the .001 level for both groups comprise *Sd*. In their meta-analysis of measures of underreporting, Baer, Wetter, and Berry (1992) found across six studies an average effect size of 1.60, the highest of the measures they included. This value compared favorably with that for *Mp* at 1.42, and was more than twice that for $F - K$ (.71), which, in turn, was lower than the effect size for *K* alone (.94). The weight of subsequent research tends to confirm *Sd* as the best of the measures of impression management.

Both *Mp* and *Sd* are highly effective measures of impression management. They share 13 items and are highly correlated (.75), however, three features of *Sd* differentiate it from *Mp*. First, unlike *Mp*, for which 58% of the items are keyed *False*, 73% of the *Sd* items are keyed *True*. Second, both *Mp* and *Sd* deny flaws and assert virtues that most people need neither to deny nor assert when taking the MMPI-2, but *Mp* emphasizes the denial of negative attributes, whereas *Sd* emphasizes the assertion of positive attributes. Thus, the images portrayed of the self in these two scales differ, with *Mp* emphasizing virtue and stability in the context of relaxed, pacific, quiet self-assurance, and a placid if not imperturbable emotionality, and *Sd* emphasizing virtue and vitality in the context of a strong-willed, outgoing, constructive, engaged, and poised social presence. Finally, *Sd* has considerably more top than *Mp*, with *T*-scores peaking above 100 rather than at about 80. (See Rapid Reference 5.12 for a summary description of *Sd*.)

Interpretation

Sd items combine to create a portrait of a model citizen, one who is extroverted and outgoing, free of worry and self-doubt, assertive, self-directed, and in full control of his or her mental faculties; who is orderly, confident, capable, decisive, cool under pressure, and oriented to success; and who is composed but friendly, buoyant, energetic, up-to-the-task, and actively engaged in living—but also one who is straightlaced, hypervirtuous, prudish, and unrealistic in self-portrayal.

≡ Rapid Reference 5.12

Summary Descriptive Features of *Sd*

Number of Items: 33
True/False Balance: 24/9
Overlap: *Sd* shares 13 items with *Mp*, 7 with *L*, and 4 with *DIS*, scored in reverse.

Content: *Sd* items are subtle and cover a wide variety of content, including a high level of cognitive speed and alacrity in decision making; conventional (if not conservative) but socially responsible moral and political values; freedom from worry, self-consciousness, and self-doubt; high self-confidence, drive, and energy; persistence and self-control; sociability and loyalty; broad interests; and an absence of health concerns. Both masculine and feminine interests are represented, unlike on *Mp*, which includes only masculine interests.

Relations with Other Scales: *Sd* is correlated highly with *Mp* (.75) and moderately with *L* (.54) and *Ma3* (.44). It is negatively correlated with *Mf2* (−.50), *LPE* (−.50), and Scale *0* (−.44).

As with *Mp*, *Sd* scores should be evaluated in the context of scores on *L*, *K*, *S*, *Ss*, and *Sd*. It is appropriate to interpret *Sd* most confidently when it is elevated, is accompanied by an elevation on *Mp*, and is of greater elevation than *K* and *S*, and when *Ss* is below *T*-55. Spuriously high scores may be the result of extreme values for *T%* and generally should not be interpreted when *T%* exceeds 50. Such profiles are not uncommon among manics, who are prone to higher values for *T%* than other diagnostic groups and whose responses to many of the highly self-positive items on *Sd* may be determined by grandiosity or psychomotor acceleration rather than by impression management.

Sd scores at or above *T*-60 suggest an intention to present oneself unrealistically, claiming a variety of positive but cumulatively unrealistic attributes, especially when accompanied by equal or greater elevations on *Mp*. As *Sd* scores reach *T*-65, especially when *Mp* is of equal or greater elevation, or when both exceed *K*, impression management is strongly suggested and interpretation should proceed with caution.

🪶 TEST YOURSELF 🪶

1. **VRIN and/or TRIN are primarily useful for determining**
   (a) response consistency.
   (b) a preference for *True* or *False* responses.
   (c) exaggeration or malingering.
   (d) the accuracy of responses to test items.
   (e) a and b.
   (f) b and c.
   (g) c and d.
   (h) b and d.

2. **As one of the validity scales, F is largely insensitive to psychopathology.** True or False?

3. **Which statement is true?**
   (a) F_B is sensitive primarily to psychotic item content on the last half of the MMPI-2.
   (b) F and F_B are not affected differently by different kinds of psychopathology.
   (c) F items have a psychotic bias whereas F_B items have an affective bias.
   (d) F and F_B are both sensitive to problems in reading comprehension.
   (e) F and F_B are both sensitive to response inconsistency.
   (f) a, c, and d
   (g) b, c, and e
   (h) c, d, and e

4. **Which statement is true?**
   (a) The item content of F has a psychotic bias.
   (b) The item content of F_B has a psychotic bias.
   (c) The item content of F_P has a psychotic bias.
   (d) The item content of Ds has a psychotic bias.
   (e) a and c
   (f) a and d
   (g) b and d
   (h) c and d

5. The scales in which set are the most similar to one another?

(a) L, S, and Ss

(b) K, Ss, and Mp

(c) L, Mp, and Sd

(d) K, S, and Sd

6. Which pair of scales is the most sensitive to conscious, deliberate faking?

(a) F and K

(b) F_p and Sd

(c) L and Ds

(d) S and Ss

7. Which pair of scales is the most sensitive to genuine psychopathology?

(a) F and F_B

(b) K and F_p

(c) F and K

(d) S and Ss

Answers: 1. e; 2. False; 3. h; 4. a; 5. c; 6. b; 7. a

Six

THE STANDARD CLINICAL SCALES

The standard clinical scales include the eight basic scales developed from Hathaway's pathological criterion groups and the *Masculinity-Femininity (Mf)* and *Social Introversion (Si)* scales. Although originally named after the constructs (hypochondriasis, etc.) that determined membership in each of the criterion groups, the accumulation of external correlates gleaned from decades of MMPI research, along with shifts in the original diagnostic constructs themselves over the same period of time, made these designations progressively more misleading. Correlates from samples in which the base rate for hypochondriasis is known to be quite low (e.g., college students) could hardly be said to contribute to the construct validity of hypochondriasis as such, even though such correlates did contribute to the construct validity of the *Hypochondriasis* scale. Thus, the current clinical scale constructs embrace more—and less—than their clinical psychopathological labels imply. These labels may also distort the clinician's feedback on test results, because diagnostic terminology may often be received as pejorative, dreaded (e.g., paranoia), or obscure (e.g., psychasthenia). Because scales like those on the MMPI/MMPI-2 have the same basic format as a thermometer, it is tempting to speak of them in terms that invoke concepts of quantity rather than those of probability (e.g., "How much hypochondriasis has he got?"). For these and other reasons, users of the MMPI/MMPI-2 identify and speak of the standard clinical scales by scale number rather than scale name—hence, Scale *1* rather than *Hypochondriasis*. This convention also facilitates coding and the handling of code patterns.

THE "NORMAL" VERSUS "CLINICAL" RANGE

For both the MMPI and the MMPI-2, scale elevations exhibit psychopathological significance at 1.5 standard deviations (SD) from the mean. This point has been subject to some confusion, however, because of an apparent difference between the MMPI and the revised MMPI-2. On the MMPI, a T-score of 70 reflected this amount of deviation *plus* an additional increment that can be traced to three major causes: (a) the hypernormalizing effect on the original normative sample of their service as the controls for clinical scale development (Pancoast & Archer, 1989); (b) the failure to discourage of the use of the *Cannot Say (?)* category in the earlier work; and (c) the decision to exclude from the normal sample anyone "under a physician's care" (Hathaway & McKinley, 1940/1980, p. 10). None of these three factors were operative in the restandardization, and the movement of the line of demarcation between normals and patients from T-70 to T-65 on the MMPI-2 therefore represents a change less than it does a point of continuity.

Although a T-score value of 65 may represent the point at which normal and pathological groups are most reliably discriminated, this value has often erroneously been treated as an absolute line of demarcation rather than as a point of reference that lies in the center of the area within which the distributions of normal and pathological samples most densely overlap. Some clinicians tend to identify scale elevation with problem severity. Scale and profile elevation may be influenced primarily by the severity of the examinee's symptoms and distress, but they are also significantly influenced by factors related to response style. That is, the person's attitude toward taking the MMPI-2—his or her biases or dispositions to overreport or underreport problems and complaints and to approach the test self-critically or self-protectively—can also have a dramatic effect on elevation. Estimates of the proportion of variance in elevation that can be traced to response style vary with the particular index used. The correlation between the mean elevation of the basic clinical scales (*1–4* and *6–9*) and the $F - K$ Index at .66 is representative, however, indicating that 44% of elevation is related to response style.

For example, when scales L and/or K are substantially higher than F, scores on the standard clinical scales rarely reach a T-score of 65, regardless of the severity of an individual's disorder or disability. Because the items of the content scales are generally more obvious, and because of the lack of any correction (such as K) for these scales, scores greater than T-50 are rare under the same circumstances. Conversely, when F is substantially elevated over L and K, the extent and severity of the individual's problems may be grossly overstated by both the elevations of the highest scales and by the number of scales elevated above T-65. Under these conditions, the content scales are also subject to rapid and concerted elevation, which, in turn, complicates interpretation. For this reason T-65 should be considered a point on a band, the width of which is determined by assessing the person's test-taking attitudes, the context of the testing, the nature and duration of the relationship between examiner and examinee, the examinee's stake in producing valid and accurate results, and other external or situational factors that may influence response style. For overreporting response styles, T-65 will form the lower border of a band that reaches upward so that interpretive efforts focus on only those scores for which elevations are extreme. For underreporting response styles, T-65 will form the upper border of a band that extends downward to catch and include scales for interpretive attention that might otherwise be neglected. The $F - K$ Index (raw scores) may be the most acceptable general measure of overreporting and underreporting, with 0 to −10 indicating a normal range.

UNIFORM *T*-SCORES AND PERCENTILE RANKS

The concept of uniform T-scores was introduced in Chapter 4. Table 6.1 aids in translating uniform T-scores into percentile ranks for the eight basic clinical scales. The table also expresses these relationships for the MMPI-2 content scales. Note that the percentile values are approximate rather than exact. For the basic and content scales these approximations are very close for the combined restandardization sample, but they conceal small differences between men and women. For all other scales, these approximations are crude, if not very crude. They may provide the interpreter some degree of orientation, but should be avoided in formal reports.

The elevation classifications at the margin are given for convenience. Note that these levels are slightly overlapping, such that a T-score of 55 might be called "average" in some circumstances and "moderately high" in others. This overlap/ambiguity is a reminder that, just as a T-score of 65 will not always best classify any given examinee or set of respondents as normal or abnormal, the same principle holds at all levels of elevation. For example, a T-score of 55 on Scale *8* might be classified as "moderately high" when $F - K = -15$, but as "average" when $F - K = 0$.

Table 6.1 Percentile Equivalents of Uniform T-Scores

	Uniform T-score	Percentile Equivalent
Extremely High	90	> 99.9
	85	> 99.8
Very High	80	> 99
	75	98
High	70	96
	65	92
Moderately High	60	85
	55	73
Average	50	55
	45	34
Moderately Low	40	15
	35	4
Very Low	30	< 1

SUBSCALES

Because the standard clinical scales were derived by the method of contrasted groups, their item content tends to be heterogeneous and their structures multidimensional. In the contrasted groups approach (as opposed to the rational approach to inventory construction), criterion group members, not scale developers, select the items. The items appear on scales because criterion group members endorse them preferentially over normal controls. Moreover, items are selected for scale membership solely on their ability to discriminate criterion cases from controls. It is this circumstance that tends to bias the clinical scales of the MMPI/MMPI-2 in the direction of heterogeneity and multidimensionality. Once items are combined in a scale, inspection of the scale's item content may reveal any number of themes or organizing principles that permit rational or statistical subdivisions among the items to be discovered.

Another important reason for the multidimensionality of most of the standard clinical scales is that the psychiatric syndromes that characterized Hathaway's criterion groups were themselves multidimensional. Depression, for example, is often spoken of as a symptom (i.e., depressed mood), but the term is also used diagnostically to denote a severe condition characterized not only by depressed mood but also by certain vegetative (e.g., weight loss/gain, disturbed sleep, psychomotor slowing), cognitive/attitudinal (e.g., impaired concentration, forgetfulness, preoccupation, pessimism, worthlessness), and personological (e.g., inhibition of aggression, passivity) features. Obviously, a scale that failed to take such symptomatic diversity into account would be poorly attuned to the condition it seeks to measure. For this reason, the multidimensionality of most of the standard clinical scales is not only inevitable, given the method of contrasted groups, it is highly desirable. Because depressive illnesses vary so much in their symptomatic manifestations from one patient to another, a scale dominated by item content related to one class of symptoms (e.g., mood) but lacking content related to a different but equally common class of symptoms (e.g., cognitive) would perform poorly at best. Such a test would tend to overclassify as "depressive" patients with depressed mood but no other signs or symptoms of depression (i.e., false positives), and underclassify depressives whose diagnostic status rested primarily on signs and symptoms other than depressed mood (i.e., false negatives). Thus it is helpful to think of the basic scales not only as measures of their respective constructs, but also as *models* of them. In this sense, the basic scales may be thought of as *syndrome* scales, each containing a number of items that correspond to important but disparate features that characterize the major psychiatric syndromes.

The Harris and Lingoes (1955, 1968) subscales provide a convenient means for gaining access to the various dimensions contained within six of the eight basic scales. Depending on the parent scale, the content of each may be assessed with reference to scores from three to six subscales. These subscales can contribute to the clinical description of the syndromes signified by elevations on the parent scale. However, their contribution to understanding trends in the patterns of item content endorsed that underlie the entire profile of clinical scales may be even more important. For example, two patients may have

---

DON'T FORGET

The basic scales may be thought of as *syndrome* scales, each containing a number of items that correspond to important but disparate features that characterize the major psychiatric syndromes.

identically elevated scores on Scale *3* without having endorsed any of the Scale *3* items in the same way! One patient may have endorsed only those items reflecting somatic complaints, discomfort, and inefficiency, whereas the second overwhelmingly preferred items reflecting social interest and comfort, trust and friendliness, and the avoidance of hostility and unpleasantness. For most purposes it would be unwise to describe these two patients in similar terms, even though many of the empirical correlates of high Scale *3* scores might apply to both. Rather, the interpreter should heed each patient's specific pattern of item endorsements in the choice of empirical correlates selected in order to maximize the uniqueness, cogency, and precision of their respective clinical descriptions in the report of findings.

The Harris-Lingoes subscales were developed by rational means. The authors separately examined the items scored on Scales *2, 3, 4, 6, 8,* and *9*. Items that seemed similar in content, or that seemed to reflect a single attitude or trait, were gathered into a subscale which was then named to reflect the items' underlying theme. Harris and Lingoes considered Scales *1* and *7* to be unidimensional and therefore unsuitable for subscales, but their reasons for not attempting subscales for Scales *5* and *0* are unknown. Such subscales have been developed for the MMPI-2 by Martin and Finn (1992), Martin (1993), and Ben-Porath, Hostetler, Butcher, and Graham (1989), respectively, using a combination of statistical (primarily factor analysis) and rational techniques. Along with the Harris-Lingoes subscales, these will be presented in the discussion of the standard clinical scales.

Wiener and Harmon (1946; Wiener, 1948) developed a different set of subscales based on whether the items of each basic scale indicated emotional disturbance easily or only with difficulty. Those easily indicating disturbance were aggregated into an *Obvious* subscale; the remaining items constituted the obvious subscale's *Subtle* counterpart. No attempt was made to make the subtle and obvious subscales of equal length, and the obvious items outnumber the subtle items 145 to 108. Wiener and Harmon developed subtle and obvious components for five of the basic scales: *2, 3, 4, 6,* and *9*.

The role of subtle items in personality measurement is controversial; the literature surrounding this controversy has been recently and skillfully reviewed by Hollrah, Schlottman, Scott, and Brunetti (1995). The thrust of the literature critical of the subtle subscales is that their scores typically fail to converge with other inventory or ratings-based measures of the parent construct. For example, the subtle component of Scale 2 often fails to correlate significantly with external measures of depression or with other inventory measures of depressed mood. Such failures are hardly surprising, however, because both kinds of measures tend to reflect obvious features of the depressive syndrome. Indeed, the correlation between *Depression-Obvious (D-O)* and *Depression-Subtle (D-S)* is –.23 on the MMPI-2. Most of the literature on the subtle-obvious scales fails to consider the proper role of the subtle items: that of enhancing the discriminant validity of the clinical scales. The subtle items tend to be somewhat resistant to response styles, whereas the obvious items are highly vulnerable to them. Burkhart, Christian, and Gynther (1978) and Dubinsky, Gamble, and Rogers (1985) commented extensively on the "paradoxical" relationship of the subtle versus obvious items, such that attempts to suppress endorsement of the obvious items tends to be accompanied by an *enhanced* rate of endorsement of the subtle items. Thus the subtle items counteract a defensive approach to the obvious items, thereby suppressing the total scale score, by pushing it back up because of an increased endorsement rate for the subtle items.

In this fashion, the subtle scales appear to operate in much the same way as the *K*-correction, and three of the five scales with subtle subscales (*2, 3,* and *6*) have no *K*-correction; for the two scales that do receive *K*-corrections (*4* and *9*), the corrections are small, .4 and .2 respectively. These proportions are even smaller when reckoned on a *K*-per-scale-item basis. For example, the maximum correction for Scale *4* is 12 items ($30 \times .4 = 12$); dividing this number by the number of items on Scale *4* ($12 \div 50$) yields a *K* per-item value of .24. Recall that the purpose of adding proportions of the *K* score to some of the basic scales was to increase those scales' ability to discriminate between normal and criterion subjects. The role of the subtle items, then, appears to be analogous to that of *K*. It is helpful to think of the subtle items as a kind of built-in *K*-correction for those scales that do not need the amount of suppression required by scales such as *1, 7,* and *8*, which have no subtle items of their own. As might be expected from this analysis, Hollrah and colleagues (1995) found that, on the whole, the subtle subscales fared better when studied in the context of discriminant validity, whereas the obvious subscales fared worse. Regardless of the true dynamic function of subtle-obvious scales in relation to their parent scale scores, they do possess empirical correlates that can assist in interpreting the basic scales.

SCALE 1: HYPOCHONDRIASIS (Hs)

Development

Hypochondriasis was the first of the basic scales to be developed because there was widespread agreement on the construct, which was fairly simple, and because many cases were available for study. The criterion group for Scale *1* consisted of 50 cases manifesting "abnormal . . . concern over bodily health" (McKinley & Hathaway, 1940/1980) and carrying a diagnosis of Psychoneurosis, Hypochondriasis. The cases were carefully selected to exclude patients with symptoms of psychosis, and all had been thoroughly screened to exclude medical, neurological, or other psychiatric illness. The items that discriminated between this group and two comparison groups (262 [109 men, 153 women] of the 724 Minnesota Normals who had been roughly matched to the criterion group for age, and 265 [151 men, 114 women] students entering college) were gathered into a preliminary scale that was then tested against two other groups: 50 patients who were hospitalized on medical wards of the University hospital for physical illness, and 45 patients hospitalized for psychiatric treatment for conditions other than hypochondriasis. These procedures reduced the influence on scale scores of demographic variables such as age, marital and socioeconomic status, and education, and tested the ability of the scale to discriminate hypochondriacs from other patients with whom they might be confused, whether medical patients suffering the pain, discomfort, inconvenience, and stress of organic disease (and hospitalization), or psychiatric patients who may manifest hypochondriacal features in the context of other psychiatric disorders. The scale was cross-validated on a new sample of 25 hypochondriacs, and these cases proved to separate themselves adequately from the normal, medical, and psychiatric samples.

Interpretive Implications

General

Concerns center around health and somatic functioning. These concerns tend to persist despite disconfirming medical opinion and negative findings from diagnostic procedures, with the latter bringing not relief, but a continued conviction of illness and decreased confidence in the physician who ordered them. Patients with bona fide illnesses generally score near *T*-60, but may obtain

≡ Rapid Reference 6.1

Summary Descriptive Features of *Hs*

Number of Items: 32

True/False Balance: 11/21

Overlap: Scale 1 overlaps Scale 3 by 20 items, Scale 2 by 9 items, and Scale 8 by 4 items.

Content: Somatic Complaints. Items reflect head and sensory complaints; poor general health; upper gastrointestinal complaints; weakness, tiredness, and easy fatigability; and cardiac complaints. Specific complaints or symptoms exceed vague complaints at a ratio of about 2:1.

Relations with Other Scales: Among the basic clinical scales, Scale 1 is most highly correlated with Scale 2 (with which it shares 9 items), at .82, and Scale 3 (with which it shares 20 items), at .80. The latter correlation is decreased with the addition of the .5K that is added to Scale 1. Correlations with subscales are, in descending order, Hy-O (.96), Hy4 (.94), Hy3 (.88), D-O (.86), D3 (.82), D1 (.80), Sc6 (.80), and D4 (.79). Scale 1 is also highly correlated (.97) with the content scale HEA (36 items), with which it shares 23 items, and with its component scales HEA2 (.87), HEA3 (.81), and HEA1 (.80). High raw (i.e., uncorrected by K) scores will tend to raise Scales 2, 3, 7, and 8.

scores that are considerably higher if the illness is life-threatening and engenders fear and anxiety. Scores on Scale *1* never rule out a disease or illness of medical significance. (See Rapid Reference 6.1 for a summary description of Scale *1*.)

Presenting Problem

Concern about one's health and physical integrity, with a need that a visible sign or internally experienced sensation (e.g., pain, weakness) be placed in a medical context. The concern may focus on disease, disability, physical damage, or on the implications of one's symptoms for deterioration, morbidity, or mortality. Insomnia or other sleep difficulties are often mentioned. The presenting problem is characteristically difficult to localize and classify and the physical complaints are often accompanied by a detailed narrative of the patient's medical history that may include an extensive technical vocabulary of symptoms, diseases, and so forth (the hypochondriac's "organ recital") and diagnostic and treatment procedures that have brought no relief. There may be considerable and bitter criticism of previous physicians ("quacks," "charla-tans," "pill-pushers") for their incompetence, greed, or lack of care ("just in it for the money"). Earlier doctors missed or bungled the diagnosis, failed to or-der the correct lab test, gave medication that didn't help, made the problem worse, or produced intolerable side effects.

Among psychiatric patients, the symptoms of concern are much less stable over time unless they are connected with delusional ideation. Cases of pure hypochondriasis are now virtually never seen in psychiatric hospital settings, but patients who are hypochondriacal on a comorbid basis are not especially uncommon.

Symptomatic Pattern

These patients tend to be sensitized to interior somatic sensations or to the potentially dire health implications of visible signs. Although not typically de-pressed or anxious, high scorers tend to be cheerless, dissatisfied, and some-what pessimistic or cynical in their outlook. Anxiety, when present, is apt to take the specific form of nervousness. Patients are sluggish and unenthusi-astic, difficult to excite, and lacking in drive and ambition. Cognitively, they tend to be rather narrow, unimaginative, uncreative, conventional, and bound by habits and routines. Despite their self-centeredness, they are not character-istically self-indulgent. To the contrary, they are cautious and self-denying in many areas and view many pleasures as frivolous. Their dealings with others outside the family are distant but responsible and conscientious. They are gen-erally polite, sincere, and considerate, observe rules and regulations (albeit somewhat resentfully at times), and do not act out in antisocial ways. Incapac-ity is rare. These patients are usually able to function but suffer a reduced level of efficiency.

Interpersonal Relations

These patients tend to form long-term, dependent attachments of an extrac-tive kind onto another person, typically a spouse. Their relations with others tend to be limited, utilitarian, and controlling. They place excessively high ex-pectations and demands on intimates, and become sullen or whiny when oth-ers fail to provide them adequate levels of attention, consideration, or service. At the same time, they are emotionally reserved and stingy where others are concerned and often appear stubborn, bitter, self-centered, selfish, ungiving, ungrateful, and difficult to please. Their anger (especially hostility) tends to be expressed indirectly through dissatisfaction, demandingness, and controllingness. Somatic symptoms and disabilities can also be used manipulatively to intimidate others, instill guilt and a heightened sense of obligation, or both. Over time their behavior pattern creates an accumulation of resentment in others who may, in turn, meet the person's needs more sparingly, grudgingly, or both. Nevertheless, their marriages tend to be stable. Carson (1969) noted that these patients "appear readily to adopt a paranoid posture when pressured" (p. 284).

Behavioral Stability
This pattern can be extraordinarily stable over time. Scale *1* is considered to be one of the character scales of the MMPI-2.

Defenses
Displacement of depression, anxiety (including anxiety about having a serious or life-threatening illness), or dependency onto physical symptoms/illness/disability. Rationalization (e.g., for failure to achieve). Conflicts; denial of other problems. Projection of selfishness and self-centeredness. Somatization may afford a way out of undesirable activities and situations such as social or sexual interaction. Finally, counterphobic denial of illness or injury may be seen with low scores.

History
Look for multiple previous medical contacts, physical examinations, laboratory tests, invasive diagnostic procedures (laparoscopies, spinal taps, etc.), treatments, and surgeries. The patient may have had a great many medical contacts, both recently and over many years ("doctor shopping") without relief.

These patients often come from underprivileged backgrounds in which the family of origin was impoverished or subject to economic instability either because of external factors, such as layoffs and periods of unemployment, or internal factors, such as an absent or alcoholic father. Often the family provided an environment conducive to the learning of illness behavior either indirectly—through the illness or death of a parent, sibling, or other close relative, or through the hypochondriacal modeling of an important adult—or directly, through the patient's own experience of frequent illness, life-threatening disease, or catastrophic accident. Intelligence and educational attainment are generally lower than average, although occupational attainment may be fair (e.g., skilled tradesperson).

Diagnostic Considerations

Diagnoses tend to be among the Somatoform Disorders such as Somatization Disorder or Hypochondriasis, but comorbidities may be extensive, especially substance abuse (often of alcohol, prescription drugs, or both for pain or sleep) or depression.

Treatment Considerations

In a medical context these patients are best treated conservatively and without extensive workups and diagnostic tests. Issues of medication should be handled carefully because these patients are quick to experience side effects due to their somatic focus and sensitivity to internal sensations. Medications need to be monitored closely to insure that they are being consumed according to prescription. There is some potential for the development of abuse.

These patients are often referred to psychiatrists or psychologists after their primary physicians have become exasperated with them, deciding that they are not real patients, but "crocks." Consequently, patients are likely to view the initial contact skeptically, as being unjustified and possibly demeaning. In particular, they are apt to be overwhelmingly resistant to any idea of psychological causation, which the hypochondriac is likely to interpret as meaning that the problem is "all in my head." Not to be discounted is the possibility that the patient has encountered real scorn in contacts with previous doctors, and this, and the psychologist's understanding of it, can often create an initial foothold for treatment.

There may be a number of effective initial approaches, but all tend to require attention, sympathy, and support. Time, appointments, and attentive listening help the clinician assess general attitudes toward illness, mortality, and relationships, both in their substantive dimensions and through their revelation in the patient's use of language. Many of these patients lack verbal fluency and a suitable vocabulary for conventional psychotherapeutic efforts, and may feel significantly disadvantaged in any context in which the primary medium is talk. The therapist's ability initially to mirror the patient's language can be helpful. Reassurance tends to be counterproductive as patients view it as oppositional; moreover, it was likely attempted in the past without benefit, and its use will tend to identify the therapist with earlier doctors who were unable to help. These patients tend to draw reassurance from the availability of the therapist and the continuity of relationship and support. They also tend to gain confidence from the therapist's focus on the patient's coping problems due to anxiety, fear, misunderstandings, and so on, and from a de-emphasis on their actual health status.

In addition to establishing therapeutic rapport, an initial goal of treatment is to achieve a shift from somatic to interpersonal language; the use of metaphors such as "tension" and "stress" may be useful here. The hypochondriac's language often conspicuously lacks references to family, friends, and other relationships. "Stress" and "tension" can serve as bridge metaphors that provide a path from initial discussions of tension as a cause of pain and discomfort to later explorations of the effects of the patient's stress on the spouse and others. Initial feelings of anger, frustration, and bitterness should over time give way to fear, disappointment, and helplessness. Where present, this transition can be a sign of progress in the treatment.

Cognitive interventions may center on the patient's persistent tendency to construe innocuous somatic sensations as signs of illness, and on the anxiety stimulated by such misinterpretations. Directive interventions generally are best offered pessimistically, with ample permission for rejection. For example, "I doubt that this will be much help, but I've seen it work before when I didn't expect to. You could give it a try if you want." Exercise and behavioral treatments such as relaxation, biofeedback, hypnosis, and chronic pain programs can be helpful for some patients, but treatment for patients with substantial hypochondriacal histories tends to be long term.

Some of the foregoing considerations apply poorly to patients with somatization patterns of recent or traumatic onset. Such patients can often be treated much more aggressively and may respond well to reassurance, explanations, and strategies for reducing or coping with stress (Kellner, 1991).

Low Scores

There are two fundamental ways to achieve a low score on Scale *1*. First, a low raw score on Scale *1* with an average score on *K* is preferred, and suggests an overall sense of comfort in one's "own skin." Freedom from somatic ailments; greater initiative in physical and social activity; positive enjoyment of embodiment in general; a sense of pleasure in exercise, exertion, and activity; and an ability to accept challenges and opportunities without trepidation are all consistent with this pattern. There may be a lack of attention given to matters of health and safety, with the assumption of imprudent risk-taking in physical activity. Low scores may also be achieved by endorsement of few items on *both* Scale *1* and *K*. In this pattern, the freedom from somatic ailments is joined with the self-criticism, dissatisfaction, inefficiency, and social awkwardness of low *K*. There may be neglect of illness or injury until such problems become worse and more debilitating.

SCALE 2: DEPRESSION (D)

Development

The criterion group for Scale *2* consisted of 50 cases manifesting "a clinically recognizable, general frame of mind characterized by poor morale, lack of hope in the future, and dissatisfaction with the patient's own status generally" (Hathaway & McKinley, 1942/1980, p. 25). Most were considered to be in the depressed phase of manic-depressive psychosis and had been thoroughly evaluated to rule out nonpsychiatric causes of depressed mood. The authors recognized and tried to allow for instability in the construct by requiring that the criterion cases be considered depressed only at the time of testing, regardless of whether such mood was rooted in endogenous or situational factors. A preliminary scale of 70 items was devised by comparing the criterion group with 339 (139 men, 200 women) of the 724 Minnesota Normals, who had been roughly matched to the criterion group for age, and 265 (151 men, 114 women) students entering college. Scores on the preliminary scale were then obtained for 413 randomly selected psychiatric cases ("random psychiatrics") and 690 of the Minnesota Normals. On the basis of these comparisons, a group of 50 psychiatric patients who scored high on the preliminary scale but showed no depressive features clinically ("nondepressed"), and a group of 40 of the normals who scored high on the preliminary scale ("depressed normals"), were selected for further study. The items for the final scale were selected on the basis of a progressive increase in endorsement frequency from 690 of the Minnesota Normals, through the depressed normal group, to the criterion group. This procedure yielded 49 items. Eleven items that differentiated the nondepressed psychiatric cases from the criterion group were then added to the other 49 items and scored in the direction of the criterion group, for a total of 60 items on the final scale. This scale was then cross-validated on a new sample of 35 depressives, and these cases proved to separate themselves

≡ *Rapid Reference 6.2a*

Summary Descriptive Features of *D*

Number of Items: 57

True/False Balance: 20/37

Overlap: Scales *1* (with which *D* shares 9 items) at .82, and Scale *7* (with which it shares 12 items) at .80.

Content: Unhappiness, anxiety and worry, apathy and lethargy, nonimpulsiveness, physical symptoms, and low self-esteem.

Relations with Other Scales: Among the basic clinical scales, Scale *2* is most highly correlated with Scales *1*, with which it shares 9 items, at .82, and *7*, with which it shares 12 items, at .80. These correlations are decreased with the addition of .5K to Scale *1* and 1.0K to Scale *7*. Correlations with subscales are, in descending order, *D-O* (.95), *D1* (.95), *D4* (.90), *Hy3* (.90), *Hy-O* (.87), *D5* (.82), *Sc4* (.81), and *D3* (.80). Scale *2* is also highly correlated (.80) with the content scale *DEP* (36 items), with which it shares 8 items, and with its component scales *DEP2* (.79) and *DEP1* (.77), and moderately correlated with *DEP3* (.64) and *DEP4* (.55).

adequately from the 690 Minnesota Normals. They also achieved higher mean scores than the 50 nondepressed psychiatrics, the 413 randomly selected psychiatric patients (which included none of the criterion depressives), a subgroup of 223 of the latter patients who manifested some depressive symptoms but were given diagnoses other than depression ("symptomatic"), and 229 general medical patients. The order of these groups in terms of mean Scale *2* scores was: Criterion > Cross-Validation > Nondepressed > Symptomatic > Random psychiatrics > Medical patients > Minnesota Normals. Three items were dropped from Scale *2* in the transition to the MMPI-2. Scale *2* is described in summary in Rapid Reference 6.2a; the subscales for Scale *2* are described in Rapid Reference 6.2b.

Interpretive Implications

General

Carson (1969) describes Scale *2* as "the best single—and a remarkably efficient—index of immediate satisfaction, comfort, and security" (p. 285). Con-

≡ Rapid Reference 6.2b

Subscales for *D*

The five Harris-Lingoes subscales for Scale 2 are extensively overlapping. *D1*, for example, overlaps with *D2* (8 items), *D3* (3 items), and *D4* (12 items), and contains all 10 of the *D5* items. Five *D2* items overlap with *D4* and 2 with *D5*; *D4* and *D5* overlap by 4 items.

D1 (Subjective Depression—32 items): "A negation of joy in doing things; pessimism, poor morale and low self-esteem; complaints about psychological inertia and lack of energy for coping with problems" (Harris and Lingoes). One of the mood components of Scale 2, *D1* appears to operate as an analog of the full *D* scale. It is the longest of the *D* subscales, containing more than half of the items on *D*. It contains the most obviously depressive of the Scale 2 items and is almost completely contained in and virtually identical to *D-O* ($r = .98$). It is highly correlated with *Hy3* (.91), *Sc4* (.89), *Sc3* (.81), *Sc2* (.78), *Pd5* (.79), and MMPI-2 content scales *DEP* (.89; *DEP1* [.86]; *DEP2* [.86]), *ANX* (.86), *WRK* (.85), *TRT* (.79; *TRT1* [.78]), *LSE* (.78; *LSE1* [.79]). *HEA* (.75), *OBS* (.72), and *SOD* (68), as well as *LPE* (.79) and *NEN* (.75). *D1* is probably the most sensitive MMPI-2 scale to short-term fluctuations in mood.

D2 (Psychomotor Retardation—15 items): "Non-participation in social relations; immobilization" (Harris and Lingoes). *D2* is the inhibition component of Scale 2, and only weakly correlates with its contrastingly named Scale 9 counterpart, *Ma2*, at −.15. It is composed of items whose content suggests withdrawal from social participation, lethargy/anergia, and denial of anger. The inhibitions involved appear to be more emotional than behavioral, judging from correlations with *R* (.52) and *DIS* (−.32). *D2* appears to be sensitive to passivity and submissiveness (Friedman et al., 2001). *D2* is moderately correlated with *LPE* (.66). Levitt (1989) has speculated that low scores on *D2* may suggest sufficient energy for suicide, and this would seem to apply especially when scores on the other Scale 2 subscales are high.

D3 (Physical Malfunctioning—11 items): "Complaints about physical malfunction; preoccupation with oneself" (Harris and Lingoes). This subscale encompasses the somatic component of Scale 2. Content predictably reflects the vegetative features of depression, such as loss of appetite, change in weight, weakness, and constipation, but is unusual in that two of the items (117 *True*; 181 *True*) deny somatic problems. *D3* is highly correlated with Scale 1 (.82), *Hy3* (.82), *Hy4* (.72), and *HEA* (.76; *HEA3* [.76]; *HEA1* [.68]; *HEA2* [.67]). Caldwell (1988) speculated that *D3* may touch on the fear that one may never be restored to health, that there is nothing to look forward to but further physical decline.

(continued)

D4 (Mental Dullness—15 items): "Unresponsiveness; distrust of one's own psychological functioning" (Harris and Lingoes). D4 reflects the cognitive debility of depression; it is the mental counterpart of D3. The items overlap with those of several other subscales, including D5 (40%), Sc3 (40%), and Sc4 (36%), and describe an inability to comprehend one's reading; distractibility; lapses in judgment; problems with memory; low energy; a lack of self-confidence and initiative; and a sense of the futility of caring and trying. It is highly correlated with D1 (.94), Sc4 (.90), Hy3 (.88), and Sc3 (.87). Eight of its items (53%) overlap with those of Scale 7. High scores imply a loss of interest, a sense of mental failure or decline, and the depletion of energy needed to accomplish mental work. Thinking and problem solving are experienced as effortful, and as subject to going off course even when significant effort is made. The patient is likely to view his or her thinking as impaired and unreliable, and to have the sense that "I can't seem to get my mind to work right."

D5 (Brooding—10 items): "Ruminativeness; irritability" (Harris and Lingoes). The second of the mood subscales of Scale 2, D5 is the most heavily saturated with obvious depressive content of the Scale 2 subscales. Eight of its 10 items overlap DEP (half of these on DEP1), amounting to the total number of items shared by Scale 2 and DEP. D5 is highly correlated with Scale 7 (.89), Hy3 (.81), Pd5 (.82), Sc4 (.85), ANX (.84), DEP (.92; DEP2 [.91], DEP1 [.86], DEP3 [.80], LSE [.80]), and NEN (.80). It combines a sense of being easily upset with those of misery and agitation. For interpretative purposes, it is most useful when compared with D1 rather than the full Scale 2. D5 is more angry and extrapunitive than D1.

D-O (Depression-Obvious—39 items): D-O contains 28 of the 32 items of D1 (r = .98) and is nearly identical to the latter.

D-S (Depression-Subtle—18 items): D-S is a subtle measure, not of depression as such, but of the inhibition of crude affect. It reflects passivity, sub-assertiveness, and tolerance for domination/subordination. It is moderately correlated with ANG (−.59), Re (.57), ANG1 (−.57), Ma4 (−.57), TPA (−.56), TPA2 (−.55), and ASP (−.55) and is the best MMPI-2 measure of inhibited aggression.

cerns center around mood, morale, and efficiency. Scores have implications for experienced physical health and well-being; the level of interest and engagement with the environment, including the social environment; and general feelings of satisfaction, contentment, and security. Scale 2 scores tend to be highly responsive to fluctuations in mood and to the situational factors that may influence such changes, and are generally more sensitive to true health/illness status than Scale 1 scores. Scale 2 is rarely elevated in isolation and its interpretation is *highly* dependent on its patterns of combination with other scales. For example, many of the aforementioned correlates actually reverse when Scale *2* is paired with Scale *4;* this configuration predicts externalization, undercontrol, and much higher levels of substance abuse, acting out, aggression, anger, and hostility than when Scale *2* shows an isolated spike. Elevations on Scale *8* tend to emphasize endogenous features whereas elevations on Scale *3* tend to deemphasize them.

Presenting Problem

The presenting problem is highly variable. Complaints of depression and depressed mood are probably most frequent, but physical symptoms and illness (so-called "masked depression"); insomnia or hypersomnia; weight loss or gain; weakness, fatigue, and exhaustion, or a lack of energy and vigor; guilt, low self-esteem, and a lack of self-confidence; distractibility, forgetfulness, and indecision; tension, anxiety, and worry; and irritability, being easily upset or agitated, and even anger, are all common as well. Situational or interpersonal problems often lead to the initial contact, which may be incited or even arranged by others. The presenting complaint often involves a profound sense of loss or grief that precedes the onset of symptoms and has adversely affected the patient's security and self-esteem. Not uncommonly, the crisis involves the loss of a loved one through separation or death, the loss of employment, financial reverses, the collapse of a cherished aspiration, or the failure of some strongly desired achievement.

Symptomatic Pattern

These patients feel unhappy, sad, blue, and dissatisfied with themselves and their life situations. They take little pleasure in events and activities that they formerly enjoyed, feel discouraged and pessimistic about the future, and are slowed down in their thinking and movement. They also lack motivation and initiative, find it difficult to overcome a sense of inertia to "get going," or to resume a task once it has been interrupted or set aside, and tend to give up in the face of obstacles. Problems with appetite and sleep disturbance are common. Guilt, self-depreciation, and low self-esteem impair self-confidence, and past accomplishments are disparaged for no good reason. They withdraw from normal physical and social activities into silence and self-absorption. Turning inward avails them little, however, because their mental function is compromised. Problems with attention, concentration, memory, judgment, and indecision make thinking and problem solving effortful, taxing, stereotyped, and often fruitless. They may focus on minor matters as if they were important, "making mountains out of molehills." Information is processed slowly and incompletely, and is often given a gloomy bias. Patients tend to turn away from present and future concerns, with an unavailing focus on the past. Ruminative worry, preoccupation, and self-recrimination create a downward spiral leading to despair and thoughts of suicide.

These patients' coping styles tend to be highly internalized. Emotionality is constricted and overcontrolled, and they tend to be impassive, conventional, unassertive, nonaggressive, and unlikely either to act out in self-defeating or antisocial ways or to engage in substance abuse. Most patients experience weakness, tiredness, and fatigue; have little energy or initiative; and manifest some degree of psychomotor slowing or retardation. In such cases, aggression and hostility are strongly inhibited. In a minority of cases, however, tension, agitation, impatience, irritability, an intolerance for frustration, and short-lived angry flare-ups occur, about which the patient may experience an exaggerated sense of guilt afterwards.

At higher elevations, these patients may feel defeated and utterly useless, helpless, hopeless, and worthless. Moreover, they may feel that their physical health has embarked upon an inexorable decline toward ruin and permanent physical suffering, especially when coupled with elevations on Scale *1*. Objectively, such patients tend to be severely withdrawn emotionally, immobilized, and even mute.

An assessment of suicide risk is generally indicated when Scale *2* is elevated. Reference to the patient's responses to the Koss-Butcher Depressed Suicidal Ideation set of critical items, and specifically to items 150, 303, 506, 520, and 524, are recommended in this regard.

Interpersonal Relations

Retiring and socially reserved, these patients tend to shrink from conflict and confrontation and are generally seen as timid. Intimates and others find them distant and difficult to reach emotionally, which tends to create stress in the lives of those close to them. Although not necessarily dependent on a characterological basis, their passivity and gloominess often result in others' having to take responsibility for them by default. Those close to them are likely to feel that they must offer assistance, propose solutions, and take up responsibilities that the patient has dropped, as well as provide reassurance that the patient is cared for and that things will improve and make efforts to boost the patient's self-esteem. The patient's lack of response to these well-intended ministrations may create a sense of alarm and exasperation in the caretakers. However, the patient's self-criticism tends to blunt and frustrate caretakers' candid expressions of annoyance, so that words and acts designed to comfort and encourage the patient will often become more grudging and resentful with the passage of time. This trend may lead to the rejection and abandonment the patient has both feared and longed for, confirming the patient's view of him- or herself as hopeless, worthless, and an unworthy burden to others.

Patients often report school or work problems, such as difficulty completing work on time; conflicts with other students or coworkers or with a teacher/supervisor because of underperformance, excessive absences, inattentiveness, and related difficulties. They may also report problems with the spouse (including a lack of sexual interest) or letting financial obligations slide. Such problems are often internalized by the patient as guilt or feeling like a failure.

Behavioral Stability

The behavior pattern is inherently unstable and subject to a wide variety of influences—environmental, interpersonal, and biochemical. Scale 2 is highly sensitive to such instability and tracks changes in symptom status fairly well. As such, it tends to function more as a state than a trait scale.

Defenses

The defensive patterns associated with high scores on Scale 2 are many and varied, depending on other features of the profile. In general, Scale 2 elevations tend to signal some degree of failure, if not a breakdown of whatever defensive posture preceded it (Trimboli & Kilgore, 1983). Many defenses, such as intellectualization, rationalization, or reaction formation may be observed as the patient deals with anger. Other defenses, such as denial, displacement, suppression, and repression may be directed at the anger or the depression itself. Somatization, too, may be directed at the depression, thereby masking it from the patient and others.

History

Look for the loss or death of a parent or other loved one in childhood; exposure to neglect, abuse, or emotional cruelty, whether at first or second hand, while growing up; the experience of being frequently uprooted; or the loss of what was felt to be a major opportunity, especially if the patient responded to such losses passively. More recent losses that may be relevant include separation from an important source of emotional support or companionship such as a spouse or close friend, as through death or desertion; losses related to employment or economic security; and losses related to accident, injury, or loss of function due to illness or disease.

Diagnostic Considerations
Diagnosis is generally within the mood disorders: Dysthymic Disorder, Major Depression, Depressive Disorder NOS, or Adjustment Disorder with Depressed Mood.

Treatment Considerations
Elevations on Scale 2 are associated with favorable treatment outcomes using a wide variety of treatments. The cognitive and interpersonal therapies have established a good track record in this regard, especially when accompanied by antidepressant medication. However, many patients will respond well to much more conservative measures, including exercise and environmental manipulation (e.g., transfer to a different department), and the simple passage of time.

The patient's level of discomfort is generally favorable to establishing rapport. These patients require an initial level of support commensurate with the severity of depression. In the more severe cases (e.g., Major Depression), the onset of psychotherapeutic work may have to await at least partial response to antidepressant medication because the patient may be too immobilized and emotionally withdrawn for productive interaction with the therapist. At a minimum, the patient must have passed beyond the period of greatest suicide risk and be largely restored to a normal sleep cycle.

Early goals in treatment include providing for the patient's safety through supervision, continuing contact with intimates and close friends, suicide contracts, and restoring morale. Supportive family can be especially important in the initial stages of treatment. Excessive support from the therapist may be counterproductive, however, potentially undermining the development of a more independent and assertive coping style.

Much of the treatment process may involve the review and correction of maladaptive cognitive and emotional reaction patterns and working through grief and loss. In particular, helping the patient gain release from an overly passive, inhibited, and conscientious emotional style and from the tendency to internalize stresses may be helpful. These patients are overly quick to accept blame and responsibility for circumstances over which they may have little or no control. Learning a style of relating that enables greater self-expression and a sense of enhanced self-determination, including the expansion of the patient's ability to make "selfish" or self-indulgent choices, to decline excessive or unwanted responsibilities, and to pursue his or her rights and preferences assertively in relationships with others is the usual end goal of therapy.

Low Scores

Low scores reflect optimism, cheerfulness, and a capacity for enthusiasm; heightened activity and social interest; and mental alertness and facility. With very low scores, however, these trends can become problematic. Excessive optimism can lead to poor judgment; excessive cheerfulness can take on a relentless and impervious character; excessive activity or enthusiasm can lead to disinhibition and recklessness; an excess of social interest can lead to superficial and opportunistic relationships, ostentation, fickleness, insensitivity, or intrusiveness; excessive mental facility can lead to ill-considered judgment and an impressionistic or careless style of information processing. The quick-wittedness of emotional buoyancy and cognitive facilitation may lead to expressions that are irrepressible but inappropriate, or at the expense of others' feelings. Although they occur infrequently, low scores on Scale 2 can reflect the euphoria and undercontrol seen in mania.

SCALE 3: HYSTERIA (Hy)

Development

McKinley and Hathaway (1944/1980) mentioned several criterion groups, but the final primary group contained 50 cases, most diagnosed with Psychoneurosis, Hysteria. Then, as now, the clinical concept of hysteria was ill-defined and controversial. Hathaway tried to emphasize cases with "a simple conversion symptom such as aphonia, an occupational cramp, or a neurologically irrational anesthetic area" (1944/1980, p. 46), but so few such patients were available that several probable but less clear-cut cases had to be included. A set of discriminating items was identified early, and these repeatedly surfaced in various group comparisons, although these comparisons are not described. It was immediately evident that most of the items fell into two categories: so-matic complaints and "statements tending to show that the patient considered himself unusually well socialized" (p. 46). Because of the conceptual similarity between the hypochondriasis and hysteria constructs, a great deal of effort went into testing Scale 3 against new cross-validation samples of hysterics and cases of hypochondriasis to ensure that the appropriate conceptual similarities were preserved without rendering the two scales excessively redundant. This goal proved elusive, however, and the decision to adopt Scale 3 rested primar-ily on the insistence of clinicians that the scale performed well in classifying hysterical and hypochondriacal cases based on which scale was higher in the profile. Considerable consistency existed in the trend for those patients with hypochondriasis to manifest neurotic features, whereas the hysterics more fre-quently appeared to be psychologically normal but manifesting a more specific set of symptoms that tended to wax and wane in response to stress. Scale 3 is described in summary in Rapid Reference 6.3a; its subscales are described in Rapid Reference 6.3b.

Interpretive Implications

General

Scale 3 is intended to identify persons who are prone to respond to life stresses by developing conversion-like symptoms, such as fits (e.g., absences, faint-ing, blackouts, and pseudoseizures), abdominal pain, and stress vomiting; am-nesia, fugue, and somnambulism; paralysis; contractures (e.g., writer's cramp); tremors; speech irregularities (e.g., aphonia/mutism, stammer, stutter, lisp, whispering, or other mannerisms/affectations); spasmodic movements; awk-ward or impaired gait; episodic weakness and fatigue; anesthesia, deafness, blindness, and blurred or tunnel vision; and cardiac crises (e.g., palpitations). In fact, the range and variety of conversion symptoms are endless; hysteria has been called "the great imitator" for its ability to simulate the signs and symp-toms of organic illness. Although often diagnostically ambiguous when seen initially and in isolation, such symptoms may come to be viewed in the context of conversion (a) when they are observed to be recurrent but transitory and re-versible; (b) when they are judged to be related to some significant emotional stress that preceded symptom onset, or to serve some communicative func-tion (e.g., emotional appeal) or to have iconic significance; (c) when the symp-

≡Rapid Reference 6.3a

Summary Descriptive Features of *Hy*

Number of Items: 60

True/False Balance: 13/47

Overlap: Scale 3 overlaps Scale 1 by 20 items, Scale 2 by 13 items, and K by 10 items.

Content: Somatic complaints; denial of cynicism and mistrust, health dysphoria, anxious depression, and social inadequacy.

Relations with Other Scales: The relations between scale 3 and other scales are misleading when based on correlations obtained within psychiatric samples because symptoms and complaints within such samples will be overweighted relative to those aspects of the scale that reflect social interest and comfort, a trusting and positive self-portrayal, and a distaste for aggression and conflict. However, correlations between the obvious *(Hy-O)* and subtle *(Hy-S)* components of Scale 3 and other scales will be discussed along those scales. Among the basic clinical scales, Scale 3 is most highly correlated with Scales 1, with which it shares 20 (mostly somatic) items at .80, and 2, with which it shares 13 items at .72. Its configural relation to Scale 1 has a variety of implications: 1 greater than 3 suggests more somatic complaints, greater pessimism and defeatist attitude, and greater extractiveness and abrasiveness in relations with others; when 3 is greater than 1, the Scale 1 trends are moved in the direction of fewer somatic complaints, more optimism and poignancy, more social skill, and a more appealing if not seductive approach to others. Content scale correlates of Scale 3 are highly disparate between normal and abnormal samples. The high *(HEA)* and moderate *(ANX, DEP, WRK)* correlations seen in psychiatric samples collapse or reverse in normal samples, whereas the negative moderate *(ANG, CYN, ASP, TPA)* content correlates within normal samples collapse or reverse in psychiatric samples. Elevations on L and K, especially when combined with low scores on Scales F, 7, 8, and 0, emphasize the success of defensive operations in warding off anxiety.

tom appears in some way to resolve or comment upon a conflict deemed to follow or be otherwise related to the precipitating stressor; or (d) when the medical diagnostic pursuit of symptoms has nonconfirmatory outcomes. The classical psychodynamic view tends to associate motor symptoms with the symbolic regulation of behavior (disavowed impulses and actions), sensory symptoms with the symbolic regulation of awareness (repudiated memories or images), and interoceptive symptoms with the symbolic regulation of emotion

Subscales for *Hy**

The 5 Harris and Lingoes subscales for Scale *3* are entirely nonoverlapping.

Hy1 (Denial of Social Anxiety—6 items): "Extroversion" (Harris and Lingoes). *Hy1* is the extroversive component of Scale *3* and the shortest of its subscales. Five of its six items are contained within *Si1* (r = −.88) and three within *SOD2*, in both cases keyed oppositely. Four of its items overlap *Pd3* (r = .90) and two overlap with *Ma3*. Because of its limited length, it is a less reliable measure of extroversion than Scales *0* and *SOD*. *Hy1* correlates negatively with *A* at −.65, suggesting unusual freedom from social anxiety and fear of embarrassment; these items convey the "social butterfly" aspects of the histrionic personality construct, and emphasize social disinhibition. It is one of the *K*-correlated subscales (r = .61).

Hy2 (Need for Affection and Reinforcement from Others—12 items): Harris and Lingoes state that this subscale reflects an "(obtuse) denial of a critical or resentful attitude toward other people; impunitiveness; overly protested faith and optimism in other people." *Hy2* is the "Pollyanna" component of Scale *3*. The items deny negative traits such as cynicism, mistrust, hostility, and rebellious attitudes, feelings, and impulses. This subscale is closely related to *Pa3* (r = .76), with which it shares three items. However, whereas only three (33%) of the *Pa3* items begin with "I," nine (75%) of the *Hy2* items do so. The *Hy2* items emphasize the denial of negative traits in the self; the *Pa3* items deny negative traits in others. Thus, whereas the thrust of most of the *Pa3* items is that "*Most people* are virtuous and constructive," the thrust of *Hy2* is that "*I am virtuous and constructive.*" The low level of cynicism connoted in high *Hy2* scores implies the kind of impunitive detachment and naive lack of normal skepticism of the motives of others that some may view as immature and unrealistic. In the aggregate, these items suggest strong needs for approval, or at least an abnormally strong aversion to giving offense or to drawing negative attention from others. A high score reflects an overly gracious and beguiling style of relating to others and apparent blind trust in their integrity and innocuousness, suggesting passivity/dependency, a lack of a sense of personal power, and an unnecessarily roundabout style when it comes to seeking affection. *Hy2* is strongly correlated with *K* (r = .77) and, negatively, with *CYN* (−.84) and *CYN1* (−.83).

Hy3 (Lassitude-Malaise—15 items): "Complaints about functioning below par physically and mentally; effortful keeping up of a good front; need for attention and reassurance" (Harris and Lingoes). *Hy3* is the depressive component of Scale *3*. Ten of its items overlap with Scale *2* (r = .90), eight with Scale *1* (r = .88), seven with *D1*, five with *D3*, three with *D4*, and one each with *D2* and *D5*. Four items overlap with *Pd4*. Not quite half of the items are somatic/health related, but most of these have clear depressive overtones. The somatic complaints tend to be vague rather than specific; see *Hy4*. Elevations connote a broad lack of vitality and physical discomfort without freedom from distress. The neurasthenic syndrome of weakness, tiredness, and easy fatigability is strongly represented in *Hy3*.

Hy4 (Somatic Complaints—17 items): Harris and Lingoes describe these items as being "Of a kind that suggest repression and conversion of affect." Hy4 is the somatic component of Scale 3. Twelve of its items overlap Scale 1 (r = .94), and 13 overlap HEA (.94); 6 overlap HEA2 (.89). Only 2 items overlap Sc6, but the scales are highly correlated (.80). The items refer to symptoms that are fairly discrete and dramatic; specific complaints outnumber vague complaints in a ratio of about 3:1, and emphasize head complaints, pain and discomfort, vascular and cardiorespiratory problems. About half of the items refer, implicitly or explicitly, to spells or attacks. Just over half of the symptoms lend themselves to iconic or metaphoric use, especially through wording like, "lump in my throat," "attacks of nausea," "I feel hot all over," "pains over my heart," "my muscles twitching," "a tight band around my head," "dizzy spells," "my hand shakes," and "my heart pounding," and so forth. The language of these items is more dramatic—even flamboyant—than is typical for the somatic portion of the MMPI-2 item pool. These items have an arresting quality and are subject to colorful elaboration on interview. That is, they are easily pressed into service as components of a story that the patient wishes to relate, and one that is likely to have a relatively easily discernible latent message.

There is much less implied distress in Hy4 than in Hy3; hence Hy4 greater than Hy3 suggests a "working" conversion with probable la belle indifference, provided Hy4 is not too high. However, at about five to seven raw items, Hy4 begins to suggest somatization over conversion, regardless of the Hy4–Hy3 difference.

Hy5 (Inhibition of Aggression—7 items): This brief subscale lacks internal consistency and appears to have been inaptly named. Harris and Lingoes noted that the inhibition of aggression is "Expressed by concurrence with others, disavowal of violence." Only one of the items (number 29) fits the label at all well (but see D-O and D2). Judging from its correlations with R (.39) and DIS (−.28), such inhibitions as there may be appear to be biased toward the emotional. Hy5 is only moderately to weakly related to measures of aggression (e.g., AGG, −.27), anger (e.g., ANG, −.45), and hostility (e.g., TPA2, −.33); it does not appear adequate for contributing to judgments about aggression or the inhibition thereof. However, at least three of the items appear to reflect distaste, abhorrence, revulsion, or noninterest in vicarious violence and aggression. Thus, the high Hy5 scorer seems to be saying that crime news, detective stories, swearing, the sight of blood, and so on are morbid and disgusting and are implicit threats to the patient's sensory inhibition. Hy5 is moderately correlated with K (.46). Low scores may suggest interest or even morbid fascination with violence, but the scale is a weak basis for clinical inferences.

Hy-O (Hysteria–Obvious—32 items): Hy-O contains 32 items and encompasses Hy3 and Hy4. Hy-O is highly correlated with Hs (.96), HEA (.92), D-O (.92), Pt (.84), Sc (.83; Sc4, .81; Sc6, .79), ANX (.83), and DEP (.80), and moderately with K (−.55). This subscale is highly saturated with the First Factor (correlation with A = .78) and thus will be raised by any of the distress scales.

Hy-S (Hysteria–Subtle—28 items): Hy-S contains 28 items and encompasses subscales Hy1, Hy2, and Hy5. It is highly correlated with K (.82) and negatively with CYN (−.79; CYN1, −.77) and A (−.70). Hy-O scores, then, will be increased by K and will, in turn, suppress scores on Scales 7, 8, and 0.

*nonoverlapping

(displaced sorrow or longing, fear/terror, anger/hostility, etc.). These categories are oversimplified and are not intended to be mutually exclusive.

There is no implication that symptoms will be present at elevated scores unless these are at a sufficiently high level (e.g., T-75) to have forced the endorsement of some of the somatic items. Conversely, false negative predictions can easily occur when conversions are singular, localized, and uncomplicated, even when active and manifest.

The scale embraces two fairly distinct groups of items: the first a set of somatic complaints, many with dysphoric overtones, and the second a set of items that affirm freedom from emotional difficulties and a friendly, gregarious orientation to others. Rapid assessment of the relative strength of these two components of Scale 3 may be made with reference to Scale 1 (non–K–corrected T-score) and K, respectively. The same distinction may be made with reference to the difference between Hy-O and Hy-S, or between $Hy3$ and $Hy4$ versus $Hy1$, $Hy2$, and $Hy5$. The pattern of correlates and clinical predictions can vary markedly, depending on the relative emphasis the examinee places on one of the components versus the other. When the first group of items is clearly ascendent in the total Scale 3 score, the patient (Type 1) is likely to manifest a clear somatic focus and experience significant discomfort and distress in the form of depression, anxiety, or nervousness. With the opposite pattern (Type 2), the latter problems are largely denied, but often with some residual but focal source of unhappiness or discontent and a limited somatic symptom that is fairly well delineated, at least in the patient's description. The patient is much more likely to be optimistic, socially outgoing, responsive, engaging, and enthusiastic, and to express lively, positive, and generous views about others and about life experiences in general—but also to be somewhat immature, prone to worry, and inhibited around aggression and anger. *La belle indifference* (the patient's apparent lack of concern for or indifference to the somatic symptoms and their related disability, despite normal concern, worry, or anxiety about other matters) is more common and striking in this pattern. In both patterns, self-centeredness is common, but tends to be expressed demandingly in the former and appealingly or seductively in the latter.

In normals and psychiatric patients in general, these two components, most readily indexed by Hy-O and Hy-S respectively, are uncorrelated if not slightly *negatively* correlated, such that the two patterns described are not commonly combined. The first pattern is relatively frequent in abnormal samples; the second is rare in such samples unless determined by a defensive response style, but is common in normal samples, especially when there is a perceived incentive to create a positive impression, such as among job applicants. It is the coincidence of the two components that defines Conversion Disorder, with the symptomatic focus drawn from the somatic items, and the corresponding "normal," "rational" presentation and *la belle indifference* drawn from the remaining social-interest items.

Hy-O tends to have high convergent validity with intratest measures and external ratings, and with diagnostic judgments of somatization and its related distress and discomfort; but it also has poor discriminant validity due to its insensitivity to the social and interactional features of the conversion syndrome. *Hy-S*, conversely, shows high convergent validity for the latter features but low discriminant validity for the former features. Consequently, when *Hy-O* dominates Scale *3*, the profile is more highly elevated and Scale *3* scores are likely to be accompanied by elevations on Scales *1, 2, 4, 7,* and *8,* along with a self-critical pattern on the validity scales; whereas *Hy-S* domination of Scale *3* usually accompanies a profile of lower general elevation, fewer peaks, and a self-favorable validity scale pattern.

Elevations on Scale *3* do not rule out medical illness. Follow-up studies of patients diagnosed with conversion disorder have commonly found high rates of organic pathology (see, e.g., Merskey, 1995).

Presenting Problem

The presenting problem is highly variable. Many patients are seen on referral from medical services, especially neurology, or from lawyers representing the patient in a personal injury/compensation claim. In self-referred patients a somatic focus is not unusual, but is often not obvious in initial interview. Some of these patients will present with a more or less immediate disclaimer of freedom from emotional/psychological problems (e.g., "I don't really know why I'm here. Things are basically going fine. There's just one problem . . ."). Often the patient's relations with others have overtones of rejection, such as the break-up of a valued relationship, the death or illness of a loved one, a marital conflict or argument, a pregnancy or the birth of a child, or a feeling of not being fully accepted or included by a desired group of peers. There is often an inchoate sense of disharmony between the way patients see themselves and the way others see them. For example, the high Scale *3* scorer may view his or her social conduct as friendly and approving, whereas others see it as superficial and seductive; his or her speech as positive and kindly, whereas others see it as ungenuine and insincere. Problems with scholastic performance that risk separation from school or placement on academic probation, or on-the-job failures that risk dismissal, are also evident, as are problems with anxiety, especially anxiety attacks or "spells." Among men, the presenting problem may involve conflicts with teachers, supervisors, or other authority figures. A complaint of pain is probably the most common somatic symptom.

Symptomatic Pattern

The symptoms may be of either recent or distant onset. Symptoms of recent onset often appear suddenly in response to stresses that have profound emotional significance, or that replicate or remind the patient of some previous emotionally traumatic event. La belle indifference may be present to the extent that the symptom is effective in keeping the stressful event and the anxiety surrounding it out of awareness—the so-called "working conversion." (When pain is the major symptom, the presence of la belle indifference does not apply to the pain as such, but to its consequences in the patient's life, the adaptations and limitations [e.g., being home-bound] that the pain has imposed.) Symptoms tend to be few in number and to wax and wane over time. In cases of distant onset, the precipitating event is often obscure or unknown, and the emotion surrounding it blunted. Symptoms are typically more numerous, less dramatic, and apparently disabling, and seem intended to confirm or legitimize the patient in a sick role. In such cases, la belle indifference is typically absent, and the patient may exist as an invalid, freed of all responsibilities apart from seeking treatment. Such cases often manifest secondary depression and tend to shade into the symptom pictures characteristic of hypochondriacal or somatization disorders.

The social style in the Type 2 pattern at least tends to be cheerful, animated, and talkative if not vivacious and flamboyant, and approving if not seductive. There is a positive emphasis and outlook with an avoidance of topics deemed negative, unpleasant, offensive, or disgusting. These patients tend to adhere to the principle that "If you can't say something nice, don't say anything at all," in an effort to make themselves as socially appealing and attractive as possible. They tend toward dramatization in social situations as well as at the level of symptom(s) and mood. Expressions may be somewhat exhibitionistic and often appear calculated to achieve specific social effects. Likewise, speech may be laden with superlatives in an effort to command attention and interest; but others tend to find this overreaching and tedious. Despite an outward appearance of strength and self-possession, suggestibility is also common, with the high Scale *3* scorer being subject to influence, imitativeness, and marked shifts in feeling and mood, and to the rapid embrace or abandonment of attitudes and convictions, often seemingly dependent on the person with whom the patient last spoke.

Where present, sexual provocativeness or seductiveness in dress, speech, and movement often appear contrived to attain assistance, protection, security, and nurturance rather than intimacy and sexuality. In some cases, the reciprocation of seductive blandishments is met with shock, indignation, and accusations of misunderstanding or selfishness. In others, sexual follow-through will occur but without a satisfying level of awareness, participation, or mutuality.

Emotionality tends to be labile and capricious. Whether angry and petulant or tearful and appealing, the emotionality often appears highly demonstrative, staged, and indirectly coercive. Such expressions are typically self-limiting, however, because they interrupt the patient's preferred cheerful, nice, and agreeable social role. They tend to dissipate quickly without leaving a residue of resentment. In extreme cases, emotional outbursts subside coincidentally with the emergence or exacerbation of somatic symptoms, as if the soma had been given proxy to carry on the patient's part of the emotional dialogue.

Cognitive functioning is mixed. In general, psychotic ideation is less likely when Scale *3* is elevated, regardless of the profile pattern or the elevation of other clinical scales. There tends to be a high level of comfort in matters of choice and decision, and a subjective conviction that judgment is sound and thinking is unfettered, clear, and rational—but with a feeling that his or her mental functioning should never be put to the test. Others, however, are likely to view the patient's thinking as undisciplined, flighty, impressionistic, superficial, fanciful, poorly focused, uncritical, and illogical. Their opinions often appear to be formed hastily and on the basis of information that made a strong emotional impression, but with little concern for perspective, accuracy, or corroboration. They are also inclined to embellish or fabricate events or experiences, sacrificing truth and accuracy in the hope of greater audience appeal. There are often particular problems in the way everyday information is gathered from the environment, with attention tending to be diffuse and perception tending to be selective and overly casual, rather than searching and discerning. They are often viewed as looking but not seeing; listening but not hearing, as if their information processing is hampered by sensory inhibition. In many cases they actively avoid information considered "negative" or potentially upsetting, such as that found in newspapers and news magazines, as if greater exposure would risk popping their balloon of cheer and optimism. Where such information cannot be avoided, it will be encapsulated, misrecognized, or disregarded. As a consequence, despite having broad interests, their actual knowledge within their areas of interest is often thin, spotty, and poorly developed, and they are likely to pass off gaps in their knowledge as unimportant "details." Their inattention and carelessness may protect them emotionally by limiting their exposure to unpleasantness and emotional upset; unfortunately, overlooking or failing to register important details in the environment that must be heeded in one's day-to-day activities will often cause these patients trouble. For example, temporary traffic detours, the opening and closing times of businesses, various features of packaging, product specifications, the location of keys, the level of fuel in the tank—these and a host of similar details may often be overlooked, requiring extra trips, greater expense, the return of unsuitable products, needs to reschedule, and similar remedies and adjustments that complicate daily living, reduce satisfaction, increase stress, and engender impatience and conflict with others.

They often have trouble anticipating the consequences of their actions because their inattention, trust in others, and desire to be "in the spirit of things" causes them to overlook or miscalculate risks and get carried away. They may have sexual and antisocial misadventures while remaining consciously ignorant of the motives or significance of them, and despite having values and prohibitions that would ordinarily lead to their avoidance; in the aftermath, the patient may feel perplexed and ashamed.

Interpersonal Relations
The Type 2 Scale *3* scorer is concerned that others find him or her pleasing to be around, but covertly (if not overtly) demands attention, affection, reassurance, and support, and implicitly insists that these be provided unselfishly, in a way that requires no reciprocation. This lack of reciprocity vis-à-vis the interests and wishes of others renders all of the patient's relationships potentially unstable. Trusting, open, and optimistic in relationships but also self-centered

and immature, the high Scale *3* scorer tends to seek out others who are highly patient, nurturant, and undemanding. Relations with others tend to be somewhat superficial and immature. They are easily disappointed when others fail to live up to their expectations and may drop relationships as suddenly as they were formed. Their relationships with intimates tend to be dependent and one-sided, and they may make multiple and infantile demands upon the partner. Often, symptoms and powerful emotional reactions, real or feigned, are deployed manipulatively, to avoid responsibilities and to provide cover for selfish choices (e.g., "Would you take care of that? I know I could do it myself, but if I tried it would make me sick [throw up; faint; stress my sore arm; etc.]."). When these maneuvers are pointed out, the reaction is often one of wounded incomprehension, with projections of selfishness and meanness: "How could you be so selfish and unfeeling?" Expressions of aggression, anger, and hostility are generally infrequent and handled poorly. Such reactions in general are strongly inhibited but may occur when demands are not met.

Behavioral Stability
In cases of recent onset, symptoms may appear and disappear relatively quickly, and in accord with the patient's overall level of satisfaction and security. In cases of distant onset, however, the symptom pattern tends to be relatively stable, chronic, and disabling.

Defenses
In addition to conversion itself, the classic defenses here are denial and repression. Denial can be especially striking. Many such patients deny problems and difficulties that others would recognize as emotional or psychological in nature—in effect, denying psychic reality. Some patients, however, flatly deny evidence of their own senses, or aspects of external reality of which others have no doubt. For example, the patient may deny frank and disabling illness, documents bearing his or her signature, well-documented events in his or her history, a large dress size, pregnancy, a spouse's alcoholism or imprisonment, or divorce, even in the face of clear, graphic, and incontrovertible evidence. The patient appears simply to bypass such evidence, to glide over it in a way that prevents effective confrontation. The manner of denial generally is not to argue that the evidence is unproven, but rather is flat, unequivocal, and final. Repression (keeping painful feelings and images out of awareness) appears to be the central defensive operation in Scale *3*.

History

Look for the early loss of a parent, especially the father, through death or desertion, or for other experience(s) of painful rejection; the lost parent is often idealized. Other patients may have experienced fierce if not violent altercations between his or her parents as overwhelming in intensity, leading to emotional anguish and an acute need to escape sensory overload. The circumstances surrounding these events—a parent who was otherwise preoccupied, or a family norm of inhibition—often will have discouraged the expression of unpleasant or disruptive (though candid) feelings in favor of those that, however ungenuine, were considered "nice" and as advancing family harmony. In this context, pain or other physical symptoms may have become a compromise between rejection, because of honest but disruptive expressions of feeling, and silence about internal anguish. In some cases the history may reveal someone who served as a model for the patient's symptom(s). In still others, there was general emotional neglect that contrasted with excessive and indulgent attention during periods of illness.

Diagnostic Considerations

The typical diagnosis is Conversion Disorder, but secondary or even primary diagnoses of Psychogenic Pain Disorder, Dysthymia, Depressive Disorder NOS, and Adjustment Disorder with Depressed Mood or Disturbance of Conduct are also seen. Psychotic disorders are infrequent, as are most personality disorders, but histrionic, paranoid, borderline, and dissociative disorders do occur in some cases when Scale 3 is elevated with other scales. Substance abuse is also infrequent but, when present, is usually limited to prescribed medications for pain, anxiety, or sleep.

Diagnostic judgments involving Scale 3 are rendered unusually difficult by the diversity of its item content. Overall, the greater the Scale 3 elevation above about T-65, the less likely is conversion disorder. Also, to the extent that Hy-O exceeds Hy-S, diagnosis among the mood (especially depressive) disorders, the somatoform disorders *other than Conversion Disorder,* and the personality disorders, becomes more likely. Unless Hy-S exceeds Hy-O, conversion syndromes are unlikely. Unfortunately, this pattern is far more commonly produced by persons adopting defensive response styles than by patients with Conversion Disorder. Thus, for both patterns, the diagnostic interpretation of Conversion Disorder is apt to be severely limited by the unfavorable base rates for this disorder.

Treatment Considerations

Medical as opposed to psychological explanations and treatment modalities are generally preferred, but this is less firm than is typical for hypochondriasis. With their optimistic outlook and need for approval, these patients' initial attitudes toward therapy tend to be highly positive and hopeful. They tend to have unrealistically high expectations of the therapist, who will be treated as knowledgeable, wise, and generous but will be evaluated primarily on the basis of patience and tact. As treatment proceeds, the patient's expectations may begin to clash with the therapist's. Therapist pressure for the patient's analysis of his or her own feelings, thoughts, motives, and behavior, and of those of important others in his or her life, are at odds with the patient's desire for concrete, practical solutions to problems and the prompt relief of symptoms.

Therapy should generally follow a defense-accommodating rather than a defense-challenging pattern. Measures to increase insight are likely to be actively resisted, and the therapist's persistence along such lines may result in early termination. Limitations in psychological-mindedness and a reluctance to introspect should be respected and recognized as part and parcel of the patient's disorder; efforts to expand the patient's awareness must be modest and carefully graduated to protect the patient from anxiety or other disconcerting emotionality. By contrast, environmental manipulation and measures that depend on reassurance, suggestion, practical advice, and therapeutic directives are often helpful, especially if these are in accord with the patient's reasons for being in therapy and with his or her own views of how things work. When such measures are effective, especially when promptly so, concerns about saving face with family and physician can suddenly emerge because of the implication that nonmedical relief "proves" that the symptom was "all in my head." Here, as in the case of hypochondriasis, using the stress metaphor, among other measures, may be helpful.

In some cases, a period of active listening occasionally interspersed with empathic requests for clarification will open up sources of emotional pain or grief that can then be addressed more conventionally. Involvement of the family often helps gather relevant historical information that the patient may overlook, and helps provide needed support and reduce secondary gains.

In general, retention in treatment and prognosis will be related to the patient's level of distress and discomfort at the time of contact, the recency and variability of symptoms, and the premorbid level of functioning, including the level of functioning between symptomatic periods. The instability of la belle indifference; limited secondary gains; and the ability to tolerate some degree of anxiety and to achieve psychological distance from symptom(s) and upsetting emotional experience, are all prognostically favorable.

Low Scores

Low Scale 3 scores are achieved by avoiding somatic complaints and asserting of social interest and friendliness. Thus, it is not surprising that low scorers should be described in terms suggesting personal comfort and self-sufficiency, but also as unfriendly and socially isolated. They seem to have a generally misanthropic outlook, are seen as cold, aloof, and hard to get to know, and are somewhat cynical and suspicious of others. They are likely to be unpretentious or indifferent to social approval. Their style of interaction ranges from candid and direct (though blunt, unsympathetic, and hard-hearted) to abrasive or caustic. They are likely to lack a sense of industry or purpose, to have few interests, and to live lives that others may view as relatively routinized and unengaged.

SCALE 4: PSYCHOPATHIC DEVIATE (Pd)

Development

McKinley and Hathaway (1944/1980) did not report the size of the criterion sample, but indicated that members were young, mostly within an age range of 17 to 22 years, and that women outnumbered the men, probably because the court had diverted more of the women to the hospital and more of the men to jail. The main criterion cases chosen were diagnosed Psychopathic Personality, Asocial and Amoral Type, using recent descriptions of the syndrome by Henderson (1939) and Cleckley (1941). Hathaway (1944/1980) noted that

> The symptomatic backgrounds of the criterion cases were highly varied but ... most often the complaint was stealing, lying, truancy, sexual promiscuity, alcoholic overindulgence, forgery and similar delinquencies. There were no major criminal types. Most of the behavior was of the commonly described poorly motivated and poorly concealed sort. All of the criterion cases had long histories of minor delinquency. Although many of them came from broken homes or otherwise disturbed social

backgrounds, there were many in whom such factors could not be seen as particularly present. (p. 57–58)

Hathaway's emphasis on the persistence and consistency of the behavior pattern, rather than on the severity of any particular aspect of conduct (e.g., theft, lying, promiscuity, etc.) appears to have been central in his conception of the scale. The initial Scale *4* was the survivor of five trial scales that had been devised by comparing criterion group responses with those of a married subgroup of the Minnesota Normals and with the college applicants. By studying the discriminating items, Hathaway was able to divide them into subgroups: "home difficulty," "social trouble," "over-perfect tendencies," "depression and the absence of strongly pleasant experiences," and "paranoid trends." The scale was then cross-validated on a sample of 78 cases from the hospital and 100 men from a federal prison, each of whom had received a diagnosis of Psychopathic Personality. These comparisons led to a revision of the initial scale, which resulted in the final version of Scale *4*. Staff physicians viewed the final scale as clearly valuable and able to detect at least half of the cases of psychopathic personality seen at the university hospitals.

Dahlstrom, Welsh, and Dahlstrom (1972) pointed out that there were probably unavoidable biases in the criterion group that would render it somewhat unrepresentative of psychopathic deviates at large. In some ways, the circumstance of confinement in hospital for the criterion cases may have adversely affected the sensitivity and specificity of Scale *4* for the psychopathic personality. For example, the depressive/guilty items on the scale, mostly *Pd5,* might have differentiated the criterion group on the basis of the purely situational discomforts that attended hospitalization, or they might have represented feigned remorse and contrition calculated mollify parents' qualms about allowing patients to return home, or to win early release (W. G. Dahlstrom, personal communication). Rapid Reference 6.4a contains a summary description of *Pd;* its subscales are described in Rapid Reference 6.4b.

Interpretive Implications

General

Scale *4* was intended to identify asocial/amoral psychopathy. Decades of research and use have made clear its limited validity for this narrow purpose,

≡Rapid Reference 6.4a

Summary Descriptive Features of *Pd*

Number of Items: 50

True/False Balance: 24/26

Overlap: Scale 4 overlaps with Scale 3 by 10 items, Scale 8 by 10 items, Scale 6 by 8 items, Scale 2 by 7 items, Scale 9 by 6 items, and Scale 0 by 5 items and, negatively, 6 items.

Content: Family conflict, antisocial behavior and attitudes, social fearlessness, social alienation, and unhappiness, dissatisfaction, and guilt.

Relations with Other Scales: The interpretation of Scale 4 is heavily dependent on its relationships with other scales in the profile. Among the basic clinical scales, Scale 4 is most highly correlated with Scales 8, with which it shares 10 items (at .76), and 7, with which it shares 6 items (at .73). Content scale correlates of Scale 4 include *DEP*, with which it shares 5 items (.76), and *FAM*, with which it shares 6 items (.73). These relationships are determined by *Pd-O* and by the fact that these correlates are drawn from a psychiatric sample; in this sample, the correlation between Scale 4 and *Pd-O* is .92, while that with *Pd-S* is only .37. This pattern of correlations would be substantially different in a correctional sample, and somewhat different in a normal sample.

but have also exposed its value in a broad spectrum of personality and symptom disorders. Elevations on Scale 4 have been reported regularly in studies of patients with antisocial, borderline, dependent, histrionic, narcissistic, paranoid, and passive-aggressive personality disorders; alcoholics and substance abusers; correctional inmates; and patients with psychotic disorders.

The general construct embodied in Scale 4 appears to be one of an ingrained, durable, and mostly maladaptive pattern of personality organization and behavior that tends to narrow the range and stability of interpersonal satisfactions; impair educational and occupational achievement; impede attainment of long-term goals; and limit the harmony, flexibility, or efficacy of social functioning. The pattern typically involves some degree of externalization such that problems and conflicts are seen as originating outside the self, especially because of unfavorable traits and motives in others or in the social environment and its organizations more broadly, dishonesty, selfishness, bias, disloyalty, malice, or rigidity—to which the subject is merely reacting. Thus the subject's attributions onto others tend to reinforce themselves as new en-

Subscales for *Pd**

Pd1 (Familial Discord—9 items): "Struggle against familial control" (Harris and Lingoes). *Pd1* operates largely as a content scale, reporting problems and conflicts biased toward the family of origin. It has six items in common with *FAM*, three on *FAM1* and two on *FAM2*. Considerable bitterness and resentment and some projection of blame are implicit in many of the items. There is a sense of injury implicit in *Pd1* that may be the result of being controlled and disapproved of while not feeling cared for. *Pd1*, along with *Pd4* and *Sc1*, is one of the subscales most sensitive to the history of abuse, both for victims and for perpetrators.

Pd2 (Authority Conflict—8 items): "Resentment of parental and social demands, conventions and standards" (Harris and Lingoes). *Pd2* items are heterogeneous, but most share a common theme of rebelliousness and resistiveness or a sense of chafing under the constraints of authority, custom, or propriety. Major themes include historical acts of rule breaking or delinquency, rebelling against authority or conformist pressures, and argumentativeness. *Pd2* predicts behavioral undercontrol and reactive defiance of demands made by others, and is a good measure of misbehavior/rule-breaking. It can be usefully compared with *Ma4*, with which it is essentially uncorrelated. When both are elevated, issues of control avoidance, autonomy, and self-determination may be prominent.

Pd3 (Social Imperturbability—6 items): "Denial of social anxiety; blandness; denial of dependency needs" (Harris and Lingoes). *Pd3* is the extroversive component of Scale 4 and is the shortest of the Scale 4 subscales. In addition to cutting its length by half, the restandardization committee's elimination of the offscale items from Scale 4 increased the redundancy between *Pd3* and *Hy1* (r = .90), which now have two-thirds of their items in common. Both subscales connote an aggressive sociability. Four of the six *Pd3* items are contained within *Si1* (r = −.85) and three within *SOD2* (in both cases keyed oppositely), and three overlap with *Ma3*. The three offscale items dropped from the MMPI-2 version of *Pd3* combine with three of the remaining *Pd3* items to dominate the content of the seven-item *SOD2* component scale, but keyed in reverse. Thus the socially aggressive aspect of *Pd3* is also reflected in low *SOD2* scores. *Pd3* correlates negatively with *A* at −.64, suggesting unusual freedom from social anxiety and fear of embarrassment, as well as an assertive, counter-anxious attitude consistent with the image of the glib, "smooth operator." *Pd3* is one of the *K*-correlated subscales (r = .61).

Pd4 (Social Alienation—13 items): "Feelings of isolation from other people; lack of belongingness; externalization of blame for difficulties; lack of gratification in social relations" (Harris and Lingoes). *Pd4* is the paranoid component of Scale 4, but with some depressive undertones. It has six items in common with *Pa1* (r = .79) and three with *Pd5*. The primary theme of *Pd4* is social alienation: feeling apart, estranged, and misunderstood by others. Important secondary themes include resentment, deprivation, and dysphoria. Of these, deprivation may be the most important for understanding the high scorer on *Pd4*. Such patients often lacked an adequate holding environment in childhood and, as adults, carry a feeling of having been deprived and neglected by others and of their emotional needs' having been trivialized and ignored.

(continued)

Despite sharing the same label as *Sc1* (the two subscales have only three items in common), *Pd4* is different in several important ways from *Sc1* (r = .78). Whereas *Sc1* reflects a disinclination to form attachments to others, *Pd4* emphasizes an inability to do so, but with a sense of sorrow about this, unlike *Sc1*. Among the standard clinical scales and subscales, *Pd4* is probably the most sensitive to severe childhood deprivation and neglect. High scorers have come to anticipate that others will withhold the interpersonal goods of affection, support, encouragement, and similar forms of emotional nourishment.

Pd5 (Self-Alienation—12 items): "Lack of self-integration; avowal of guilt, exhibitionistically stated; despondency (e.g., these items are often answered in the scored direction by alcoholics who refer themselves to treatment)" (Harris and Lingoes). *Pd5* is the depressive component of Scale 4. *Pd5* overlaps *DEP* by six items (r = .87) and is also highly correlated with *PK* (r = .88) and *PS* (r = .86). The items tend toward a theme of self-reproach and ostentatious remorse. They have a neurotic flavor and appear distinctly out of place in a scale intended to model the psychopathy construct. Evidence exists (Voelker & Nichols, 1999) that this group of items does not contribute incrementally to the validity of Scale 4 when pitted against scores from the Psychopathy Checklist–Revised (Hare, 1991). *Pd5* appears to be an artifact of the effect of hospitalization on the criterion group cases. It may be one of the key elements in the so-called "caught psychopath" configurations, such as the 2-4/4-2 code patterns. These reflect depressive phenomena that are largely inspired by situation, as a reaction to the felt need to enact mea culpa for tactical reasons, and to the inconvenience of having to live within a restrictive, style-cramping, institutional environment with its schedules, policies, rules, privilege levels, fixed menus, and so on. Among the standard clinical scales and subscales, *Pd5* is the most satisfactory measure of guilt.

Pd-O (Psychopathic Deviate–Obvious—28 items): Two-thirds of the *Pd-O* items overlap *Pd4* and *Pd5*, with the remaining third divided about equally between *Pd1* and *Pd2*. However, *Pd-O* is thematically dominated by *Pd5* and predominantly distressed and depressive in tone. It is fairly highly saturated with the First Factor (correlation with *A* = .84) and thus will be raised by any of the distress scales.

Pd-S (Psychopathic Deviate–Subtle—22 items): *Pd-S* is a more heterogeneous collection of items than *Pd-O* and is built around *Pd3*, its largest (six) cluster of items. It achieves its highest correlations with measures of extroversion (*Pd3* = .51, *Hy1* = .44; *SOD2* = −.37; *Si1* = −.35), but has no clear central theme. It correlates with *K* at .32. The items suggest an individual who is inwardly conflicted although self-controlled, and outwardly socially insouciant, carefree, and imperturbable. Many items also assert independence and self-determination in the examinee's reactions and behavior. The overall effect is one of instability or brittleness, with a potential for stubbornness or argumentative overreaction to the assertions, demands, or complaints of others.

*The five Harris-Lingoes subscales for Scale 4 contain minimal overlap (three items overlap *Pd4* and *Pd5*). The MMPI versions of these subscales contained 14 items from an earlier version of Scale 4 that were not scored on the final scale. The restandardization committee dropped these items for the MMPI-2 versions of the Scale 4 subscales, thereby weakening one of them (*Pd3*, which lost 6 of its 12 items) substantially.

counters draw reactions from the social environment, which are seen as confirming or validating them. This perceived confirmation, in turn, prevents new learning and renders the subject's attitudes and behaviors concerning social negotiations highly resistant to extinction.

Not all of the attributes of Scale *4* are undesirable. Characteristics such as adventurousness, energy, spontaneity, self-confidence, aggression, an enterprising spirit, and even rebelliousness can serve important and highly positive social functions in certain times and circumstances. One person's recklessness, for example, may be another's courage, bravery, or daring. Some of the same traits that for many result in long prison sentences may lead to revolutionary discoveries, the breaking of previous records, or, for a few, the Congressional Medal of Honor. See, for example, Neil Sheehan's *A Bright Shining Lie: John Paul Vann and America in Vietnam* (1989).

Scale *4* elevations generally constitute a greater physical risk to the patient than to those with whom he or she may come into contact. In terms of overall mortality/morbidity, the high Scale *4* scorer tends to be more self- than other-destructive. Substance abuse and a tendency to take imprudent risks and disregard hazards renders high scorers vulnerable to mishaps that result in injury or death. However, high scorers do constitute a greater emotional risk to others through their emotional coldness, lack of availability, selfishness, and lack of responsibility, and by their indifference to the stresses they cause others by the situations into which their behavior may place them.

There are important similarities between Scales *3* and *4:* Both are complex and multidimensional, and both contain some components positively and some negatively correlated with *K*. For example, *K* correlates with *Pd-O* at $-.71$, and with *Pd-S* at .30. *Pd-O* tends to have high convergent validity with intratest measures and external ratings, and with diagnostic judgments of discomfort and dissatisfaction, guilt, self-depreciation, depression, and both fear of and alienation from others. However, it has limited discriminant validity because of its lack of sensitivity to the socially skillful, dominant, and intrepid (or counterphobic) features of the Scale *4* syndrome. Conversely, *Pd-S* shows high convergent validity for the latter features but low discriminant validity for the former features. Consequently, the domination of Scale *4* scores by *Pd-O* is likely to be accompanied by greater overall profile elevation with prominent peaks on Scales *7* and/or *8* and a self-critical pattern on the validity scales; whereas the domination of Scale *4* scores by *Pd-S* is associated with lower profile elevation, few concurrent peaks (usually Scales *3, 6,* or *9*), a low score on Scale *0,* and *K* greater than *F.*

Concurrent elevations on Scales *6, 8,* and *9* tend to accentuate the negative features of Scale *4* characteristics, whereas elevations on Scales *2, 3, 5* (low *5* for women), and *0* tend to attenuate or socialize Scale *4* expressions. For example, the *4-9/9-4* pattern accentuates the acting-out and sensation-seeking trends in Scale *4,* while in the *4-5/5-4* pattern the rebellious trends of Scale *4* are influenced in the direction of verbal expression and social consciousness by the passivity and somewhat aesthetic and intellectual orientation of Scale *5.* Elevations on *L* and/or *K* accompanying Scale *4,* especially when scores on Scales *F, 7,* and *8* are low, often reflects a more fundamentally paranoid than antisocial pattern.

Presenting Problem

It is unusual for the high Scale *4* scorer to present on his or her own initiative, for such types are typically comfortable with themselves and their behavior. These patients are usually seen under some form of duress, such as a spouse's or partner's threat to leave the relationship; directives from employers or potential employers; in the course of court-ordered or other forensic investigations; hospital commitments; and similar circumstances. In other cases, the duress is in the form of personal distress that has attended some disturbing situational event such as divorce, an unplanned or illegitimate pregnancy, being at odds with or not feeling included in the activities of friends, school failure, layoff or termination of employment, legal difficulties, motor vehicle accident, the emergence of symptoms from an Axis I psychiatric disorder, problems related to alcohol or drug abuse, and so forth. The goals in making contact with a mental health professional tend to be practical: the solution of a problem or set of problems, or the amelioration of an uncomfortable set of life circumstances. Because these patients locate the problems in their lives outside themselves, they are rarely interested in changing things about themselves, but prefer to become more skilled or better informed about how to change or avoid the behavior of others toward them.

Symptomatic Pattern

Patterns involving Scale *4* reliably predict being at odds with the social environment. This may take the form of active conflict; passive resistance; or efforts to undermine, subvert, or evade the influence of specific persons, authority figures, conventions, and rules. Patients tend to be rebellious toward anyone whom they feel may be a threat to their autonomy, even when such rebellion may be manifestly contrary to their own interests. They also tend to disregard or resent social customs and conventions and seek to evade or flaunt rules and social norms. These patients are often inattentive to or heedless of the consequences of their behaviors, and have a reckless disregard for the feelings, expectations, and convenience of those around them. They are viewed as quick to sacrifice long-term goals to indulge short-term gratifications. They have long-term difficulties learning from experience, even when adverse or punishing. The history often reveals in childhood an incorrigible response to all manner of disciplinary efforts, from admonitions and the withdrawal of privileges, to various forms of restriction, corporal punishment, beatings, suspensions or expulsions from school, to natural consequences such as accidents and injuries. A pattern of delinquency and involvement with juvenile authorities in youth becomes in adulthood clashes with legal and other authorities and the resulting sanctions—fines, imprisonment, termination of employment, and so forth. The behavior pattern often shows involvement in the same kind of difficulty (sexual promiscuity, drunk driving, forgery, etc.) on repeated occasions.

There is commonly an underregulation of emotionality and abrupt changes in mood. Emotional arousal and expression tend to be poorly calibrated to the circumstances that instigate them such that, for example, irritation becomes openly expressed anger, and anger turns into aggressive verbal or physical altercation. Tolerance for frustration and boredom are low. Expressions of affiliative emotionality, such as affection, approval, and warmth, tend to be guileful and manipulative. The same tends to be true of guilt and remorse. Affect at baseline tends to be underaroused but unstable, easily shifting into irritability, restlessness, or boredom, and the feeling tone tends to be cold or aggressive. These patients are rarely anxious; however, their restlessness, boredom, and irritability may incite in others an anxiety that they, in turn, may mistakenly attribute to the patient.

Although unlikely to experience acute distress under most circumstances, including circumstances that would typically be upsetting to others, these patients do not view themselves as especially happy or content, despite assertions to the contrary. They generally view themselves as having to operate under a greater level of stress than others, and as somehow missing out on satisfactions that others seem to be able to take for granted. They are unlikely to describe themselves as depressed, but often do experience a vague sense of purposelessness, emptiness, or futility about their lives, feelings of boredom and restlessness, and a brooding dissatisfaction with clear dysphoric overtones. With age and the accumulation of adverse consequences for their behavior, these patients are increasingly prone to moodiness, brooding, bitterness and resentment.

With the exception of judgment, cognitive functions are generally within normal limits. Attention, concentration, and memory are unimpaired, and decision making is unfettered if not fearless and bold. Judgment, however, is uneven to poor, with a chronic tendency to underestimate risk and frequent failures of anticipation and foresight. Planning ahead is often sacrificed to momentary impulse or the need for stimulation or gratification.

Motivations are typically seen by others as selfish, self-serving, self-justifying (rationalizing), and oriented to immediate gratification. Major life goals are rarely defined, and even when these can be articulated, there is a notable impersistence in efforts to achieve them. Values are expedient, self-serving, subject to rapid revision in response to changing circumstances, and weakly internalized. Truth and lying are evaluated on the grounds of expediency rather than moral commitments.

High scorers tend to be socially extroverted, outgoing, glib, and intrepid. They are talkative and able to speak easily to others, including strangers, and appear energetic and adventurous. Their lack of normal levels of social anxiety and inhibition often causes others to view them as attractive, self-confident, and exciting to be around, as their own disinhibition may free others to feel less fearful and self-conscious, and more engaged, "with it," and spontaneous. Although they are likely to make a favorable initial impression, upon more protracted acquaintance their basic self-centeredness, coldness, and unreliability become more apparent.

These patients are occasionally described in terms suggesting hostility, such as "sarcastic" and "cynical"; however, they are more reliably seen as socially aggressive, in the sense of moving into social encounters in a way others often perceive as forward, intrusive, or implicitly demanding. Hostility, as such, tends to be situational rather than consistent, especially as a reaction to frustration.

The pattern of sexual behavior is characteristically focused on sensation seeking rather than on intimacy. There is a low threshold for sexual experimentation and a relatively high need for erotic stimulation. Sexual interaction is typically spontaneous and uninhibited, but also relatively indiscriminate and promiscuous. Partners tend to be selected more for their stimulating qualities than for their suitability as companions, and selfishness and exploitiveness in this domain are common.

Interpersonal Relations

Patients with high Scale *4* scores appear chronically unable to bond—to form warm and stable attachments—with others. Even when durable, these patients' relationships are usually based on dependency, and tend to be egocentric and exploitative. Whether durable or not, their insensitivity to others' needs and feelings leads their relationships to be viewed as superficial and parasitic. There is often a sense of carelessness or indifference in the way they relate to people even when not behaving toward them in especially manipulative or exploitive ways. For example, they can be impatient, demanding, and overbearing, not because of any intention on the part of others to frustrate them, but simply on the basis of having a different tempo or timetable. They are often dishonest in their relations with others, with frequent opportunistic lying, withholding important information, or otherwise misleading them, and tend to assume that others would be as dishonest as they are were it not for their weakness and lack of courage.

Family relationships may be turbulent, and marital relationships are subject to discord due to improvident habits such as substance abuse or gambling, or to problems related to aggression, disloyalty, thoughtlessness, carelessness, and unreliability. They tend to describe their families of origin as critical and controlling. Their adult heterosexual relationships are often especially stressful to the partners as the patient may change plans or keep odd hours without informing the partner, squander financial resources or refuse to pay bills, seek extramarital liaisons, fail to follow through on agreements and appointments, repeatedly lie to or mislead the partner, refuse to engage areas of conflict and dissatisfaction within the relationship, and in other ways leave the partner "holding the bag."

Other Problem Areas

Substance abuse of one kind or another is very common and typically causes long-term financial/occupational difficulties, including unemployment and homelessness. In older patients there are often health problems as well, such as diabetes, cardiovascular/pulmonary diseases, and closed-head injuries. The physical consequences of their recklessness, their exhausting or alienating interpersonal support, or both can precipitate depression and create ideation and impulses to suicide.

Behavioral Stability

This pattern is highly resistant to change with or without treatment. The trend toward behavioral and social deviance of the kind predicted by Scale 4 generally becomes consolidated by late childhood or early adolescence and tends to remain stable and persistent until early middle age. Scores on Scale 4 are known to decline with age, just short of a standard deviation over the course of adult life.

Defenses

Rationalizing, intellectualizing, and transferring blame are characteristic. Defensive operations are typically directed toward avoiding responsibility and the consequences of their behavior, rather than toward the reduction of anxiety, depression, or other internal sources of discomfort.

History

They typically manifest a history of underachievement in education due to disobedience and disruption, or to dropping out, or both, and in employment due to conflicts with supervisors over tardiness, abuse of sick leave, theft, intoxication on the job, insubordination, quarrels and disagreements with coworkers, and similar infractions. A pattern of lying, cheating, truancy, and stealing is often well established by mid-adolescence, and there is usually, but not always, a record of run-ins with school or juvenile authorities.

There is often a history of family conflict and instability, emotional neglect, and unreliable or indifferent parenting. The home environment was often lacking in affection and warmth, with insufficient attention to the child's physical and emotional needs. The child may have been pressed into service for his or her own caretaking prematurely and without sufficient guidance, resources, support, or supervision for him or her to feel safe and protected. In other cases there was a permissive or incompetently corrective reaction to the child's aggressiveness. One or both parents may have implicitly approved of and obtained vicarious satisfactions from the child's misbehavior by repeated rescues and intercessions with authorities ("Boys will be boys"), thereby reinforcing deviant social development.

Diagnostic Considerations

The primary diagnosis tends to fall on Axis II, with Antisocial, Borderline, and Narcissistic Personality Disorder being typical. On Axis I, disorders involving substance abuse are most common, and usually involve alcohol, street drugs, or both, but Adjustment Disorders with Depressed Mood or Disturbance of Conduct are also possible. Psychotic disorders are infrequent but not rare, and usually involve paranoid elements when they occur. When Scale *4* is highest and is combined with the validity scale pattern $L > K > F$, encapsulated paranoid and delusional disorders are common.

Treatment Considerations

Prognosis for treatment is generally poor, but may vary considerably depending on such factors as age, gender, the availability of family support, occupational skills, employment, chronicity, substance abuse, and the patient's level of subjective (not situational) discomfort/distress. The poorest prognosis seems to attend those patients who abuse substances and have drained their social environment of persons who care about them. Prognosis is more favorable when the patient retains some sources of emotional support, however exhausted or shaky these may be, and feels some genuine motivation to repair and maintain them. Younger and female patients have better outcomes than older and male patients. Outcome appears to bear a curvilinear relationship to intelligence: Those at the upper end of the distribution tend toward various forms of rational self-defense and keeping the therapist at an emotional distance, and those at the lower end have trouble incorporating and deploying new learning and greater difficulty leaving a peer culture that reinforces their prior maladaptive habits of thought and action.

The apparent intelligence, verbal fluency, and professed interest in treatment displayed by some of these patients can often mislead therapists to make overly favorable prognoses in the initial sessions, but these impressions tend to give way rapidly to discouragement as the persistence of acting-out and the entrenched patterns of shifting and avoiding responsibility become evident.

Many of these patients will seek to prey on a therapist's humanity by trying to convert him or her into an ally against the people or forces arrayed "against" them. In this strategy, the patient will dwell artfully on accounts of his or her unfair or callous mistreatment by others or institutions (often "the system") in an effort to create sympathy and a sense of outrage in the therapist. Others will use flattery and seek to seduce and compromise therapists by trying to place them in a position to receive vicarious gratification from the patients' acting-out. Often these manipulations are subtle and can be convincing initially. When they fail to have the desired effect on the therapist, the patient tends to abandon treatment promptly.

Effective therapeutic strategies tend to emphasize detachment in the context of steady optimism and care for the patient. However, the therapist's detachment must be intellectual/attitudinal rather than emotional, as too little warmth and emotional support will drive these patients from treatment. The therapist must often take the role of an empathic "broken record" in which the patient's choices and evasions are repeatedly fed back to her or him, along with the probable (if not actual) practical consequences in his or her life. It may help to couch commentary on the patient's behavior as though the behavior is understandable (in terms of expediency) but unwise (i.e., short-sighted, selfish), thus preventing the patient's feeling blamed or rejected by the therapist. The therapist may appeal to the patient's wisdom of experience as a way to direct his or her aspirations toward less self-defeating life choices, encourage longer time horizons for goal attainment, and develop understandings about how others obtain those satisfactions that the patient envies.

Initial efforts are best focused on resolving whatever in the patient's situation creates or maintains stress; such efforts usually meet the patient's desire to focus on external aspects of the situation without requiring an overwhelming or intolerable level of self-examination. Short-term, behaviorally focused goals and interventions that effectively reduce stress may only set the stage for early termination for some patients, but should not be deemed valueless on that account. Such success, although limited, can leave the patient with a satisfying experience of therapy that may favor a later return. For other patients, initial short-term success may create a sense of therapeutic momentum and set the stage for greater commitment to treatment that involves self-examination and emotional change.

Low Scores

Persons with low scores on Scale 4 tend to be at peace with themselves and others. They are easygoing and have a cheerful, good-natured outlook. They may be shy, modest, and unassuming. Sincere and trusting in relations with others, they often show a great capacity for loyalty and steadfastness. They are trustworthy in the sense that they value trust in their relations with others and experience a sense of moral obligation to live up to their agreements, both explicit and implicit. They are gentle and reasonable in their approach to working out the conflicts that arise in their relationships, and seem to value harmony and stability highly. Conscience and ethical sensibilities tend to be integrated. Sexual inhibitions or a lack of heterosexual interest and adventurousness has been noted for some low Scale 4 scorers, especially among men. This may range from excessive modesty and concerns over public displays of affection to actual fears of sexual activity. They are noncompetitive and do not seek advantage over others. To the contrary, they are often seen as obliging, passive, submissive, and unassertive, easily able to accept advice and suggestion and to subordinate their own preferences to those of others, although they may be seen at times as overly willing to do so. They tolerate routine well and are dependable and persistent in their pursuit of their goals and duties, but are also somewhat conventional and unspontaneous. At the extreme, low Scale 4 scorers may be rigidly conforming and conservative as well as overly accepting of authority, and may have narrow interests, a high tolerance for boredom, a preoccupation with status and security, and a fear of change and the unfamiliar.

SCALE 5: MASCULINITY-FEMININITY (Mf)

Development

Hathaway's description of the development of Scale 5 is especially sparse, covering only two paragraphs (1956/1980). The criterion group consisted of "13 homosexual invert males," by which he meant men whose homosexual preference rested on a constitutional, rather than a neurotic, psychotic, psychopathic, or other basis. The men were not described with respect to age, education, or other demographic variables. Fifty-five items adapted from "sections 5, 6, and 7 of the Terman and Miles's Attitude-Interest Analysis Test"

(Dahlstrom et al., 1972, p. 5; Terman & Miles, 1938) were added to the original pool of 504 items based on their "promise in identifying sexual inversion as shown in the studies of Terman and Miles" (Dahlstrom et al., 1972, p. 201; Terman & Miles, 1936). Because the responses of the Minnesota Normals to these new items were unavailable, two new normal contrast groups, consisting of 54 male soldiers and 67 female airline employees, were created (Dahlstrom et al., 1972). The soldiers provided the initial, primary contrast group. Constantinople (1973) has suggested that only those items that discriminated between the men and women of the Minnesota Normals, plus the 55 new items, were eligible for scale membership with those items discriminating the inverts from the soldiers being retained. Hathaway then apparently contrasted the 54 soldiers with an unknown number of men who had obtained high scores on the Terman and Miles Inversion score of their Attitude-Interest Analysis Test. The latter comparison likely cross-validated, at least in part, those items separating the criterion cases from the soldiers, but nowhere is this stated explicitly. Finally, the items surviving the previous comparison were checked to make sure they separated the soldiers from the female airline employees. The final scale of 60 items consisted of 37 items from the original item pool and 23 of the 55 newly added items (Dahlstrom et al., 1972). Of these, 56 were retained for the MMPI-2. Perhaps because of characteristics of the homosexual criterion group that Hathaway left unspecified, and/or the characteristics of the samples used in the development of the Attitude-Interest Analysis Test, Scale 5 is sensitive to measured intelligence. Its relation to education and SES is also positive among normal samples, but is negligible among psychiatric samples. Rapid Reference 6.5a contains a summary description of Scale 5; its subscales are described in Rapid Reference 6.5b.

Interpretive Implications

General

Although in its core aspects Scale 5 is based upon the responses of Hathaway's 13 "inverts," it has never performed well in separating homosexuals from controls (e.g., Manosevitz, 1971; Wong, 1984). Nor, at least in recent times, has it been important that it be able to do so. In most circumstances, information regarding a patient's sexual preferences can be had for the asking. Moreover, in terms of their bearing on sexual preference, the items of Scale 5 are sufficiently

≋Rapid Reference 6.5a

Summary Descriptive Features of *Mf*

Number of Items: 56

True/False Balance: 25/31

Overlap: Scale 5*f* overlaps GF by 16 items positively and GM by 8 items negatively; Scale 5*m* overlaps GF by 13 items positively and GM by 8 items negatively.

Content: Heterogeneous but tending to divide about evenly between (a) sex role–related interests, activities, and occupations, and (b) a mix of items reflecting sexual concerns, conflict, worry, sensitivity, denial of cynicism and mistrust, and social reserve.

Relations with Other Scales: With the exception of GF (.70) and GM (−.52), Scale 5 is only weakly correlated with most other MMPI-2 scales. Three scales, Nelson's Ss, Barron's Es, and Scale 4, are important moderators. High scores on Ss, Es, and Do all tend to emphasize favorable aspects of Scale 5 scores, whether the latter are high or low. Scores on Scale 4 strongly influence the interpersonal aspects of high Scale 5 raw scores. For men, the strength of the patient's basic attachment to others, his commitment to the maintenance and repair of close relationships, and his capacity for trust, optimism, warmth, and forgiveness are indicated by the extent to which Scale 5 exceeds Scale 4, provided that 4 does not exceed T-55. For women, the same pattern of positive trends is given by the extent to which Scale 4 exceeds Scale 5, provided that 4 does not exceed T-60.

As Scale 4 is elevated beyond these limits, especially as it exceeds Scale 5 for men, there tend to be chronic problems in the quality, strength, and stability of attachments. Such patterns tend to predict passive-aggressive struggles; significant conflicts around dependency-independency; a tendency to react to requests as if they were demands; and a quickness to feel dominated (especially with men feeling dominated by women), and to reflexively rebel against this feeling. With high scores on Scale 5, elevations on Scale 4 are more benign than otherwise. Scale 5 tends to focus the rebelliousness and authority conflict that accompany Scale 4 and give them an intellectual/philosophical basis, such that many men with this pattern are better described as anti-authoritarian than anti-authority.

obvious that examinees can easily slant their responses to emphasize or deemphasize stereotypically masculine or feminine patterns of interests, pastimes, and occupational preferences, just as they might do in interview.

Scale 5 has been criticized in its role as a measure of masculine versus feminine interests (Constantinople, 1973) because of its contamination with homosexual preference, and because of its presumed bipolarity, with high raw

≣*Rapid Reference 6.5b*

Subscales for *Mf**

Mf1 (Denial of Stereotypical Masculine Interests—11 items, including 5 offscale items): This is one of the two interest subscales. It is moderately correlated with GF (.55), R (.45), and CON (.32), indicating a secondary theme of circumspection, control, and timidity.

Mf2 (Hypersensitivity/Anxiety—13 items): This is the neuroticism/negative emotionality component of Scale 5. Mf2 is highly correlated with other measures of this dimension such as NEN (.76), A (.75), and ANX (.71). It reflects worry, self-doubt, a sense of vulnerability to hurt feelings, and guilt.

Mf3 (Stereotypical Feminine Interests—6 items): The second of the two interest subscales, Mf3 is moderately correlated with GF (.47) and GM (−.33), but unlike Mf1, contains no subtheme.

Mf4 (Low Cynicism—6 items): These items deny cynicism, antisocial attitudes, and suspiciousness. Correlations with similar measures of these constructs are moderate to high: CYN1 (−.76), ASP1 (−.75), and Pa3 (.65).

Mf5 (Aesthetic Interests—5 items): These items suggest openness to experience, culture, and sophistication. Low scores on this subscale may suggest passivity in patients with high *raw* Scale 5 scores, especially among persons with little education.

Mf6 (Feminine Gender Identity—5 items, including 3 offscale items): These items are in the spirit of "I enjoy being a girl." Mf6 is moderately correlated with GF (.64) and GM (.38). High scores suggest homoerotic fantasy in men, but low scores are without homoerotic implications in women (Martin, 1993).

Mf7 (Restraint—6 items): This subscale suggests emotional and behavioral constraint. It has moderate correlations with R (.50) and CON (.45). Interestingly, its correlations with measures of fear and discomfort are very close to zero.

Mf10 (Composite Femininity-Masculinity—22 items, including 8 offscale items): Mf10 is a simple composite of Mf1, Mf3, and Mf6. High scores for men and low scores among women suggest non-normative gender identity.

*Scale 5 is multidimensional. Factor analyses have typically found from five to seven factors relating to feminine interests, masculine interests, introversion, hypersensitivity, distress/discomfort, and trust. The Martin-Finn subscales were developed from the MMPI-2 restandardization sample and include eight offscale items to increase the reliability of two of the subscales.

scores signifying an extreme feminine interest pattern and low raw scores signifying the opposite masculine extreme. Although Hathaway (1956/1980) appears to have considered masculinity-femininity a bipolar dimension, the current consensus is that masculinity and femininity are better understood as separate and independent dimensions. As a result, Peterson and Dahlstrom (1992) developed separate gender-role scales for males and females, *GM* and *GF,* from the MMPI-2 restandardization sample; these will be discussed in Chapter 7.

Regardless of the details of its origins, the construct underlying Scale *5* is not pathological, at least in the same sense that the basic scales are considered to model psychopathological constructs. It is not free of psychopathological variance, however, nor does it lack relevance for psychopathological description. However, its raw scores are normally distributed and it appears to function primarily as a measure of an individual difference variable. Scale *5* can make an important contribution to clinical description, particularly in the way it may modify descriptions based on the other clinical scales, and to issues related to treatment.

Scale *5* reflects a general dimension of activity-passivity, with high-scoring men and low-scoring women tending toward behavioral control and nonaggressiveness. Rather than thinking of Scale *5* as a single dimension, however, it is convenient to think of it as a family of dimensions related to the overall activity-passivity construct, with unique characteristics (see Table 6.2). The fact that one characteristic on the active pole is unusually descriptive does not mean the other characteristics on the active pole will likewise describe the person better than all or most of the characteristics on the passive pole. Nevertheless, most people tend toward one or the other pole.

Another dimension of Scale *5* scores is the breadth versus the narrowness of the examinee's pattern of interests. For both sexes, low scores tend to reflect a narrow interest pattern that may be overly tied to sex-role constraints, expectations, and identifications. High scores suggest a broader, more inclusive range of interests, which, at the extreme, may reflect identity diffusion or may become chaotic. In schizophrenia, the identity disturbance may involve a sense of uncertainty such that the boundary between what are and are not one's interests becomes highly permeable. In mania, the identity disturbance may involve expanding the experience of the self to encompass an unrealistically overinclusive endorsement of interests.

Table 6.2 Possible Characteristics of *Mf* Scores

Active Pole (low males, high females)	Passive Pole (high males, low females)
Dominance	Submission
Succorance	Dependency
Competition	Cooperation
Exhibitionism	Spectatorship
Participating	Observing
Intrusiveness	Receptiveness
Physical-Somatic-Motor	Mental-Cerebral-Sensory
Action/Movement Preferred	Thought/Contemplation Preferred
Mobile/Vigorous (e.g., hunting)	Stationary/Sedentary (e.g., fishing)
Outdoor Pastimes	Indoor Pastimes
Pragmatic	Aesthetic
Mechanical	Artistic
Practical	Theoretical
Realistic	Idealistic
Tough	Tender
Behavioral	Verbal
Crude/Coarse	Refined/Delicate
Vulgar	Sophisticated
Ostentation	Circumspection
Acting-Out	Intellectualizing
Mechanistic	Humanistic
Values Self-Sufficiency	Values Nurturance
Values Independence	Values Relatedness
Values Self-Reliance/Autonomy	Values Mutuality
Values Utility	Values Style/Appearance
Father Identification	Mother Identification

In males, higher raw scores are associated with higher T-scores; among women this relationship is reversed. For both men and women, T-scores must enter the range of 80–85 to indicate that the person is responding in a manner characteristic of the opposite gender. For this reason, T-65, the level of elevation that is usually the most convenient point for separating clinical from nonclinical ranges of elevation, can be misleading, especially if one wishes to characterize scores by such locutions as masculine, feminine, masculinized, effeminate, and so on.

The love relationships of low-scoring men and women may have a highly personal focus on amorous behavior and sentiment, with an intense and romantic emotional attachment. By contrast, at least for men, high scores may be characterized by a broader, civilized altruism, in which tender and affectionate sentiments are more inclusive, extending well beyond the spouse or primary partner. Such scorers are apt to emphasize companionate over romantic-erotic relationships.

The adjectives used to describe high-scoring men are overwhelmingly positive. They are seen by others as mature and effective, self-controlled and inner-directed, insightful and self-aware, and as feeling comfortable with themselves and their lives. Intellectually able, they tend to value clear and logical thought. Although they are imaginative, they are also well-organized planners, are able to foresee the consequences of their actions, and exercise common sense and good judgment. They have wide-ranging interests and are curious about others and the world at large. They show concern about moral issues, are tolerant and fair-minded in their approach, and are able to become socially involved to influence the fate of issues they deem important. In this and other regards they have the advantage of being verbally fluent, of communicating clearly, and of being persuasive in argument. They are able to take satisfaction in their work and accomplishments, set ambitious goals, and show perseverence in achieving them even though they may be seen as more serious and exacting than necessary. Their relations with others are characterized by sensitivity and skill. They are receptive to feelings and nuance in relationships and capable of expressing affection and care. However, they are uncomfortable with conflict and confrontation and will generally go out of their way to avoid them. This may include shrinking from disagreement, withholding opinions, and a quickness to compromise, make concessions, or yield to the will or opinions of others, especially when Scales *4* and/or *9* are low. They are aware of their own stimulus value and accurate in their perceptions of others. Others, in turn, tend to view them favorably, as capable, reasonable, sensitive, and practical, but also at times as overly cautious, fussy, and submissive.

High-scoring women also tend to be described in positive terms but less richly, possibly because such scores occur infrequently. These women describe themselves or are seen by others as physically robust and adventurous, logical, creative, balanced and poised; as relaxed and easy-going; and as facing life. They may be more self-assured in situations requiring competition and leadership than are women in general. They are likewise more comfortable being involved in vigorous outdoor activities, in watching or participating in sports, and in mechanical pursuits, than most other women are. At times they may be seen as direct, controlling, loud, overly assertive, or willful, such that they may generate discomfort or resistance in others—perhaps especially in men with relatively fixed and narrow expectations of womens' "proper" roles.

These women often feel confined by traditional feminine roles such as those defined by marriage, home, and child rearing. Although they may value one or more of these roles highly, they seek to broaden their areas of activity and influence, and are often oriented to achievement and competitive careers in business and industry. They are typically self-confident and outgoing, and comfortable with values that emphasize skill, practical know-how, mastery, and competition, and may prefer the company of men. They may also be somewhat forward socially, interpersonally brusque, and impatient with small talk.

Low-scoring men are described in mixed terms. They are viewed as cheerful, balanced, self-confident, and independent, but also as stereotyped and unoriginal in their approach to problem solving, possessing a narrow range of interests, avoiding difficult or unpleasant situations, and lacking in self-awareness regarding their motives and stimulus value. In fact, the adjectives used to describe these men suggest a puerile, happy-go-lucky approach to life, in which contemplation and self-examination are assiduously avoided in preference to action, however hasty, reckless, or ill-considered. Less intelligent than high-scoring men for the most part, low Scale 5–scoring men appear to lack flexibility and resourcefulness. In some cases, their apparent insensitivity and lack of refinement along with their concern to project a "macho" image may be defensively motivated by past failures, embarrassments, or other experiences that involved a painful sense of awkwardness or impotence in social situations, particularly those requiring verbal facility. Some of these men appear to harbor significant doubts about their own adequacy as men, for which their exaggerated masculinity may be an unwitting expression.

Low-scoring women tend to identify with the traditional feminine role, with their loyalties and interests centered around home and family. Although their interests may well extend beyond the domestic into employment and social issues, their choices in the latter areas are often influenced by nurturant values and concerns with family, neighborhood, and community. In contrast with high scorers, women with low Scale 5 scores tend to gravitate toward occupations in education, social service, and medical care, or to occupations related to beauty and fashion, and to avoid occupations in the competitive areas of corporate business. The traditional correlates for low-scoring women have emphasized their passivity, sensitivity, responsiveness, social reserve, and idealism.

Some of these women, especially the most impoverished and least educated, may indeed manifest high levels of constriction, deference, submissiveness, hypersensitivity, affected modesty, timorousness, and self-pity. A few may exhibit a long-suffering and perverse inability to feel and express pleasure, happiness, and satisfaction. This could be a consequence of learned helplessness and limited opportunities for economic advancement and social efficacy. However, given the past half-century's changes in women's level of educational attainment, the extent of their participation on the work force, their economic independence, and the availability of oral contraceptives, such descriptors may no longer be accurate. On the other hand, the description of low-scoring women depend heavily on their levels of education. Graham and Tisdale (1983) found that educated women who obtained similar low scores were described in much more adaptive terms (e.g., insightful, considerate, conscientious, easy-going, capable, and intelligent). Such women appear able to integrate many cultural features of the feminine gender role with a broad set of interests, intellectual strength, and competency. In terms of the ability to tailor their gender roles to gain the benefits and pleasures of femininity without having to constrain their potential for effectiveness across a broad array of non–gender prescribed social roles, these women appear liberated.

A second implication of low Scale 5 scores for women concerns their handling of important relationships. Clinical experience has found unusually high levels of commitment and endurance in these women's relationships, such that they have been able to bear with their partners in the face of considerable conflict and hardship, and even of neglect and mistreatment by them. In some cases, these women stick with their partners, often because of a lack of economic resources or social supports, but become embittered, fault-finding, resentful, and chronically aggrieved. But for others, attachments to their children and other involvement, such as extended family, church, or neighborhood, allow them to accept or resolve the problems that weigh upon their marital relationships without a sense of permanent injustice and resentment. In a few cases, the husband's occupation (e.g., truck driver) entailed relatively long periods away from the home, which may have been helpful. These women, through forgiveness, a strong sense of optimism, a generosity of spirit, or an orientation to service and devotion in the face of the spouse's selfishness, breaches of trust, and unkind treatment, were able to endure without divorce or extreme adjustments, provided that their mistreatment was not severe. These attitudes appeared, over time, to be repaid by a stronger and more enriched relationship than onlookers would have predicted. Thus, at least in retrospect, the "low-5 strategy" seemed to pay off for these women. They first achieved a degree of happiness that seemed to issue from their resolution and devotion during times of hardship; later, after the stormy period in the relationship had passed, they found a more stable happiness that flowed from a renewed sense of mutuality in the relationship; from a feeling of accomplishment through their loyalty and persistence in seeking opportunities for repair and reconciliation; the vindication of their optimism; or from some combination of these.

Presenting Problem

Males with high Scale 5 scores usually present with sexual problems or concerns, dysphoric mood, problems with self-image, or relationship difficulties. They may feel pressured by others' expectations, particularly in regard to enacting roles that make them feel uncomfortable or ill-prepared. For example, pressures placed upon the patient by superiors on the job to discipline subordinates may clash with the patient's more tolerant, egalitarian, and easy-going management style. Others present as having conflicts with coworkers, neighbors, or others due to harassment or hostile teasing that leave the patient frightened and angry. Still others present with sadness or depression, often centered on a sense of alienation or frustration and the inability to have their needs met. Regardless of the primary presenting problem, problems in the area of sexuality are usually present.

The situation is similar with women who have high Scale 5 scores, but sexual problems and dysphoria occur much less frequently than among high Scale 5 men. These women often experience conflicts between their core values and the roles they are expected to perform. They experience a variety of interpersonal problems, including difficulties because of what others perceive as their insensitivity, feelings that their motives are misunderstood, feelings of rejection and marital and child-rearing problems. In women with limited education, problems with underachievement, acting-out, and occasionally violence are seen.

Low-scoring men rarely present themselves for treatment as outpatients but sometimes accompany (usually reluctantly) their wives for marital counseling or to address problems with a child, especially problems with discipline or rebelliousness that trace to the father's lack of sensitivity to the child's needs and an overreliance on corporal punishment.

Low-scoring women present with a wide variety of difficulties, often focusing on the marital relationship, with communication and assertiveness problems, feeling overwhelmed with responsibilities, and acting-out on the part of the spouse or children. These women often seem to internalize stresses and not infrequently present with somatic problems such as headache.

Symptomatic Pattern
Heavily dependent on relations with other scales.

Interpersonal Relations
Heavily dependent on relations with other scales.

Behavioral Stability
The basic pattern of behavior tends toward stability, but scores can fluctuate considerably depending on currently experienced (or expressed) levels of stress or discomfort.

Defenses
High-scoring males tend toward adaptive and mature defenses, such as humor and sublimation. They tend to be intellectualized and intellectualizing; defenses like rationalization and suppression (Trimboli & Kilgore, 1983), as well as minor denial, idealization, devaluation, and passive-aggression are also relatively frequent.

Low-scoring females likewise tend toward adaptive defenses but show a considerable range of constriction, with the less constrained tending to rely on humor and sublimation, and the more constrained relying on suppression (Trimboli & Kilgore, 1983), rationalization, intellectualization, reaction formation, and even denial and projection.

The defensive postures of high-scoring women and low-scoring men are less well understood, but acting-out is not uncommon.

History

Little is known about the histories of patients with high and low Scale 5 scores. Some (e.g., Caldwell) have speculated that the pattern of parental identification is formative, with a primary maternal identification tending to favor high scores in men and low scores in women, and primary paternal identification favoring low scores in men and high scores in women. However, it is likely that roles are played by a host of other factors, including temperamental characteristics, such as activity level, sociability, emotionality, and impulsiveness; family demographics, such as the education and income of the parents; matters related to family atmosphere, such as the availability and interest of the parents in caretaking, their intelligence and breadth of interests, and their own role flexibility; and birth order, inasmuch as it may interact with opportunities (or demands) for the caretaking of younger by older siblings.

Diagnostic Considerations

Scale 5 scores show no particular relationship to traditional diagnostic constructs. For patients seeking psychotherapy, Adjustment Disorder or Adjustment Disorder with Depressed Mood are common diagnoses. For high-scoring men, an additional diagnosis among the sexual disorders may be appropriate. For low-scoring women, a secondary diagnosis among the somatoform disorders may fit some patients.

Treatment Considerations

Scale 5 scores have important implications for treatment. High-scoring men and low-scoring women tend to understand the concept of psychotherapy as a relationship-based instrument of symptom relief or personality/behavior change, for which the primary medium is verbal exchange. They are able to accept that the therapeutic process requires time and the endurance of emotional discomfort to achieve its desired effects, and tend to have realistic expectations of the therapist and treatment outcome. They also accept the idea that therapy will expose them to new perspectives and sources of insight, and that they will be responsible partners in the process of converting these to change. Low-scoring men and high-scoring women, on the other hand, tend to approach therapy unrealistically, sometimes with preconceived and cynical notions that it is "just talk" and "a waste of time," sometimes as a kind of "advice station" or "mental repair shop," expecting the therapist will solve a problem, then tell the patient what to do or propose a practical course of action. In treating patients of the latter group, the therapist may have to adapt the treatment approach in the direction of the patient's expectations so that the patient will not feel placed at an intolerable disadvantage, risking premature termination. A supplemental strategy for these patients is to involve them in some pretreatment activity that can reduce their fears and shape their expectations in ways that will allow them to feel better informed, more competent, and more realistic about what therapy is and how it will work. Advice, homework, directives, and educational and action/active methods generally produce better results than methods that depend on talk and introspection.

Patients in the former group may also present significant therapeutic challenges. These include a potentially excessive willingness to adopt a passive role and to invest the therapist with oracular powers, to substitute the therapist for the patient's real relationships as an outlet for his/her strivings for intimacy, and to place the therapist in the role of repository for a variety of other dependency gratifications. The patient may work hard to please the therapist by engaging the verbal work of therapy, exploring new ideas and developing new insights, but may be notably slow to implement therapy-acquired learning outside the treatment setting. The latter problem is based partly on the fear that behavior change in vivo may fail to bring about the desired response from the environment, and partly on the fact that the transfer of learning outside therapy may seem like a threat to the dependency supports within the patient-therapist relationship. Many of these patients benefit from existentially or rationally-based therapies and are typically able to tolerate fairly narrow limits on therapeutic regression. Because the men in this group tend to intellectualize, techniques that mobilize feeling are preferred. Many also benefit from training in assertiveness. Assigning such patients to group therapy may be helpful to diffuse an excessively dependent focus on the therapist.

SCALE 6: PARANOIA (Pa)

Development

Hathaway (1956/1980) reported neither the size nor any demographic information on his criterion group of paranoid cases. Like the criterion group for Scale 2, with its emphasis on symptomatic rather than syndromal depression, the paranoid criterion group was diagnostically heterogeneous, with "paranoid state, paranoid condition, and paranoid schizophrenia" the most common. Hathaway's emphasis was on paranoid symptoms, including "ideas of reference, feel[ing] that they were persecuted by individuals or groups, and ... grandiose self-concepts. Milder symptoms included suspiciousness, an excess of interpersonal sensitivity, and an underlying rigidity of opinions and attitudes" (p. 73). Several provisional scales were derived using various contrast groups and cross-validated on new test cases, but the contrast groups were not identified and the numbers and origins of the test cases were not given. The various provisional scales performed poorly on cross-validation. The final version of Scale 6 was the best that could be developed but was considered weak. Its publication was justified primarily because it was associated with a low false positive rate: "When a person had a high score, he tended to be diagnosed as paranoid or at least he was felt to be sensitive and rigid in personal relationships" (p. 73). Another justification, which went unmentioned but which probably entered into Hathaway's decision to release the scale, was that when sufficiently organized, paranoid patients are notoriously able to evade detection on mental status and interview. Nevertheless, even a weak scale can contribute to enhanced accuracy in classification, especially if, as in Scale 6, false positives are rare. Rapid Reference 6.6a contains a summary description of Pa; the Pa subscales are described in Rapid Reference 6.6b.

Interpretive Implications

General

Scale 6 is sensitive to a pattern of felt vulnerability caused when one feels oneself to be mercilessly and relentlessly opposed by hostile forces, or subject to facing such opposition suddenly and without warning. High scorers feel trapped, as if they've been "pushed into a corner," their "back to the wall," and "without a leg to stand on," or potentially so; they feel as if they face annihila-

≡Rapid Reference 6.6a

Summary Descriptive Features of *Pa*

Number of Items: 40

True/False Balance: 25/15

Overlap: Scale 6 overlaps with Scales 8 (13 items), F (9 items), 4 (8 items), PSY (9 items), and BIZ (8 items).

Content: Externalization; persecutory ideas; resentment; denial of normal skepticism regarding others' motives/honesty; delusions of reference, persecution, and control; sensitivity; emotional lability.

Relations with Other Scales: Concurrent elevations on Scales 4, 8, and 9 tend to accentuate the negative features of Scale 6 characteristics, whereas elevations on Scales 2, 3, and 7 tend to attenuate and soften them. Among the basic scales, Scale 6 is most highly correlated with 8 (.75), with which it shares 13 items. Scale 8 influences Scale 6 scores in the direction of greater disorganization, profuseness, bizarreness, and incoherence. When Scale 8 is low and Scale 6 is high, the delusions tend to be systematized and focused on a specific enemy. Scales 6 and 4 overlap by eight items and correlate at .66; elevated together, these two scales emphasize the coldness, resentment, and provocativeness of Scale 6 and the family animosity of Scale 4. Content scale correlates of Scale 6 include DEP, with which it shares four items at .70, and BIZ, with which it shares eight items at .68. Scale 3 is correlated at .48 with Scale 6, with which it shares four items. To the extent that Scale 3 exceeds Scale 6 when both are elevated, the paranoid manifestations tend to be better socialized. The patient manifests a socially positive and compliant attitude on the surface, and rarely becomes overtly angry or hostile. Covertly, however, there are often preoccupations with control, power, and secrecy. These people command but do not inspire loyalty, and tend to be seen as conniving, calculating, two-faced, and ruthless. Scale L sometimes acts as a proxy for Scale 6. In psychiatric populations, unelevated profiles with distinct elevations on L, especially when coded 34/43, almost invariably reflect a paranoid condition.

tion if they fail to stand what little ground they believe they have left, and shame, humiliation, and defeat if they do stand their ground—a catch-22. These patients maintain a strong focus on rationality, ethics, and morality as they try to apply their minds to the threats and dilemmas they face, knowing that their own physical strength cannot save them. Their speech may magnify the power and size of the forces arrayed against them (the FBI, the CIA, atomic weapons, lasers, etc.), their corruption (the Mafia, drug dealers, crooked cops, etc.), or

⟰ Rapid Reference 6.6b

Subscales for *Pa**

Pa1 (Ideas of External Influence—17 items): "Externalization of blame for one's problems, frustrations, failures; in the extreme degree, persecutory ideas; projection of responsibility for negative feelings" (Harris & Lingoes). Eight items overlap *F* and *8*; six items overlap *Pd4*. *Pa1* contains three related and somewhat overlapping subsets of items: (a) *Persecution/Paranoia* (items 99, 138, 144, 259, 314F, and 361). These items express the idea that one is an object of interest to hostile forces. (b) *Delusions of Control/Subversion of the Will* (42, 162, 336, 355, and 361). This set reflects ideas (delusions) that one's will and mind are being weakened and undermined (e.g., by hypnosis or poisoning). (c) *Resentment and Ideas of Reference* (17, 22, 145, 234, 259, 305, and 333). These items reflect fixed ideas of mistreatment and victimization; many have a secondary depressive theme (e.g., 22, 234, 305). Unless *T*-scores on *Pa1* are equal to or greater than *T*-100, it is possible that the patient endorsed items on one or two of these subgroups without having endorsed any items on a third. The implications for psychosis vary from weak in the third subgroup, to strong in the second, to intermediate in the first. The first and third subgroups are sensitive to actual (as distinct from delusional) plotting and persecution. For example, persons awaiting trial may respond to a number of these items with reference to the prosecuting attorney as the latter builds a case and plots strategy to try to ensure a verdict of guilty and punishment for the defendant.

High *Pa1* scorers report feeling beset by hostile forces. These forces are generally experienced as implacable and far more powerful than the subject. Implicit in *Pa1* is the disposition to projection and the externalization of blame.

Pa2 (Poignancy—9 items): "Thinking of oneself as something special and different from other people; high-strung; cherishing of sensitive feelings; overly subjective, 'thin-skinned'" (Harris & Lingoes). *Pa2* is the depressive component of Scale 6. The items connote extraordinary emotional sensitivity or vulnerability that is dysphoric in tone. These items have a "poor little me" flavor, portraying the self as meek and innocuous, emotionally fragile, incapable of being a threat to others, and perhaps as being entitled to special concern and consideration for one's tender sensibilities. There is an implicit theme of resentment and a lack of forgiveness ("for the way you hurt me"), however, and high scorers nurse grudges and are viewed as "injustice collectors."

Pa3 (Moral Virtue [formerly Naivete]—9 items): "Affirmation of moral virtue, excessive generosity about the motives of others; righteousness about ethical matters; obtuse naivete; denial of distrust and hostility" (Harris & Lingoes). Similar to Hy2 (shares three items and the theme of denied cynicism), Pa3 is nevertheless distinctive. Whereas 9 of the 12 Hy2 items make explicit reference to the self ("I"), only 5 of the 9 Pa3 items do so. For most of the Pa3 items, the focus is on others ("Most people") rather than the self. Thus, whereas Hy2 denies negative dispositions in the self, Pa3 denies such traits in others. Pa3 also denies normal paranoia about the level of selfishness, expediency, and dishonesty that one may reasonably, however regrettably, expect to encounter in the social environment. Notwithstanding their denial of paranoid attitudes, high scorers tend to be viewed as hostile and as manifesting paranoid ideation (Graham et al., 1999). Pa3 is independent of scores on Scale 6 (–.02), but moderately negatively correlated with Pa1 (–.44), and raised by K (r = .64).

Pa-O (Paranoia–Obvious—23 items): More than three-quarters of the Pa1 items are contained in Pa-O—making up more than half of the latter's items, with an additional five items coming from Pa2. None overlap with Pa3. It is thematically dominated by Pa1 and is largely redundant with it (r = .93). Pa-O may be thought of as the psychotic component of Scale 6; it is highly correlated with PSY (.86), Scale 8 (.85), and BIZ (.82), but also contains a subtheme of vulnerability.

Pa-S (Paranoia–Subtle—17 items): All of the Pa3 items are contained in Pa-S and dominate its content (r = .79); four of the remaining items overlap Pa2. It is most highly correlated with measures of cynicism (CYN1 = –.61, ASP1 = –.59, CYN = –.56, ASP = –.53) and is essentially independent of Pa-O (r = –.09) and Pa2 (r = .00). It correlates with K at .32.

*The three Harris-Lingoes subscales for Scale 6 contain minimal overlap (one item scored on both Pa1 and Pa2).

their ruthlessness, savagery, and heartlessness (witches, warlocks, sorcerers, the devil, and their malevolent human incarnations—various characters portrayed as evil, wicked, cruel, sadistic, brutal, vicious, spiteful, vengeful, and vindictive). They are likewise inclined to claim greater strength, resources, and knowledge to oppose such forces than they actually possess or even *feel* they possess. There is a general tendency to equate resolution, tenacity, and certainty with strength, whereas equivocation, flexibility, and doubt are equated with weakness. They exhibit a drive to elevate the self as the arbiter of what is fair, righteous, good, honorable, and moral as a way of laying claim to a higher form of strength or insight to compensate for physical vulnerability.

However, the patient's focus typically is not on physical vulnerability but on a sense of identity, will, and autonomy. The high Scale *6* scorer demands to be treated as a full citizen with inalienable rights and a good name, and dreads being reduced as a locus of action and free choice to the status of a cipher or slave. Following the principle that eternal vigilance is the price of liberty, the high scorer is quick to notice interpersonal events that may carry pejorative implications for self and status; to construe oversights and inadvertencies as deliberate, malicious discourtesies; and to read slights as indications of disrespect, insult, and scorn. That is, patients remove themselves from the world of ordinary social give-and-take in which the inevitable lapses and indiscretions are buffered by humor, the benefit of the doubt, graciousness, and forgiveness, because in the patient's experience, the level of threat makes the game too serious and the stakes too high. Tending to construe all interactions as potential contests for dominance, as zero-sum games, patients are suspicious that others will take advantage of any weakness to advance the goal of their control and subjugation. In this context, giving in is giving up; compromise is experienced as weak-willed on the part of the self and as deceitful when proffered by others. Status and power are viewed as illegitimate and coercive unless reposed in those seen as allies. Even such allies may well remain objects of ambivalence and suspicion, however, because the status differential involved does not favor the patient. Persuasion, regardless of whether its appeal is rational or sentimental, is viewed as a weapon to undermine and weaken the patient's will, resolve, or resistance. The patient's attention is so attuned to the implications of interaction as contest, that the context of interaction is often lost. Put another way, these patients do not choose their fights very well, so that self-righteous and hyperrational refusals to grant minor concessions early in their disputes lead to escalations that end with major concessions, defeat, and humiliation—reinforcing the patient's attitude that he/she is the object of the coercive designs of others, and that giving in earlier in the interaction serves only to legitimize illegitimate authority. Friends must be distinguished from enemies quickly and unequivocally; failure to do so is a threat to survival. Thus, hurt is "deliberate," indignities are "willful," anger is "malicious," demands are "atrocious," unkind words are "venomous," discipline is "cruel," disrespect is "calculated," injustice is "flagrant." Even kindness may be seductive and undermining.

Their sense of vulnerability has further consequence in chronic feelings of tension and an intolerance of ambiguity and suspense. The coincidence of vulnerability and perceived threat inclines the patient toward an unstable and edgy affect, such that a state of emotional neutrality can quickly shift to anger or tears with minimal provocation.

Scale 6 is a scale in conflict with itself. *Pa1* items assert paranoid symptoms (persecution, etc.), whereas *Pa3* items deny them (specifically suspiciousness). Although *Pa3* appears to play the role of a suppressor variable, analogous to that of *K* for those scales receiving *K*-corrections, it appears to function better at suppressing false positives (yet Scale 6 is already biased against false positives) than false negatives (which are in greater need of suppression). If one conceives paranoia as a syndrome marked by symptoms that include ideas of external influence *and* suspiciousness, *Pa3* content should be added to *Pa1* rather than subtracted from it. The consequences of not doing so are: (a) Elevations into the clinical range on Scale 6 tend to underestimate total paranoid symptomatology; and (b) guarded and defensive attitudes toward revealing paranoid symptoms generally keep Scale 6 scores well below the clinical range because *Pa3* alone is barely able to suppress such effects and reelevate the score. *Pa-S* is somewhat more effective in this regard, having more "top" to identify paranoid dynamics and elevate Scale 6 even when obvious items *(Pa-O)* are completely avoided.

Normals tend to be described more positively than psychiatric patients. High Scale 6 scorers among normals are seen as sensitive, emotional, kindly, and trusting, but also as high-strung and prone to worry. They tend to be attuned to the reactions of others and, for this reason, strive to present an attractive, neat, and well-groomed appearance and to behave so as not to elicit negative impressions and judgments. They are somewhat egocentric, in the sense of having difficulty identifying others' motives and expressing others' points of view, and ego-involved, in the sense of having difficulty setting aside their own perspectives and impartially evaluating situations of which they are a part. Consequently, when the latter become problematic, perceived misunderstandings and the attendant emotions get to them, leading to crying, upset, and a tendency to rehash the troublesome events. They often seek the sympathy of others and approval for their own interpretations and points of view. Among high-scoring psychiatric patients, Scale 6 is associated with such signs and symptoms as guardedness, suspiciousness, contentiousness, irritability, hostility, temper outbursts, delusions, and hallucinations.

There is an uncertain and variable area of elevation within which the more subtle aspects of paranoia shade into more dramatic and unequivocal manifestations. Thus, a few aspects may be evident even at low levels of elevation (e.g., T-55 to T-60), and tend to grow in number and strength with increasing elevation through T-60 to T-65, by which point the patient has often manifested some of the following qualities or behaviors: egocentrism; touchiness and hypersensitivity to perceived slights or criticism; a fragile sense of autonomy; a heightened concern with the motives of others and an alertness for occult meanings and disguised intentions; humorlessness, with forced or attenuated laughter; argumentativeness, hyperrationality, and an underlying rigidity in beliefs, values, and attitudes; a quickness to take offense and a tendency to transfer blame/responsibility and judge others harshly; angry flareups; an unusual preoccupation with power relations, their abuse, and injustice; a quickness to feel wronged and a slowness to forgive; and a tendency to collect injustices and feel resentment.

Presenting Problem

Presenting problems associated with Scale *6* scores depend heavily on elevation, such that the rate of self-referral tends to fall off markedly as elevation increases. At lower elevations, relationship problems are the most common instigation for referral. The loss or threatened loss of friends or a spouse leads to dysphoria and apprehensions for which the patient desires relief, understanding, and support. The threat may be covert or implicit, as when the spouse decides to enter the work force or return to school. In some cases the complaint is of an inability to maintain desired relationships, with new relationships lasting a few months at most. At times patients will express concern about their anger or resentment and its consequences in important relationships, recognizing that "we fight too much," but with an implicit demand that the therapist take his or her side. Consideration of divorce or other legal proceeding, such as a child custody action or lawsuit against a neighbor or employer, may lead patients to seek the therapist's blessing, particularly with reference to the patient's rightness in taking the action and an assessment of the patient's case in terms of evaluating the strength of the opposition, their likely strategy, and the therapist's estimate of the patient's chances of prevailing.

A second common reason for referral is problems at work, such as difficulties getting along with coworkers or problems with a supervisor. Such problems usually involve feelings of being harassed, excluded, or mistreated by coworkers, or of being unfairly targeted, watched too closely, or criticized by the supervisor. In some cases the complaint involves dysphoria or bitterness over a failure to be recognized adequately or credited with some contribution to the organization, or, alternatively, over the failure to achieve some cherished or anticipated goal or promotion. There is often some valid basis for the patient's complaints, but the patient's account typically excludes the ways he or she has aggravated these problems by being unfriendly, overreactive, inflexible, sullen, provocative, ungracious, argumentative, polarizing, and so on.

With higher scores there is an increasing likelihood that contact with the clinician has been mandated by legal or mental health authorities because of behavior in the community that is viewed as deviant and possibly dangerous, such as incidents of violence or threatening others, disruptiveness, bizarreness, seclusiveness, or a suicide attempt. Such behavior may result from an accumulation of environmental stresses such as academic failure, the loss of a job, a work injury, the death of a friend or relative, or the loss of an important relationship, especially a heterosexual rejection. In a few cases, the breakdown followed a sexual or other physical assault on the patient. Often the event was seen as confirming a painful sense of inadequacy that the patient had been trying to overcome or overlook.

Symptomatic Pattern

Scale *6* elevations predict a broad range of feelings, attitudes, and behaviors related to a central issue: that of safety versus vulnerability to the enmity of others, especially as such enmity seems potentially to bear on the individual's autonomy, status, and identity. Symptomatic manifestations tend to follow elevation, with expressions related to general personality function predominating at lower levels and paranoid psychotic expressions at the higher levels. At virtually any level of elevation greater than T-55, there is some concern that the patient's sense of personal security and well-being is subject to adverse influence by the sentiments and actions of others. At mild elevations, the experience of disapproval may create only mild discomfort, activating only proportionately mild defensive or self-protective maneuvers that are well within the range of normal face-saving. With increasing elevation come increasing distortions in social perception, such that ordinary gestures of disapproval or displeasure on the part of others, even when inadvertent, are experienced as the product of determined malice. The patient's self-protective reactions become increasingly more visible and maladaptive. Such visible reactions gain observers' notice and subsequent counterreactions, which in turn reach the patient's sensitive attention, create an increased sense of threat, and bring forth even more conspicuous and more alarming self-protective reactions—and the cycle continues.

Mood and affect tend to fall into two main patterns, both relatively unstable, corresponding to flight or fight, and to high versus low levels of self-control. Tension, fear, irritability, and resentment are common to both. In the first pattern, tension and apprehensiveness express feelings of anxiety and dysphoria. The patient tends to avoid confrontations and internalize stresses, seeks to ingratiate or withdraw from others, and may be suicidal. Features of projection or resentment influence the coloring of these affective signs. In the second pattern, emotionality is more externalized and controls are compromised. Suspicion, edginess, anger, resentment, hostility, hatred, rage, and vindictiveness dominate the affective picture. Confrontations are provoked, stresses are externalized, and temper outbursts and assaults are a risk. These patterns are not mutually exclusive and are commonly seen to co-occur, especially as oscillations between ingratiation and suspiciousness. Fear is typically concealed behind one or another facade because overt expressions are felt to only enhance the patient's vulnerability to threat.

Feelings of affection and tenderness tend to enhance the patient's sense of vulnerability to hurt and deception and are therefore subject to rigid control. The patient tends to see yielding to any emotional appeal as a sign of weakness and a threat to rationality and the capacity for self-protection. Thus expressions of kindness and consideration directed toward the patient may be received as seductive and condescending.

Although largely driven by mood and affect, the cognitive features of the paranoid pattern appear most directly to influence the empirical correlates of Scale 6 scores. It is the aberration of rationality that marks high Scale 6 scorers most distinctively. The outlook of these patients is marked by suspiciousness and a malign set of expectations that others seek to deceive, trick, or harm them; to deprive them of dignity; to make them look small; or to expose, humiliate, coerce, or overpower them. Yet the patient's rationality is deployed in a way that decommissions the falsifying function of rational inquiry in favor of an uncompromising confirmatory bias. Obvious and consensually valid features of the situation and stream of events are specifically disregarded in favor of subtle, hidden, and occult features. Facts and arguments that others say disprove the patient's theses are viewed as a threat to the rational basis of the patient's self-esteem and as a measure of the power and resourcefulness of enemies, who seem able to create a set of surface conditions designed both to mislead onlookers and discredit the patient. An outstanding feature of high Scale 6 scorers is hypervigilance, a watchful sensitivity for signs of hostility or confirmation of fixed beliefs. This sign is considerably less common following delusion formation and among patients in whom cognition is disrupted and disorganized (see 6-8/8-6).

High Scale 6 scorers are inclined, however, to describe their own thinking as unusually free of impairment. They view their attention, concentration, memory, decision making, and judgment as normal and free of disruption. However, when accompanied by elevations on Scales 1, 2, 3, 7, or (especially) 8, items admitting problems in thinking are endorsed more frequently. Regardless of whether other scales accompany Scale 6, problems in thinking and especially judgment are almost always present and usually obvious to others. Because attention is narrowly focused on features of the environment that seem to confirm threats or ill will, while features that would disconfirm the reality or severity of such threats are ignored or discounted, the patient's judgment is reflexive and misguided.

These patients commonly have significant trouble in role-taking, such that their difficulties with others are substantially aggravated and amplified by their inability to feel empathy for them. The patient is thus a kind of prisoner of his or her own limited, often isolated, point of view, one that is shared with others not as a confidence but as an accusation or rebuke. Often patients are unable even to state the grievances others may have against them, much less entertain the possibility of their truth; even being asked to do so may feel like a concession to views which they have determined to be anathema and erroneous.

Typical behaviors and attitudes related to Scale 6 scores can be tied to zones of elevation more reliably than is possible for other basic clinical scales, yet they should not be considered a basis for cutting scores. The adequacy of descriptions for any given level of elevation will be significantly influenced by the validity scales and the other clinical scales. Concurrent elevations on Scales 2, 5, and 7 tend to raise the level of elevation at which the features given for a particular zone become maximally descriptive; whereas elevations on Scales *4, 8,* and *9* often favor the descriptive accuracy of features given for a higher zone. For example, in a profile showing Scale *2* or *7* elevated and Scale *6* between *T*-60 and *T*-65, characteristics of this level of elevation may fit the patient less well than those given within the *T*-55 to *T*-60 range, where the kinds of paranoid characteristics show the softening and attenuating effects of dysphoric or anxious mood. Similarly, in a profile showing elevations on Scale *4* or *8* (and perhaps *F*) and Scale *6* at *T*-55 to *T*-65, the features may apply less well than those characteristic of elevations between *T*-65 and *T*-75, because the features within the latter range are more likely to reflect the hardening effects of alienation and possible capitulation to psychosis.

At lower levels of elevation, *T*-55 to *T*-60, the behavior pattern is usually dominated by moral rigidity, hypersensitivity to rejection and betrayal, and mild but persistent resentments. Patients are cognitively flexible, rational, and productive. They are not overtly cynical or mistrustful, but do tend to evaluate others in terms of their loyalty and are quick and harsh in judging others, reluctant to admit mistakes, and slow to forgive. They tend to be controlling in relationships, and often use information for this purpose (i.e., they calculate how much and with whom information is shared). Resentments are usually focused on intimates who are regarded as demanding, inconsiderate, selfish, or unsupportive. Overt expressions of anger tend to be withheld unless they can be self-righteously justified. These patients are often socially skilled but lack flexibility in resolving their differences with others. They are rarely classified as paranoid.

At moderate levels, *T*-60 to *T*-65, the indications of paranoia in the patient's makeup begin to emerge more clearly and visibly. Tension and rigidity are more pervasive, and overt suspicion and mistrust are evident. Cognition is grossly intact but arbitrary; having only a few, fixed ideas is not uncommon at this level. The patient's hypersensitivity now tends to include any hint of devaluation or hostility. Such offences are routinely interpreted as deliberate and willful, as maliciously intended, and the patient is easily angered. Patients are quick to transfer blame and to rationalize their conduct. Argumentativeness, stubbornness, resentment, and an inability to "roll with the punches" interfere with the patient's ability to get along with others. Concerns about control and being controlled and about the legitimacy of authority become an added dimension of the patient's conflicts with others. Women with scores in this range often show symptoms of dysphoric, anxious, and unstable mood; are generally less likely to react with anger; and appear better able to tolerate hurt feelings than men. Delusional beliefs first make an appearance at this level but are not particularly common. In some cases, suspicion and mistrust are denied but the patient will admit to multiple fears and phobias (check *FRS*).

Moderately high scores, *T*-65 to *T*-75, are associated with guardedness, suspiciousness, and hypervigilance. Significant cognitive distortions are evident in social perception. There may be preoccupation with secrecy and firm refusals to grant releases of information, even when these are manifestly in the patient's interest (e.g., to apply for housing or Social Security Disability income). The patient's attitude is obstinate and irascible, with a very low threshold for perceiving the words and actions of others as a threat to autonomy. The patient is attuned to hidden meanings and intimations of danger, and may actively provoke conflicts with others to "make them show their true colors," and to release tension. They fear being subjugated, regard hostile motives as pervasive in the social environment, and view authorities as instruments of injustice. Resentments accumulate rapidly; family, friends, and acquaintances are cut off for perceived offences; and the patient seems unable to let go of things that are upsetting. Argumentativeness shades into litigiousness as grievances are righteously and doggedly pursued. Ideas of reference and persecutory or other delusional ideation occur but affect only a minority of cases. Women in this range are again viewed as less visibly and actively paranoid than men. They are less likely than men to provoke confrontations or to become assaultive, tending to express their anger in verbal tirades, accusations, hostile glares, and resentful gestures of defeat.

High scores, *T*-75 to *T*-85, suggest the presence of delusional beliefs, although they are not uncommonly contained by the patient's guardedness. Hypervigilance is less constant because patients have typically (delusionally) identified and localized the threats against them. Cognition may remain fairly well organized, even though the perception of social reality is distorted in a variety of ways. Although the patient may feel less generally vulnerable to others, the sense of vulnerability to identified enemies is heightened, leading to an increased risk of assault, which he (rarely she) typically views as a preemptive strike.

Very high scores, *T*-85 and above, suggest reduced guardedness and increased disorganization and bizarreness. Such patients are often unusually can-

DON'T FORGET

It is both possible and advisable to interpret scores on Scale 6 at elevations below T-65. Check the subscales for *Pa*.

did about divulging delusional ideation, but their beliefs tend to have a much reduced emotional charge at these levels and may be related matter-of-factly. They are more likely to be withdrawn, unkempt, and neglectful of grooming and hygiene. Levels of depression and anxiety tend to be high, and suicidal ideation is not uncommon. In some of these cases, reality testing is so impaired that the patient may act upon delusional ideas, which may include threatening and attacking others.

Interpersonal Relations

The domain of interpersonal relations is almost always severely affected if not disrupted among high Scale 6 scorers. They tend to see all others as potential antagonists, bent on undermining or interfering with them, weakening their will, or assaulting their dignity, and seek to compensate for these risks by hypersensitivity to slights and signs of threat. Their dread of coercion is so great that they tend to equate even minor compromises and concessions as intolerably submissive, tantamount to being forced to stoop and crawl. In the most typical case, the patient's suspiciousness and attempts to expose the perfidy of others, followed by his or her ill-tempered reactions to the inevitable discovery of evidence for it, leaves others initially exasperated and fearful—and ultimately angry, exhausted, alienated, or terrified. Thus, the patient's core belief that he or she inhabits a threatening and unsupportive interpersonal environment is partly paranoid and partly realistic. Even at modest levels of elevation, the accumulation of frustrations, misunderstandings, arguments, and resentments, combined with the obstacles the patient places in the way of reconciliation (his or her rigidity, self-righteousness, and stubborn unwillingness to forgive) often create extreme stresses for those most closely involved with the patient, even when the former are unusually patient and understanding.

With some patients (those with significant dependent and dysphoric or histrionic features), close relations are much better preserved. These patients, usually women, have better controls, are less fixed in their anticipations of malice from others, and are less intrusive and provocative in their interactions. They are less egocentric and less driven. Although they may be rigid and self-righteous, their hypersensitivity tends to focus on rejection rather than attack, and they may make significant concessions to retain relationships of value to them.

Behavioral Stability

At elevations below T-65 and above T-75, the behavior pattern tends to be more stable than at elevations between these values.

Defenses

Projection is the overriding defense among high Scale 6 scorers. The scale is sensitive to both implicit (e.g., moral self-righteousness) and explicit (e.g., transfer of blame) operations to place responsibility and socially undesirable or ego-alien motives and other personal attributes outside the self. Rationalization of anger, resentment, and loss of control is also common if not pervasive. One sees rigid self-justification in the accumulation and hostile use of "evidence" to authorize suspicion, accusation, and even attack. Depending on other features of the profile, a range of secondary defenses, including intellectualization, reaction-formation, and denial, are seen.

History

The most typical history involves various kinds of oppression. The home atmosphere was often tense and embattled, with one parent, usually the father, a tyrannical and sadistic figure who was both rigid and distant, while the other, usually the mother, was weak, depressed, and ineffectual as a source of protection from the spouse's brutality. In some cases the mother was seen as controlling, fault-finding, intrusive, demanding, perfectionistic, and seductive, while the father, when not absent, was passive, weak, remote, and ineffectual in protecting the child from the mother's abuse. Discipline, even when not violent, often harshly disregarded the patient's feelings, and was unexpected, capricious, and out of proportion to the infraction. In either pattern, the patient often felt rejected by both parents. There was often a pattern of chronic enmity between the parents, ranging from emotional alienation to open warfare, with frequent loud verbal feuding if not physical violence. The patient felt unable to please the persecuting parent without risking being undercut, discredited, ridiculed for his or her submissiveness, or abandoned. No performance was good enough to merit unqualified approval or gratitude, leading to feelings of personal inadequacy and inferiority. One or both parents seemed to be threatened by any sign of autonomy in the patient and reacted by attacks that were often directed at the patient's sense of self-esteem or status, seeking to make the patient feel crushed and small through ridicule, shame, and humiliation. To the patient, autonomy and independence collided with the experience that relations with the parents could be maintained only through submission, leading to chronic feelings of anger, resentment, and rage. Perhaps paradoxically, the patient may also feel frustrated longing for closeness with the persecuting parent.

In some cases, the history will reveal indications of paranoid dynamics on a traumatic basis. The most common of these are rape with a threat to kill, prolonged domestic abuse, and/or other assault in which the patient felt utterly at the mercy of his or her assailant.

Diagnostic Considerations

Diagnosis is influenced by elevation, with association of mild and moderate elevations with personality disorders and mixed conditions. Paranoid, Schizotypal, Antisocial, Narcissistic, Histrionic, and Passive-Aggressive personality disorders are the rule at these levels. Psychotic conditions also occur, including Delusional Disorder and some mood disorders, especially Bipolar Disorder, Manic, with paranoid features. At higher levels of elevation, psychotic thought and mood disorders predominate, including Paranoid or Undifferentiated Schizophrenia; Bipolar Disorder; Schizoaffective Disorder; and Major Depression, all with paranoid features.

Treatment Considerations

Therapy with high Scale 6 scorers is considered arduous and unrewarding because of the patients' characteristic rigidity and distrust. The best candidates for treatment are those who are relatively well organized but in appreciable discomfort and who have at least some history of successful relating, as to a favored and interested teacher. Perceived differences in status between patient and therapist will likely create an obstacle to gaining the patient's trust and confidence, and the initial stages must be devoted to building dependable rapport. The therapist's neutrality, formality, dependability, self-control, and willingness to be bound by a firm set of rules tend to reassure these patients. Avoid overly friendly or familiar expressions as these tend to incite fears of being "set up," whereas courteousness and kindly, thoughtful handling are distinctly helpful. Therapists should avoid feeling pressed or recruited into confirming the patient's beliefs and interpretations of events. These patients are often identified with both victim and persecutor, so taking sides in an effort to empathize with the patient-as-victim may make the patient-as-persecutor feel guilty or condemned. Be aware that the patient's outward display of arrogant pride, even grandiosity, and attitudes of certainty and of possessing special or privileged information and insight that confers inviolate authority tend to cover underlying feelings of shame, doubt, inferiority, impotence, and vulnerability. Patience is essential, as is the ability to withstand being the target of the patient's suspiciousness, hostility, and ambivalence; these patients are inclined to test the therapist repeatedly for coercive or retaliatory inclinations. The therapist's readiness to acknowledge oversights, errors, and misunderstandings serves to model both candor and cognitive (and moral) flexibility. Middle stages of treatment often focus on history, the restoration of cognitive flexibility, and training in role-taking skills. Exercises that help the patient to accurately state the point of view of others, however mistaken or malicious from the patient's own point of view, are often helpful in loosening rigid cognitive habits and decreasing the patient's sense of isolation. Likewise, carefully exploring recent and relatively nontraumatic interactions can help the patient appreciate the role that his or her own antagonism plays in creating and maintaining the atmosphere of fear and mistrust to which he or she feels vulnerable. Exploring together the patient's grievances and concepts of loyalty establishes the therapist's role as a witness to episodes of mistreatment and helps form a treatment alliance. This alliance increases the patient's tolerance for considering painful emotions (fear, hurt, sadness), allows greater independence from anger, hatred, hostility, and fears of loss of control, and increases tolerance for ambiguity. In this phase, frustrated longings for closeness and safety may be uncovered. For example, the patient may express sorrow at not having a loving father/mother "like the other kids had," and this may inaugurate a phase of sadness and depression. Transference-countertransference issues often center on sadism and impotence. The patient often places the therapist alternately in the position of chief tormenter and the role of the patient as the helpless recipient of others' cruelty.

Low Scores

Clinical lore would suggest that patients scoring high and low on Scale 6 can be described similarly (e.g., Carson, 1969), but there is no firm evidence on this point. In fact, Boerger, Graham, and Lilly (1974) found that psychiatric patients with low Scale *6* scores tended to be rated in terms opposite those describing high scorers. It has been speculated that some paranoids are able to "psych out" the items of Scale *6* and could obtain low scores for this reason. This, too, seems unlikely, however. For such a scenario to work, the patient would have to endorse most of the *Pa3* items in the non-keyed direction—that is, in the direction consistent with cynicism and mistrust. This may be the key to the survival of the impression of paranoia in low-scoring patients in clinical lore. Scores below *T*-35 can be achieved only by avoiding items that affirm trust and confidence in the motives of others. In this sense, such scores may implicate at least one element of the paranoid attitude, that of cynicism if not suspiciousness. Implications of low scores on Scale *6* are not dissimilar to those of low scores on Scale *3*. Both are associated with having little regard for the feelings of others and with showing little inclination to try to make encounters with others smooth and comfortable.

SCALE 7: PSYCHASTHENIA (Pt)

Development

Psychasthenia is an obsolescent term from late 19th-century French psychiatry, coined by Janet to separate neuroses dominated by "doubting, agitation and anxiety and by obsessional ideas" (Berrios, 1985, p. 174) from the bloated category of neurasthenia. Itself an overinclusive category, psychasthenia was intended to designate essentially all neurotic disturbances other than neurasthenia, most hypochondriasis, and hysteria. Following the end of World War I, the categories of both neurasthenia and psychasthenia were dismembered and largely disappeared, their members reallocated to smaller and more parsimonious groupings. These were, in the case of psychasthenia, anxiety, phobic, and obsessive-compulsive neuroses. Just why the category of psychasthenia persisted at the University of Minnesota Department of Neuropsychiatry and Psychopathic Hospital is not clear, but the *Outline of Neuropsychiatry* (McKinley, 1944) applies the term "to those psychoneuroses which are characterized by obsessions, compulsions or phobias. Psychasthenic conditions are often spoken of as compulsive neuroses, obsessive-compulsive states, or obsessive ruminative tension states" (p. 194). Hathaway and McKinley (1942/1980) expanded this definition in his description of the development of Scale 7: "thinking is characterized by . . . unreasonable fears . . . by great doubts as to the meaning of his reactions in what seems to be a hostile environment . . . [feeling] forced through fear to compulsively perform needless, disturbing or personally destructive acts or to dwell obsessively upon lines of thought which have no significance for his normal activities [and] to perform them without regard to rational considerations. Obsessive thinking is . . . accompanied by anxiety so that the patient may be tense and anxious over the content of his thoughts . . . [or] find[s] himself anxiously obsessed with such ideas as . . . that he will faint or that something terrible or threatening is about to happen, [or that] he may be forced to think things which . . . secondarily produce an anxious reaction; for example, compulsive counting. . . . The general reaction type characterized by these compulsive and obsessive acts and thoughts is called psychasthenia. The word derives from the concept of a weakened will that cannot resist the behavior, regardless of its maladaptive character" (34–35).

Hathaway's criterion group included only 20 inpatient cases who had been subject to intensive medical and psychiatric study. He compared their item responses with those of normal married subjects (200 women, 139 men) between ages 26 and 43, and of a group of 265 college students, to evaluate the effect of age on endorsement rates. Because the preliminary scale based on these frequency contrasts was unusually homogeneous, a group of additional items that fell short of meeting the initial selection criteria was added to the preliminary scale, and item-total tetrachoric correlations were calculated within another sample of 100 normals and a sample of 100 randomly selected psychiatric patients. Items were considered valid if they achieved sufficiently high item-total correlations within either group. The results of this analysis determined the item composition of the final scale. This scale was then tested against a new sample of 50 variously diagnosed psychiatric cases. These were not cross-validation cases in the usual sense, and none received a final diagnosis of Psychasthenia. However, Hathaway's staff considered each to manifest "symptomatic evidence of obsessions or compulsions" (Hathaway & McKinley, 1942/1980, p. 40). Only 10% of these cases obtained scores below the mean of a normal group of 397 women and 293 men, ages 16 to 45. The mean for these symptomatic cases was about 20% below that for the criterion psychasthenics, but 30% higher than for an unselected sample of psychiatric patients, and nearly twice that for the normal group, even though their

≡ *Rapid Reference 6.7*

Summary Descriptive Features of *Pt*

Number of Items: 48

True/False Balance: 39/9

Overlap: Scale 7 overlaps with Scales 8 (17 items), 2 (13 items), and 0 (9 items).

Content: Anxiety, fear, worry, self-dissatisfaction, obsessiveness, compulsivity, dysphoria, apathy, self-consciousness, agitation, and impaired concentration and memory.

Relations with Other Scales: The most important configural relationship of Scale 7 is with Scale 8. The relative elevation of these two scales is a good predictor of psychotic versus nonpsychotic diagnostic status. In the original MMPI, this relationship was best judged using T-scores; for the MMPI-2, raw scores should be used. To the extent that the raw score on Scale 7 exceeds the raw score on Scale 8 by more than three, 7 is likely to reflect a struggle against the disorganizing effects of 8. The patient struggles to maintain relations with others, to follow a daily routine, to ignore psychotic experience (e.g., hallucinations) to limit its effects on functioning, to live up to obligations, to maintain employment, and to retain insight. To the extent that the raw score on Scale 8 exceeds the raw score on Scale 7 by more than three, 7 is likely to reflect defeat or a yielding to psychotic influences, such that what may formerly have been experienced as struggle and resistance is now experienced more passively as apathy, anxiety, alienation, or helplessness.

Scale 7 is correlated in the .90s and high .80s with A (overlap 13 items), PK (17 items), PS (16 items), Mt (14 items), 8 (17 items), DEP (9 items), ANX (6 items), OBS (5 items), and WRK (3 items). These correlations are reduced when Scale 7 scores are K-corrected. The relative elevations of ANX, FRS, OBS, and DEP are helpful in understanding the role of Scale 7 in the profile and in shaping its interpretation.

psychasthenic symptoms were relatively mild or equivocal. A summary description of *Pt* is found in Rapid Reference 6.7.

Interpretive implications

General

Although no listing of the items from the preliminary scale derived from group contrasts has survived, it probably did not differ significantly from the final

Scale 7, except perhaps in its homogeneity. Hathaway reported the homogeneity of the preliminary scale, but estimates of the internal consistency of Scale 7 have consistently placed it among the highest of the clinical scales. Whether because of the excessive breadth of the psychasthenia construct, the small number of criterion patients, or an insufficient number of items in the total pool explicitly referencing obsessive and compulsive phenomena, the group contrasts employed in the development of the scale failed to net sufficient numbers and kinds of items specific to obsessional or phobic conditions. Even granting sufficient numbers of items having relevant content, the potential number and variety of corresponding symptoms within the small criterion group could have prevented many or most of such items from being endorsed with sufficient frequency among the psychasthenics to meet the group separation requirements for inclusion on the scale.

Given the strength of its statistical relationship to measures of the First Factor, such as Welsh's A ($r = .95$), there is reason to doubt that Scale 7 bears a strong relationship to any particular psychiatric disorder, including Obsessive-Compulsive Disorder. Rather, Scale 7 reflects: a highly general disposition toward negative emotionality or a vulnerability to anxiety, apprehension, dread, and fearfulness; tension, discomfort, and distress; moodiness, turmoil, and agitation; being high-strung, jumpy, and overreactive; ambivalence, uncertainty, self-doubt, and a lack of confidence; obsession and rumination; vacillation, indecision, and immobilization; guilt, regret, and remorse; self-criticism, self-recrimination, self-reproach, and self-devaluation; feelings of insecurity, inadequacy, and inferiority; and social reserve, awkwardness, and self-consciousness. It is less anxious than anxiety-prone, less phobic than vulnerable to fear, less obsessive than inhospitable to productive thinking, less compulsive than subject to compulsion, and so on. The particular form a symptom may take depends on other factors, some of which may be discerned from other features of the profile, particularly the content scales.

The primary symptom associated with high Scale 7 scores is worry. The patient worries as a precaution against error or unpreparedness. Although worry is partially directed outward against feared events and others' influence, it is primarily directed against the patient's own psychic life, measuring thoughts for their correctness or appropriateness, their motives for signs of baseness or other taint, and their impulses for any sign of growing strength that could compel catastrophic action. Doubt and ambivalence pervade the review of past decisions and future choices. There is a relentless concern that any acts or events involving the patient will not play out well. These characteristics appear to be rooted in self-mistrust, leading to rigid self-control. Mistrust of their own judgment and agency is compensated by meticulousness, perfectionism, a grim conscientiousness, and slavish rule-following. Their approach to problem solving is inflexible. They dread making mistakes and consider these the inevitable consequence of spontaneous, self-willed action. Thus they seek to conform their conduct to guidelines, standards, and principles imposed from without as though these were eternal verities. While they may seek the guidance of others for decisions or to affirm their own, already-established inclinations, they stubbornly resist unsolicited advice and directives. Notwithstanding, such influences later combine with the patient's own oversupply of "shoulds" and "musts," and his or her doubt and ambivalence, to reestablish an anxious state of uncertainty.

Among the MMPI-2 clinical scales, 7 and 2 are most clearly associated with subjective distress. Whereas Scale 2 reflects an inner sense of slowing and depletion that typically corresponds to outward signs of fatigue and reduced motor activity, Scale 7 reflects a mental life at odds with itself, in which ego-alien experiences are met with ego-syntonic counter-thoughts. The experience—whether of anxiety, fear, belief, doubt, image, idea, word, or impulse—originates within the self but is viewed as an unwelcome intrusion to be monitored, resisted, or banished by the means and resources of the patient's better self. Even when outwardly impassive, the high Scale 7 scorer tends to be inwardly active and alert, checking, reviewing, worrying, second-guessing, critiquing, planning, and struggling in an effort to stay on top of things and to be prepared for the unexpected. High scorers fear that memory, concentration, and judgment will fail to perform as desired, leading to errors or oversights with catastrophic consequences. In turn, this relentless fear leads the patient to feel overwhelmed and exhausted, and vulnerable to social embarrassment. The consequences of this busy internal self-absorption and apprehension include an exaggerated startle response and being knocked off-balance by emotional arousal or unanticipated events.

The interpretation of Scale 7 is strongly influenced by various of the other basic scales, especially 2 and 8, and by several of the content scales. As noted previously, Scale 7 reflects a highly generalized disposition toward emotional discomfort; important clues to the specific nature of the discomfort and its symptomatic expression can be obtained from the content scales. *ANX, FRS, OBS, DEP, HEA,* and *BIZ* are the most useful in this regard, and can contribute significantly to the differential diagnosis. Provided that Scale 7 is among the two or three highest scales in the code and is elevated to about *T*-60, considerable importance attaches to the relative effects of the *raw Pt* items and the items contributed by the *K*-correction to the total score. Recall that 1.0*K* is added to the raw *Pt* score. Figured as the amount of *K*-correction on a *per-item* basis, *Pt* obtains the largest correction among the basic scales. For example, although both *Pt* and *Sc* receive corrections of 1.0*K,* the correction for *Pt* is about 40% greater (30 *K* items ÷ 48 *Pt* items = .63) than that for *Sc* (30 ÷ 78 = .38) on a per-item basis. Since the raw *Pt* score correlates at –.75 with *K,* the "push" (or "pull" in the case of very low *K* scores) exerted upon *Pt* scores when *K* is elevated is substantial. To the extent that Scale 7 is dominated by *Pt* items, the total score is likely to reflect the range and severity of symptoms and the patient's resulting incapacity. To the extent that the Scale 7 score is dominated by the *K*-correction, interpretation is likely to focus on personality style and traits, with a relative deemphasis on symptoms.

Presenting Problem

These patients seek treatment for an exceptionally wide variety of specific symptoms, either because these are intrinsically distressing and uncomfortable or because of problems they cause at work or within their important relationships. The presenting problem may or may not be a symptom. Younger patients may present with academic difficulty or with a crisis brought on by the loss of someone on whom he or she depended for emotional support. In others, the presenting problem is a situation that results from the influence of symptoms. For example, a patient may present with difficulties in finding a suitable partner for marriage, but examination reveals that the patient's symptoms, inhibitions, or peculiarities discourage or alienate eligible prospects. Symptoms typically create significant inefficiencies in how patients go about their daily lives, as greater and greater adjustments must be made to accommodate them. Situations that may stimulate anxiety or fears are increasingly avoided, creating disruptions in normal routines at home and employment. Problems at work may include the postponement of important decisions, an inability to delegate responsibility to subordinates, a tendency to micromanage (including an excessively controlling or intrusive approach to the work of others), inflexibility about how tasks are to be performed, and various other perseverative, pedantic, or rigid characteristics leading to conflicts and resentments. In some cases, promotion may create a crisis because of the prospect of more responsibility, more (and more important) decisions to make, and more subordinates. Occasionally, men will present with homosexual concerns, especially with concurrent elevations on Scale *5*.

Symptomatic Pattern

A rather weak relationship exists between Scale *7* and Obsessive-Compulsive Disorder (OCD) and Obsessive-Compulsive Personality Disorder (OCPD), with indications of the latter preceding the former in no more than a third of cases. OCPD is thus neither a necessary nor a sufficient condition for the development of OCD. The pattern of characteristics in patients with OCD may bear little resemblance to that seen in OCPD, although the co-occurrence of certain features of one with certain features of the other (e.g., tension and perfectionism) is not unusual. Elevations on Scale *7* are most typically seen in the anxiety and phobic disorders but are not uncommon among the psychoses, except for mania. Regardless of the type of disorder, the features associated with Scale *7* scores include tension, fear, and anxiety; problems in concentration; rumination and worry; the inhibition of hostility; insecurity, underassertiveness, and a lack of self-confidence; and early insomnia and nightmares. Somatic complaints are not uncommon and include cardiac complaints such as racing or pounding heartbeat and fears of heart attack, asthma, tension headaches, and gastrointestinal complaints such as acid stomach or ulcer. Elevations are usually accompanied by elevations on two or three of the other basic scales, especially *2* and *8*. Such profiles usually show *F* greater than *K* and the number of raw Scale *7* items exceeding the number of items added in the *K*-correction. In short, in these contexts, Scale *7* operates primarily as a symptom scale.

When the Scale *7* score is achieved primarily on the basis of the *K*-correction, the clinical picture tends to be dominated by personality rather than symptomatic features. These people may function well in a variety of situations and even excel in their achievements. They set high standards for themselves; are disciplined, persistent, and controlled; are neat, clean, frugal and orderly in their personal habits; are systematic, methodical, and precise in their approach to work; and are formal, punctual, reliable, scrupulous, conscientious, dutiful, self-effacing, and obliging in their relations with others. Regardless of whether these trends rise to the level of personality disorder, such persons are limited in a variety of ways by their caution and lack of spontaneity and by their tendency toward fixed routines. They tend to live a bland, humdrum, colorless existence and are vulnerable to failures to live up to their own rigid expectations. They also tend to harbor inflexible expectations of others, and while they may be intropunitive in reaction to their own shortcomings, they may be self-righteous and extrapunitive in their responses to others' failings and weaknesses. Among these patients, *K* usually exceeds *F,* and the subtle scales exceed their obvious counterparts; *Pa3* and *Re* are often *T*-60 or greater.

At relatively low levels of intensity this pattern of traits is largely favorable and consistent with satisfaction and success. When *Es* and *K* are both elevated, socialization and adjustment are especially likely to be favorable. At greater intensity, however, this pattern of traits becomes increasingly disabling. Failures to live up to (perfectionistic) expectations may occasion self-recrimination, apprehension, and a loss of confidence. A rigid preoccupation with neatness and orderliness in one area may become so demanding that other areas fall into disarray. Perfectionism stalls into indecision as the best becomes the enemy of the good. Persistence and self-control may be emphasized to the point of dogged, blinkered determination and an imperviousness to others' needs. A respect for rules and regulations may devolve to pettiness and a tendency to apply those rules mechanically, failing to recognize individual needs or extenuating circumstances. This may leave others feeling they have been treated unfairly. As these vulnerabilities expand and encounter stresses within the environment, the likelihood increases that symptoms will emerge, and the MMPI-2 profile will begin to take on a symptomatic pattern of scores.

Coping style tends to be highly internalized. Emotionality is attenuated, distantiated, and excessively filtered through intellect or a set of moral/ethical imperatives; emotional expression is characteristically inhibited and restrictive. Activities that most people pursue spontaneously out of interest, desire, or enjoyment are apt to be forsworn as frivolous unless they can be justified on some rational or moral basis, one elevating them to a level of obligation. Patients rationalize their actions not on the basis of feeling and desire, but on the basis of a rule or some external standard, such as their estimates of what others would consider proper. Thus, patients tend to experience the motives for their acts as imposed from outside the self, and feel driven (e.g., by a fear of guilt, failure, anxiety, or disapproval) rather than free and autonomous in initiating action. There are often rigid controls governing the expression of anger and hostility, which, when expressed openly, are likely to be well rationalized and confined within the family, or directed toward someone deemed to be of lower status.

High Scale 7 scorers tend to be introspective and pessimistic. They overly anticipate improbable and dire outcomes, lack confidence in their ability to cope with or adjust to difficult or stressful situations, and are prone to give up easily. There are often problems with distractibility and forgetfulness and an overall decline of cognitive efficiency. Their cognitive style emphasizes analysis over synthesis. They tend to be rigid and unimaginative in their approach to problems, get bogged down in detail, split hairs, and lose track of the larger picture. They have difficulty distinguishing the relevant and essential from the gratuitous and trivial. Their lack of ingenuity and resourcefulness combined with their quest for absolute solutions often leads to procrastination, indecision, and finally immobilization. In times of stress or when the demand for decision is high, the patient may suddenly and inexplicably abandon all of his/her previous deliberations and decide the issue impulsively.

High Scale 7 scorers are prone to magical ideation in that their thoughts and ideas are often invested with a degree of power or reality reserved for acts, and symbolic gestures may be considered to have a degree of efficacy that is the equivalent of direct action. They often feel intruded upon by ideas and images that they view as obscene, horrific, or blasphemous, that create a sense of alarm or panic, and that they may see as evidence of impending disintegration and insanity.

The pattern of social behavior tends to be constrained, either through formality and overconventionality (mild and moderate elevations) or through apprehension and self-consciousness (higher elevations). In either pattern, a dread of embarrassing awkwardness or missteps that may elicit attention or disapproval from others drives conformity. They tend strongly to prefer formal, structured social situations in which status and role expectations are clear. Unfamiliar, spontaneous, and informal gatherings make them uncomfortable and self-conscious because of a fear of saying the wrong thing or of being caught unprepared in some other way.

Interpersonal Relations

When the total Scale 7 score is based primarily on the K-correction, interpersonal relations are usually smooth and untroubled, although formal and routinized. Difficulties sometimes arise as others react to the person's inertia, lack of adventure and emotional expression, or indecision. More rigid and moralistic individuals may create discord by their inflexible expectations of those around them, for, while they may be intropunitive in reaction to their own shortcomings, they tend to be self-righteous and extrapunitive in their judgments and responses to others' failings and weaknesses.

There are often conflicts between the patient's need for support and reassurance and an equally strong need to maintain independence. This can lead to stress and instability in close relationships as the patient alternates between being willful and stubborn and being contrite and self-condemning.

These patients take an over-ideational approach to emotional problem solving. They fear and distrust feelings and may become anxious when strong emotion threatens to break through their rational controls. Similarly, although they may be able to sympathize with others, they often feel at a loss as to how to put their knowledge of others' feelings and attitudes to use in negotiating conflicts. As patients' mental status is increasingly dominated by anxiety, apprehension, or preoccupation, they become less accessible to others. The spouse is often highly distressed by the patient's symptoms and attitude, and the ways these disrupt and stress the marital relationship and interfere with feelings of closeness and common cause. The patient's loss of warmth and spontaneity and a generally altered set of priorities may adversely affect sexual interest or availability, diminish the sexual desire of the spouse, and lead both to a sense of emotional abandonment.

Behavioral Stability

At mild elevations the behavioral pattern is remarkably stable. Increasing elevation, however, marks the behavior pattern with a series of exacerbations brought on by situational stresses and by changes in the patient's experienced level of threat and vulnerability. Behavioral stability tends to increase with the relative proportion of the K-correction to the total Scale 7 score.

Defenses

The defensive operations of high Scale 7 scorers center around ratio-

> **DON'T FORGET**
>
> Scale 7 is likely to reflect personality over symptomatic features when scores are elevated primarily due to the K-correction.

nality and logic. Intellectualization, rationalization, reaction-formation, isolation of affect, displacement, and undoing are all common.

History

There is no typical history. Scale 7 is a marker for neuroticism/negative emotionality, a trait of fairly high heritability. Thus, it is not uncommon to find manifestations of this trait among genetic relatives. However, such manifestations may take an almost infinite number of forms.

Clinical lore suggests that parental attitudes and family atmosphere contribute to the condition, such that the patient's rearing environment stressed emotional continence (especially in expressing anger), circumspection and politeness in public, and normal virtues such as hard work, cleanliness, good grammar, cooperation, respect for authority, honesty, correct table manners, taking responsibility, thrift, and so forth. However, even when the inculcation of such attitudes and habits may have been rigid, intrusive, and domineering (possibly the expression of obsessional trends on the part of the parent[s]), no strong association between such experience and unfavorable adult outcomes is proven. Those who manifest anxiety disorders in adulthood do not necessarily report such a pattern in their descriptions of their parents' conduct during development. Some have speculated that hostile teasing by older siblings or classmates might create a fear of unanticipated events and an excessive emphasis on planning, worrying, and vigilance (Lewak, Marks, & Nelson, 1990). The most parsimonious childhood environmental factor conducive to developing anxiety disorders in the adult is probably imitation and modeling. Many cases feature an association between symptom onset and stress caused by changes in employment or in close relationships (e.g., death, pregnancy, or divorce).

Diagnostic Considerations

Scale 7 is elevated in so many different profile patterns as to be consistent with most Axis I and many Axis II diagnoses, depending on overall profile configuration.

Treatment Considerations

These patients typically seek treatment long after symptom onset, when symptoms either can no longer be concealed or when they begin to disrupt employment or close relationships. By the time they seek treatment their symptoms are usually disabling. As a result patients tend to enter treatment highly motivated. Concurrently, they often dread making concrete changes and may postpone behavior change for as long as possible. They respond to a wide variety of treatments. Cognitive-behavioral psychotherapy is often preferred, but systematic desensitization, implosion, and paradoxical procedures have all proven successful with some patients. Insight-oriented therapies can be helpful but are vulnerable to patients' tendencies to intellectualize their problems and the treatment itself. Already overly introspective, such patients are prone to engage in much unproductive self-examination, often developing insights that they are persistently unable to translate into behavior change. These patients tend to resist interpretation and confrontation, which stimulate intellectualization and rationalization and may lead to anger and hostility toward the therapist. Because the patient may harbor catastrophic expectations around the expression of insufficiently processed emotions, the emergence of such expressions in treatment affords the clinician a valuable opportunity to promote new learning.

Low Scores

As a marker for the First Factor for the MMPI-2, Scale 7 is a unipolar scale in which scores indicate the level of general maladjustment and subjective distress, from low to high. The primary interpretive implication of low scores is the absence of those symptoms and traits associated with high scores. That is, low scores should be associated with self-confidence and security; a generally relaxed attitude; comfort with subjective initiatives; and freedom from anxiety, worry, and fear. However, the K-correction complicates this picture. Scores in the range T-40 to T-55 may be obtained on the basis of high to very high elevations on K, with few or no raw Pt items. To the extent that Es approaches or exceeds K, persons with scores in this range may be described as natural and balanced; cheerful and friendly; responsible, adaptable, and realistic; aspiring, competent, and efficient; and able to deploy their resources to address the tasks before them without inhibition or delay. This favorable pattern of traits is less convincing and partially obscured when K substantially exceeds Es. Such persons are apt to be less relaxed and flexible, and more inhibited, timid, and wary. Scores lower than T-40 are infrequent and are achieved by lower K scores with a reappearance of raw Pt items. In this pattern, the patient appears awkward and unstable, and may exhibit obvious signs of disturbance, especially mania.

SCALE 8: SCHIZOPHRENIA (Sc)

Development

Hathaway (1956/1980) described the criterion samples as "two partly over-lapping groups of 50 patients who had been diagnosed schizophrenic" (p. 71), of which about 60% were women. At least four preliminary scales were de-vised from the 152 items derived from the comparisons between these groups and normals, and 12 differential scales were devised in an effort to distinguish the schizophrenics from other psychiatric groups (hypochondriacs, depres-sives, etc.). Regardless of scale and cutting score, none of the scales could iden-tify more than 50–60% of the criterion cases, and the false positive rate could not be kept below 10–15%. Hathaway then sorted the criterion cases into di-agnostic subtypes of catatonic, paranoid, simple, and hebephrenic, and devel-oped new scales for each of these groups. These scales were tested both independently and in various combinations with the preliminary and differen-tial scales, but all failed to increase the ratio of true-to-false–positive identifi-cation rates. Hathaway then examined the false negative cases, those among the criterion patients that failed to obtain high scores on the preliminary scales. These cases were used as a separate criterion group to develop "test miss" scales, which were tested independently and appended to the preliminary scales to achieve better identification rates. Unfortunately, this strategy also proved fruitless. The final scale was the fourth of Hathaway's preliminary scales. It was considered the best that could be created by the means at hand even though it performed only slightly better than the other preliminary scales.

Hathaway speculated that at least two factors could be responsible for his inability to produce a better Schizophrenia scale: diagnostic unreliability and differences in symptomatic status (i.e., psychotic vs. nonpsychotic states). An explanation based upon symptomatic status is unlikely, because psychotic item content amounts to only about 10% of Scale 8 items (the overlap between Scale 8 and scales explicitly developed to emphasize psychotic content such as BIZ [eight items] and PSY [five items], for example, is minimal). More promis-ing is an explanation based on diagnostic practices.

Until the FDA approved lithium carbonate for treating manic-depressive illness in 1970 and cross-national studies of diagnostic practice were com-pleted, psychiatrists in the United States tended to resolve any manifestation of psychosis in favor of schizophrenia. Pope and Lipinski (1978) concluded from their review of the extant research bearing on the differential diagnosis of schizophrenia and manic-depressive illness that an estimated 40% of previously constituted groups of American schizophrenics were misdiagnosed and suffered from affective illness, particularly mania. This estimate may apply to Hathaway's criterion cases, and Hathaway himself hints at the possibility that some of his potential criterion cases for the mania group could have been assigned to his schizophrenia group: "Care was exercised to exclude [from the manic group] individuals with delirium, confusional states, or with excitements associated with other psychoses such as schizophrenia; the agitated depressions were likewise excluded" (McKinley & Hathaway, 1944/1980, p. 52).

Subsequent research and clinical experience have amply confirmed that Scale 8 lacks diagnostic specificity, with elevations common in psychotic forms of both mania and depression; in PTSD and some other anxiety disorders; and in severe personality disorders, especially borderline and schizotypal, as well as in schizophrenia. Nevertheless, Scale 8 is useful for differential diagnosis on the basis of patterns it forms with other scales and for personality description (see, e.g., Gottesman & Shields, 1972, p. 273). Rapid Reference 6.8a contains a

≡Rapid Reference 6.8a

Summary Descriptive Features of *Sc*

Number of Items: 78

True/False Balance: 59/19

Overlap: Scale 8 overlaps with Scales 7 (17 items), F (15 items), 6 (13 items), 9 (11 items; 10 on *Ma-0*, 4 on *Ma2*), 4 (10 items), 2 (9 items), *BIZ* (8 items), and *PSY* (5 items).

Content: Alienated relationships with others (especially parents), motor and sensory complaints, apathy and depressive withdrawal, loss of impulse control, strange or dissociated experience, paranoid ideation, cognitive disruption, impaired concentration and memory, and sexual concerns.

Relations with Other Scales: Scale 8 is most highly correlated with general measures of distress such as *PS, PK,* Scale 7, and *A* (all > .85). As suggested in the discussion of *Sc6,* Scale 8 contains rather little psychotic or positive symptom content. It shares only eight items with *BIZ*—barely 10% of the items on Scale 8 (two on *BIZ1* and six on *BIZ2*)—and five with *PSY*. Elevations on the latter scales may therefore contribute significantly to the interpretation of Scale 8 scores, particularly with respect to current symptomatic status.

summary description of Scale *8;* its subscales are described in Rapid Reference 6.8b.

Interpretive Implications

General

Despite the uncertainties surrounding the accuracy of the diagnoses for Hathaway's criterion schizophrenics, Scale *8* has generally performed adequately in separating samples of schizophrenics from normal and pathological groups. Its performance in the clinic for the individual assessment of patients is less reliable for a number of reasons, including its sensitivity to various depressive phenomena, particularly depressive cognition and feelings of helplessness, hopelessness, and worthlessness; to thought disturbance and disorganization in mania; to various personality disorders, especially borderline and schizotypal disorders, in which vulnerability to psychotic episodes and interpersonal alienation are relatively severe; to PTSD and other severe and potentially disabling anxiety disorders that adversely impact identity and self-esteem; and to efforts to minimize or exaggerate psychopathology for various instrumental purposes. Nevertheless, Scale *8* provides essential insights into a variety of psychopathological conditions by way of its implications for the individual's sense of identity and self-esteem, cognitive and behavioral organization, pattern of relating to others, and quality of ordinary experience.

Most patients who score high on Scale *8* experience the self as damaged, alienated, estranged, afflicted, or defective. They also tend to experience the material world as alien and beyond their ken. They feel presented with challenges that seem perversely antagonistic and frustrating. From social customs and conventions to finding one's way from here to there; from managing financial affairs to performing assigned duties; from attending to the repair of broken or malfunctioning appliances to making social arrangements; from waiting in line to replacing exhausted commodities, patients tend to find the ordinary experience of living strewn with pitfalls, the avoidance of which requires that their range of communication and behavior be contracted to a point that is consonant with the need to avoid both social gaffes and offenses, and problems encountered in the material world that exceed their capacity to cope and resolve.

Their words and actions may feel awkward, stilted, and out of place, as if the

Subscales for *Sc**

Sc1 (Social Alienation—21 items): "A feeling of lack of rapport with other people; withdrawal from meaningful relationships with others" (Harris & Lingoes). Eight items overlap Scale 6, five items overlap *F*, and three items overlap *Pd4*. Compared with *Pd4* the degree of interpersonal estrangement is more extreme. The content is heterogeneous, and a secondary paranoid theme is evident; six items overlap *Pa1*. Five of the items imply strong family antipathy (all on *FAM* with three on *FAM1*; only one on *Pd1*), hatred toward parents in particular. *Sc1* conveys an impression of irremediable social disability about which the patient is largely apathetic. The patient is cold and interpersonally adrift, and demonstrates both projected and internalized hatred. Identity is contaminated, alien, and defective. This scale is saturated with nuclear schizophrenia, but also rises in suicidal depression, PTSD, and Borderline Personality Disorder. Given its heterogeneity, examining the actual items endorsed to rule out the selective endorsement of a few items (e.g., those concerning parents) that may be related only partially or indirectly to the theme of *Sc1* as a whole is helpful.

Sc2 (Emotional Alienation—11 items): "A feeling of lack of rapport with oneself; experiencing the self as strange; flattening or distortion of affect; apathy" (Harris & Lingoes). Along with *Sc4*, with which it shares 8 items, *Sc2* is one of the two deficit or negative symptom subscales of Scale 8. *Sc2* reflects a depressively toned, core schizoid element that other scales do not capture well. The central quality is one of emotional deadness, dysphoric detachment, and apathy, in which life is endured without any sense of participation or care. Nothing generates interest or a sense of positive anticipation. Whereas *Sc1* indicates a severe emotional withdrawal from other people, *Sc2* reflects a compromised attachment to life itself. Its outlook is bleak and pessimistic, but also indifferent. Although some content reflects suicidal ideation (e.g., item 303), the scale as a whole suggests apathy even to suicide.

Sc3 (Lack of Ego Mastery: Cognitive—10 items): "The admission of autonomous thought processes, strange and puzzling ideas" (Harris & Lingoes). The cognitive dyscontrol component of Scale 8, *Sc3* has three items in common with *Sc4* (r = .86), four with *D4* (r = .87), and six with Scale 7. It is dominated by items reflecting problems with memory and concentration and includes items expressing the fear of losing one's mind. Whereas *D4* emphasizes the difficulty of and a lack of confidence in performing normal cognitive operations despite will and effort, the major theme of *Sc3* is of having lost control of one's cognitive processes because of alien, unbidden, and sometimes frightening thoughts and ideas that intrude upon and disrupt thinking.

Sc4 (Lack of Ego Mastery: Conative—14 items): "Feelings of 'psychological weakness,' abulia, inertia, massive inhibition; regression" (Harris & Lingoes). The second of the negative symptom subscales, *Sc4* is more overtly depressive in content than *Sc2* and *D4*, with which it shares five items. It combines items describing mental inertia, memory and concentration difficulties, and dysphoria; it is the motiva-

(continued)

tional dyscontrol component of Scale 8. As with Sc2, the depressiveness of Sc4 is apathetic rather than sad. Unlike Sc2 or D4, Sc4's emphasis is not on mental breakdown but on a depleted or deanimated will (abulia), listlessness, loss of interest, and anhedonia that defeats the completion—even the initiation—of mental and behavioral projects. The high scorer is disabled by the lack of a "psychic starter," and lapses into regression and apathy.

Sc5 (Lack of Ego Mastery: Defect of Inhibition and Control—11 items): "A feeling of not being in control of one's impulses, which may be experienced as strange and alien; at the mercy of impulse and feeling; dissociation of affect" (Harris & Lingoes). The content is heterogeneous, with items referring to losses of consciousness, depersonalization and dissociation, motor difficulties (uncontrolled movement and speech), agitation, and impulsiveness. These disparate items connect around a theme of strong internal (and some external) menace to the patient's composure, such that he or she may be set off by even mild internal or external events. The threat is immanent in the discrete failures of control described in each item: acting without awareness, motor "attacks," fits of uncontrollable laughing, extreme touchiness, sudden excitements, restlessness, shocking or harmful urges, irrational fears. High scores predict actual losses of control as impulses (especially rage) overpower normal defenses, or a catastrophic sense of crumbling, coming apart, or disintegrating. Although rage is not manifest in the item content, it is implicit in many of the items, and appears to be unfocused and primal (blind rage). Thus, high scorers feel at the mercy of internal and external forces that may at any time incite an act or reaction that they feel no power to direct or suppress.

Sc6 (Sensorimotor Dissociation—20 items): "A feeling of change in the perception of the self and the body image; feelings of depersonalization and estrangement" (Harris & Lingoes). In their 1955 description of the subscales, Harris and Lingoes named Sc6 "Bizarre Sensory Experiences." The revised (1968) label recognized the content of this subscale more clearly. Most of the items refer to motor or sensory experiences that may be unusual and even distressing, but are not bizarre. Their implications are more clearly neurological than psychiatric. Four or five of the items suggest schizotypal cognition, but even these are not bizarre. An additional several items refer to losses of consciousness and may suggest dissociation. Both in theme and content, the scale is largely somatic. Six of the items overlap HEA, all on HEA2, and five overlap BIZ, four on BIZ2. Sc6 consistently achieves higher correlations with the somatic scales (HEA2 [.86], HEA [.83], Hy4 [.80], Scale 1 [.80]) than the psychotic scales (BIZ [.75]; BIZ1, .63], PSY [.72], Pa1 [.64]). The significance of this set of items on a scale intended to measure schizophrenia rests with the frequent reference to soft neurological signs that may be manifestations of the central neural deficit that Meehl (1962, 1972) has called "schizotaxia" and postulated as the inherited substrate for schizophrenia.

*The six Harris and Lingoes subscales for Scale 8 contain some overlap, particularly between Sc2 and Sc4 (eight items), Sc5 and Sc6 (five items), and Sc3 and Sc4 (three items). The subscales break down into two relatively distinct divisions: detachment and disconnection, and dyscontrol and malfunction. Sc1 and Sc2 reflect severe alienation from others, and alienation from the self, the nonhuman environment, and the future, respectively. Sc3, Sc4, Sc5, and Sc6 reflect malfunctions of cognition, motivation, impulse, and neurology, respectively.

product of miscues. Whether kindly or hurtful, their expressions are experienced as tinny and mechanical, and seem to create echoes instead of resonances. They are perplexed by the apparent effortlessness of others' words and actions, which seem to have a harmony and an integrity to which the patient feels unable to aspire. Thus, the self is felt to be ill-equipped and incompetent for transactions with the world and other people. Where others seem engaged and excited, the patient feels untouched and strangely indifferent. Eventually this alienation leads to self-contempt and inchoate rage.

Whether the cause or consequence of this alienated experience of self, the high *8* scorer has trouble making and executing rational plans. Cognitive activity is effortful and unreliable, and patients are often strikingly ignorant of information needed to solve a variety of practical problems. Although intelligence and simple problem solving may be well preserved, the sustained intellectual performance required for prolonged or complex projects in the real world is out of reach. Thinking may be productive on a piecemeal basis, but the patient has difficulty organizing the materials and results of thought coherently. Information is gathered haphazardly and patients are unable to judge the relevance of facts to the task at hand. Thus, the process of thinking is compromised at the level of its raw materials. Information is then processed in a disorganized fashion, with elementary failures of logic and sequence; condensations, inappropriate juxtapositions, and arbitrary combinations; purposes confused with means; misplaced concreteness; the confusion of part-whole relations; fantastic intrusions; idiosyncratic biases and overvalued concepts; gaps and sudden leaps; mixed or arbitrary metaphors; metonymy; and a host of other lapses and missteps that render the product labyrinthine, capricious, and impotent. Moreover, the process of thinking itself is subject to disruptions (e.g., blocking) that cause patients to lose their way and drift off into other directions.

Given these difficulties in thinking, the process by which ideation and intention are translated into behavior becomes short-circuited. As thinking can no longer achieve complex or distant goals, the motivational system becomes impoverished. Goal-directed behavior becomes fractured unless focused on immediate appetitive aims. Nonappetitive behavior begins to be guided by impulse and magical ideation. Most commonly, the behavior pattern becomes slack and withdrawn, with increasing periods of inactivity or of activity that appears repetitive, stereotyped, and aimless, such as wandering, pacing, or chanting.

The disrupted and ineffective reasoning is an opening for many of the anomalies of thought characteristic of schizophrenic psychosis: the belief that one's thinking is being influenced by radio waves, laser beams, or satellites; that others are putting thoughts into one's head via telepathy, microchips, television, and the like; or that it is somehow ordained that the patient must abandon customary approaches to understanding the world in favor of some "deeper," more revelatory, esoteric, or occult science or discipline, based on numbers, fasting, the Bible, crank physics, and so on. Even at lesser, nonpsychotic degrees of disturbance, features of magical ideation, superstition, and privileged sources or insights that characterize the patient's functioning exist. In some cases the patient may claim foreknowledge of future events or of the behavior of others, and the power to influence them. Although such features may limit competent performance in the real world, they often afford the patient a feeling of power or potency in information and explanation, a feeling that would otherwise be denied by conventional cognitive processing.

Cognitive organization problems may not be immediately evident in the patient's speech, but may manifest in the patient's behavior over time. His or her life patterns are difficult to follow and lack any intelligible plan. Changes in activity, employment, associates, and residence may seem self-defeating and made for no good reason. Although the patient can often supply a retrospective account if asked to do so, clinicians find these choices and their rationale nonetheless arbitrary and unconvincing. This phenomenon is common among high Scale 8 scorers who are nonpsychotic.

These problems in cognitive and behavioral control have commonly been thought related to the difference in elevation between Scales 7 and 8 (see discussion in Rapid Reference 6.7b under *Relations with Other Scales*). When Scale 7 is the higher, the patient appears to struggle to preserve organization and contain psychotic expressions. When Scale 8 exceeds Scale 7, he or she loses concern over inappropriate behaviors. When the 8 is much higher than 7, it is increasingly likely that symptomatic expressions will be bizarre and that behavioral dyscontrol may reach destructive proportions.

Relations with others reflect a degree of alienation greater than that felt vis-à-vis the self; thus intimate and durable relationships are rare. Patients are aloof, apprehensive, and secretive around others, fearful of saying or doing something that will expose incompetence and mark them as different or weird and elicit uncomprehending responses that risk embarrassment and chagrin. As a result, patients avoid interacting with others because they feel at a disadvantage. In some cases they react to this fear counterphobically. When they do approach others their interactions often lack vitality and animation, and a sense of co-presence. They may seem to talk *at* others, their words sounding rehearsed like lines from a script. Thus their transactions may appear stilted, distant, abortive, or futile.

Social contacts tend to be fleeting and instrumental. A sense of decorum, respect for personal space, and such basic social amenities as "please" and "thank you," answering greetings, and refraining from staring, are often severely limited or haphazard. Tone of voice and volume are often inappropriate or offensive. The patient's fear of ineptitude, embarrassment, and frustration tends to draw considerable confirmation from the environment, thereby reinforcing negative self-attitudes, expectations of indifference or rebuff, and social withdrawal. Because patients are unaware of having committed an impropriety, they view disapproving responses from the environment as gratuitously obtuse if not hostile.

Schizophrenic high Scale 8 scorers sometimes seek relations with objects rather than people. Portable radios, T-shirts, the Bible, insignia buttons, photographs, and even scraps of paper or food are cherished, repetitiously reviewed, and sometimes hoarded, perhaps as a way of retaining external support for cognitive organization and an external outlet for emotional attachment.

The specific manifestations of this pattern of difficulties, their severity, and the extent to which they are disabling vary widely. Other features of the profile provide clues to the form these manifestations will take—Scale 8 should not be interpreted in isolation. However, it can be a fairly good indicator of the severity or chronicity of disturbances described in the profile pattern, regardless of how it is combined with other scales and features of the profile.

Presenting Problem

Scale 8 elevations are more associated with the need for hospitalization than any of the other basic scales. Although such elevations are not rare among outpatients, they do tend to reflect visible levels of disorganization and debility that are difficult to stabilize in the community. Often, the behavior of these patients is considered to pose a threat to self or others, sufficient that civil commitment procedures are initiated. The specific behaviors vary considerably among patients—wandering into traffic, soiling oneself in public, menacing passers-by on the sidewalk, precipitous weight loss, drug overdose—but they generally conform to commitment criteria that, in most states, involve some combination of being dangerous to oneself or others and an inability to provide for one's own basic needs. Under the current situation of mental health care in the United States, the presenting problem is often a minor criminal offense such as trespassing, vagrancy, criminal mischief, or prostitution; minor drug offenses; creating a public nuisance; minor assault; or theft of service (e.g., "dine and dash").

The presenting problems among outpatients are likewise variable, but usually involve symptoms of depression or anxiety. Among younger patients who are self-referred, there are often problems with academic achievement or motivation, difficulties settling on a career or major, conflicts with peers, or concerns regarding sexuality or sexual identity. When referred by others, there are often conflicts at home with parents or siblings or a concern about the patient's spending too much time alone, having no friends, or refusing to seek employment. Among older patients, problems at work, conflicts with coworkers, job loss, marital conflicts, the breakdown or loss of an important supportive relationship, and obsessions are common.

Patients with high Scale 8 scores have difficulty articulating their presenting problems in a way that is immediately comprehensible to the clinician. The latter may have to listen for a considerable time before the patient's problems come into focus. Outside informants are often better sources of information about the problems the patient is having than is the patient.

Symptomatic Pattern

Scale 8 is commonly elevated in disorders that bear strong features of chronicity, severity, intractability, or disorganization, regardless of formal diagnosis. It is rarely elevated in isolation. Core features include dysphoria and deanimation, problems with thinking, negative self-attitudes, and interpersonal alienation. Somatic complaints, where present, are often chronic and peculiar, and may have delusional aspects.

When Scale 8 exceeds T-65, the role of K appears to provide a cover for symptoms, especially as the raw score on K exceeds the raw score on Sc. Such patients tend to appear more skilled and better integrated socially than those with identical T-scores but a predominance of raw Sc items, in spite of feelings of being different and apart from others, and showing subtle problems in thinking, judgment, and task completion.

Mood and affect vary considerably over time, but tend to center around a muted and cheerless baseline. These patients tend toward anhedonia; manifestations of happiness and unrestricted pleasure are rare to nonexistent. Laughter, for example, tends to appear forced, ironic, localized, or mirthless—almost never lively, full, merry, or hilarious. Among patients with chronic disorders, affect tends to be blunted or flattened, with mood tending to be apprehensive, dysphoric, or anxious. Patients in an acute phase may show intense turmoil, with acute anxiety or terror, or they may become counterphobically enraged and assaultive. Their difficulty in modulating emotional expressions extends to anger and hostility, such that these tend to occur either as outbursts or not at all.

Common cognitive features include problems in attention, concentration, memory, judgment, and organization, which can be observed on interview even when not evident to the patient. Patients have trouble supplying a linear account of events. Often the patient loses track of the end point or of the initial question that prompted a narrative, or may get one narrative confused with another. Both the sequence and the context of events are likely to be disrupted as the patient tries to relate them. Odd preoccupations, overvalued ideas, or references to esoterica intrude into the patient's speech, sometimes to the point of incoherence. Speech, even when not grossly disorganized, is often allusive, abstract, elliptical, digressive, and hard to follow. Factual signposts are often missing, such as firm links between names and the pronouns attached to them, and clear referents for times, places, and events, so that the context and implications become vague or lost. Among patients of high intelligence, the inability to use that intelligence to the same good effect as before the onset of illness may be a source of painful frustration and shame.

Abnormal perception, including hallucinations, and unusual thought content, including delusions, is often evident among patients, especially when they are seen in hospital. They may talk or whisper to themselves, speak and gesture to unseen others, and display bizarre mannerisms or postures. They are quick to retreat into fantasy and daydreaming when under stress, and may at times manifest a tendency to ascribe fantasy-derived attributes to real situations.

Interpersonal Relations

High Scale 8 scorers are typically remote, unengaged, and avoidant in their interpersonal relations. They feel inferior to and misunderstood by others, and are apprehensive around new people and situations for fear that they will not be accepted or understood, that they will be pressed into loyalties or acts of submission that deprive them of a sense of separateness or independence, or that they will be called upon for some performance or task that they will not be able to handle without awkwardness or embarrassment. Their fear of others is often accompanied by envy at the ease with which others engage in interpersonal transactions, an ease that appears wholly inaccessible to the patient. They tend to have long histories of social failure, as others have seized upon their appearance or behavior to hurt or reject them, or to attract the ridicule of onlookers. The response to such history varies, with some patients adopting a pattern of withdrawal and inaccessibility, and others adopting a more aggressive, counterphobic pattern in which odd features of grooming, dress, or behavior are cultivated, even accentuated, as a means of calling attention to themselves and their individualities.

The high Scale *8* scorer feels strongly motivated to avoid the control of others, fearing that such control will be irrational and abusive. There is no corresponding desire to exert coercive control over others, however. These patients show very little investment or interest in what others do, and can be remarkably accepting of difference. Wanting to be let alone, they seek to control others' access to them by their own secretiveness and odd manner or dress.

Affiliative feelings such as affection and tenderness are infrequently expressed verbally and, when they occur, tend to be either overly direct and inept, or subtle, disguised, or tentative in a way that retains "plausible deniability." More often, such feelings are acted out through small gifts and other gestures, or via sexual interest or contact, as if their verbal expression would risk intolerable vulnerability.

Despite their alienation and aloofness, these patients are subject to developing strong dependencies. These often appear to rest on their sense of interpersonal incompetence and their need for connection with a competent proxy to negotiate with others and the world at large. Such dependency is sometimes transferrable to institutions, but usually involves a parent, spouse, friend, or therapist that the patient can use as an anchor to tether him or her to the world. These relationships are usually ambivalent and conflicted, however, with the patient often making critical and disparaging remarks about the proxy's domination, selfishness, dishonesty, malice, or other perceived shortcomings.

Behavioral Stability

Scale *8* is associated with chronic malignant patterns of maladjustment. High scorers tend to show exaggerated and maladaptive reactions to stress, and the core, non–mood-related features (e.g., negative self-concept) tend to be resistant to influence and change.

Defenses

Scale *8* elevations signal strained or collapsing defensive operations; thus particular defensive postures are rigid and unstable. Psychotic-level defenses such as projection and denial predominate and are often accompanied by a retreat into fantasy. The risk of regression in psychotic conditions is high.

History

As in the case of Scales *4* and *7*, Scale *8* possesses considerable genetic variance. Although clear cases of schizophrenia are not common in the family histories of these patients, peculiarities in their first- and second-degree relatives are frequent. The observed patterns of family life defy concise description. Some families of schizophrenic patients are seen as warm and supportive, others as cold and rejecting. The families of these patients often impress the clinician as being somehow much more attached to one another than the frequency and quality of their interaction would lead one to expect. While the patient is in hospital, the family are often faithful visitors, yet the rate of interaction between patient and family member is relatively low, and its quality often distant and formalized, lacking features of coziness and affection. The facial expression of the visitor may be as deanimated as that of the patient, and their verbal expressions delivered in flat voices and unaccompanied by gesture. Eye contact is infrequent and seemingly is sought no more often by the visitor than by the patient; physical contact is typically limited to stiff greeting and parting exchanges, or is absent altogether. Mothers will sometimes report that the patient was "different" from birth or shortly thereafter, rarely smiled, could be content but never happy, or seemed indifferent to affection. Later, the child is sometimes described as being overly fearful or fearless, overly passive or stubborn; as awkward or accident-prone, or "not good at sports"; or as having few close friends. Where the patient was able to form peer friendships, these were often abnormally exclusive, with the patient being overinvested, sometimes jealous, and deeply vulnerable to a change in or loss of the relationship. Yet for a great many patients, including schizophrenic patients, this description fits poorly, if at all.

Diagnostic Considerations

Scale *8* is routinely, although not invariably, elevated in schizophrenia, in depressive disorders with psychotic features (and sometimes without), in PTSD, and in Borderline and Schizotypal personality disorders. It is also commonly but less frequently seen in mania. The differential diagnosis of schizophrenia versus mania can be aided with reference to the formula: $(Ma - D) - (Sc - Hy)$, with positive scores being in the manic direction.

Treatment Considerations

Antipsychotic medication tends to help a wide range of these patients. Psychotic features are a clear indication for such medications, but a variety of nonpsychotic patients with high Scale 8 scores are helped as well. Benefits include improved cognition, restored affect, better mood, a greater outward focus (i.e., less internal preoccupation and time spent in fantasy/daydreaming), improved self-care (e.g., hygiene and grooming), increased interaction with others, more competent functioning, and increased self-esteem. These benefits are evident even when psychotic symptoms such as hallucinations and delusions continue.

Psychological treatment of these patients can vary considerably, depending on their histories and functional competencies. The more intact among them can benefit from conventional psychotherapies, especially the cognitive and interpersonal varieties. Among more disabled patients, formal psychotherapy is often unavailable and is less reliably helpful than are treatment programs with a problem-focused approach that provide structure and support, skill-building and socialization experiences, and recreational and/or vocational activities. Nevertheless, even severely disturbed patients can respond well to psychotherapeutic measures when symptoms are under partial psychopharmacological control and when an adequate treatment alliance between therapist and patient can be formed.

For most patients, the illness and its consequences deal an overwhelming blow to self-esteem—a blow that both renders him/her incompetent in bewildering ways and creates what is often experienced as an unbridgeable gulf between the self and others. In a certain sense, the oft-noted withdrawal of the schizophrenic is not a willful act at all, but a mere accommodation to a fait accompli, a recognition that one has lost standing when one no longer has a place to stand. In this context, patients may regard the therapist's bid for a therapeutic relationship as irrational. Because the proposed therapeutic relationship is not one between equals, from the patient's point of view, making him or herself accessible to the therapist by letting go of denial or granting trust is a matter of giving further ground.

The key ingredients in forming a therapeutic alliance are kindness, patience, and therapeutic optimism. Patients often respond well to initial acts of kindness, provided they are brief, relatively unobtrusive, and require little patient response. Stimulation, expectations, and demands for information and interaction should be minimal at this stage, opening the patient to the possibility of relatedness without an overwhelming burden of reciprocity.

The patient's experience of time is likely to be quite different from that of the therapist. Patients often experience themselves as if frozen in time, and may be indifferent to time markers (e.g., weekends, holidays, birthdays, and anniversaries), that others find significant, and lack the normal short-term temporal structures that shape time spent with others, as in meetings and appointments—the very events with which the therapist must be routinely preoccupied. Consequently, the patient's and the therapist's respective perceptions of and stakes in treatment time and progress are usually out of balance. Therapeutic movements that may seem slow, trivial, or mundane to the therapist may be felt as precipitate, important, or dramatic by the patient; and therapist impatience is likely to seem critical and even irrational to the patient, and can provoke severe anxiety. Hence, a necessary part of establishing a therapeutic alliance involves working out a temporal rhythm with the patient that respects both participants' sensibilities where time is concerned.

Therapists and high Scale 8 scorers are also poorly matched in terms of therapeutic optimism. The therapist-patient encounter is one in which, by definition, a history of interpersonal failure meets with a history of interpersonal success. Thus, the assumptions of the two parties as to the probable outcome of their engagement are likely to be diametrically opposite. This can be tempered if the patient had a previous relationship that was successful and a few previous kindly contacts with the therapist, on the one hand, and if the therapist remembers that treating these patients is challenging and arduous, on the other.

When the psychosis clears enough that a significant degree of normal functioning is restored, these patients often have unrealistic preoccupations about their potential for harming the environment or others in various ways. At the same time, they tend to mistrust the therapist deeply. Occasionally these trends may have distinct therapeutic benefit, such as when the patient blows up at the therapist and the therapist is able to survive without punishing the patient or pulling away.

For full benefits of psychotherapy to be achieved, 2 to 4 years are required, with the initial stages devoted to building the relationship to the point of a therapeutic alliance. Therapist reliability and punctuality are crucial and supportive measures may emphasize the identification of practical problems and stresses, with the therapist taking the lead in their management and resolution. This may mean performing services for the patient such as negotiating with staff or family and in other ways serving as the patient's advocate and assistant. In the middle stages, greater emphasis may be placed on the patient's understanding of illness and its consequences, and on promoting reflection on habitual thoughts, feelings, behaviors, and interactions, especially as responses to stress. Cognitive-behavioral techniques for mood (anxiety, anger, etc.) management are helpful in these stages. In addition to continuing to build skills in self-reflection and stress and mood management, the latter stages of treatment can emphasize interpersonal techniques for understanding and responding to the moods and behavior of others, the management of conflict and criticism, self-appraisal, establishing and maintaining friendships, and related matters.

Low Scores

Low Scale *8* scorers see themselves and are seen by others as friendly, cheerful, good-natured, mannerly, peaceable, trusting, responsible, and adaptable. The picture is one of contentment, but also conventionality, status consciousness, timidity, caution, and an inclination to yield to the will of others, especially those of higher status or authority. The tendency to avoid conflict and subjective intensity would be expected to limit both the range of relationships and the levels of intimacy achieved in them. These low scorers are likely to be seen as competent in a pedestrian way rather than highly skilled or imaginative in problem solving. At the same time, they would seem to have an interest and aptitude for task-oriented pursuits. Alert, precise, and not easily distracted, they are likely to measure themselves on the basis of accomplishment and productivity, rather than in terms of more personal (or interpersonal) attributes. As with Scale *7,* low scores on Scale *8* are uncommon. Scores below *T*-30 can only be obtained by extremely low raw scores on *Sc* and by below-average scores on *K.*

SCALE 9: HYPOMANIA (Ma)

Development

Scale *9* was the last of the basic scales to be developed. It took Hathaway 5 years to gather the 24 criterion cases. All were intensively studied inpatients from the psychopathic unit at the University of Minnesota Hospitals and diagnosed with Hypomania or Mild Acute Mania. Although Hathaway did not describe specific criteria for inclusion, he did provide an extensive general description of such patients: They manifested symptoms of "elated but unstable mood, psychomotor excitement, and flight of ideas" (McKinley & Hathaway, 1944/1980, p. 52). Among characteristics seen in milder cases, Hathaway referred to their egocentricity, energy, restlessness, unstable mood, distractibility, and inefficiency; and their being full of ideas but trying to do too many things at a time and being unable to bring tasks through to completion. In addition he noted their "egocentricity, lack of appreciation of the ineptitude of [their] behavior . . . and a certain obvious disregard for others" (p. 52). The number of cases was too small to analyze the effects of gender, age, marital, and socioeconomic status, as was attempted for most of the other basic scales. Nevertheless, the group was considered sufficiently homogeneous for scale construction, and several preliminary scales were derived. The final scale was tested against 38 cross-validation cases, of which only 5 carried diagnoses of manic-depressive psychosis. Most carried diagnoses of schizophrenia, but ward staff considered these patients to manifest some degree of overactivity or elation. In retrospect, many of the latter cases were probably false negatives for mania or hypomania (see discussion under *Development* for Scale *8*). In evaluating the records of more than 900 clinic cases, only 30 obtained scores exceeding *T*-69, and many of these were psychopaths or chronic alcoholics, or had "organic deterioration of the brain." The final scale performed adequately well in separating the criterion and cross-validation cases from 690 of the normals and 300 randomly selected psychiatric clinic cases, respectively, and would have performed better had the former cases been in a clearly manic or hypomanic state at the time of testing. However, since these disorders are intrinsically unstable, it is not clear whether Scale *9* would perform better in routine clinical use had all criterion cases been tested at the apogee of the mood cycle. Such procedures might have resulted in an overly state-like measure that lacked sensitivity to important longitudinal and characterological features of the manic/hypomanic syndrome, including instability of mood. The scale quickly proved useful. It assisted in identifying "the juvenile delinquent, the overactive adult, and the agitated depression with ambivalent affect" (p. 57).

Subsequent research has consistently supported the sensitivity and specificity of Scale *9,* much of which is reviewed by Nichols (1988). Scale *9* scores are routinely elevated in both absolute and relative (to other scales) terms among manic patients, and tend to be somewhat higher among bipolar than unipolar depressives. Just as in Hathaway's experience in developing Scale *9,* the scale is vulnerable to state-dependent effects and tends to lead or follow the shifts in mood cycle commonly observed in patients with Bipolar Disorder. Consequently, scores often understate or overstate the clinically observed manifestations of mania at the time of testing. As noted under the discussion of the development of Scale *8,* cases with manifestly psychotic features were largely excluded from the criterion group. Research and clinical experience have shown, however, that hallucinations and delusions are so common in mania as to obviate their utility in the differential diagnosis of mania and schizophrenia. Symptoms of formal thought disorder, such as Schneider's First Rank symptoms (1959), have likewise been found to occur at least as often in mania as in schizophrenia, thereby obviating their value in this differential diagnosis as well. According to the current view of the clinical phenomenology of mania, therefore, Hathaway's criterion group must be considered a distinctly unrepresentative sample of manic cases. However, this probably should not be considered a weakness. The absence of those features of the manic syndrome that are shared with other disorders (e.g., schizophrenia) in the original criterion group undoubtedly contributes to the discriminant validity of Scale *9,* thereby enhancing its value in a differential diagnosis that often is extremely difficult. A summary description of Scale *9* is found in Rapid Reference 6.9a; subscales are described in Rapid Reference 6.9b.

Interpretive Implications

General

The primary characteristics of high Scale *9* scorers are increased energy; an accelerated physical and mental tempo and reduced need for sleep; increased rate, volume, and amount of speech; irritable or elevated mood; increased perceptual acuity; increased extroversion and rates of social approach; greater sexual interest and activity; impulsiveness; and volatility. They strongly convey an impression of freedom from the constraints that inhibit aggression or risk taking. Relations with others are prone to significant strain because of the patient's excesses, whether of talk, loudness, activity, temper, financial prodigality, or sexual adventuring. The degree of elevation is not well calibrated to observed levels of activity and disturbance; some patients with scores near *T*-65 may manifest severe manic symptoms and psychosis, whereas others

≡ Rapid Reference 6.9a

Summary Descriptive Features of *Ma*

Number of Items: 46

True/False Balance: 35/11

Overlap: Scale 9 overlaps Scale 8 by 11 items, distributed across Sc1 (3 items), Sc5 (6 items), and Sc6 (5 items). Ten of these 11 items overlap *Ma-O*.

Content: Hypomanic excitement, imperturbability, inflated self-esteem, amorality/cynicism, family discord.

Relations with Other Scales: When Scale 9 is accompanied by unusually low scores on Scale 2, especially when the lowest scales are 2 and 0, mood tends to be buoyant if not elated and euphoric. Concurrent low scores on Scale 7 tend to enhance this effect. When Scale 2 is elevated with 9, mood tends to be turbulent and unstable, and the patient is prone to periods of agitation. Concurrent elevations on Scales 4, 6, or 8 limit if not prevent euphoria, and mood tends to be irritable. High scores on Scale 9 tend to raise scores on *MAC-R*, increasing the likelihood of false positive *MAC-R* scores unless higher cutting scores are used as a basis for predicting substance abuse.

with higher scores may remain relatively functional and controlled. Hypomania tends to shade into mania, and here, too, elevations on Scale *9* are not of much help in discriminating between them. However, the relative elevations of *Ma-O* and *Ma-S* are useful in this respect. When *Ma-S* exceeds *Ma-O*, hypomania and euphoric mania are common but irritable mania is rare. *Ma-O* greater than *Ma-S* shows the opposite pattern.

Presenting Problem

These patients present with a limited but typical range of problems, including sleeplessness, increased alcohol consumption, extravagant or ill-advised spending, hyperactive behavior, overtalkativeness, sexual excesses, hallucinations and delusions, and assault. Often the patient will present with several of these problems; rarely with only one or two. Precipitating events are difficult to isolate from processes related to the illness itself, but the onset of illness often follows a buildup of work-related stresses, the failure to achieve an occupational objective or deadline, some anticipated or coveted aspiration such as a raise or job promotion, admission to a prestigious educational institution or

Rapid Reference 6.9b

Subscales for *Ma**

Ma1 (Amorality—6 items): "A callousness about one's own motives and ends and those of other people; disarming frankness; denial of guilt" (Harris & Lingoes). Four items overlap *ASP1*. These items are attitudinal rather than behavioral in character and espouse an expedient if not opportunistic morality in which egocentric desire supplants moral scruple. High scorers are unsympathetic to if not contemptuous of weakness in others. Graham and colleagues (1999) found histories of substance abuse among men and women high scorers; the men often had histories of convictions for domestic violence.

Ma2 (Psychomotor Acceleration—11 items): "Hyperactivity, lability, flight from 'inner life' and anxiety; pressure for action" (Harris & Lingoes). *Ma2* is the core subscale of Scale 9 and reflects impulses to act in preference to contemplation or the experiencing of feeling, as a means of resolving psychomotor tension (and this would seem to include feelings of impending depression), and of breaking through perceived or anticipated obstacles. The pattern of correlates found by Graham and colleagues (1999) is similar to patterns describing high scores on *Ma1*, including histories of substance abuse and domestic violence (men).

Ma3 (Imperturbability—8 items): "Affirmations of confidence in social situations; denial of sensitivity; proclamation of independence from the opinions of other people" (Harris & Lingoes). The extroversion component of Scale 9, *Ma3* overlaps *Hy1* by two items and *Pd3* by three items but is less saturated with this dimension than the other two subscales. The items reflect "cool" and composure under various social stresses. Like *Ma1*, *Ma3* involves a denial of sensitivity to the plight of others, and like *Ma2*, involves pressures to press ahead in the face of obstacles and uncomfortable feelings. Graham and colleagues (1999) found stronger stereotypically masculine interests among their female outpatients with high *Ma3* scores. Low scores suggest vulnerability, especially of the type seen in Avoidant Personality Disorder.

Ma4 (Ego Inflation—9 items): "Feelings of self-importance to the point of unrealistic grandiosity" (Harris & Lingoes). This subscale is heterogeneous in item content and resists concise thematic description. It reflects a tendency to resist influence and domination by experts and authority, and by others generally, and to be intolerant of and to rebel against a passive position in relationships. High scorers adhere to a defensive but pugnacious autonomy, however, moderate elevations (T-60 to T-70) may imply concerns about self-determination and a need to do things "my own way." The highly unflattering portrait of high *Ma4* scoring women (sociopathic, narcissistic, histrionic, whiney, difficult to motivate, etc.) given by Graham and colleagues (1999) raises the question of an excessively dominant or overbearing approach taken by the therapists assigned to these outpatients.

Ma-O (Mania–Obvious—23 items): This is the psychotic component of Scale 9. It is dominated by *Ma2* and is thematically distressed/dysphoric, in contrast to *Ma-S*. The correlation between *Ma-O* and *Ma-S* is only .15. The items reflect tension, drivenness, impulsiveness, volatility, and feelings of being out of control, both mentally and physically.

Ma-S (Mania–Subtle—23 items): These items are more heterogeneous than those on *Ma-O*, and reflect inflation, euphoria, and freedom from distress. *Ma-S* is a more characterological than symptomatic component of Scale 9, and is dominated by *Ma3*. High scorers portrays themselves as aggressively outgoing and gregarious, emotionally buoyant, morally unconstrained, physically energized, and behaviorally uninhibited (as "feelin' good and ready for anything!").

*The four Harris and Lingoes subscales for Scale 9 are entirely nonoverlapping. Subscales *Ma2* and *Ma4* appear more distinctly related to mania than *Ma1* and *Ma3*, which may partially overlap the psychopathy construct. Only 34 of the 46 items appear on one or another of the Harris subscales for Scale 9.

program, or falling below the cut on an examination. In many cases, the patient had gone without sleep to advance progress on a project, meet a deadline, or prepare for an exam. In other cases, onset may follow a financial setback or some important interpersonal event such as the loss (real or threatened) of an important relationship or source of support and approval through separation, divorce, death, or the delivery of a child. The circumstances leading to hospitalization are often dramatic, such as arrest, the loss of a job, or a serious breakdown in the marital relationship. Usually such patients manifest clear psychotic symptoms, especially paranoia, but grandiosity, hallucinations, delusions, and hyperreligiosity are also frequent.

Newmark (1985) mentions the "empty nest syndrome" as a presenting situation among women in their fifth decade who redirect their energies to group and community involvements in order to distract themselves from feelings of loneliness and loss after their children leave home. He describes this dramatic and excessive reorientation of energy and activity as often creating concern among family and friends who press for a professional consultation and noted that brief interventions are usually effective.

Symptomatic Pattern

Whether as initial onset or relapse, manic symptoms often develop suddenly, with the time between the first symptomatic manifestations and a full manic syndrome only a matter of hours or days.

In most cases, the mood of high Scale 9 scorers is predominately irritable or unruly, with the patient becoming angry, hostile, and at the extreme, assaultive when crossed. In fewer cases, mood is elated/euphoric and exalted, especially early in the manic cycle, but these patients are often described as cheerful, happy, enthusiastic, sunny, vivacious, or exhilarated. Such mood is typically thin and fragile, however, with an undercurrent of irritability that can become readily manifest in the face of contradiction, opposition, or rebuff. In still other patients, mood is notably unstable and labile, with rapid shifts through elation, irritability, and profound sadness. In these cases, the patient's mood seems reactively to mirror the expressions of others in the immediate social environment. When mood is euphoric, the patient is often seen, and sees him- or herself, as sharp-witted and in the possession of a gifted sense of humor, and speech may be peppered with quips, brisk satire, gags, puns, and wisecracks. The effect of the patient's wit on others is often not one of gaiety, however, and ill-considered expressions may be hurtful, intrusive, or offensive. Tolerance for frustration tends to be low. When obstacles are encountered, regardless of whether their source is temporal, material, or human, the patient tends to feel thwarted and reacts dramatically with angry flare-ups, sudden giving up ("throwing in the towel"), or destructive rages.

High Scale 9 scorers also tend to have enhanced feelings of cognitive competence, in which the grasp of ideas and the ability to reason are felt to be powerfully expanded. Ideation is mobile and overproductive, memory is sharp and easily accessed, and speech is strong and articulate. The patient experiences him- or herself as intellectually limitless, and as having unique access to deep and profound insights. The range of interests widens and becomes more inclusive. Thinking is rapid and commonly experienced as racing thoughts, which may be distressing as normal cognitive controls are overcome. At the extreme, the train of thought becomes jumpy and easily disrupted; in mania proper, simple distractibility gives way to flight-of-ideas, in which thoughts rapidly follow upon one another but become progressively more tenuously connected until the stream of thought becomes incoherent. Acceleration of thought is not always accompanied by motor hyperactivity. Judgment is often grossly impaired and manifested in ill-advised commitments and liaisons, reckless and dangerous behavior, immoderate speech, and conspicuous dress.

Thought content is not infrequently focused on matters of high principle, whether ethical, moral, or religious. The patient may act as an expositor of particular values or ideals but take an overly aggressive role in pressing them on others and rendering harsh judgments on self and others for their violation. In this the patient often appears to have embraced a set of principles or standards rather suddenly, possibly as a source of structure to substitute for a preexisting set of values that are poorly organized and consolidated, or by which the patient has felt poorly served. Notwithstanding, the patient's approach to these values is often selective and expedient with respect to both their observance and their rationale.

The patient's buoyant energy and accelerated cognition may be combined in the production of voluminous writings (hypergraphia), to which profound importance or even messianic significance are attached. These are characteristically written in a bombastic style with frequent signs of emphasis such as capitalization, underlining, and exclamation points; and as proclamations, polemics, spiritual inspirations, legal briefs, ideological tracts, and jeremiads. These may vary considerably in coherence from highly detailed and organized to rambling, repetitious, and scribbling, but grandiose or paranoid themes (or both) are usually apparent.

Although not represented in the item content, Scale 9 elevations are often associated with conventional signs and symptoms of psychosis, including conceptual disorganization, thought disorder, hallucinations and delusions, a decline in self-care, and a tendency to lose track of concerns and commitments even when these are extremely important, such as paying rent or managing diabetes.

Self-concept is inflated and unrealistic if not grandiose, but also highly vulnerable. Patients often view their gifts and possibilities as unlimited; hence aspirations are poorly grounded. Brimming with self-confidence, boundlessly optimistic about their potential for greatness, and feeling entitled to the limitless deference, approval, and favors of others, they paradoxically court disappointment and failure. At first these attitudes may be supported by the patient's energy and euphoria, but over time they become progressively more fragile and precarious, and often collapse in the later stages of the manic cycle. Without the support of euphoria and grandiose self-attitudes, self-esteem is unusually dependent on others' affection and approval.

Behavioral

The patient's behavior pattern tends to follow mood. Intolerant of boredom, and impatient with detail and routine, the patient's behavior tends to be directed to broad themes, big realizations, and daring initiatives. At hypomanic levels, behavior is overactive and indefatigable, becoming erratic and frenzied as thinking becomes increasingly disorganized. Aggression and disinhibition are often central characteristics. The patient moves into situations boldly, with neither appraisal or trepidation, and may be quick to test limits.

Impulsive judgment tends to follow an overly optimistic surface appraisal of situations. Projects tend to be engaged enthusiastically but rather unrealistically, with little attention to planning and the details of execution. Consequently, the patient is unable to sustain them. As thought becomes increasingly disjointed, task focus tends to be capricious and fickle. Patients may generate multiple schemes but efforts to realize these lack constancy and persistence. They are unable to sustain an enthusiastic focus, and as obstacles are encountered or execution becomes complex, projects are quickly set aside or abandoned, only to be replaced by others with the same fate. At moderate score levels, there may be a pattern of overcommitment, with the patient taking on more projects or responsibility than he or she can realistically manage. The stress of impending failure or defeat as progress begins to lag behind overly optimistic expectations may, especially when combined with lost sleep, precipitate a manic episode. With increasing levels of severity there is a breakdown in behavioral controls leading to improvident risk-taking, if not recklessness, in sexual and financial matters, walking and driving, and the management of conflict.

Dress may be colorful, gaudy, and unconventional, and makeup may be garish and ostentatious. Beads, patches, stickers, buttons, slogans, scarves and sashes, hats, and similar accessories may be worn in profusion to attract others or to support a grandiose self-concept.

Interpersonal Relations

These patients are extroverted and tend to manifest social hunger and a high rate of social approach. They typically try to dominate in relationships and engage others for lopsided interactions in which they monopolize the conversation, are demanding, interrupt frequently while being themselves difficult to interrupt. At lower levels, their high spirits, quick wit, and mild disinhibition can be attractive and infectious, and often create favorable first impressions. Yet there is often a quality of superficiality, tactlessness, and a lack of sensitivity and restraint in their interactions that eventually leaves others feeling hurt, used, and exhausted, or angry and exasperated. Despite their attractiveness and craving for affection, these patients are typically emotionally distant. They tend to be inconsiderate of others' needs and motives, while being quite sensitive to their soft spots. Their relations with others can be seen as exploitive, as these patients employ flattery and seduction to draw attention, support, praise, favors, and even goods from them. The patient may skillfully manipulate the weaknesses, goodwill, self-esteem, and guilt of others to ensure their loyalty, to gain advantage, or for self-aggrandizement. At the same time, his or her indiscriminate embrace of others' ideas or admiration may subject them to their influence. In many patients, outward bravado is a cover for underlying self-doubt, apprehensiveness, and dysphoria. At the extreme, these patients can be so intrusive, presumptuous, and demanding that both seductive and exploitive means become ineffective as instruments of influence and are superceded by nakedly coercive methods that drive others away or provoke their anger. Paranoid symptoms often begin to manifest themselves at this point, as the patient begins to feel increasingly spurned and isolated.

Interpersonal flexibility is often significantly compromised. Interactional style and behavior tend to become homogenized as the patient fails to observe differences between people in terms of degree of familiarity, role, and status. Thus strangers or casual acquaintances, individuals they encounter in commercial or service roles, such as a salesperson or doctor, may find themselves the recipients of overtures, conversation, requests, and confidences normally reserved for a spouse or close friend.

The manic state is typically very stressful to the marital relationship, especially when the spouse is unaware that the patient's behavior is the product of illness. The spouse tends to view the patient's conduct as not only disruptive but as willfully inconsiderate and obnoxious. Overspending, threats, and sexual advances to others are particularly stressful, with the spouse often being both angry at the patient and fearful that the patient's behavior poses an imminent threat to the family's reputation or financial security. The spouse often feels pushed away except for sexual relations, powerless to set limits, and forced to initiate divorce as the only means to escape a relationship that has become chaotic and unmanageable.

Behavioral Stability

Elevations on Scale *9* predict an unstable and erratic behavior pattern with both short- and long-term fluctuations in mood, activity, excitability, risk taking, and so forth. Patients with mood disorders tend to show greater instability than those with substance use and personality disorders; many of these latter patients manifest a stable behavior pattern.

Defenses

The pattern of defense in high Scale *9* scorers is externalizing. To a large extent in hypomania and an even greater extent in mania, the patient believes nothing is impossible and that defeat is unthinkable. In this sense, denial and mania are coextensive. The patient is impervious to hindrance or bad news, ignoring, dismissing or aggressively challenging anything that looks like an impediment. Two closely related defenses are omnipotence and devaluation. Omnipotence is often an outgrowth of the patient's elation, euphoria, and intellectual potency, such that he or she feels exalted and invulnerable to threats to self-esteem. Devaluation is commonly enlisted to help the patient cope with goals that grow increasingly out of reach, as obstacles that stand in the way of their realization become evident. This may be especially obvious in the patient's reaction when those who are sought for his or her projects or for romantic attachments fail to reciprocate the patient's interest. Friends and associates who were formerly idealized may be summarily dropped or derided as lacking in vision. In such instances, the line between devaluation and persecutory ideas can be fine. Projection of responsibility and transfer of blame are common, often transparently used to protect or rescue the patient's self-esteem from failure, including moral failings. Acting out is common in high Scale *9* scorers, both as an outlet for high energy and as a defense against feared loss or defeat. Psychomotor acceleration may afford the patient little or no mental space for true reflection on feelings and impulses, or on the formulation of plans for dealing with them. Consequently, these feelings and impulses are rapidly shifted into the motor sphere to become manifest in behavior. In this sense, acting out may be better understood in the context of disability than in the context of defense. However, the typical behavior pattern is one in which the consumption of stimulation may be seen as a kind of race against lost opportunity, as in the case of hypersexuality, gambling, intoxication, and similar excesses; or against defeat, as in the case of hostility and assaultiveness. Sooner or later, the patient may experience the encroachment of depressed mood or begin to appreciate the destructive consequences of his or her behavior earlier in the manic cycle, and these may stimulate acting out as a flight from insight. In hypomania, where disorganization is minimal or absent, the patient's intellectual mobility is conducive to intellectualization. Among patients without mood disorder, acting out appears to be the primary defense, but denial, rationalization, and projection are also common.

History

The histories of high Scale *9* scorers tend to vary considerably with diagnosis. Patients with substance use and personality disorders often show instability, underachievement, and conflicts with others; however, the historical antecedents of these problems do not follow a predictable pattern. Patients with Bipolar Disorders tend to have more stable family backgrounds, higher levels of achievement in education and employment, and more relatives with mood disorders. Cohen, Baker, Cohen, Fromm-Reichmann, and Weigert (1954) found a consistent constellation of factors that characterized the rearing environment of 12 private hospital manic-depressive patients. These included placing excessive responsibility on the patient to restore the family's reputation in the community, especially through pressures to conform and achieve and to be a credit to the parents. The findings of Cohen and colleagues were generally supported by Gibson, Cohen, and Cohen (1959) in a comparison of 27 manic-depressives and 17 schizophrenics from a public hospital. Despite their small *N*s and methodological limitations, these do provide a provisional basis for understanding the possible role of early pressures to achieve and later vulnerability to failure and loss that are not uncommon in the personal histories of manic-depressive patients. Even in non-bipolars with high Scale *9* scores, aspects of the patient's childhood experience in some cases were conducive to vulnerability to loss or failure, such as parental death, illness or alcoholism, frequent relocations, and overindulgence.

Diagnostic Considerations

Diagnoses associated with high Scale *9* scorers vary by setting, but are divided mostly among mood, substance use, and personality disorders. In hospitals, Bipolar I Disorder is the most distinctive and most similar to Hathaway's criterion patients. Patients with Bipolar II Disorder (major depressive episodes with a history of or alternating with hypomania), unipolar manics, and schizoaffectives are also seen. Defensive paranoid schizophrenic patients will rarely but occasionally obtain elevations on Scale 9. In outpatient settings, patients with personality disorders (antisocial, narcissistic, atypical borderline) and cyclothymia are more common. In both settings, substance use disorders are frequently seen, especially alcohol and sympathomimetic abuse. Comorbidities between the substance use disorders and both mood disorders and personality disorders tend to run high.

Treatment Considerations

In patients with Bipolar Disorder, suicide is a significant risk and can dramatically increase in the wake of, or possibly in the anticipation of, depression, failure, or loss. Substance use substantially enhances the risk for all these factors. Although suicide in the manic state is rare, some studies have found the rate in mixed states to be particularly high (Goodwin & Jamison, 1990) because depressive mood and cognition may temporarily coincide with residual energy and impulsiveness. This pattern of symptoms may be a particular contraindication for hospital discharge.

Mania is untreatable by psychotherapy alone; thus concurrent treatment with anti-manic agents, mood stabilizers, or both should be offered. The initial goals of therapy should support adherence to the patient's medication regimen. Even when symptoms are under some degree of control by medication, therapists tend to find patients with high Scale 9 scores challenging and difficult. They tend to be oriented toward action and quick to become bored and impatient with treatment approaches that emphasize exploration and contemplation. They are also intolerant of the kinds of discomfort typically induced by such approaches. Finally, such patients tend to find the development of dependency within the therapeutic relationship threatening. The patient's need for the therapist's interest, support, and approval is often in conflict with his or her need to avoid emotional discomfort. Patients may try to save face by explaining things away, stalling, distracting, prematurely siding with the therapist's opinions, keeping the therapist enthralled, and in other ways trying to keep the therapeutic interaction on the surface and away from areas that risk emotional discomfiture. For these reasons, methods that emphasize the patient's task orientation by providing challenge and stimulating interest and problem-solving skills are often helpful. The initial challenge in most cases is to retain the patient in treatment, making it necessary to anticipate impulses to discontinue therapy, and to prepare him or her to cope with these. These patients are usually more fragile than they appear, and are vulnerable to therapist aggression or lack of consideration. They tend to overestimate their tolerance for emotional discomfort and may seek to escape from treatment to gain relief from such discomfort unless the therapist provides sufficient structure, support, and reassurance to enable the patient to endure the inevitable periods of upheaval. These patients seem to do best with therapists who project a relaxed strength and are able to combine activity and directness with support. Loss, failure, frustration, difficulties in maintaining relationships, and the clarification of intrinsic versus extrinsic motives are common themes in the therapy of these patients. They often need considerable help in learning to distinguish and achieve a normal balance between acting to please or meet others' expectations and acting on behalf of their own needs, pleasures, interests, and enjoyment, and between present satisfactions and future aspirations. Specific techniques that these patients find helpful include relaxation, role playing, teaching, and homework because these provide structure and rapid feedback.

Difficulties during therapeutic interaction with these patients provide valuable clues to the nature of his or her interactions with significant others. By the same token, therapist countertransference feelings can provide insight into the emotional climate patients encounter in these relationships. For example, patients who refuse to take responsibility for their behavior in therapy are likely to do so in other relationships and to stimulate feelings of frustration, exasperation, or hostility in the spouse or parent as well as in the therapist.

Low Scores

Low scores on Scale 9 in patient populations are usually associated with depression, psychomotor retardation, and overcontrol. These patients may feel lethargic, listless, and immobilized. In some cases of depression, Scale 2 may fail to elevate, leaving the low Scale 9 score as one of the only indicators of depression on the MMPI-2. In these cases, the depressive picture tends to be dominated by behavioral manifestations, such as psychomotor retardation or loss of interest, rather than by affective/mood features, such as the manifest sadness and dysphoria that dominate Scale 2. Unipolar depressives commonly obtain very low scores unless agitation is present. Bipolar patients usually but not consistently tend to score higher than unipolars. Among less impaired patients, low scorers are stable and well adjusted, controlled, steady, reliable, even-tempered, and nonaggressive, and tend to conserve energy.

SCALE 0: SOCIAL INTROVERSION-EXTROVERSION (Si)

Development

Drake (1946) developed the final clinical scale using female college students at the University of Wisconsin, and later cross-validated it on college males. Membership in the criterion and comparison groups was determined by subjects' percentile ranks on the Minnesota T-S-E Inventory (Evans & McConnell, 1941). The T-S-E Inventory was a factor-analytically derived inventory of three measures of introversion-extroversion: Thinking (T), Social (S), and Emotional (E). The responses to the MMPI item pool of a criterion group of 50 students who obtained percentile ranks of greater than 64 on the social scale of the T-S-E Inventory were compared with those of another group of 50 students with percentile ranks lower than 35. The items selected for the preliminary MMPI *Social Introversion-Extroversion (I.E.)* scale met the same criterion Hathaway used in developing the earlier clinical scales: "a difference between the percentage responses of the upper and lower groups of at least twice the standard error of the difference" (p. 77). Items deemed too frequently or too infrequently endorsed by the two groups were dropped and the remaining 70 items were retained for Drake's MMPI *I.E.* scale. Cross-validations were carried out by evaluating the correlations between *I.E.* and T-S-E *S*-scale scores for 87 new female and 81 male students. Hathaway found the *I.E.* scale useful in assessing patients, and adopted it as Scale *0*. Sixty-nine of the original 70 items survive in the MMPI-2 version of the scale. Rapid Reference 6.10a gives a summary description of Scale *0;* its subscales are described in Rapid Reference 6.10b.

Interpretive Implications

General

Introversion-extroversion is a normal individual difference variable of high heritability, and Scale *0* has consistently achieved high correlations with other

≡Rapid Reference 6.10a

Summary Descriptive Features of *Si*

Number of Items: 69

True/False Balance: 36/33

Overlap: Scale *0* overlaps the standard scales by several items, except for Scales *F, K,* and *1*. In all cases positively overlapping items exceed negatively overlapping items, but for Scales *L, 3, 6,* and *9,* the difference is slight. The highest net overlap with Scale *0* is found on Scales *2* and *7*. Scale *0* shows strong overlap with the following subscales: *D1* (seven items), *D5* (three items), *Hy1* (five items; negative), *Pd3* (five items; negative), and *Ma3* (three items; negative).

Content: Social inhibition, group avoidance, circumspection, somatic and mental symptoms, low self-confidence, self-consciousness, and cynicism.

Relations with Other Scales: Among the basic clinical scales, Scale *0* is most highly correlated with Scales *7, 8,* and *2,* in that order. It is highly correlated with *SOD,* with which it shares 18 items. The most important configural relationship of Scale *0* is with Scale *9,* with which it correlates .14. In patients with Bipolar Disorder, these two scales often cross in the transition between depressed and manic states. Low *0* and high *9* are synergistic with respect to social hunger. When both Scales *9* and *0* are elevated, *0* tends to dominate, whereas Scale *9* features are confined to those suggested by *Ma-O, Ma2* and *Ma4.* When both are low, Scale *9* tends to be dominated by *Ma3* and *Ma-S,* which mostly blend in with and augment the low *0* characteristics.

measures of this variable. However, it is also highly correlated with scales reflecting general maladjustment and subjective distress, particularly depressed mood and feelings of personal inadequacy. In this sense, it is not considered a pure measure of introversion. On the other hand, Scale *0* is sensitive to a pattern of malaise not readily reflected in the other MMPI-2 scales—a blend of shyness, self-consciousness, and discomfort in group situations with a broad range of psychological distress, including dysphoric mood; tension, anxiety, and fearfulness; problems in cognition (e.g., attention, concentration, memory, decisiveness, and judgment); physical vulnerability; convictions of inefficacy, incapacity, incompetence, and ineptitude; and a nagging, ambivalent, and unstable quality of alienation from others. This alienation is such that one's isolation is experienced now as a blessing, now as a curse; now as a cynical reflection on others, now as a disparaging reflection on oneself. In addition to being

Subscales for *Si*

Scale *0* is heterogeneous in item content and factorially complex. Graham, Schroeder, and Lilly (1971), for example, found six interpretable factors, but Ben-Porath and colleagues (1989) believed subscales based on these factors lacked internal consistency. The subscales also overlapped extensively and were difficult to interpret. Ben-Porath and colleagues developed three subscales for Scale *0* that obtained coefficient alpha estimates of .75 or greater among college men and women. Although these subscales have the advantage of high reliability and zero overlap, they account for only 39 of the 69 items on Scale *0*, or only 57% of the total, whereas the previous MMPI subscales accounted for 66 of the 70 Scale *0* items. The consequences for interpretation are considerable. Theoretically at least, a patient may achieve *T*-scores of 65 or more on both *Si1* and *Si2*, the subscales most highly saturated with the introversion dimension, and not exceed a *T*-score on Scale *0* of 50, provided that *Si3* is low. Conversely, *T*-scores of 70 or more on Scale *0* may be obtained without endorsement of any items on *Si1* or *Si2*. For some purposes, therefore, *SOD* may provide a better estimate of pure social introversion than Scale *0*.

Si1 (Shyness/Self-Consciousness—14 items): These items reflect the subjective aspects of introversion: bashfulness, feelings of social awkwardness and inadequacy, and fears of embarrassment. Such feelings are likely to be acute in new and unfamiliar situations. High scorers tend to be socially timid and quick to feel inept and conspicuous, the focus of disconcerting attention. They tend to lack social skills, and feel disadvantaged when interacting with others, especially strangers. *Si1* overlaps *SOD* by 10 items, 7 on *SOD2*. Low scorers are socially intrepid and are comfortable being highly visible in social situations.

Si2 (Social Avoidance—8 items): This subscale reflects the objective aspects of introversion. It is more behavioral in its focus, and emotionally more neutral. *Si2* overlaps *SOD* by eight items, all on *SOD1*. The items admit the dislike and active avoidance of crowds, parties, dances, and social gatherings and, when these cannot be avoided, a preference for remaining on the periphery and uninvolved. Low scorers like to join in with others for social activity; they like "being where the action is." Occasionally, a low score on *Si2* will be seen with a high score on *Si1*, suggesting a highly self-conscious person who likes to "get lost in the crowd."

Si3 (Self/Other Alienation—17 items): This set of items reflects the neuroticism component of Scale *0*. The emphasis is on personal rather than social inadequacy, with a secondary theme of cynicism, hypersensitivity, and a sense of being in conflict with others. None of the items overlap *SOD*. Many of the items suggest implicit comparisons of how the individual measures up against others. These disparate threads come together as a general inability to function competently in social situations; forgetfulness, irritability, distraction, self-conscious misery, a lack of confidence, or "the way other people are" will prevent the individual from performing effectively. Scores on this subscale are suppressed by *K*.

uncomfortable in groups and crowds, high Scale *0* scorers also tend to be sensitive to sound and overstimulation. Loud voices, boisterousness, and noise from any source tend to seem oppressive and distracting. Not unexpectedly, patients are likely to speak in a soft, well-modulated voice that may be slow and halting.

Presenting Problem

These patients are typically concerned with social functioning. Worries include lack of social skills; unassertiveness; social fearfulness; self-consciousness; fear of public speaking; concerns about weight or some other aspect of physical appearance; problems meeting and feeling close to others; feeling awkward or blocked in initiating sex or grievances; difficulties in expressing feelings; feeling bottled up; and problems with self-confidence in a variety of situations. The problems tend to be specific rather than diffuse. Marital problems may be an outgrowth of excessive Scale *0* differences between spouses. Leisure time activities of the more introversive spouse (e.g., reading, gardening, fishing, movies, collecting) may be incompatible with those of the more extroversive partner (e.g., having company over, sewing or discussion groups, clubs, live sports).

Symptomatic Pattern

It is often difficult to discern the full pattern of symptoms and situation of high Scale *0* scorers because of their difficulty in opening up and confiding to others. Their fear of misunderstanding and embarrassment makes them concerned about timing and about expressing themselves in "the right way," which can result in omitting important facts and circumstances as well as the feelings that attend them. At times these omissions are defensively motivated, but more often they result from uncertainty as to when—and lack of confidence as to how—these topics should be raised. This difficulty is often integral to the patient's stated presenting problem, and symptomatic of his/her functioning in a variety of areas. That is, the patient typically has long-standing difficulties in making his/her feelings known to others, a function of introversive inhibition and a fear of being misunderstood. Often this reluctance is abetted by a concern that the patient will be unable to respond appropriately if asked for elaboration, rationale, background, and so forth. Confiding feelings is seen as a potential can of worms that the patient would prefer to avoid. One consequence is that he or she may be frequently hurt or offended by others who are unaware of the patient's sensitivity, which in turn makes the patient more apprehensive and reluctant to confide.

Mood is highly variable among high Scale *0* scorers and heavily influenced by other scales. Emotional expression tends to be tightly controlled, with these patients being more emotionally active than they appear on the surface. They harbor concerns that others may consider their feelings inappropriate. They tend to experience at least mild dysphoria and apprehensiveness and tend to suffer a painful self-consciousness to which they feel prisoner. A component of this self-consciousness is the awareness that the patient is unable to interact in the spontaneous and carefree manner that he or she observes others doing, creating feelings of sadness, deprivation, and envy. This distress is chronic and tends to coexist with other moods.

Cognitive functioning usually is largely intact, apart from chronic or obsessive self-doubt, a tendency to ruminate about situations and events, and problems with decision making, especially for decisions with social consequences. These problems do not necessarily prevent the patient from being reliable and productive, but they do tend to interfere with a creative and original approach to solving problems. These patients tend toward cognitive rigidity and are prone to freeze, give up, or become upset when their usual approaches don't solve the problem. Within the patient's areas of competence and skill, however, he or she brings a seriousness of purpose, dedication, focus, and dependability to work and achievement-related pursuits that, in the absence of greater satisfactions in interactions with others, is often a very important support for self-esteem.

These patients tend to dwell excessively on social comparisons. Their self-confidence tends to be low and their self-esteem precarious. They are overly sensitive to what others think of them and take note of the appearance of others, and of their skill and comfort in interaction, their friendliness and generosity, the amount of attention paid to them and paid by them to others, and so on. And in these assessments, of course, the patient usually comes up short. Competitive situations therefore tend to create considerable discomfort and are avoided. Social visibility tends to be aversive—another area of calculation in the high Scale *0* scorer's decisions about activities to be engaged in or avoided, and the amount of interaction that can be accommodated without exceeding his or her comfort level.

The behavior patterns of these patients are characterized by moderation, caution, and conventionality. They tend to accept authority and avoid conflict. Their tendency to avoid antisocial conduct rests mostly with their avoidance of peer groups that might engender or support it.

The social behavior of high Scale 0 scorers is marked by shyness, reserve, bashfulness, uneasiness, fear of embarrassment, circumspection, and conversational reticence. They typically avoid group and social situations because these make them feel anxious or overwhelmed. Even relatively anonymous circumstances such as standing in line may be marked by discomfort and urges to flee. When group activities cannot be avoided, these patients prefer to be on the periphery and to take the role of observer. They tend to be passive, retiring, and self-effacing. Others find them quiet, standoffish, timid, and difficult to get to know. These patients are often not in on the events and enthusiasms that engage their peers, and are vulnerable to being relegated to the sidelines of social activity. Although they tend to gravitate toward the sidelines anyway, being seen by others as "square," "nerdy," or "out of the loop" can nevertheless aggravate their self-consciousness and sense of inadequacy.

Interpersonal Relations

High Scale 0 scorers are uncomfortable with others but do not necessarily wish to be alone or uninvolved. They form relationships slowly and deliberately, often after an initial period of considerable hesitancy and awkwardness. Once formed, however, these relationships may be highly stable, loyal, and intimate. These patients may be particularly uncomfortable dealing with members of the opposite gender, owing to deficits in heterosexual social skills, which, in turn, are due to their own shyness and past avoidance of situations (e.g., school dances) within which such skills are often learned. In relatively close social interaction, these patients are peaceable and avoid conflict or unpleasantness. Even when safeguards are strong, they are quick to make concessions or submit, rather than expose themselves to the stimulation that comes with conflict and skills they view as inadequate to its management. Resistance, if any, tends to be passive, and these patients may find fault with their own attitudes and conduct, or even fall into self-criticism or self-deprecation to prevent or abort confrontation.

Behavioral Stability

In most patients, the behavior pattern (and scores) of high Scale 0 scorers is highly stable and persistent, although at moderate levels the patient can acquire social skills and adaptations that will permit increased comfort in routine interactions and, in some cases, allow him or her to pass as sociable. Patients with Bipolar Disorder are an important exception to this rule, and it is not unusual to see Scale *0* scores shift by 30 *T*-scores or more between manic and depressive states.

Defenses

The overall defensive pattern tends to be internalizing, with feelings and impulses being processed within rather than expressed or acted out. The chief defense is stimulus reduction/avoidance, which usually translates into social withdrawal. Secondary defenses include intellectualization and emotional constriction.

History

The history is typically one of relative isolation, few close relationships outside family, and limited socialization experiences, primarily due to the patient's avoidance of these. In some cases, there is a history of an acutely embarrassing social calamity that engendered a subsequent phobic/avoidant response to similar circumstances.

Diagnostic Considerations

Diagnosis is highly variable, depending on the other scales of the MMPI-2. Elevations on Scale *0* alone are associated with adjustment disorders and social phobias. When elevated in combination with other scales, Scale *0* is most often associated with anxiety and depressive disorders but is not uncommon in Schizophrenia. Among Axis II disorders, Scale *0* is most commonly associated with avoidant, dependent, schizotypal, and schizoid trends.

Treatment Considerations

Patients with high Scale *0* scores are typically slow to seek treatment because of their reluctance to initiate new relationships, especially when under stress. As a result, treatment tends to be sought only after numerous procrastinations as symptoms and discomfort become progressively more severe and disabling. Directive methods are usually preferable to those focused on exploration, at least initially, because of their reticence and constriction and because of their typically high immediate level of distress. The patient is likely to view the therapist as an authority and an expert and is inclined to follow the treatment plan. Patience and reassurance on the therapist's part are important in helping the patient feel comfortable, as are efforts to help place the presenting problem in perspective. Because of their relative isolation, these patients often are unaware that many others may have similar problems, and thus may be unrealistically pessimistic about their prognosis. Patients often have significant difficulty expressing themselves. Speech is often tentative, overly deliberate, overqualified, slow, and halting, and the patient is often conflicted or uncertain about what information should be shared with the therapist. These patients are therefore helped to express their concerns by periods of frequent but minimally intrusive questioning, interspersed with periods during which the patient can be silent and regroup.

Many of the problems high Scale *0* scorers bring to therapy are amenable to behavioral and skills-training procedures, such as relaxation, assertiveness training, and time management, in addition to general interactional and social skills methods taught by role-playing/rehearsal. Given the high stability of this largely genetically determined dimension, it is generally more realistic and helpful for patient and therapist to think in terms of making small but effective adaptations to the patient's introversive style than to resolve or eliminate problems. Bibliotherapy can augment and expedite treatment. These patients are often able to gain a better perspective on the nature of introversion and may better learn and retain information on how to cope with it through reading than they can in the therapy session. The former can be pursued quietly and alone, whereas the therapeutic interaction can be intrinsically anxiety-provoking and distracting for them.

Low Scores

Low Scale *0* scorers are described in terms that suggest favorable overall adjustment, such as expressive and responsive; cheerful and enthusiastic; active, energetic, and vigorous; enterprising and ambitious; adventurous and courageous; frank and assertive; adaptable, versatile, and ingenious; talkative and witty; friendly and affectionate. They are socially gregarious, outgoing, self-confident, intrepid, and able to take the initiative in meeting others and forming relationships, and are comfortable and effective in a broad variety of social situations. However, they may also be regarded as opportunistic, self-indulgent, and impulsive. Their eagerness to seek out others can be forward if not aggressive, and they can be perceived as flighty and undiscriminating. Their difficulty (or lack of interest) in appreciating and acknowledging the individuality of others tends to render their relationships superficial and causes them to be viewed as insensitive and insincere. In like manner, their lack of social inhibition and self-consciousness may contribute to self-seeking and exhibitionistic behavior. They tend to take an ascendent role in relationships and are seen as persuasive, but they may use this position to serve manipulative, selfish, and deceitful ends. Thus they are capable of stimulating interest and engagement with others, but also of inciting anger and resentment. Their need for social stimulation often interferes with their ability to focus long enough to establish and maintain secure and intimate relations with others. Such relations are also obstructed by the patient's tendency to sacrifice genuine emotional expression to what will play to the audience.

In profiles having significant elevations on other scales, low Scale *0* scores tend to be prognostically favorable. These patients are better able to attract support from others and are more able to establish a working relationship in treatment. They are often better informed and more confident and optimistic, and have fewer idiosyncratic beliefs and attitudes that can complicate therapy. Moreover, they are generally more willing and able to make the indicated behavior changes. However, they also tend to be more oriented toward action than contemplation and have difficulty reflecting on their problems.

🐿 TEST YOURSELF 🐿

1. **Considering the differences between the Minnesota Normals and the MMPI-2 restandardization sample, a *T*-score of 70 on the MMPI represents about the same level of deviance as a *T*-score of 65 on the MMPI-2.** True or False?

2. **In general, the basic scales of the MMPI-2 are more likely to model psychiatric syndromes, whereas the content scales are more likely to represent discrete groups of symptoms.** True or False?

3. **Among the basic scales, those least heterogeneous in item content are**
   (a) *2* and *9*.
   (b) *1* and *7*.
   (c) *6* and *8*.
   (d) *4* and *9*.
   (e) *1* and *3*.
   (f) *3* and *6*.

4. **Among the subtle subscales of the MMPI-2, which best reflects the inhibition of aggression, anger, and hostility?**

   (a) D-S

   (b) Hy-S

   (c) Pd-S

   (d) Pa-S

   (e) Ma-S

5. **Which of the basic scales receives the largest K-correction on a per-item basis?**

   (a) Scale 1

   (b) Scale 4

   (c) Scale 7

   (d) Scale 8

   (e) Scale 9

6. **For which of the basic scales does the K-correction most clearly oppose the scale's content?**

   (a) Scale 1

   (b) Scale 4

   (c) Scale 7

   (d) Scale 8

   (e) Scale 9

7. **The amount of obvious psychotic content among the basic scales**

   (a) is greatest for Scale 6.

   (b) is greatest for Scale 8.

   (c) is about the same for Scales 6 and 8.

8. **Which of the basic scales contains item content that most clearly opposes other item content on the same scale?**

   (a) Scale 2

   (b   Scale 3

   (c) Scale 4

   (d) Scale 6

   (e) Scale 9

Answers: 1. True; 2. True; 3. b; 4. a; 5. c; 6. c; 7. c; 8. d

THE CONTENT & CONTENT COMPONENT, PERSONALITY PSYCHOPATHOLOGY–5 (PSY-5), AND SUPPLEMENTARY SCALES

≡Rapid Reference 7.1

Content and Content Component Scales: *Anxiety (ANX)*

Items: 23; 18 keyed *True*

Major Internal Correlates: Saturated with the First Factor of the MMPI-2, ANX is highly correlated with A, Scales 7 and 8, D1, D4, D5, D-O, Hy3, Hy-O, Pd5, Sc3, Sc4, OBS, DEP, DEP1, DEP2, WRK, TRT, NEN, Mt, PK, and PS, and negatively with Es.

Description: Items reflect generalized anxiety, including excessive worry, nervous tension, disturbed sleep, and problems with attention and concentration.

Interpretation: A fear of mental collapse that is close to panic. Feeling "stressed out" and extremely vulnerable to upset by disappointment, financial difficulties, or decisions that don't work out. Dread that a sudden unanticipated event will cause one to "go to pieces."

Positive Aspects: Insight; desire for relief.

Low Scores: Relaxation; nonapprehensiveness.

Most Useful Comparisons: High scores: Scales 7, OBS, DEP, DEP1, DEP2, BIZ, LSE. Low scores: Scales 4, 9, Pd1, Pd2, Pd3, Pd4, Pd5, Ma1, Ma2, Ma3, Ma4, ASP, ASP2, AGG, DIS.

Components: None

≡Rapid Reference 7.2

Content and Content Component Scales: *Fears (FRS)*

Items: 23; 16 keyed *True*

Major Internal Correlates: *Es* and *GM*; both negative correlates.

Description: Items reflect general fearfulness and specific phobias. The word *fear* and its cognates (afraid, dread, frightened) appear in more than three-quarters of the items. The several groups of items include: (a) specific fears of classically phobic type (darkness, heights, open and closed spaces); (b) animals such as mice, snakes, and spiders; (c) natural phenomena such as earthquakes, lightning, storms, fire, and water; (d) loss of physical integrity, especially through germs and tissue damage; and (e) admissions of general neurotic fearfulness and a low threshold for feeling fearful that is likely to be incapacitating.

Interpretation: Fearful, apprehensive, easily frightened. High scores suggest displacement/condensation of anxiety onto situations and phobic objects. Not infrequently elevated in defensive Paranoid Schizophrenia (especially *FRS2*).

Positive Aspects: Harm avoidant; not inclined to take risks; relatively mature defense structure (e.g., avoidance, displacement, condensation).

Low Scores: Intrepid but potentially reckless; judgment may be poor; look for bravado; mania.

Most Useful Comparisons: Scales *1, 6, 7, 9, Pd2, Pa1, Pa2, Pa3, ANX, HEA, CYN, ASP2, SOD, GM*. With high scores, possible paranoid trends. With low scores, look for indications of fearlessness, recklessness, and poor judgment, such as might be seen in psychopathy or mania.

Components: 2

Generalized Fearfulness (FRS1) (12 items; 11 keyed *True*). *FRS1* encompasses most of the items in groups (a), (d), and (e) above, with a theme of broad apprehensiveness in the approach to daily living, with emphasis on the dangers or potential harmfulness of objects and circumstances in the environment. Phobic anxiety.

Multiple Fears (FRS2) (10 items; 4 keyed *True*). *FRS2* encompasses most of the items in groups (b) and (c) above. Specific common phobias.

≡ *Rapid Reference 7.3*

....

Content and Content Component Scales:
Obsessiveness (OBS)

Items: 16; all keyed *True*

Major Internal Correlates: Saturated with the First Factor of the MMPI-2, OBS is highly correlated with A, Scales 7 and 8, D5, Pd5, Sc3, ANX, DEP, DEP3, LSE, LSE1, WRK, TRT, TRT1, NEN, Mt, PK, and PS, and negatively with K and Es.

Description/Interpretation: Items reflect indecision and the potentially endless supply of considerations that may be brought to bear in decision making: obsessiveness, worry, intrusive thoughts, preoccupation with detail, timidity and self-doubt, and a fear of taking or committing oneself to concrete, practical action. Overly busy but massively inefficient cognitive activity. High scores when ANG2, TPA1, or both are also high may suggest passive-aggressive motivation, with nonperformance via indecision, obsession, and preoccupation with detail being used as a means of coping with the demands and expectations of others, and, in turn, engendering responses of impatience, frustration, and exasperation in them.

Low Scores: Suggest an opposite trend, with decisions being made with self-confidence and dispatch, possibly reflecting a histrionic cognitive style (high Hy-S). Very low scores may imply overconfidence and a hasty and incautious approach to decision making such as often is seen in mania (low Scale 2, high Scale 9).

Limitations: The items of OBS are ego-dystonic in character, and therefore closer to Obsessive-Compulsive Disorder (OCD) than to Obsessive-Compulsive Personality Disorder (OCPD). Internal consistency strictures employed in developing OBS may have prevented it from incorporating the range of content (i.e., content related to symmetry, checking, cleaning, ordering, perfectionism, concerns about contamination, overcontrol, restriction of affect, stinginess, overconscientiousness, preoccupation with details, and forbidden aggressive, sexual, or sacrilegious thoughts and actions) that would have enabled it to function better as an indicator of obsessive trends, despite the availability of many suitable items in the MMPI-2 pool (e.g., items 136, 322, 447, 507, etc.).

Most Useful Comparisons: Scales 2, 3, 7, 8, and 9, D4, Hy-S, Sc3, Ma3, ANX, FRS, HEA2, ANG2, and TPA1. Scores on these scales may be especially informative when OBS is greater than ANX and FRS. With high scores, look for impaired cognitive/neuropsychological functioning. With low scores, look for signs of impulsive decision making.

Components: None

CAUTION

Inferences based on *OBS* for Obsessive-Compulsive Disorder, especially Obsessive-Compulsive Personality Disorder, should be made cautiously, if at all, and never in isolation.

≡ *Rapid Reference 7.4*

Content and Content Component Scales: *Depression (DEP)*

Items: 33; 28 keyed *True*

Major Internal Correlates: Saturated with the First Factor of the MMPI-2, *DEP* is highly correlated with A, Scales 2, 7, and 8, D4, D5, D-O Hy3, Hy-O, Pd5, Pd-O, Sc1, Sc2, Sc3, Sc4, Si3, ANX, OBS, LSE, LSE1, WRK, TRT, TRT1, NEN, Mt, PK, and PS, and negatively with Es.

Description: Items reflect brooding, dysphoria, moodiness, apprehension, worry, fatigue, pessimism, loss of interest, self-criticism, and irritability, with an emphasis on the cognitive and attitudinal components of depressive syndromes, including helplessness, hopelessness, and worthlessness. Only nine items overlap Scale 2. Ben-Porath and Sherwood (1993) showed that *DEP1, DEP2,* and *DEP3* all reflect aspects of diagnostic criteria for Major Depressive Episode.

Interpretation: High scorers (following the component scales; see below) report despair, a loss of interest, and feelings of fatigue, apathy, and exhaustion *(DEP1)*; they are unhappy, blue, and quick to cry *(DEP2)*; they show a collapse in self-efficacy and self-regard to the point that they feel guilt-ridden, useless, unpardonably sinful, and condemned *(DEP3)*; and they feel hopeless, wish for death, and contemplate suicide *(DEP4)*. The empirical correlates of high *DEP* and component scores found by Graham and colleagues (1999) confirm these features. Their outpatients often had histories of prior suicide attempts and psychiatric hospitalizations, in addition to profuse depressive symptomatology with hopelessness, suicidal ideation, and disturbed sleep.

Low Scores: Suggest the absence (or denial) of depressiveness rather than the presence of elated or expansive mood, but some low scorers will be seen as defensive, euphoric, irritable, or overactive, especially in psychiatric settings.

Most Useful Comparisons: Scales 2, 7, and 8, ANX, OBS. Higher Scale 2 than *DEP* suggests greater psychomotor retardation, inhibition of aggression, and vegetative symptoms such as sleep disturbance, anorexia, and weight loss (or gain); higher *DEP* than Scale 2 suggests convictions of worthlessness and futility, along with a view of the self as inadequate or inferior, greater chronicity, and characterologic features.

(continued)

Components: 4

Lack of Drive (DEP1) (12 items, 9 keyed *True*). Items report despair; a loss of pleasure, interest, and motivation in living; and lethargy. High scores reflect apathy, anhedonia, an inability to accomplish routine tasks of daily life, and a sense of having given up. Low scores suggest optimism and zest, with active interests, aspirations, and plans for the future.

Dysphoria (DEP2) (6 items; 4 keyed *True*). Items reflect dysphoric/depressed mood in the form of subjective unhappiness, especially brooding, feeling blue, and moody spells. Four of the six items overlap *D5 (Brooding)*. Low scores assert happiness and freedom from "the blues."

Self-Depreciation (DEP3) (7 items; all keyed *True*). Items reflect self-dissatisfaction, guilt, a sense of moral failure, and a negative self-concept. High scorers admit to feelings of guilt, helplessness, hopelessness, regret/remorse, uselessness, and worthlessness. Low scorers deny such feelings.

Suicidal Ideation (DEP4) (5 items; all keyed *True*). DEP4 functions as a critical item list for suicidal ideation and despair, but does not exhaust the supply of such items in the MMPI-2 item pool (see items 150, 524, and 530). None of the DEP4 items appear on Scale 2. Not all are explicitly suicidal in content, but they do imply a level of pessimism about the future that supports a wish to die and thoughts of suicide. High scores raise the question of suicide potential, the need for its assessment, and the probable wisdom of initial precautions against suicidal acts or gestures.

≡ Rapid Reference 7.5

Content and Content Component Scales: *Health Concerns (HEA)*

Items: 36; 14 keyed *True*

Major Internal Correlates: Scales *1*, *3*, and *8*, *D3*, *Hy3*, *Hy4*, *Hy-O*, *Sc6*, and *ANX*, and negatively with *Es*.

Description: Items consist of somatic complaints and health worries. Content is strongly redundant with Scale *1*, with 23 overlapping items, and a correlation of about .95.

Interpretation: High scores reflect concern or preoccupation with health, and a tendency to develop physical symptoms in response to stress. Patients may also manifest fatigue, insomnia, nervousness, fearfulness, and characterological features such as pessimism, bitterness, and problems expressing anger.

Low scores: See discussion of low scores under Scale *1*.

Most Useful Comparisons: Scales *1*, *3*, and *8*, *Hy3*, *Hy4*, *Hy-O*, *Sc6*; *ANX* and *DEP* (presence or absence of distress accompanying somatic complaints); *BIZ* (possibility of somatic delusions).

Components: 3

Gastrointestinal Symptoms (HEA1) (5 items; 3 keyed *True*). Items report upper gastrointestinal distress, including nausea, vomiting, stomach pain and discomfort (stomachache), and constipation. All items overlap Scale *1*.

Neurological Symptoms (HEA2) (12 items; 5 keyed *True*). Items report sensory and motor problems, losses of consciousness, and other head complaints. Two-thirds of the items overlap Scale *1*. When *HEA2* is higher than Scales *2*, *8*, *HEA*, *HEA1*, and *HEA3*, consider neuropsychological evaluation.

General Health Concerns (HEA3) (6 items; 1 keyed *True*). Items report poor health and health worries and preoccupations. Two-thirds of the items overlap Scale *1*.

≡ *Rapid Reference 7.6*

Content and Content Component Scales: *Bizarre Mentation (BIZ)*

Items: 23; 22 keyed *True*

Major Internal Correlates: Scales *6*, *8*, and *9*, *D4*, *Pa1*, *Pa-O*, *Sc1*, *Sc3*, *Sc5*, *Sc6*, *Ma-O*, *OBS*, and *PSY*, and negatively with *Es*.

Description: Items report peculiar and unusual ideation, including ideas/delusions of control, persecution, and reference. *BIZ* is the content analogue of the 86/68 profile type. About one-third of the items are paranoid in content. Scores are easily suppressed by intent to appear nonpsychotic. Does not discriminate well between Schizophrenia and other psychotic conditions such as psychotic depression.

Interpretation: High scorers report being beset by intrusive and disruptive ideas and experiences that they typically attribute to the malevolence of others. They experience a severe loss in the control of their thinking and feel highly vulnerable to being injured or undermined by others' actions.

Low Scores: Reflect the absence (or denial) of these experiences.

Most Useful Comparisons: Scales *F*, *1*, *6*, and *8*, *Pd4*, *ANX*, and *DEP* (presence or absence of distress accompanying psychoticism), *LSE* (question of grandiosity when low), *AGG*, *DIS*, *PSY* (possibility of somatic delusions). *BIZ* is a useful standard for judging the extent to which psychotic content has contributed to elevations on Scales *F*, *6*, *8*, and *PSY*.

(continued)

Components: 2

Psychotic Symptomatology (BIZ1) (11 items; all keyed *True*). Items report frankly psychotic content reflecting positive or accessory symptoms characteristic of Schizophrenia and other psychotic conditions (e.g., auditory, visual, or olfactory hallucinations; delusions of persecution and control; and such other first-rank symptoms as thought broadcasting and thought withdrawal). Nearly half of the items refer to paranoid symptomatology.

Schizotypal Characteristics (BIZ2) (9 items; all keyed *True*). Items are less obviously psychotic in content than *BIZ1*, but are nevertheless unusual, odd, peculiar, and weird, such as ideas of reference, derealization, intrusive thoughts, and uncanny sensory experiences as are sometimes seen in prodromal or residual phases of Schizophrenia, dissociative conditions, and mood disorders with psychotic features.

≡Rapid Reference 7.7

....

Content and Content Component Scales: *Anger (ANG)*

Items: 16; 15 keyed *True*

Major Internal Correlates: Scales 7 and *8, Pd-O, Ma-O, Si3, A, ANX, OBS, DEP, TPA, TPA1, WRK, NEN, Mt, PK,* and *PS,* and negatively with *K, S,* and *S4.*

Description: Items report angry impulses and episodes, which have often been pursued aggressively or secondary to a breakdown of inhibitory emotional or behavioral controls, and which have at times resulted in property destruction, injury to others, or both. Angry feelings are at times reported to be distressing and the violence of their expression inexplicable.

Interpretation: High scorers are irritable and volatile, underregulate crude affect, are intolerant of frustration, issue angry expressions at a high rate, and are prone to angry tirades and destructive outbursts. They have strong needs to discharge their ire and if they feel constrained by external circumstances from discharging in expansive ways through temper tantrums, bouts of yelling and cursing and the like, they will do so in more controlled ways through frequent bugging, nagging, picking, carping, quibbling, belittling, discrediting, deriding, needling, ridiculing, shaming, irritating, taunting others, sadistic teasing, demanding, imposing, intruding, and being stubborn.

Most Useful Comparisons: Scales 4, 6, and *8, Pd4, Pa1, Sc1, Sc5, ANX, DEP, BIZ, BIZ1, BIZ2, TPA, TPA1, TPA2, AGG, DIS, PSY.* Angry/hostile variance characterizes both *ANG* and *TPA,* but the former is "cool" whereas the latter is "hot." When accompanied by elevations on *TPA* (especially *TPA2*), and on *AGG, ANG* connotes hostile and sadistic, not merely angry, motivation. Concurrent elevations on *ANX* and *DEP*, however, especially when *ANG2* is higher than *ANG1*, *TPA1* is higher than *TPA2*, and *NEN* is higher than *AGG*, suggest *ANG* is a component of a general pattern of negative emotionality, and that angry expressions are an occasion for guilt, remorse, and self-criticism. This pattern may be associated with a special risk for dramatic suicide, including provoked homicide and murder-suicide. Low *ANX* and *DEP* when *ANG* is high suggests instrumental aggression and the use of anger, and the threat thereof, to intimidate. When elevated with *BIZ*, especially when *ANG1* is higher than *ANG2* and *BIZ1* is higher than *BIZ2*, the instigation to angry expressions may be psychotic, appear unprovoked, and, when *Pa1* and *AGG* are also elevated, may be extremely violent.

Components: 2

Explosive Behavior (ANG1) (7 items; 6 keyed *True*). Items report explosive and violent episodes that have been directed to both persons and property and have likely resulted in injury and damage; these items are reminiscent of the criteria for Intermittent Explosive Disorder. Behavior is emphasized over impulse; the opposite emphasis characterizes *ANG2*. High scorers experience an irresistible need to express and discharge angry feelings when these are aroused. That is, they feel unable to control and contain anger when it is present. Low scores on *ANG1* emphasize the denial of undercontrolled violent expressions over the denial of anger per se. That is, low *ANG1* scorers are more likely able to assert better control than an absence of angry emotionality.

Irritability (ANG2) (7 items; all keyed *True*). Items report high levels of anger and irritability, but also a sense of distress and perplexity about these reactions. The emotional tone of *ANG2* is more dysphoric than hostile, which may inhibit the extremity of the behavioral outbursts that characterize high *ANG1* scorers. The combination of anger and inhibition themes in *ANG2* suggests that it may be responsive to partial or attenuated expressions of anger that are emitted within a context of self-justification such as argumentativeness, disagreeableness, annoyance, frustration, stalling, pettiness, impatience, complaining, criticism, and passive-aggressive or passive-paranoid maneuvers. Low scores reflect a serene and peaceable temperament.

≡ *Rapid Reference 7.8*

Content and Content Component Scales: *Cynicism (CYN)*

Items: 23; all keyed *True*

Major Internal Correlates: *Si3, ASP, ASP1, PSY*, and negatively with *K, S, S1, Hy2, Hy-S,* and *Pa3*.

(continued)

Description: Items appear as points on a dimension extending from naive altruism and an obtuse absence of skepticism regarding others' motives; through normal prudent regard for one's vulnerability to deceit, mendacity, and chicanery at the hands of others; to the unqualified misanthropic conviction that people are unprincipled and corrupt, invariably acting out of motives that are selfish, perfidious, or craven. Seven items overlap *ASP*, all on *ASP1*.

Interpretation: High scorers assert that others are to be distrusted because they act only from self-interest, resort to honesty only to avoid detection, and act friendly only because it makes others easier to exploit. They see life as a jungle in which one must be constantly on the lookout for any competitive advantage because they expect others, given the opportunity, will use any means at their disposal to claim such advantage for themselves. They therefore have no qualms about resorting to deception, hypocrisy, subterfuge, and manipulation to get away with whatever they can. They justify their expedient if not exploitive approach to others with the (projective) rationalization that others are equally selfish, dishonest, and amoral.

Low Scores: Deny normal levels of skepticism regarding the good will of others, by maintaining that they are completely trustworthy and driven solely by prosocial and altruistic motivations. At the same time, they portray themselves as bastions of benevolence, holders of an unshakable belief in the goodness of their fellow men and women. These sentiments are not infrequently expressed in the context of defensive response styles in which there is some focus on portraying themselves as enjoying consummately harmonious relationships, in which conflict and ill will are unheard of.

Most Useful Comparisons: For high *CYN* scores, *Pd2, Pd4, Pa1, Pa3* (low), *Sc1, Sc3, BIZ, BIZ1, ASP, ASP1, ASP2, LSE, PSY,* and *Re.* These measures permit an estimate of the extent of influence of alienation, antisocial attitudes and conduct, psychotic ideation, or a combination of these, on *CYN.* For low scores: *Hy2, Hy-S, Pa3, K, S, Mp, Sd.* These measures permit an evaluation of response style on *CYN* scores and an impression of whether naive, trustful attitudes expressed reflect primarily on the self (*Hy2*) or others (*Pa3*). With low *CYN,* high *LSE/LSE2,* and other indications of dependency (e.g., *Si3, Do* [low], *GM* [low]) present, there may be an unusual aversion to giving others offense for fear of rejection or the loss of dependency supports. A peak on *FRS* when *CYN* is low signifies the displacement of fears of others onto phobic objects.

Components: 2

    Misanthropic Beliefs (CYN1) (15 items; all keyed *True*). Items reflect a view of others as deceitful, selfish, untrustworthy, manipulative, unsympathetic, and disloyal. High scorers are likely to be "burned out" on relations with others and unwilling to exert significant efforts to improve them. Low scorers reflect a naive, optimistic, and overly positive view of others.

Interpersonal Suspiciousness (CYN2) (8 items; all keyed *True*). More dysphoric than *CYN1*, these items reflect a theme of feeling oneself to be a particular target of others' cynical, hostile, manipulative, or exploitive actions leading to suspicious and guarded reactions. High scorers feel "under fire" and vulnerable to others, especially superiors, who are thought to be stingy with recognition and understanding, and to be trying to disadvantage them. Low scores reflect excessive self-confidence and a conviction that their relations with others are marked by unusual harmony, mutual understanding, and an absence of competitiveness.

≡Rapid Reference 7.9

Content and Content Component Scales: *Antisocial Practices (ASP)*

Items: 22; 21 keyed *True*

Major Internal Correlates: Scales 4 and 9, *Ma-O, Si3, DIS*, and negatively with *K, S, Hy2, Hy-S, Pa3*, and *Re*.

Description: Items reflect cynicism and insensitivity toward the motives and feelings of others; sympathy with violations and violators of established order, rules, and social conventions; and admissions of past rule breaking and trouble with authorities. *Antisocial Practices* is a misnomer because the items referring to actual misbehavior, all on *ASP2*, amount to less than a quarter of the items on the full *ASP* scale. Moreover, the two components are only weakly correlated (at .34) and the correlation between *ASP* and its components (*ASP* × *ASP1* = .95; *ASP* × *ASP2* = .63) is divergent; thus *ASP* is better thought of as an antisocial attitudes scale. Nevertheless, Graham and colleagues (1999) found that their high *ASP* outpatients frequently manifested antisocial features, including histories of arrest, hostility, antisocial behavior, acting out, low frustration tolerance, substance abuse, and physical abusiveness. Seven items overlap *CYN*, all on *CYN1*.

Interpretation: High scorers subscribe to a wide range of antisocial attitudes and dispositions, are cynical about and rebellious toward conventional behavioral standards, and admit past delinquency and conflicts with authority. Low scorers assert the opposite pattern of beliefs and behaviors.

Most Useful Comparisons: Scales 4, 6, and 9, *Pd1, Pd2, Pd3, Pd4, Pd5, Pa1, Pa3* (low), *Sc1, Sc5, Ma1, Ma2, Ma3, Ma4, ANX, FRS, OBS, DEP, ANG1, CYN, CYN1, CYN2, AGG, DIS, PSY, R, Re*. Examination of the configuration of *CYN* and *ASP, CYN1* and *ASP1*, and *CYN2* and *ASP2* permits fairly detailed inferences about individual sentiments and dynamics and may be especially useful in interpreting the 46/64 codetype and its variants (462, 468, 469). *ASP, ASP1, CYN,*

(continued)

CYN1, and CYN2 are all correlated in a range of .50 to .62 with Pa1, suggesting potential paranoid trends given high scores on these scales. CYN > ASP, CYN2 > CYN1, ASP1 > ASP2, and especially CYN1 > ASP1, suggest a predominance of paranoid over antisocial features, especially when ASP2 and DIS are low. The opposite pattern suggests the predominance of antisocial trends. Elevations on ANX, FRS, OBS, DEP, or a combination of these may reflect the presence (when high) or absence (when low) of distress over antisocial attitudes/conduct. Scores on Sc5, ANG1, TPA2, R, DIS, and AGG may help refine inferences regarding control and aggression/sadism.

Components: 2

Antisocial Attitudes (ASP1) (16 items; all keyed *True*). Items reflect the belief that most people lie and cheat to get ahead in life, steal because others tempt them, and resort to honesty chiefly to avoid trouble. High scorers endorse a code of silence with authorities, a disdain for the rule of law, a willingness to steal given the opportunity, sympathy for those who treat others rapaciously, and a kind of vengeful joy when others are "catching it." There is thus a strong implicit theme of defective empathy in this set of items and a tertiary theme of generalized rage at others. Low scores reflect an unusually if not naively favorable view of others' honesty, altruism, and good will, and a view of the self as honest, trusting, friendly, agreeable, responsible, and nonaggressive.

Antisocial Behavior (ASP2) (5 items; 4 keyed *True*). Items report a history of delinquency, including theft, truancy, school suspensions, and conflict with school and legal authorities. Reflects historic behavioral features consistent with Antisocial Personality Disorder.

≡Rapid Reference 7.10

Content and Content Component Scales: *Type A (TPA)*

Items: 19; all keyed *True*

Major Internal Correlates: Scales A, 7, 8, and 9, Pd-O, Ma-O, Si3, ANX, OBS, ANG, ANG1, ANG2, CYN1, CYN2, ASP1, FAM1, WRK, PSY, NEN, PK, PS, and negatively with K, S, Hy2, Hy-S, and Re.

Description: The concept of the Type A or coronary-prone personality has been described in the Jenkins Activity Survey (JAS; Jenkins, Rosenman, & Friedman, 1967) as comprising three components: Speed and Impatience, Job Involvement, and Hard-Driving Competitiveness. The first focused on the time-urgency aspect of the Type A syndrome, the second with the extent of occupational demands and the person's dedication or determination to meet or exceed them, and the third with a serious, competitive, and hard-driving self-concept. The items of the *TPA* scale fail to cover this domain adequately, for reasons discussed in Friedman and colleagues (2001). Briefly, although the first component may receive a rough approximation in MMPI-2 items (i.e., *TPA1*), the second is represented by, at most, two items (507, 531), and the third is saturated with hostility at the expense of its intended themes of competitiveness, and self-imposed demands for performance. The only correlate found among both the male and female outpatients studied by Graham and colleagues (1999) to be associated with high *TPA* scores was interpersonal hostility. Both *TPA1* and *TPA2* reflect angry emotionality; in *TPA1*, the anger is "hot" and closer to the irritable-angry emotionality of *ANG*, whereas in *TPA2* it is "cool" and more calculating, controlled, hostile, vengeful, and sadistic than in *ANG*. Because *TPA2* is the larger of the two components, containing half again as many items as *TPA1*, the quality of *TPA2* is imparted to the full *TPA* scale, making it "cooler" than the full *ANG* scale.

Interpretation: High scorers have a low threshold for experiencing hostility and vengeance. They are self-centered, resentful, irritable, suspicious, spiteful, and lacking in empathy. They tend to treat others in a cold and dismissive fashion, as necessary evils at best, or, perhaps more typically, as obstructionist nuisances, and may take pleasure in their pain and misfortune.

Most Useful Comparisons: Scales A, Ma-O, Si3, OBS, ANG, ANG1, ANG2, CYN, CYN2, ASP, ASP1, ASP2, WRK, NEN, 4, 6, and 9, Ma-O, Si3, ANX, OBS, ANG, ANG1, ANG2, CYN1, CYN2, AGG, DIS, and negatively with K, S, Hy2, Hy-S, and Re. Scores on these scales help to refine inferences for high *TPA* scores, particularly with respect to whether they may be driven by anxiety, perfectionism, cynicism, mistrust, overarousal/hyperactivity, or sadistic aggression, and whether vengeance is likely to be confined to fantasy or acted out aggressively. Note level of *Pa3*. The Type A behavior pattern appears more likely when *TPA1* > *TPA2*, *CYN* > *ASP*, *CYN* > *TPA2*, *CYN1* > *CYN2*, *CYN1* > *TPA2*, and *WRK* < *T-60*, than when these relationships do not obtain (Friedman et al., 2001).

Components: 2

Impatience (TPA1) (6 items; all keyed *True*). Items reflect a sense of time urgency along with delay-stimulated irritability, such that having to wait in line, being interrupted, or having people upon whom one depends fail to do their work on time stirs one to annoyance if not anger.

Competitive Drive (TPA2) (9 items; all keyed *True*). Items convey less a spirit of competitiveness than of resentment, vengefulness, and sadism. Two additional items appear thematically displaced from *TPA1* (510, 545), and a third refers to job overinvolvement (531). High scorers admit to wanting to win a point against or pay back people who oppose them, opposing people for trivial reasons, relishing the misfortunes of people whom they dislike, resentment when they feel taken in, and gloating over their competitive advantages.

≡Rapid Reference 7.11

Content and Content Component Scales: *Low Self-Esteem (LSE)*

Items: 24; 21 keyed *True*

Major Internal Correlates: Scales A, 7, 8, and 0, D1, D4, D5, D-O, Pd5, Pd-O, Sc1, Sc4, Si3, ANX, OBS, DEP1, DEP3, WRK, NEN, Mt, PK, PS, and negatively with Es.

Description: Items admit personal and interpersonal shortcomings, a severe lack of self-confidence, a low threshold for self-blame and self-criticism, and a tendency to give up in the face of even minor adversity. It is the most sensitive of the content scales to ego-syntonic pathological dependency.

Interpretation: High scorers feel slower; less capable, intelligent, coordinated, attractive, likeable, self-confident, and resolute; and, in many ways, less adequate than others. They feel so overwhelmingly flawed, incompetent, and inferior to others that the independent management of daily life may seem out of the question, necessitating dependent and self-abasing attachments onto others.

Low Scores: Suggest relative freedom from negative self-attitudes, especially in the context of social interaction. Such scores affirm personal adequacy, self-confidence, competence, and independence. Within psychiatric populations, very low scores may reflect an inflated self-concept and possible grandiose ideation or delusions.

Most Useful Comparisons: High scores: Scales A, 7, and 8, Sc1, Sc2, Sc3, Sc4, Sc5, Sc6, Si3, OBS, DEP, DEP3, BIZ, WRK, TRT, NEN. LSE may be contrasted with DEP in terms of the locus of control construct, with LSE being more external than DEP. Whereas high DEP is worthless, more active, demanding, and relatively extrapunitive, high LSE is helpless, and more passive, dependent, and intropunitive. LSE is highly intercorrelated with OBS, DEP, WRK, and TRT. An underlying theme in each of these scales is an inability to perform. OBS stresses the inability to make decisions and act on them; DEP stresses the inability to mobilize sufficient personal resources to engage life; WRK stresses the inability to produce output in the context of employment; and TRT stresses the inability to rise above helplessness and despair to grapple with personal problems. Together, these scales form a quintet for which the theme of motivational disability may be almost as significant as their common core of negative emotionality. That is, the respondent showing peaks on these scales is reporting feeling immobilized and helpless. Reference to LSE and BIZ can be especially useful in interpreting high Scale 8 scores, with these two content scales reflecting the contributions of negative self-attitudes and psychotic thinking, respectively. Low scores: Scales 9, Pd1, Pd2, Pd3, Pa1, Pa3 (low), Ma1, Ma2, Ma3, Ma4, Ma-S, Ma-

O, ANG1, ANG2, CYN1, CYN2, ASP1, ASP2, TPA1, TPA2, AGG, PSY, DIS. Low *LSE* scores reflect inflated self-esteem that may have a basis in narcissism, psychopathy, paranoid ideation, or mood disorder (mania).

Components: 2

Self-Doubt (LSE1) (11 items; 8 keyed *True*). Items are all negative self-attributions that are mostly phrased in such a way as to convey, not self-doubt, but the *conviction* that one is inferior and inadequate. That is, these items assert negative self-attitudes that are relatively fixed, and that sum to an overall negative or devalued identity. Low scores reflect a positive if not exalted and aggrandized self-concept. Look for overconfidence and grandiosity.

Submissiveness (LSE2) (6 items; all keyed *True*). Items reflect passivity, a servile obedience to others, and, by implication, an avoidance of responsibility. Low scores reflect independence, social confidence, and a sense of inner strength and competence.

≡ *Rapid Reference 7.12*

Content and Content Component Scales: *Social Discomfort (SOD)*

Items: 24; 13 keyed *True*

Major Internal Correlates: Scales A, 7 and 0, D1, D-O, Hy1, Pd3, Ma3, Si1, Si2, DEP, LSE, WRK, TRT, LPE.

Description: A bipolar scale, with high scores connoting introversion and low scores connoting extroversion. Three-quarters of the items overlap Scale 0. Items express shyness and self-consciousness; fears of embarrassment, awkwardness, and ineptitude; conversational reticence; a desire for low social visibility; the avoidance of crowds, parties, and strangers; and a preference for being alone. The theme of interpersonal aversiveness is stronger in *SOD* than in Scale 0.

Interpretation: High scorers seek to avoid other people, both individuals and groups, because they feel uneasy and awkward in such situations, and because they say they are happier being alone. The high scorer is not claiming loneliness, although this failure may represent a defensive denial of loneliness in some respondents.

Low Scores: Suggest a gregarious, outgoing style, with an enjoyment of interaction whether with individuals or in groups. They have a high level of social comfort and confidence, and are regarded as friendly, fun-loving, participative, and flexible. Sizeable SOD2 – SOD1 differences tend to identify individuals who

(continued)

have difficulty feeling at ease either alone or in the company of others. Very low scores on both components suggest a glib but superficial interactional style and are consistent with those manic/hypomanic syndromes that have high social hunger (and high social turnover) as a cardinal feature.

Most Useful Comparisons: Scales A, L, F, K, 2, 6, 7, 8, and 9, D5, Hy1, Hy2, Pd2, Pd3, Pa1, Sc1, Ma3, DEP, BIZ, CYN, ASP, ASP1, ASP2, AGG, PSY, DIS, NEN, LPE, Re, GF. With Scales 2 high and 9 low, high SOD reflects the kinds of anergic withdrawal and social anhedonia seen in depressive syndromes. With primary elevations on Scales F, 6, and 8, high SOD may indicate schizophrenia-spectrum interpersonal aversiveness and social withdrawal, the avoidant wariness that is grounded in paranoid suspiciousness and concerns for one's personal safety, or both. SOD scores in a region of 55T to 65T, when SOD2 exceeds SOD1, are seen in borderline syndromes. Low SOD scores, especially when SOD1 is low, can indicate warmth and a capacity for closeness with others when Scales L, 2, 7, and 8 are relatively low; K is in a 55T to 65T range; and raw K exceeds the non–K-corrected raw score on Pt. Low SOD scores in which SOD1 exceeds SOD2 are consistent with socially aggressive (see Pd3), if not narcissistic (check scores on LSE, Scale 9) and psychopathic (check scores on Pd2, ASP2, Re, GF; ASP > CYN), features, as well as with manic/hypomanic states.

Components: 2

Introversion (SOD1) (16 items; 8 keyed *True*). Items emphasize the avoidance of group and social situations, an aversion to interpersonal interaction, and a preference for being alone. More behavioral than SOD2, SOD1 contains all of the items of Si2. Ben-Porath and Sherwood (1993) have suggested that a low score on SOD1 coupled with a high score on SOD2 may reflect an aspiration to be more socially involved and a desire for an increased sense of personal comfort and control in interaction. This pattern is akin to stage fright, in which others are not rigidly avoided but simply approached with a sense of anxious trepidation. Very low scores may reflect a drive to become lost in the crowd and an intolerance of being alone.

Shyness (SOD2) (7 items; 4 keyed *True*). Items reflect self-consciousness, social inhibition, bashfulness, ease of embarrassment, and discomfort in social interaction. High scorers lack self-confidence and dread being the center of attention. They fear that they will be regarded as awkward or inept. Others view them as reticent and standoffish. Low scores reflect self-confidence and an uninhibited outgoing style. In some cases, low scores may reflect social fearlessness, aggressive sociability, and psychopathic insouciance.

≡Rapid Reference 7.13

Content and Content Component Scales: *Family Problems (FAM)*

Items: 25; 20 keyed *True*

Major Internal Correlates: Scales A, 4, and 8, Pd1, Pd4, Sc1, Si3, MDS.

Description: Items reflect family disharmony and dissension, in which conflict, neglect, jealousy, and misunderstandings contribute to a turbulent and unpleasant family atmosphere and to alienation among family members. By implication, the family emerges as an unsuitable venue for emotional nourishment because of a lack of attention, affection, and support, leading to feelings of deprivation, bitterness, and hostility toward family members.

Interpretation: High scorers not only feel deprived and mistreated by family, but appear to have acquired or augmented a set of dispositions that maintains both intrafamilial and more generalized enmity and insecurity into adulthood. Others are apt to consider them immature and overreactive people who harbor grave doubts and deeply negative attitudes toward themselves, but who are equally mistrustful and disparaging of others. This pattern of correlates is reminiscent of Borderline Personality Disorder. The pattern is also common to alcohol and other substance abuse. Ben-Porath and Sherwood (1993) suggested that high scores on FAM2 when FAM1 is low indicate disengagement from family. This pattern would also seem to suggest a much greater sense of indifference, perhaps with some feeling of sorrow about the shortcomings of family as a source of emotional provisions. The opposite pattern suggests the persistence of attachment in the midst of enmity and discord. When both components are elevated, a state of resentful alienation is suggested in which physical ties (i.e., association) have been severed but unresolved emotional attachments continue.

Most Useful Comparisons: Scales 4 and 8, Pd1, Pd4, Sc1, Si3, CYN, CYN1, CYN2, ASP1, ASP2, MDS. FAM and Pd1 have somewhat different interpretive implications for the primary nature and locus of family conflict, with FAM referring to current family and family of origin in about equal measure, whereas Pd1 refers more to the parental home in content, giving it a clear though not strong bias toward the family of origin. Pd1 shows a relatively greater emphasis on the parents as restricting freedom, independence, and efforts toward emancipation. MDS tends to emphasize current home conflict. FAM conveys a relatively greater sense of family turbulence, pathology, and estrangement. MDS > FAM > Pd1 may better reflect current family difficulties, whereas the reverse pattern suggests that family strife may be largely confined to the parental home. The patient's age, family history, and current family circumstance may bear importantly on interpretations of Pd1, MDS, and FAM and its

(continued)

component scales. Peak elevations on *CYN* when *FAM* is also high imply a distrust and dissatisfaction with intimates that has apparently generalized to others. Distrust and dissatisfaction may reach paranoid proportions when *FAM* and *BIZ* are peaked. The pattern of high scores on *FAM* and *ASP* when *ASP* exceeds *CYN* and *SOD* is low (and *SOD1* is higher than *SOD2*) appears to be the content scale equivalent of the psychopathic 4-9 profile type. Clinically, this pattern is associated with immaturity and substance abuse, and with assaultiveness and destructiveness.

Components: 2

Family Discord (FAM1) (12 items; 11 keyed *True*). Items stress intrafamilial conflict and animosity, with members being viewed as quarrelsome and disagreeable, oppressive and disapproving, annoying and ill-tempered. The theme is one of the family as an unpleasant, noxious environment from which one would like to escape.

Familial Alienation (FAM2) (5 items; two keyed *True*). Items reflect an emotional detachment from family. The items are phrased descriptively and have low emotional valences. They report factual states of affairs that, in some, would be associated with longing, loss, and anger, but in others with a sense of at least partial equanimity or indifference. In either case, high scores imply that the respondent severed ties in order to cut his or her losses with family for their inability or disinclination to provide a center of belonging and emotional support. The empirical correlates found by Graham and colleagues (1999) among their outpatients suggest that for high *FAM2* scorers, the severing of emotional attachments to family is not followed by the formation of alternative attachments. Thus, these patients were described as lonely, having few or no friends, and self-destructive, either through suicide attempts (women) or through chronic alcohol and marijuana abuse (men). These investigators also found histories of physical (men) and sexual (women) abuse among high *FAM2* scorers.

≋*Rapid Reference 7.14*

Content and Content Component Scales: *Work Interference (WRK)*

Items: 33; 28 keyed *True*

Major Internal Correlates: Scales A, 7, 8, and 0, D1, D4, D5, D-O, Hy3, Pd5, Pd-O, Sc3, Sc4, Si3, ANX, OBS, DEP1, DEP3, LSE1, TRT1, NEN, Mt, PK, PS, and negatively with Es.

Description: Items reflect a broad range of problems and impediments to performance in employment, including tension, worry, fearfulness, and feeling overwhelmed; defeatist and pessimistic attitudes; fatigue, inertia, and lack of initiative; distractibility and indecision; lack of self-confidence and self-esteem; irritability, rebelliousness, and oppositionality; and a tendency to give up in the face of obstacles. Almost 40% of the items contain the word "work" or one of its cognates. Saturated with the First Factor, WRK is a general measure of distress and disability that has been shaped to the context of work, emphasizing the kinds of problems that have adverse effects on productivity. The interferences covered in WRK include both interpersonal difficulties and the attitudes and symptoms that impair efficiency and impede output.

Interpretation: High scorers either feel impaired and incapacitated or wish to be viewed that way.

Low Scores: Suggest self-confidence; perseverance; an adequate fund of energy; the capacity to marshal one's abilities in the service of productivity on the job, ability to cooperate with coworkers (i.e., teamwork), and an ability to limit the influence of personal problems and symptoms on job performance.

Most Useful Comparisons: Scales A, 4, 7, 8, and 9, D4, Pd2, Pd4, Pa1, Sc3, Sc4, Ma1, ANX, OBS, DEP, ASP1, ASP2, TRT, DIS, NEN, Re, MAC-R, APS, AAS. Because of its saturation with the First Factor, the interpretive implications of WRK are most likely to be realized when it exceeds Scale A in elevation. Although problems that may interfere with employment performance are suggested by elevations on WRK alone, such elevations cannot be taken to indicate occupational malfunctioning specifically. The requirement that WRK exceed A strengthens the implication of specific work interferences to the extent of this difference. Recalling the high intercorrelations among OBS, DEP, LSE, WRK, and TRT, scores on WRK should always be compared with those on the other scales in this group to gain additional insight into the kinds of problems at work. High scores on Scales 4 and 9, Pd2, Ma1, ASP1, ASP2, DIS, Re, and MAC-R raise the question of exaggeration of disability and compensation seeking. High scores on MAC-R, APS, and AAS may suggest disability on the basis of substance abuse.

Components: None

≡Rapid Reference 7.15

Content and Content Component Scales: *Negative Treatment Indicators (TRT)*

Items: 26; 23 keyed *True*

Major Internal Correlates: Scales A, 7, and 8, D5, Sc1, Sc4, Si3, OBS, DEP1, DEP3, LSE1, WRK, NEN, Mt, PK, PS, and negatively with Es.

(continued)

Description/Interpretation: *TRT* is saturated with depressive variance; the correlation between *TRT* and *DEP* among psychiatric patients can be as high as .89. The empirical correlates of these two scales are likewise nearly identical (Butcher et al., 1990; Graham et al., 1999). Its items, six of which overlap *DEP* (four of these on *DEP1*), reflect a range of dysphoric feelings and attitudes, including hopelessness about making plans and decisions, effecting changes, or reaching goals; feeling unhappy, apathetic, guilty, and irritable; feeling that others do not care or understand; and pessimism about and aversion to confiding in others, including doctors. Given the extensive shared variance between these two scales, it is doubtful that *TRT* scores can predict treatment outcome reliably among any common diagnostic group, and such scores may lead to unusually and unrealistically negative prognostications among patients diagnosed with depression for reasons discussed in Friedman and colleagues (2001) and Greene (2000). *TRT* may serve as a measure of depressive severity and immobilization, however. The interpretation of low scores on *TRT* and its components is equally problematic. Although some low scorers on *TRT* may be adequately motivated, self-confident, planful, and persistent, they are likely to be less distressed and therefore less motivated for psychotherapy on that basis. Others obtaining low scores may appear grandiose and overconfident, and may take an insouciant and unreflective approach to self-disclosure and thus be impervious to psychotherapeutic efforts even when tolerant of them. The mere capacity to disclose personal information affords no guarantee that the material revealed can be discussed productively or insightfully (e.g., manic- and psychopathic-spectrum patients). Such patients, despite a tendency to obtain low and even very low scores on *TRT*, may pose challenges to the psychotherapist that are every bit as forbidding as those posed by high *TRT* scorers. For these reasons, both the positive and the negative predictive power of *TRT* are highly suspect. Until evidence of the validity of *TRT* for its intended purpose is forthcoming, this scale should be interpreted with caution.

Most Useful Comparisons: Scales 7 and 8, *Pd5, Sc1, Sc2, Sc4, Si3, DEP1, DEP3, LSE1, NEN*. See *DEP.*

Components: 2

Low Motivation (TRT1) (11 items; 10 keyed *True*). Items reflect apathy, an external locus of control, and a tendency to give up quickly in the face of obstacles because of a depletion of personal resources. The high scorer feels helpless and motivationally destitute to the point that struggle against adversity, or even planning to do so, is felt to be futile. Low scores reflect energy, optimism, self-confidence, and perseverance.

Inability to Disclose (TRT2) (5 items; all keyed *True*). Items reflect a disinclination to volunteer personal information and significant discomfort when asked to do so. *TRT2* extends the theme of the futility of efforts at amelioration to the realm of discussion. High scorers do not wish to reveal information about personal problems, perhaps because of depressive immobility, hopelessness (in which case *TRT1* is also high), or both, or because previous attempts to confide in others have not produced relief. Low scorers report eagerness to discuss their problems.

≡ Rapid Reference 7.16

Personality Psychopathology–5 (PSY-5) Scales: *Aggression (AGG)*

Items: 18; 15 keyed *True*

Major Internal Correlates: Scales 9, D-S (low), Ma4, ANG1, CYN2, ASP1, TPA2, R (low), GF (low), MAC-R.

Description: AGG is unique among MMPI/MMPI-2 scales in reflecting offensive or predatory aggression, and the hostile urge to dominate, vanquish, and destroy others. Items emphasize a theme of superiority and control avoidance, with additional subsets reflecting sadism and vindictiveness. AGG expressions of aggression, hostility, and control/domination are more apt to reflect cruelty than rage and are more apt to appear calculated, deliberate, methodical, and cold. By contrast, similar expressions from high scorers on ANG, TPA, and the like are more likely to be considered reactions to frustration or other provocation, and as rash, reckless, or ill-considered. AGG suggests several paranoid dynamisms, including the defense mechanism, identification with the aggressor, the tendency to see interactions as moves in a zero-sum game, and, possibly, the authoritarian complex of submissiveness with superiors and tyrannical relations with subordinates.

Interpretation: High scorers control others through the threat of their tempers. The self-concept is inflated, grandiose, and resentful, with a dread of being subject to another's control and a willingness to act sadistically and vindictively to avoid it. Relations with others are marked by aggressive efforts to control and dominate through fear and the threat of violence, and by resentment, hostility, and sadism.

Low Scores: Reflect the absence of a hostile orientation toward power, domination, and sadism characteristic of high AGG. Low scorers may manifest relatively high levels of social aggression by approaching and engaging others readily and without trepidation, but such aggression is free of hostile motive and a drive to dominate. Such scores may be compatible with the acceptance of relations with others on egalitarian terms, in which the mutual achievement of individual goals and fluctuations in hierarchical position (one-up; one-down) are considered to be natural and expected.

Most Useful Comparisons: Scales A and 7, ANX, DEP, ANG, TPA, LSE, PSY, DIS, NEN, LPE. Elevations on the distress scales (A, 7, ANX, DEP, NEN), or the lack thereof, are useful in distinguishing between hostile outbursts instigated by stress and those that are the product of calculated vengeance or instrumental aggression. Perspective on the issue of calculated versus precipitate aggression may also be aided by referring to the relative elevations of AGG and ANG. When AGG is high and A and LPE are low, the control, domination, and harm that issues

(continued)

from the high AGG scorer may be associated with pleasure, enjoyment, and a sense of well-being. Selfish and self-centered, yet envious of others, the high AGG scorer has a hostile narcissism that is heavily dependent on the attention and recognition of others. But the self-concept is so unrealistic, grandiose, and entitled that the desired reflections are forthcoming only under conditions of coercion. In this context, the combination of high AGG with high DIS or high PSY would appear to be especially dangerous. In the case of high AGG and high DIS, there is a synergy between sadistic motivation and deficits in behavioral control. Conjoint elevations on AGG and PSY suggest a risk for hostile action in the context of disordered thinking, such as bizarre and violent fantasy, command hallucinations, or ego-syntonic delusions, especially when DIS and LPE are high. In relation to low AGG scores, low DIS suggests underassertion, passivity, and a high threshold for resisting domination. In this context, elevations on NEN (or similar distress scales such as A, Scale 7, ANX, and DEP) may indicate patterns of behavior suggesting self-sabotage and self-defeat. Such a pattern is also consistent with symptoms of Obsessive-Compulsive Disorder. Low scores on AGG with low LPE scores create a vulnerability to being played for a patsy by misplacing trust in others and approaching situations with a credulous confidence that most others would avoid.

≡ Rapid Reference 7.17

Personality Psychopathology–5 (PSY-5) Scales: *Psychoticism* (PSY)

Items: 25; 23 keyed *True*

Major Internal Correlates: Scales A, F, 6, 7, and 8, Pd-O, Pa1, Pa-O, Sc1, Sc5, Sc6, Si3, Ma-O, BIZ1, BIZ2, CYN2 and negatively with S.

Description: Highly similar to BIZ, with which it shares 14 items and correlates at .94, the two largest groupings of items have active psychotic and active persecutory content, respectively. Additional subsets of items concern unusual experience/magical ideation, daydreaming, and suspiciousness.

Interpretation: At moderate elevations (55–65T), PSY reflects mostly unusual beliefs or experiences and a tendency to overindulge in daydreaming. Any elevation may be taken as a sign of reluctance to engage the world and other people in conventional terms. Even at mild and moderate elevations, PSY reflects disharmony in one's relations with the physical and social worlds such that functioning is compromised and relationships are alienated. At these levels, the person may give the appearance of being *in* the world but not *of* it. At higher elevations one encounters severe distortions in the way the individual interacts with his or her social and physical worlds, such that these interactions appear, respectively, hostile, provocative, offensive, or inept; and incompetent, irrelevant, bizarre, or self-defeating. At elevations greater than T-65, however, true psychotic phenomena make an appearance, including Schneiderian symptoms, fixed persecutory if not frank delusional ideation, and suspiciousness. In general, the high PSY scorer presents as odd in appearance, behavior, and belief. He or she appears to be preoccupied with fantasy and daydreaming, and seems out of touch with reality. Relations with others are apt to be minimal, distant, and covertly hostile, with a readiness to feel mistreated and resentful.

Low Scores: These are largely without symptomatic significance apart from the absence of those features associated with high scores.

Most Useful Comparisons: Scales A, F, 6, 7, and 8, Pd4, Pd-O, Pa1, Pa-O, Sc1, Sc5, Sc6, ANX, BIZ1, BIZ2, AGG, DIS, NEN. Because the content of about 40% of PSY items is persecutory or suspicious in character, reference can be made to Pa1 to estimate the contribution of paranoid ideation to PSY elevations. Elevations on A, 7, ANX, and NEN suggest distress associated with psychoticism, or the lack of such distress when these scales are low. Scales Pd4, Pd-O, and Sc1, and scales Sc5, AGG, and DIS reflect accompanying levels of alienation and hostile dyscontrol, respectively.

≋Rapid Reference 7.18

Personality Psychopathology–5 (PSY-5) Scales: *Disconstraint (DIS)*

Items: 28; 17 keyed *True*

Major Internal Correlates: Scales 9, D-S, Pd2, Ma1, ASP1, ASP2, AGG, MAC-R, AAS, and negatively with R, Re, and GF.

Description: A broad dimension of behavioral undercontrol. The largest subset of items reflects an expedient, anything-goes morality. Items of a somewhat smaller group admit delinquent conduct. Four additional groups of items concern sexual disinhibition, sensation seeking, activity, and fearlessness (two items). The main theme is undermodulation of impulse, spontaneity, broad interests, cognitive and moral flexibility, insufficient delay of gratification, and an independence from familiar rubrics. Scores are suppressed by age.

Interpretation: High scores reflect an unconventional, disinhibited personality structure with insufficient delay and modulation of impulse, a nonconforming and rebellious attitude toward rules and regulations, sensation seeking, shallow and self-centered loyalties, a hedonistic moral compass, indifference to or disdain for legal and ethical constraints, a fearless or reckless disregard for

(continued)

potential physical hazards, and a tendency to sacrifice long-term goals for short-term satisfactions. The high *DIS* scorer may present initially as energetic and spontaneous, but upon closer acquaintance comes to appear unreliable, reckless, and rebellious. Relations with parents and authority figures tend to be conflicted; relations with peers and others tend to be exploitive, promiscuous, and unstable. Impulsive and antisocial acting out, a lack of loyalty, repeated lying and neglect of obligations, and a lack of shame or remorse eventually may disrupt all but correctional relationships. Look for substance abuse.

Low Scores: The low *DIS* scorer presents as conventional, conforming, and controlled. Relations with others may be smooth but distant, formalized, and routinized, with contacts limited to a small circle of like-minded friends. A high tolerance for boredom, sameness, and routine and a relatively rigid adherence to traditional moral standards, along with a willingness to judge others in terms of these standards, are characteristic. Very concerned with maintaining appearances, the low *DIS* scorer takes an overly deliberate if not perfectionistic approach to problem solving. Obsessive-compulsive trends may be present.

Most Useful Comparisons: Scales 4 and 9, *Pd2, Pa1, Sc5, Ma1, Ma2, Ma3, Ma4, BIZ1, BIZ2, ANG1, ASP1, ASP2, AGG, PSY, R* (low), *Re* (low), *MAC-R, AAS*. It is often helpful to determine whether behavioral undercontrol may have a psychotic basis, such as mania.

≡ *Rapid Reference 7.19*

Personality Psychopathology–5 (*PSY-5*) Scales: *Neuroticism / Negative Emotionality (NEN)*

Items: 33; 27 keyed *True*

Major Internal Correlates: Scales A, 7, and 8, D5, Pd-O, Si3, ANX, OBS, DEP, ANG2, WRK, TRT, and negatively with K, S, and Es.

Description: A broad dimension similar to the First Factor of the MMPI-2 and highly correlated with A (.89). The largest subset of items reflects worry, nervousness, anxiety, tension, and stress. A second subset reflects anger and emotional undercontrol. Two smaller groups of items denote guilt and fears, respectively. *NEN* reflects the sense of being so overwhelmed with the stress of worry, nervousness, fear, and guilt that one feels at the end of one's rope and quick to anger. Two themes are implicit in the item content: (a) a pervasively unpleasant and aversive emotional life, one that feels both relentless and intrusive, leading to (b) inner agitation and a feeling that one's controls have been taxed by this relentlessly aversive emotionality to the point of collapse.

Interpretation: High scorers present as helpless, dependent, needy, indecisive, and unstable. Relations with others are characterized by extreme passivity, fears of abandonment, and hypersensitivity to criticism. They may provoke exasperation in others as they continually fail to take initiative to improve the situation, and to act in their own best interest. Borderline attachments to others, help-rejecting complainingness, and suicidal or self-mutilative behavior may be seen.

Low Scores: Reflect a relaxed and imperturbable emotionality that may be so care- and worry-free as to suggest an impoverishment of internal experience and awareness, and raise the question of repressiveness. At the extreme, low scores reflect a placid emotional life that may be impervious to disruption.

Most Useful Comparisons: Scales 7 and 8, *ANX, FRS, OBS, DEP, HEA, BIZ, ANG, AGG, PSY, DIS.* It is helpful to compare the elevation on *NEN* with that of *PSY,* as this provides the best and most convenient quick measure of the profile's neurotic-psychotic balance.

≡ *Rapid Reference 7.20*

Personality Psychopathology–5 *(PSY–5)* Scales: *Low Positive Emotionality/Extroversion (LPE)*

Items: 34; 5 keyed *True*

Major Internal Correlates: Scales 2, 7, and *0, D1, D2, D4, D5, D-O, Hy3, Hy-O, Sc2, Sc4, Si1, Si2, DEP1, DEP2, LSE1, SOD1, SOD2, WRK, TRT1.*

Description: Items reflect social disengagement and a lack of emotional buoyancy. The largest subsets of items claim low energy and hedonic capacity, and social awkwardness/discomfort and withdrawal. Three smaller groups of items deny personal adequacy, persistence, and euphoria. An analogue of the 2-0/0-2 code type.

Interpretation: Characteristic features include anhedonia, anergy, dissatisfaction, low self-esteem, and a tendency to give up quickly in the face of difficulty. High scores suggest an impoverished emotional life more than the presence of unpleasant or aversive emotionality, as in the case of *NEN.* They may also reflect depressive withdrawal, schizoid underinvolvement, or both, depending on the particular pattern of items endorsed. The high *LPE* scorer is uncomfortable around other people and tends to avoid social situations. Relations with others are distant although not hostile. Rather, high *LPE* scorers tend to react to others impassively when interaction cannot be avoided.

(continued)

Low Scores: Present as sociable, outgoing, visible, warm, and socially attractive or charismatic. Relations with others are friendly and easy-going, based on high self-esteem, freedom from debilitating stresses, distinct pleasure in interaction with others, and mutual respect for their rights and freedoms. The low scorer describes high self-esteem; feeling liked and accepted by others; a quickness to feel pleasure and fulfillment; a deep reservoir of energy for pursuing goals; and a sense of happy connection with others that includes a desire for close and intimate relationships.

Most Useful Comparisons: Scales 2 and 0, D1, D-O, Si1, Si2, SOD1, SOD2, AGG, DIS. DIS may be an important modifier of LPE scores, with low scores on both scales suggesting that the social buoyancy of LPE is controlled and socially constructive. When DIS is high and LPE is low, the person's sociability is apt to be superficial and utilitarian. This combination suggests an especially high rate of social turnover, as the need for stimulation and novelty undermines loyalty and results in a lowered threshold for boredom in relationships. Conversely, low DIS in the context of high LPE reflects not only drastically curtailed social initiative, but a high tolerance for predictability and sameness in relations with others. This is a formula for relationships that, however long-lived, remain shallow. With moderately high AGG, the low LPE scorer may be more dominant and controlling and have significant problems with compromise.

≡ Rapid Reference 7.21a

Supplemental Scales: First Factor (Scale A [Anxiety])

Items: 39; 38 keyed True

Major Internal Correlates: Scales 7 and 8, D1, D5, Hy3, Pd5, Sc4, Si3, ANX, OBS, DEP, LSE, WRK, TRT, NEN, Mt, PK, PS, GM (low), and, negatively, K, S, and Es.

Most Useful Comparisons: See Major Internal Correlates above.

Description: Items reflect disturbed concentration and decision making; dysphoria, anxiety, and worry; fatigue, discouragement, and lack of initiative; inadequacy, inferiority, and sensitivity; and a sense of deviance and isolation. A is the best general marker for the general maladjustment/subjective distress dimension in the MMPI-2 item pool. It is most useful as an index or point of reference against which to judge the elevations of the primary internal correlates, since the latter are themselves highly intercorrelated, and are likely to elevate as a group. For example, when WRK is higher than ANX, OBS, DEP, and LSE, and also exceeds the elevation on A, it becomes more likely that the elevation on WRK relates to specific employment-related concerns rather than to more general distress, discomfort, concerns about functioning, and so on. Likewise, when *ANX* exceeds *OBS, DEP, LSE,* and *WRK,* and also exceeds *A,* the elevation on *ANX* is more likely to reflect specific anxiety-related symptoms (e.g., tension, dread, panic, worry, distractibility, shortness of breath, etc.) than general distress, dysphoria, rumination, and so forth. Because *A* begins to top out as *T*-scores reach about 80, these relationships may begin to break down at very high elevations. This scale is discussed more extensively in Friedman and colleagues (2001).

Interpretation: In general, high scorers may be described as uncomfortable, unhappy, and apprehensive. The anxiety they experience appears to be directed more toward a sense of their own incompetence than toward a sense of external threat. Their worry over the adequacy of their performances renders them hesitant, distractible, and vacillating, which makes them subject to others' influence. Under stress, they tend to become confused, disorganized, and maladaptive. They cope with their feelings of inadequacy by being cautious and standoffish, avoiding initiative and involvement, and inhibiting action. In interaction with others they tend to be timid, awkward, passive, and easily rattled. Provided that the pattern of validity indicators is not overly defensive, low scorers show confidence in their abilities, are comfortable, friendly, expressive, and assertive; they take initiative and are active, readily involved, vigorous, forceful, versatile, and achieving. In some cases, low scorers are better described as egocentric, ostentatious, overconfident, outspoken, competitive, overbearing, manipulative, reckless, and impulsive.

≣ *Rapid Reference 7.21b*

Supplemental Scales: Second Factor (Scale *R [Repression]*)

Items: 37; 0 keyed *True*

Major Internal Correlates: Scales 2, 3, and 9 (low), D2, D-S, Hy5, Ma2 (low), Ma-S (low), Si2, ASP (low), TPA2 (low), AGG (low), DIS (low), LPE, Re, MAC-R (low).

Most Useful Comparisons: See Major Internal Correlates above.

Description: A broad dimension of emotional control and inhibition. The kind of inhibition measured by *R* relates to the strength of impulse and emotionality, and to openness to experience. Items are heterogeneous in content, including poor health and physical symptoms; inhibited if not blunted emotionality, particularly with respect to "negative" feelings and feelings of energy and excitement; a lack of enjoyment in and underresponsiveness to the potential stimulation of group membership and social interaction; the avoidance of conflict, competition, and social visibility; and a denial of activities and interests in

(continued)

pursuits that may occasion fatigue or stimulation. Content suggests the suppression of emotionality and the avoidance of interactions with the human and nonhuman environment that may stimulate feeling, whether positive or negative. It also suggests a tendency to refer such feeling, when it occurs, to events in the somatic sphere. This scale is discussed more extensively in Friedman and colleagues (2001).

Interpretation: High scorers appear to be uncomfortable with more than minimal levels of stimulation and emotionality, and prefer to operate in circumstances that are conventional, predictable, familiar, and overlearned. Such preferences, in turn, suggest limitations in the individual's capacity to become aware of, identify, differentiate, and reflect upon feelings and other emotional phenomena, and form the basis for the person's constricted expression of emotionality. Low scores suggest a ready access to feeling and impulse even if not impulsively expressed, an openness to experiencing them, a prodigal and unstable pattern of interests, a high tolerance for stimulation, a willingness to entertain unfamiliar or unconventional points of view, and an ability to endure ambiguity, uncertainty, and conflict. Extremely low scores may be associated with chaotic emotionality, in which individuals feel flooded with emotionality or even euphoric, and are overinclusive and indiscriminate in their approach to expression.

═Rapid Reference 7.22

Supplemental Scales: *Ego Strength (Es)*

Items: 52; 20 keyed *True*

Major Internal Correlates: Negatively with scales *1, 2, 7,* and *8, D1, D4, D-O, Hy3, Hy4, Hy-O, Sc3, Sc6, ANX, DEP, HEA, WRK, Mt, PK, PS,* and, positively, with *GM*.

Most Useful Comparisons: Scales *A* and *K*. The interpretation of *Es* may be complicated by its covariation with the First Factor, such that *Es* and other scales having substantial First-Factor variance may be mutually affected. In psychiatric populations and among persons seeking mental health consultation, correlations between *Es* and *K* are commonly in a range of .50 to .60. Thus, high (or low) scores on one of these scales will tend to push scores on the other up (or down). As a result, a relatively low score on *K* when *Es* is substantially higher may lead to an underestimate of stress tolerance and adaptive functioning. Conversely, a relatively high *K* score when it substantially exceeds *Es* may reflect either a desire to portray greater adequacy in coping with problems and stresses than is justified, or depleted and precarious coping resources, or both.

Description: Developed by Barron (1953/1980) as a prognostic indicator for insight-oriented psychodynamic psychotherapy with "psychoneurotic" outpatients, items reflect physical functioning and physiological stability, psychasthenia and seclusiveness, personal adequacy/ability to cope, moral posture, sense of reality, and phobias/infantile anxieties. It appears to function as an indicator of control, organization, and resiliency under stress, and hence of stress tolerance. This scale is discussed more extensively in Friedman and colleagues (2001).

Interpretation: High scorers have been characteristically described as resourceful, independent, and self-reliant; possessing discipline and determination; showing initiative, flexibility, and tolerance; and as impressing others as being competent and capable and being easily accepted by them. At times they may be seen as aggressive, outspoken, and nonconforming if not rebellious toward authority. Thus they would seem to be able to use psychotherapy to supplement their own problem-solving resources, and to tolerate the self-scrutiny and confrontation that often occurs in this form of treatment without becoming upset. Little is known about the characteristics of patients (or others) who obtain very high scores (i.e., greater than T-75), but Gottesman (1959) has suggested, based on a review of several normal, delinquent, and psychiatric adolescent and adult samples, that unusually high scores may not reflect the aforementioned favorable traits, but rather be achieved by either underreporting psychopathology or by personality disturbed individuals who may be conflict-free but impulsive, such as psychopaths. Low scorers are unstable, overreactive, and subject to confusion in the face of stresses. They may be upset by seemingly minor matters; less tolerant of other people, despite being suggestible and dependent; inhibited, indecisive and procrastinating; and more rigid in their outlooks, in their choices of action, and in their approaches to problems.

≡ Rapid Reference 7.23

Supplemental Scales: *Overcontrolled-Hostility (O-H)*

Items: 28; 7 keyed *True*

Major Internal Correlates: Scales *L, K, S, Hy-S, Re,* and, negatively, *Ma2, Si3, OBS, ANG2, TPA1, TPA2, NEN.*

Most Useful Comparisons: See Major Internal Correlates above.

Description/Interpretation: Developed by Megargee, Cook, and Mendelsohn (1967) to identify prisoners characterized by high levels of hostile impulse existing side-by-side with massive, rigid, and unconscious inhibitions against hostile expression. For these individuals, assaultiveness was seen as an atypical response that would occur only rarely and unexpectedly, when the individual's

(continued)

normally hypertrophic defenses against the expression of hostility could be overcome. Whereas the undercontrolled individual's hostile reaction was typically proportional to its instigation, the overcontrolled individual's reaction was often seen as poorly calibrated to the instigating events, thereby increasing the importance of being able to identify the overcontrolled-hostile individual.

The item content of the *O-H* scale is quite heterogeneous, with few identifiable themes. High scorers portray themselves as free of tension and internal conflict, although not of occasional worries and fears; emotionally self-contained and impassive, if not underexpressive, imperturbable, and avoidant of stimulation and emotional or physical exertion. They deny impatience, irritability, and anger, and portray themselves as relaxed and tolerant of boredom and frustrations; as noncompetitive, and avoidant of willfulness and interpersonal conflict, but as nonetheless socially comfortable and able to seek advice from others. Given its origins, a major application of *O-H* is in classifying male prisoners convicted of violent offenses. Because of the low base rates for violence in most other populations, it is unsuitable as a basis for predictions of assault, violence, or dangerousness. However, *O-H* scores may be used to infer the presence or absence of a pattern of personality dynamics consisting of both hostile alienation and excessive inhibitions around the expression of aggressive or hostile impulses—both of which reside largely, if not entirely, outside of awareness. This pattern would appear to predict a vulnerability to accumulating resentments over time, and to a potential for releasing them in an explosive manner when provocations are great or when controls are diminished (e.g., due to intoxication). Quinsey, Maguire, and Varney (1983) found that their overcontrolled murderers lacked assertiveness and suggested that assertiveness training might alter the overcontrolled-hostile pattern. Fixed cutting scores have not been developed for *O-H*, and Megargee and colleagues (1967) recommended that cut-offs be established on the basis of local norms and the utilities attaching to false positive versus false negative decisions. For purposes of orientation, however, among white men raw scores of 15 or greater should raise the question of overcontrolled personality dynamics, with scores of 18 clearly indicating such dynamics, particularly when test indicators of self-favorable responding, False percentage, or both are no more than moderately elevated. Scores of 21 and above appear to be associated with strong external evidence of these dynamics, regardless of response style. There is some evidence that African-Americans and women score somewhat higher on *O-H*, suggesting the need to adjust these scores upward before inferring overcontrolled dynamics among members of these groups (Graham, 1977). Because *O-H* reflects a syndrome (hostility/resentment + impulse overcontrol + lack of awareness of these), low scores are largely without interpretive significance. That is, a low score might signify the absence of any or all of these elements. Thus, person A might be inhibited and overcontrolled but neither hostile nor resentful, while person B might be hostile and resentful but neither inhibited nor overcontrolled. This scale is discussed more extensively in Friedman and colleagues (2001).

≡Rapid Reference 7.24

Supplemental Scales: *Dominance (Do)*

Items: 25; 6 keyed *True*

Major Internal Correlates: Negatively with scales A, 7, 8, and 0, D1, D-O, Pd5, Pd-O, Sc3, Sc4, Si3, OBS, DEP1, DEP3, LSE, WRK, TRT1, NEN, Mt, PK, PS, and, positively, with Es.

Most Useful Comparisons: The Do construct appears to overlap significantly with that of Es.

Description/Interpretation: Developed by Gough, McClosky, and Meehl (1951) to identify positive social dominance (*not* domineering or autocratic behavior). Items are heterogeneous but reflect self-confidence, independence, relaxation, candor, and feelings of personal security; freedom from distractibility, indecision, worry, guilt, or preoccupations; sociability, good social skills, and social judgment; and constructive social attitudes, steadiness, and a capacity for self-restraint. High scorers demonstrate comfort, poise, initiative, and influence in social relationships. They appear secure, self-confident, self-assured, efficient, resourceful, and persevering. Their ability to elicit the confidence and social approval of others may enable them to ascend to positions of responsibility and leadership within the group. This description and interpretation appear to converge on Do, at least as measured in the MMPI/MMPI-2, as an indicator of *self-direction*. As a construct, self-direction encompasses aspects of internal locus of control and independence of judgment, but without the implications of self-sufficiency or social distancing that these concepts sometimes carry. This scale is discussed more extensively in Friedman and colleagues (2001).

≡Rapid Reference 7.25

Supplemental Scales: *Social Responsibility (Re)*

Items: 30; 6 keyed *True*

Major Internal Correlates: Negatively with Scale 4, Pd-O, Ma-O, Si3, ANG, CYN, ASP1, ASP2, TPA, FAM, MAC-R, AAS, and, positively, with K, S, Hy-S.

Most Useful Comparisons: It is noteworthy that the correlations of Do and Re with K are virtually identical, at .61 and .63, respectively, but their correlations with Es, at .68 and .38, respectively, are divergent.

Description/Interpretation: Developed by Gough, McClosky, and Meehl (1952) to identify "a ready willingness to accept the consequences of [one's]

(continued)

own behavior, dependability, trustworthiness, and a sense of obligation to the group" (p. 74). Items reflect conformity to rules and expectations; model comportment in school; low stimulation seeking and irritability; denial of self-consciousness, anger, resentment, or cynicism; the avoidance of conflict; and self-containment. High scorers are seen as conventional and conforming but tolerant and even-tempered. They have benign expectations of others, exhibit self-control, are team players, and are able and willing to pledge allegiance to the collectives of which they choose to be a part. Re measures a form of responsibility most likely to be manifested in institutional settings where creative demands are low. The institution may be as small as a family or club, or as large as a multinational corporation. The high Re scorer is one whose performance and achievement are best manifested in structured settings that place a premium on persistence, cooperation with others, and a duty-bound variety of conscientiousness. The core construct appears to be one of dutifulness. Thus, the responsible person is one on whom others can rely to observe and support the customs, norms, policies, and procedures of the institution and to advance its goals. The Re scale is widely used in employment screening (Butcher & Williams, 1992).

Although low scores can be readily interpreted in terms opposite the aforementioned qualities, guidelines for interpreting Re scores greater than 50T need further exploration and research. It appears likely, however, that as scores of about 60T are exceeded, the dispositions of high Re scorers may be less adaptive than those closer to the average range. Duckworth and Anderson (1986) speculate that higher-ranging scores may be associated with a lack of imagination and an excessive orientation to "oughts and shoulds," giving rise to attitudes that the examinee's associates may find annoying. Similarly, scorers in this range may be overly quick to identify with authority, regardless of its moral/ethical standing, and to sacrifice the interests of others, both within and outside the organization, in the pursuit of narrow organizational goals. For example, one would expect the company man to have a considerably higher Re score than the whistle blower, even though both might be seen as socially responsible. This scale is discussed more extensively in Friedman and colleagues (2001).

Rapid Reference 7.26

Supplemental Scales: *Mt, PK, and PS*

Items:
College Maladjustment (Mt): 41 items; 28 keyed *True*
Post-Traumatic Stress Disorder–Keane (PK): 46 items; 38 keyed *True*
Post-Traumatic Stress Disorder–Schlenger (PS): 60 items; 47 keyed *True*

Major Internal Correlates of All Three Scales (all > .85): Scales A, 7, and 8, D1, D4, D5, D-O, Sc4, ANX, DEP, DEP1, WRK, NEN.

Most Useful Comparisons: Caldwell (June 26, 1999, personal communication) has suggested scores on the PTSD scales be required to exceed scores
on *A* before diagnoses of PTSD are entertained.

Description/Interpretation: Scales *Mt, PK,* and *PS* are described together
because they contain virtually identical variances. They are mutually intercorrelated at .90 or greater, and all correlated with *A* and Scale 7 (raw) to the same
degree (Greene, 2000). Thus, these scales are all saturated with the First Factor, and none have features that reliably set one apart from the others, save
that *PK* may be scored completely within the first 370 items, making scores on
this scale available for the short form of the MMPI-2. *PK* and *PS* are most similar, containing 26 items in common.

Kleinmuntz (1960, 1961a) developed the *College Maladjustment (Mt)* scale
to identify college students with emotional problems that led them to seek
treatment at a university mental health clinic. The item responses of students
who sought counseling for emotional problems and remained for three or
more sessions were compared with those of students referred to the same
clinic for routine mental health screening for a teacher certification program
and who reported no previous treatment for mental health problems. Keane,
Malloy, and Fairbank (1984) developed their Post-Traumatic Stress Disorder
scale *(PK)* by testing 100 male VA Vietnam combat veterans for whom diagnoses of Post-Traumatic Stress Disorder (PTSD), often among other concurrent diagnoses, had been established on the basis of structured interviews and
psychophysiological measurements. They compared their responses with those
of 100 veterans who carried diagnoses other than PTSD. Schlenger and associates (Schlenger & Kulka, 1987; Schlenger et al., 1989) compared the item endorsements of Vietnam veterans diagnosed with PTSD (without concurrent
diagnoses) and nonpatient Vietnam veterans.

There are both empirical and conceptual reasons to doubt the utility of
these two PTSD scales for diagnosis. The chief empirical problem resides in the
absence of research demonstrating incremental validity for *PK* or *PS* over any
of several other scales with which they share substantial variance (e.g., *A* or
Scale 7). There is also no evidence that any of these scales satisfactorily discriminates patients with PTSD diagnoses from those with major anxiety and
depressive disorders. More troubling, the status of the diagnosis of PTSD is itself controversial (Young, 1995). Apart from relatively minor terminological
differences used to describe them, the symptoms of PTSD are typically indis-
tinguishable from those of better established mood and anxiety disorders.
Thus, differential diagnosis must be reckoned on the basis of etiology (i.e., putative trauma) rather than on presenting symptomatology.

Furthermore, the causal relationship between the symptoms of PTSD and
reports of traumatic events is not established (e.g., Yehuda & McFarlane,
1995), nor is the temporal stability for recall of traumatic events, even when
these are combat-related (Southwick, Morgan, Nicolaou, & Charney, 1997).
Litz, Orsillo, Friedman, Ehlich, and Batres (1997) reported that in a sample of

(continued)

Somalia peacekeepers, noncombat factors such as a lack of pride in military service and frustration with the mission were as important in predicting symptoms of PTSD as was combat experience. Presuming that a traumatic event is the etiological factor may shape the way that clinicians and patients construe familiar symptoms of depression, anxiety, panic, and so on as confirmatory bias. Furthermore, it tends to shift attention away from etiological factors (e.g., genetically influenced predispositions) that are better established as diatheses for such symptoms. Among veterans of military service, the population upon which the vast majority of PTSD research has been conducted, the potential etiological influence of disability compensation has received inadequate research attention. Pending the clarification of these empirical and conceptual issues, the clinical utility of PK and PS will remain uncertain. These scales are discussed more extensively in Friedman and colleagues (2001).

≡ Rapid Reference 7.27a

Supplemental Scales: *Gender Role–Masculine (GM)*

Items: 47 items; 19 keyed *True*

Major Internal Correlates: Scales A, 7, 8, and 0, D1, D5, D-O, Hy-O, Si3, ANX, FRS, OBS, DEP, DEP2, LSE, WRK, TRT, NEN, Mt, PK, PS, all negative.

Most Useful Comparisons: Scale 5, GF

Description: Peterson (1991; Peterson & Dahlstrom, 1992) developed the gender-role scales to serve as independent measures of masculine and feminine role identification. They sought to apply research and theory supporting a conception of masculinity and femininity as independent attributes of personality that could contribute to the understanding of both males and females. Using the MMPI-2 restandardization sample, items were selected for each of the gender-role scales if endorsed by at least 70% of members of one gender and by at least 10% *fewer* of the opposite gender. Items thus selected were then grouped into two scales. Those endorsed more commonly by men and less commonly by women comprise GM, a scale of 47 items (19 items are scored as *True*, 28 as *False*). Those with the opposite trend comprise GF, a scale of 46 items (15 items scored as *True*, 31 as *False*). Peterson's aspiration of independence for GM and GF was substantially realized in that the scales were found to correlate at only −.10 in the restandardization sample (Peterson & Dahlstrom, 1992). Note from the Major Internal Correlates (above) that GM is relatively saturated with the First Factor, with low GM scores corresponding to elevations of First Factor scales. This scale is unlikely to function well in patients with severe or active mental disorders, whether inpatient or outpatient, as scores will routinely be low in such cases.

Interpretation: High scorers tend to manifest traditional attributes of masculine strength, such as self-confidence, forthrightness, goal persistence, and freedom from fears, worries, self-consciousness, and social inhibition. Note that these attributes are somewhat culturally prescribed and stereotyped.

≡Rapid Reference 7.27b

Supplemental Scales: *Gender Role–Feminine (GF)*

Items: 46 items; 15 keyed *True*

Major Internal Correlates: Negatively with Scale 9, Pd2, Ma-O, ANG1, CYN, ASP1, ASP2, TPA2, DIS, MAC-R, AAS, and, positively, with Scale 5, D-S, Re.

Most Useful Comparisons: Scale 5, GM.

Description: See *GM*. Note from the Major Internal Correlates (above) that GF is aligned with the Second Factor, with low GF scores corresponding to elevations on most Second Factor scales (e.g., Scale 9, DIS, MAC-R). As with GM, this scale is unlikely to function well in patients with severe or active mental disorders, whether inpatient or outpatient, as scores will routinely be low in such cases.

Interpretation: High GF scores are associated with traditional feminine attributes of social circumspection, agreeableness, trust, loyalty, and the avoidance of conflict and impropriety. Such attributes are also somewhat culturally prescribed and stereotyped.

≡Rapid Reference 7.28

Addiction/Substance Abuse Scales: *MacAndrew Addiction Scale–Revised (MAC-R)*

Items: 49 items; 38 keyed *True*

Major Internal Correlates: Scale 9, Pd2, Ma-O, ANG1, CYN2, ASP1, ASP2, AGG, DIS, AAS, and, negatively, D-S, Hy5, R, Re, GF.

Most Useful Comparisons: AAS, R, DIS, and Pd-O versus Pd-S.

Description: MacAndrew (1965) developed the *MAC* scale by comparing the item responses of 200 outpatient alcoholics with those of 200 psychiatric outpatients with problems other than alcoholism. He found that a cutting

(continued)

score of 24 correctly classified about 82% of both his initial and cross-validation samples. In the transition to the MMPI-2, four items (three with religious content) were dropped. Because of the tradition of interpreting MAC on the basis of *raw* scores, these items were replaced with four new items that discriminated alcoholic from non-alcoholic psychiatric patients (McKenna & Butcher, 1987), and the revised scale was designated as MAC-R. Gottesman and Prescott (1989) criticized the use of raw cutting scores. Since the base rate for alcoholism in MacAndrew's derivation research (1965) was 50%, his cutting score of 24 is likely to produce an excess of false positives in most clinical and nonclinical settings. Gottesman and Prescott (1989) identified several groups for which classification on the basis of MAC scores is subject to large error rates. The first of these is members of the normal population such as those who may be tested as a part of employment screening or in the course of child custody disputes. For such persons, the use of MacAndrew's recommended cutting score may result in as high as three to six times as many false positives as true positives. The situation for normal women is much worse. Because the base rate for alcoholism among women in the general population is only about half of that for men (roughly 4% vs. 8%), the likelihood that a positive (i.e., a score at or above a cutting score favoring even high specificity, such as 24) will be a true positive may drop to as low as 1 in 14. Gottesman and Prescott's discussion of MAC in relation to adolescents and ethnic minorities also suggests caution when applied to these groups. Moreover, manipulating cutting scores to reduce the proportion of false positives can be achieved only by increasing the number of alcoholics who will go undetected. Even in settings with relatively high base rates for alcohol abuse, such as among psychiatric patients or correctional inmates, the development of local cutting scores is recommended to minimize misclassification.

To complicate matters further, Greene (1994) reported that profile configuration also can significantly influence MAC-R scores. In his analysis, code patterns dominated by Scales 4, 6, and especially 9 tended to have substantially higher MAC-R scores than code patterns dominated by Scales 1, 3, 7, and especially 2. As a result, for example, for any given cutting score, 4-9/9-4 code patterns will be associated with a relatively high false positive rate, and 2-7/7-2 code patterns with a relatively high false negative rate. On the other hand, scores below such a cutting score in the first instance, or above it in the second, are significantly more likely to be true negatives and true positives, respectively.

Finally, there may be some false negative cases that the MAC/MAC-R scale *should* miss. MacAndrew (1981) proposes a distinction between two kinds of alcoholics, reflecting "two fundamentally different character orientations" (p. 620). The first he designates primary alcoholics, those true positives identified by the MAC scale. From these he distinguishes a smaller group of secondary or "reactive" alcoholics, whom he describes as "neurotics-who-also-happen-to-drink-too-much" (p. 620). The extensive research on MAC/MAC-R has indicated that this scale reflects a much broader and more fundamental bipolar personality dimension, such that it may function as a measure of an important risk factor for substance abuse, rather than as an indicator of substance abuse itself. Several studies (Fowler, 1975; Kranitz, 1972; Lachar, Berman, Grisell, & Schoof, 1976; Rhodes & Chang, 1978; Sutker, Archer, Brantley, & Kilpatrick, 1979) have reported that drug abusers of various kinds (mostly heroin addicts) typically produce scores on the MAC in the same range as alcoholics, and Graham (1978) found similar scores in a sample of pathological gamblers. The outpatients studied by Graham and colleagues (1999) tended to conform in most respects with previous expectations regarding the empirical correlates of high scorers. Their patients, 75% of whom were Caucasian, tended to have long histories of abusing alcohol, marijuana, cocaine, or a combination of these. Although both men and women were seen as antisocial, acting out, and having conflicts with authority, these characteristics appeared especially strong among their women patients, who often had histories of many arrests, misdemeanor and felony convictions, impulsiveness, and a low tolerance for frustration. This cluster of traits is relatively stable over time. Hoffmann, Loper, and Kammeier (1974), for example, compared the MMPIs of 25 male alcoholics in treatment in a state hospital and the MMPIs these patients had completed as entering freshmen at the University of Minnesota. They found no differences in the MAC scores of these men, despite an average of 13 years between test administrations. A number of studies (Chang, Caldwell, & Moss, 1973; Gallucci, Kay, & Thornby, 1989; Huber & Danahy, 1975; Rohan, 1972; Rohan, Tatro, & Rotman, 1969) have reported that MAC scores show no change over the course of treatment or on follow-up. These findings provide yet another reason for interpreting MAC-R scores cautiously. The risk of misidentification cannot, in general, be circumvented through the use of such softened locutions as "potential for alcoholism" or "addiction prone" because such attributions may be equally harmful in their consequences, particularly among normals (e.g., job applicants). Although there is little doubt regarding validity of the MAC/MAC-R as a general measure of surgency, the bulk of research on its use for detecting alcoholism or addiction-proneness is equivocal, particularly for populations other than adult white men. Under these circumstances, the use of MAC scores for the prediction of substance abuse (or a liability thereto) in the individual case must be undertaken with caution. This scale is discussed more extensively in Friedman and colleagues (2001). Reviews by Gottesman and Prescott (1989), Graham and Strenger (1988), Greene and Garvin (1988), and MacAndrew (1981) are also recommended for further study.

Interpretation: High scorers are bold and energetic, self-confident and self-assertive, extroverted and sociable, uninhibited and impulsive, pleasure- and sensation-seeking, aggressive, rebellious, and resentful of authority, and may have been arrested or in trouble with the law. Low scorers are timid, anergic, inhibited, controlled, respectful of authority, and nonaggressive.

≡≡Rapid Reference 7.29

Addiction/Substance Abuse Scales: *Addiction Potential Scale (APS)*

Items: 39 items; 23 keyed *True*

Major Internal Correlates: Pd5, Ma2, ANX, ANG2, NEN, and, negatively, L, K, S, O-H, Re.

Most Useful Comparisons: AAS, MAC-R, A, R, DIS.

Description/Interpretation: Developed by Weed, Butcher, McKenna, and Ben-Porath (1992) from comparing the item endorsement rates between substance abusers and separate reference groups of normals and psychiatric patients. Items are very heterogeneous in content and difficult to characterize concisely. Like MAC-R, APS is a subtle measure of substance abuse. APS may be more sensitive to substance abuse in patients whose profiles show relatively high levels of distress (e.g., A, Scales 2, 7, and/or 8, etc.). It may better discriminate substance abusers from psychiatric patients than MAC-R, but the strength and reliability of APS for this purpose needs further confirmation. Little information is currently available for clinical description based on APS scores. The pattern of aforementioned internal correlates suggests that the high scorer may be emotionally distressed, with oversensitivity, guilt, irritability, but also acting out and irresponsibility.

≡≡Rapid Reference 7.30

Addiction/Substance Abuse Scales: *Addiction Admission Scale (AAS)*

Items: 13 items; 10 keyed *True*

Major Internal Correlates: Pd-5, Pd-O, ANG1, ASP2, FAM, DIS, and, negatively, S, Re.

Most Useful Comparisons: MAC-R, AAS.

Description/Interpretation: Developed by Weed, Butcher, McKenna, and Ben-Porath (1992) on internal consistency analyses of MMPI-2 items acknowledging substance abuse and related problems. This scale functions largely as a set of critical items for substance abuse problems, with high scorers acknowledging such problems and low scorers denying them.

Rapid Reference 7.31

Marital Distress (MDS)

Items: 14 items; 8 keyed *True*

Major Internal Correlates: Scales A, 4, 7, and 8, D5, Pd4, Pd5, Pd-O, Sc1, DEP, FAM1, WRK, TRT, NEN, Mt, PK, PS.

Most Useful Comparisons: Pd1, Sc1, FAM1, FAM2. The emphasis in MDS is on current rather than past (i.e., family of origin) family problems, so it is informative to compare elevations with scales more biased toward family of origin.

Description/Interpretation: Developed by Hjemboe, Almagor, and Butcher (1992), who determined the items based on their correlations with the ratings of couples' marital relationships (those of both normal couples and couples in marital counseling). High scorers report significant dysphoria and distress that focuses on relations within the family. MDS may not be suitable for patients not involved in committed relationships.

 TEST YOURSELF

1. The primary inference that may be justified by elevations on OBS is

   (a) obsessiveness.

   (b) indecision.

   (c) Obsessive-Compulsive Disorder.

   (d) Obsessive-Compulsive Personality Disorder.

2. The primary inference that may be justified by elevations on ANG is

   (a) the strong need to express anger.

   (b) the presence of angry feelings.

   (c) the desire to injure others.

   (d) the accumulation of resentments.

3. The primary inference that may be justified by elevations on ASP is

   (a) Antisocial Personality Disorder.

   (b) the presence of antisocial attitudes.

   (c) the admission of past antisocial behavior.

   (d) psychopathic narcissism.

(continued)

4. The primary inference that may be justified by elevations on *TPA* is

  (a) impatience with others.

  (b) job overinvolvement.

  (c) hard-driving competitiveness.

  (d) interpersonal hostility.

5. The primary inference that may be justified by elevations on *TRT* is

  (a) a lack of motivation for psychotherapy.

  (b) low self-disclosure.

  (c) depression.

  (d) antisocial trends.

6. On present evidence, scores on *TRT* justify an inference of

  (a) favorable psychotherapeutic outcome when high.

  (b) unfavorable psychotherapeutic outcome when high.

  (c) favorable psychotherapeutic outcome when low.

  (d) unfavorable psychotherapeutic outcome when low.

  (e) b and c.

  (f) none of the above.

7. Which scale among the *PSY-5* is least redundant with other MMPI-2 scales?

  (a) *AGG*

  (b) *PSY*

  (c) *DIS*

  (d) *NEN*

  (e) *LPE*

8. In evaluating the general dimension of behavioral control, which of the following scales is likely to be most satisfactory?

  (a) *R*

  (b) *ASP*

  (c) *DIS*

  (d) *TPA2*

  (e) *ANG1*

9. The Overcontrolled-Hostility scale is not suitable as a basis for predicting assault, violence, or dangerousness. True or False?

10. **The use of the Post-Traumatic Stress Disorder scales, *PK* and *PS*, for the diagnosis of PTSD is**

 (a) justified by research that establishes the *sensitivity* of these scales for this purpose.

 (b) justified by research that establishes the *specificity* of these scales for this purpose.

 (c) justified by research that establishes the incremental validity of these scales.

 (d) justified only when *PK* or *PS* exceeds *A* by at least 10 *T*-scores.

 (e) a and c.

 (f) c and d.

 (g) none of the above.

11. **The *Gender Role* scales, *GM* and *GF*, are dominated by the First and Second Factors of the MMPI-2, respectively.** True or False?

12. **For the three substance abuse measures, *MAC-R*, *APS*, and *AAS*, which statement(s) below is (are) justified?**

 (a) Only one is driven by item content.

 (b) Only one is highly vulnerable to underreporting.

 (c) Only one is traditionally associated with fixed cutting scores.

 (d) a, b, and c.

 (e) a and b.

 (f) a and c.

 (g) b and c.

Answers: 1. b; 2. a; 3. b; 4. d; 5. c; 6. f; 7. a; 8. c; 9. True; 10. g; 11. True; 12. d

Eight

PROFILE PATTERNS AND CODETYPES

DEFINING AND SELECTING THE CODETYPE

As noted earlier, the clinical scales are rarely elevated in isolation, making profiles with multiple peaks the rule, at least in clinical settings. Because of the standard error of measurement and extensive covariances among these scales, the selection of the particular codetype and how many elevated scales to include in the codetype (Spike vs. two-point vs. three-point, etc.) under which to commence actuarial interpretation is not always obvious. One simplifying strategy, the "well-defined" codetype (see, e.g., Greene, 2000) is to define the code by requiring that the highest (or second highest, etc.) exceed the next highest scale by a minimum of 5 *T*-scores to be included in the codetype. This strategy is generally sufficient to control the influence of measurement error, but may not be adequately responsive to the influences of scale covariation or response style (i.e., the tendency to over- or underreport psychopathology may affect some scales more than others). By definition, this strategy is also inadequate when the profile is not well defined. An alternative strategy, the "A-B-C-D Paradigm" proposed by Caldwell (1998), recommends arranging the five most elevated basic scales by pairs or triads according to a scheme in which the highest scale is assigned to position A, the second to position B, the third to position C, the fourth to position D, and the fifth to position E. Scale pairs are then prioritized in the following order: A-B, A-C, B-C, A-D, A-E. Thus, for a profile coded 6*27˝48′01+ −395/ F′-L/K: (see Chapter 11), the corresponding prioritized scale pairs are: *6-2, 6-7, 2-7, 6-4,* and *6-8.* Caldwell suggests that the primary codetype be defined by A-B, with the features of A-C interpreted within the context set by A-B (in this case the addition of tension and rigidity, for example), the features of B-C interpreted within the context of A-B and A-C (in this case adding features of anxious intropunitiveness, for example), and so on through

A-E. In instances where A, B, and C conform to a well-known three-point code, the first three scales (A-B-C) define the primary codetype, which may be modified in turn by scales appearing lower in the code according to the priorities, A-D, A-E, and A-F. Although the A-B-C-D strategy for codetyping remains to be established, it appears prima facie likely to extract more information from the pattern of MMPI-2 scores than the simpler "well-defined" strategy. In the absence of more validation for the A-B-C-D paradigm, it is suggested that the clinician should not feel overly constrained to follow Caldwell's sequence of priorities, especially when the pattern of scores among the subscales, content scales, and others such as *PSY-5* provides clear guidance for codetype selection/interpretation. For example, in the profile just given, the *6-8* codetype corresponds to the A-D positions and would typically be fourth in line to be integrated into the analysis of the profile pattern, after A-B, A-C, and B-C. However, clear elevations among scales like *Pa1, BIZ, BIZ1,* and *PSY* would recommend that the implications of active psychotic processes and content enter the interpretation at a much earlier point in the sequence of scale pairs.

The relative elevations of the obvious and subtle subscales may also aid codetyping decisions. In most cases, especially when underreporting can be ruled out, the order of scores on the obvious subscales can be an important vantage point for viewing the order of the basic scales in the code, whether as check or as contrast. For example, in the profile just given, the relative elevations of the obvious and subtle subscales for Scales *2, 4,* and *6* tend to confirm the importance of these scales in the code. Even though Scale *3* falls low in the code, the large difference between *Hy-O* and *Hy-S* would suggest the importance of somatization in the clinical picture, an emphasis that might be overlooked if codetype interpretation were restricted to the 5 highest scales.

Codetypes

Spike 1

- Dissatisfaction and concerns about health and physical functioning, but usually with limited emotional distress. Look for compromised efficiency in work and reduced enjoyment of leisure and recreation.
- Overly favorable in self-report, portraying him/herself as free of emotional and cognitive problems, and as confident, independent, responsible, outgoing, and identified with family.

- Check: *HEA1, HEA2, HEA3, D3, HY4, Sc6*
- Treatment: May be resistant to insight and psychological approaches.

1-2/2-1

- Concerns about health and physical functioning. Aches and pains, with accompanying emotional distress and discomfort (e.g., moodiness, unhappiness, irritability), especially somatically focused anxiety and apprehensions of serious illness, physical breakdown, and declining health. Preoccupation with somatic symptoms may obscure signs of depression (e.g., "masked depression") such as fatigue, disturbed sleep, pessimism, and dysphoria. Tend to be passive, dependent, immature, and avoidant. May be disgruntled about their medical care. Look for cognitive problems and low intellectual efficiency, depression, substance abuse, reduced efficiency in work, and a lack of interest in leisure and recreation.
- Check: *HEA1, HEA2, HEA3, ANX, DEP, DEP1, WRK, D1, D3, D4, Hy3, Hy4, Sc2, Sc3, Sc4, Sc6, AAS, APS.*
- Treatment: May be resistant to insight and psychological approaches. Prone to become impatient, frustrated with treatment, or both. Prefers medical explanations for emotional problems. May abuse medications for pain or sleep.

1-2-3

- Like *1-2/2-1* but with greater chronicity, vulnerability to stress, more somatization, (paradoxically) more optimism and acceptance of physical complaints, and better social skills. Less irritability and sleep disturbance, but greater inability to work. May be dependent, passive/submissive, passive-aggressive, conflicted about self-assertion, or a combination of these. May try to control family via symptoms/disability.

1-2-3-4/2-1-3-4/2-4-1-3

- Like *1-2/2-1* but with greater vulnerability to stress, intolerance of frustration, demandingness, and hostile-dependent relationships with intimates. Look for chronic alcoholism, hostility toward women (in men), ulcers, unstable employment histories.

1-2-3-7/2-1-3-7

- Like *1-2/2-1* but with greater vulnerability to stress and less irritability. Tense, apprehensive, fearful, and phobic. May form passive-dependent relationships with intimates and develop substance dependencies. Look for back and chest pain, cardiac complaints, and unemployability.

1-2-4

- Like *1-2/2-1* but more irritable, depressed, and alienated. Prone to complaining, bitterness, and noncompliance with treatment if not active in efforts to defeat or sabotage treatment. See *1-4/4-1; 2-4/4-2.*

1-2-7/2-1-7

- Like *1-2/2-1* but more overtly anxious, obsessive, and self-conscious, and with more disturbance in routine cognitive functions. Disturbed sleep. More dependent but fewer conflicts over dependency; higher threshold for acting out. See *1-7/7-1; 2-7/7-2.*

1-2-8/2-1-8

- Like *1-2/2-1* but more overtly depressed, with greater overall levels of distress, apprehension, weakness/fatigue, apathy, and disability, and more cognitive disruption, more impaired self-esteem, and less adequate behavioral controls. A greater proportion of neurologic-like symptoms, motor, sensory, and cognitive (e.g., concentration, memory), and a relatively high likelihood of symptoms that are peculiar if not delusional, along with disturbed sleep. There is greater alienation from others, less adequate social skills, significantly reduced efficiency, and greater anger and cynicism. See *1-8/8-1; 2-8/8-2.*

1-2-9/2-1-9

- Somatization and emotional turmoil or agitation. Possible panic over physical symptoms. Consider neuropsychological evaluation. See *1-9/9-1; 2-9/9-2.*

1-2-0/2-1-0

- Somatization and withdrawal. Schizoid features with dysphoria/depression and defeatism. Check fourth highest scale.

1-3/3-1 (1-3-2/3-1-2)

- Definition: Scale *3* must exceed Scale *2* by at least 8 *T*-scores. Ideally, Scales *1* and *3* should exceed Scale *2* by at least 10 *T*-scores and Scale *2* should exceed all other scales by at least 5 *T*-scores.
- Individuals are preoccupied with somatic symptoms and health problems about which they show mild anxiety, and are prone to develop physical symptoms under stress. Far fewer somatic symptoms than *1-2/2-1,* and these tend to be localized to the extremities or to involve problems around eating. Numbness, tremor, dizziness, and fatigue are common. Not incapacitated, but inefficient and easily tired. Socially skilled, forward, and outgoing. Expressive but also inhibited. Conventional. Wants to be seen as self-confident, upbeat, friendly, cheerful, trusting, responsible, and "normal"; prefers to have things "nice," "pleasant," and "happy," and seeks to achieve this by carrying on despite symptom(s), looking at things on the bright side and avoiding things that might be unpleasant or upsetting. Subtle avoidances of responsibility. Seen as more dependent and demanding by others than by self. Doesn't like to complain; may feel worse than appearance would suggest.
- Check: *HEA1, HEA2, HEA3, ANX, DEP, DEP1, WRK, D1, D3, D4, Hy3, Hy4, Sc3, Sc4, Sc6; Hy-O* versus *Hy-S; Hy3* versus *Hy4;* and those scales related to the nonsomatic features of the Scale *3* syndrome: *CYN1* (low), *CYN2* (low), *ASP1* (low), *ASP2* (low), *TPA1* (low), *TPA2* (low), *SOD2* (low), *Hy1, Hy2, Hy5, Ma4, Si1* (low), *R, O-H.*
- Treatment: May be resistant to insight and psychological approaches. Nonintrospective. Prefers medical explanations for emotional problems. Suggestible. Focused on symptomatic relief. Tolerates support well. Gather recent precipitating events, and look for secondary gain and a history of loss. May abuse medications for pain or sleep.

1-3-4/3-1-4

- Like *1-3/3-1* but with greater needs for approval. Manipulative, dependent, and fearful of rejection. Potential problems with anger control. See *3-4/4-3, O-H.*

1-3-6/3-1-6

- Like *1-3/3-1* but more self-centered, hypersensitive, resentful of demands, and covertly angry and suspicious. See *3-6/6-3*.

1-3-7/3-1-7

- Like *1-3/3-1* but more anxiety, tension, guilt and dysphoria. Often phobic. Anxiety may be disabling. Look for cardiac and epigastric complaints, panic attacks; dependent features such as fear of conflict, inhibition of anger, and tolerance for domination. See *1-7/7-1; 3-7/7-3*.

1-3-8/3-1-8

- Like *1-3/3-1* but with far greater emphasis on cognitive, sensory, musculoskeletal, and neurological symptoms (e.g., dizziness, tremor, blurred vision, amnesia). Depressed, with suicidal ideation; fearful, tense, possibly withdrawn. Look for paranoid/schizotypal features, religious and sexual content, and sexual identity issues.
- Check: *D4, Hy4, Sc3, Sc6, HEA2.* See *1-8/8-1; 3-8/8-3*.

1-3-9/3-1-9

- Like *1-3/3-1* but with more activity, energy, self-confidence, and social fearlessness and aggression. Lower emotional and behavioral inhibition. Look for high needs for approval, demandingness, frustration intolerance, irritability, acting out, narcissism, grandiosity, deceitfulness, and manipulations leading to family conflict. Consider neuropsychological evaluation.
- Check: *D4, Sc3, Sc6, HEA2, Ma4, DIS.* See *1-9/9-1; 3-9/9-3*.

1-4/4-1

- Emphasis on gastrointestinal symptoms not infrequently associated with alcohol abuse. Other somatic complaints and health concerns are common. Discontent and dysphoric. Very intolerant of stress; fears of disability. Immature and dependent (hostile dependency). Family estrangement and generally poor relations with others, with control avoidance, acting out, self-centeredness, entitlement, aggressiveness or passive aggression, grouchiness, dissatisfaction, demandingness, stubbornness, controllingness, complaining, blaming, bitterness, and conflict. Look for a history of drug-seeking, irresponsibility, delinquency, authority conflicts, employment instability, marital conflict, and arrests.

- Check: *HEA1, HEA2, HEA3, DEP, DEP1, ASP2, FAM2, WRK, D1, D3, D4, Hy3, Hy4, Pd1, Pd2, Pd4, Pd5, Pa1, Sc3, Sc4, Sc6, Re* (low), *MAC-R, AAS.*
- Treatment: May be resistant to insight and psychological approaches. Poorly motivated to change. Prone to authority conflicts with therapist and unreliability in the reporting of history and events.

1-5/5-1

- Men: (Uncommon) Passive, dependent, complaining, fussy; avoidant of responsibilities; rationalizing. Check third highest scale.
- Women: (Rare) Complaining, coarse, insensitive. Mild anxiety and fearfulness. Check third highest scale.

1-6/6-1

- Feelings of somatic vulnerability; wide range of somatic complaints, especially tension, fatigue, disturbed sleep, and headache, with fears that such complaints won't be taken seriously; projection, suspiciousness, resentment, and persecutory ideation. Significant anxiety; some fearfulness. Socially alienated. Sensitive and overreactive to criticism; resentful of demands; quick to feel dominated and to resist. Querulous and peevish. Chronic conflicts with others; irritable, angry, blaming; feels mistreated; stubborn and rigid. Look for somatic symptoms on a delusional basis; other signs of psychosis.
- Check: *HEA1, HEA2, HEA3, ANX, DEP, DEP1, DEP2, BIZ, BIZ1, CYN2, TPA2, WRK, PSY, D3, D4, Hy3, Hy4, Pd4, Pa1, Pa3* (low), *Sc1, Sc3, Sc6, Ma4.*
- Treatment: Quick to experience therapy as critical, demanding, and controlling; and to place therapist in no-win positions. Irritable. Fears not being taken seriously. Resentful of exploration; suspicious of support.

1-7/7-1

- Wide range of somatic complaints, especially chronic tension, cardiovascular complaints, and problems with thinking, memory, and concentration. High general distress. Apprehensive, anxious, and obsessed about physical illness and mental and physical breakdown; fears sudden onset of severe illness; fears loss of mental function and control. Some guilt and dysphoria usually present. Disturbed sleep. Feels inadequate and inferior; feels unable to perform duties and responsibilities and seeks to avoid these. Prefers others take responsibility. May be passive-aggressive and avoidant. Socially awkward, self-conscious, and unassertive, but also irritable. Look for association between accident or injury and onset of symptoms.

- Check: *HEA1, HEA2, HEA3, ANX, OBS, DEP, DEP1, DEP2, BIZ, BIZ1, ANG2, TPA1, SOD2, WRK, NEN, D1, D3, D4, Hy3, Hy4, Pd5, Sc3, Sc4, Sc6, Si1, Do* (low).
- Treatment: May be resistant to insight and psychological approaches; benefit from behavioral approaches. Intellectualized. Treatment plans initially focused on relief of anxiety and such problems as disturbed sleep are more effective than those targeting somatization. Later, may benefit from plans emphasizing "work hardening."

1-8/8-1

- Emphasis on cognitive and unusual sensory and musculoskeletal symptoms, and lethargy, but with many others as well. Multiple mental symptoms, including distractibility, forgetfulness, impaired judgment, derealization, intrusive thoughts, and cognitive disruption/disorganization. Peculiar ideas about health problems or bodily functions, if not somatic delusions, should be ruled out, as should hallucinations and ideas of reference. Spends much time in fantasy and daydreaming. Immaturity, fearfulness, anxiety, depression, and anhedonia are probable. Depression may be more evident in lethargy and apathy; vegetative signs and symptoms, including sleep disturbance; and in depressive cognition and attitudes (pessimism, helplessness, hopelessness, worthlessness) than in depressed mood. Sexual problems. Anger, hostility, irritability, and inchoate rage often significant. Severe social alienation, with suspicion and mistrust; seen by others as eccentric and peculiar. Passive-aggressive and schizotypal trends are common. Look for history of under- and unstable employment, nomadic lifestyle, rootlessness, suicidal ideation, thought disorder, and paranoid ideation.

- Check: *HEA1, HEA2, HEA3, A NX, FRS1, DEP, DEP1, DEP4, BIZ, BIZ1, BIZ2, CYN1, CYN2, LSE1, WRK, PSY, D1, D3, D4, Hy3, Hy4, Pd4, Pa1, Sc1, Sc2, Sc3, Sc4, Sc5, Sc6.*
- Treatment: Rule out schizophrenia-spectrum disorder. Resistant to insight, reassurance, and psychological approaches. Treatment plans initially focused on relief of psychotic symptoms, depression, anxiety, and problems such as disturbed sleep are more effective than those targeting somatization. Course tends to be chronic.

1-9/9-1

- Multiple somatic complaints with emotional volatility, tension, irritability, restlessness, agitation, drivenness, and behavioral undercontrol (e.g., explosiveness). May focus on physical symptoms to distract from interpersonal problems. Extroverted and outgoing but conflicted over dependency versus independence, with stubbornness and demandingness. Self-confident but unrealistic. May be grandiose. Quick to feel dominated or "bossed." Others may see them as compensating and as difficult in relationships, but with little or no insight into this. Physical symptoms may be partially embraced as an excuse for underachievement. Look for narcissistic or antisocial trends; mood disorder (e.g., mania) or reaction to physical narcissistic injury, especially one that has created a permanent change in health status, mobility, function, or appearance, and has frustrated ambition; and for possible suicidal ideation as a reaction to such injury.
- Check: *HEA1, HEA2, HEA3, DEP4, ANG1, LSE1* (low), *LSE2* (low), *SOD1* (low), *SOD2* (low), *AGG, D3, Hy3, Hy4, Pa1, Sc5, Sc5, Sc6, Ma2, Ma4, Si1* (low), *Si2* (low).
- Treatment: Rule out mood disorder. May be resistant to insight and psychological approaches. Benefits from support. Treatment plans initially focused on current difficulties and interpersonal struggles, and on major apprehensions about the future of work, relationships, and so forth are more effective than those targeting somatization. Consider neuropsychological evaluation.

1-0/0-1

- Look for somatic preoccupation and social isolation. Conventional and resigned. Check third highest scale.

Spike 2

- Mild to moderate dysphoria with sad affect and complaints of inefficiency, irritability, and a loss of interest, self-confidence, and pleasure in living. Depression may be minimized or denied. May complain of anergia and be self-critical, especially as an overreaction to perceived mistakes, or personal faults. Guilt and intropunitiveness; passivity and underassertiveness. Look for recent loss or setback (i.e., reactive elements).

- Check: *HEA3, DEP1, DEP2, DEP3, DEP4, AGG* (low), *D1, D2, D3, D4, D5, D3, Hy3, Hy4, Pa1, Sc4, Ma* (low), *Ma1* (low), *Ma2* (low), *Ma3* (low), *Ma4* (low).

- Treatment: Rule out Major Depression. Evaluate suicidal ideation. Generally responsive to a broad range of treatments, including reassurance, advice, assertiveness training, exercise, and formal psychotherapy.

2-3/3-2

- Much more frequent in women. Associated with so-called atypical depression/hysteroid dysphoria. Episodic dysphoric mood with crying and unhappiness; health concerns, fatigue, exhaustion, anxiety, insecurity, emotional overcontrol, and overreactiveness to stresses. May deny depression despite appearing manifestly unhappy. Problems with memory, concentration, and judgment, but without gross cognitive disruption. Disturbed sleep and loss of sexual interest. Conventional, conscientious, and responsible but dependent, avoidant, subassertive, and intropunitive, with self-depreciation and feelings of worthlessness, helplessness, hopelessness, and inadequacy. Excessive emotional control or constriction; feels "bottled up." Overly sensitive to criticism and rejection, but strongly inhibited in expressing aggression, anger, and mistrust. Others find them dependent, immature, self-sacrificing, and prone to martyrdom. Look for secondary or situational depression, interpersonal stresses such as marital conflict, recent losses/break-ups in relationships, and sexual maladjustment.

- Check: *ANX, DEP1, DEP2, DEP4, CYN1* (low), *CYN2* (low), *ASP1* (low), *ASP2* (low), *TPA2* (low), *AGG* (low), *D1, D2, D3, D4,*

D5, D3, Hy3, Hy4, Pd2 (low), *Sc2, Sc3, Sc4, Sc6, Ma4* (low), *R, MAC-R* (low).

- Treatment: Rule out Major Depression and alexithymia. May be resistant to insight and psychological approaches. Nonintrospective. Suggestible. May find it difficult to speak with candor about unpleasant situations, relationships, feelings, and dissatisfactions with treatment. Focused on symptomatic relief. Tolerates support well. Gather recent precipitating events. Look for history of loss or interpersonal conflict. May abuse medications for pain or sleep. See *1-2-3, 2-1-3/2-3-1.*

2-3-1/2-1-3

- Somatization in the context of anxiety, insecurity, depression, and helplessness, with inhibition. See *1-2-3, 2-3/3-2.*

2-3-4/3-2-4

- Dysphoric or depressed. Also immature and dependent. See *2-3/3-2; 3-4/4-3.*

2-3-7/2-7-3/3-2-7/3-7-2/7-2-3/7-3-2

- Like *2-7/7-2* but more dependent, helpless, and appealing, and lacking in insight. Somewhat less anxious and depressed with reduced suicide risk. More conforming, conventional, and trusting. May be docile, with clinging dependency. See *2-3/3-2; 2-7/7-2; 3-7/7-3.*

2-4/4-2

- Definition: The specific characteristics of the *2-4/4-2* code vary markedly with the third highest scale. See especially *2-4-6, 2-4-7, 2-4-8, 2-4-9,* and combinations.
- Depressed mood, anhedonia, anxiety, tension, frustration, irritability, impulsiveness, anger, and often exaggerated guilt and self-reproach. May be critical, argumentative, and resentful. Both intro- and extropunitive. Chronically poor response to stress. Depression is often externalized and situational. Interpersonally difficult, with irresponsibility, dependency conflicts, belligerence, argumentativeness, manipulations, and resentment. Look for a long-term pattern of irresponsibility and self-defeating conduct; family alienation; chronic marital discord; and a history of childhood deprivation, delinquency, authority conflicts, substance abuse, arrests, and job losses.

- Check: *ANX, DEP1, DEP2, DEP3, DEP4, HEA3, ANG1, ANG2, ASP2, TPA1, LSE1, FAM1, FAM2, DIS, D1, D2, D3, D4, D5, Hy3, Pd1, Pd2, Pd3, Pd4, Pd5, Pa1, Sc2, Sc4, AAS, MDS.*
- Treatment: Seeks symptomatic relief. Relatively low motivation for treatment despite strong expressions of regret for past conduct and desire for change. Unreliable about keeping appointments and following through on agreements reached in therapy.

2-4-3/4-2-3

- Like *2-4/4-2* but with better socialization and unstable controls. See *2-3/3-2; 2-4/4-2; 3-4/4-3.* Check *O-H.*

2-4-6/2-6-4/4-2-6/4-6-2/6-2-4/6-4-2

- Like *2-4/4-2* but more anxious. Bitter, resentful, and rationalizing, but also dependent, with strong needs for affection. Passive-aggressive, schizotypal, avoidant, or dependent features, or a combination of these. Possibility of psychotic, especially paranoid, ideation. More alienated; less adequate controls. Depression, when present, is more externalized. Look for demandingness and blaming, even blaming others for depression; marital and sexual conflict. See *2-6/6-2; 4-6/6-4.*

2-4-7/2-7-4/4-2-7/4-7-2/7-2-4/7-4-2

- Like *2-4/4-2* but with greater general distress; more anxious, insecure, and tending to be more compulsive rather than impulsive but nevertheless erratic. "Hyperresponsible but self-defeating, anxious and guilty but acting out, clinging and dependent but emotionally distancing" (Friedman et al., 2001, p. 263). More cognitive disruption and intrusive thoughts. Less overall alienation. More intropunitive. More dependent and submissive; may be self-flagellating in response to guilt, rejection, or loss; may undermine others' anger toward them with self-criticism. Tend to catastrophize stressful events. Less alienation from family but stressful to spouses. Fewer substance abuse–related legal difficulties. Look for a cyclical pattern of acting out followed by periods of relative control; alcoholism; impulsive suicide attempts. See *2-4/4-2, 2-7/7-2,* and *4-7/7-4. MAC-R* scores may be false negative.

2-4-8/2-8-4/4-2-8/4-8-2/8-2-4/8-4-2

- Like *2-4/4-2* but with much greater general distress, severe alienation from others, fear of emotional involvement, pervasive mistrust, and suicidal ideation. More somatic concern. Moderate to severe depression and pessimism, more anxiety, and greater overall sense of disability. Often unable to maintain employment. Relatively severe impairment of impulse, cognitive, and behavioral controls. More anger, resentment, irritability. Cognitive impairments ranging from forgetfulness and distractibility to intrusive thoughts, hallucinations, and delusions of reference and persecution. Chronically poor judgment. Look for a history of rejection, exploitation, or both; gross behavioral instability with substance abuse, multiple suicide attempts, self mutilation, and sexual maladjustment. See *2-4/4-2, 2-8/8-2,* and *4-8/8-4. MAC-R* scores may be false negative.

2-4-9/4-2-9

- Like *2-4* but with greater self-centeredness, immaturity, and problems in impulse control. Look for substance abuse, instability of employment, and a history of legal difficulties.

2-5/5-2

- Look for chronic anxiety or depression (men) or depression (women); problems with passivity, dependency, conflict in close relationships, accepting responsibilities, and sexual adjustment. Identity may be confused or diffuse. Check third highest scale.

2-5-8

- Passivity, apathy, dysphoria or depression, and anhedonia. Sexual maladjustment and sexual identity concerns may be severe.

2-6/6-2

- Moderate to severe depression and anxiety with hypersensitivity and resentment. Both intropunitive and extropunitive. Depression manifested in sad mood, crying, anhedonia, depressive ideation and attitudes, impairment of concentration and reasoning, weakness and fatigue, health concerns, and disturbed sleep. Seen as moody, bitter, argumentative, resentful, and often depressed "at" others. Make others angry and resentful by their own resentfulness, in a vicious circle.

May harbor fantasies of suicide to get even with others for perceived slights. Quick to take offense and feel victimized, and to interpret criticism as deliberately cruel and hostile; touchy. Projects hostility. Overreaction to imagined slights; demands for admissions of hurtful intent and reparations; these traits combined with self-defeating rigidity, hyperrationality, and a lack of impulse to forgive or reconcile often leads to hostile rejection. Look for a history of maltreatment, chronic relationship losses, feeling trapped, current conflicts in primary relationships, escalating hostilities, and temper outbursts.

- Check: *ANX, DEP1, DEP2, DEP3, DEP4, HEA3, BIZ1, BIZ2, ANG1, ANG2, CYN1, CYN2, TPA1, FAM1, FAM2, WRK, PSY, D1, D2, D3, D4, D5, Hy3, Pd1, Pd4, Pa1, Pa2, Pa3, Sc1, Sc2, Sc4, MDS.*
- Treatment: Rule out psychotic disorder. Lacks and resists insight into how behavior antagonizes others, and is quick to view therapist as critical, blaming, and unsympathetic. Exploratory/insight-oriented therapy is seen as threatening, intrusive, and critical in its aims. Treatment plans focused on mood disorder are generally more effective than a focus on history and relationships, at least initially. Cognitive-behavioral and skill-building approaches such as assertiveness training and anger management are helpful.

2-6-8

- See *2-6/6-2, 2-8/8-2,* and *6-8/8-6.*

2-7/7-2

- Definition: The specific characteristics of the *2-7/7-2* code vary considerably with the third highest scale. See especially *2-7-3, 2-7-4, 2-7-8,* and combinations.
- Moderate to severe depression with tension, anxiety, worry, foreboding, obsessions and intrusive thoughts, insecurity, apprehensiveness, agitation, and intropunitiveness. Depression is manifested in dysphoria and sad affect; feelings of helplessness, hopelessness, worthlessness, pessimism, and inadequacy; suicidal ideation; problems with concentration, memory, judgment, and decision making; and vegetative symptoms such as anhedonia, sleep disturbance, loss of appetite, weight loss, and loss of sexual interest. Guilt and themes of failure, uselessness, and being overwhelmed are common. Ruminates about

personal shortcomings and failures, overanticipates negative outcomes, and overreacts to minor problems and mistakes. May be overresponsible, inflexible, meticulous, and perfectionistic. Withdrawn and introverted; feels awkward, self-conscious, and easily embarrassed around others. Dependent, unassertive, and inhibited in expressing aggression, anger, and hostility. Look for conscientiousness, a history of self-denial, of achievement and taking on excessive responsibilities, and becoming overwhelmed. *2 > 7* more common in depressive disorders; *7 > 2* more common in anxiety disorders.

- Check: *ANX, FRS1, OBS, DEP1, DEP2, DEP3, DEP4, HEA3, LSE1, LSE2, WRK, AGG* (low), *D1, D2, D3, D4, D5, Hy3, Pd5, Pa2, Sc2, Sc3, Sc4, A, R, Es* (relative to *K*) , *MAC-R* (low).

- Treatment: Some preservation of insight, psychological mindedness, and capacity for introspection. Responds well to support, limited reassurance, structure, and graduated expectations. Cognitive and interpersonal therapies and skills training methods (e.g., assertiveness) are helpful, as are more traditional insight therapies so long as these employ measures that counteract passivity and a tendency to delay implementation of behavior change.

2-7-8 / 2-8-7 / 7-2-8 / 7-8-2 / 8-2-7 / 8-7-2

- Definition: With *2-8-7* and *8-2-7* codes, consider interpretation under the *2-8/8-2* code.
- Moderate to severe depression with suicidal ideation, anxiety, fearfulness and phobias, anhedonia, obsessional worry and rumination, compulsions, self-depreciation, psychomotor retardation, pessimism, tension, agitation, and negative self-concept. Feelings of worthlessness, hopelessness, helplessness, inadequacy, and inferiority. Severe impairment in concentration and decision making, but memory, judgment, reasoning, and problem solving are better preserved than in *2-8/8-2*. May be periodically disoriented. Tends to ruminate and obsess about own faults, guilts, and failures, and about potential future catastrophes. Markedly intropunitive; may be compulsively self-critical and self-accusatory. May gravitate toward esoteric ideas, philosophies, and religions; magical ideation. May be seen as deliberately self-defeating by setting unrealistically high standards for their

performance, but fearful about their ability to meet challenges and responsibilities. Compulsive, meticulous, and perfectionistic. Apprehensive and overreactive to minor upsets or mishaps. Vegetative signs of depression, including sleep disturbance, weakness, tiredness, and fatigue; somatic complaints such as GI problems are common. Catastrophic concerns about physical illness. Schizotypal features are common in the absence of manifest psychosis. Derealization and ideas of reference are usually tied to the patient's sense of personal sinfulness, evil, or inferiority. Introverted, socially self-conscious, and avoidant, but may seek support. Sensitive. Ambivalence in close relationships with fear of emotional involvement. Conflicted about dependency, fearful of domination, but tends to be trusting of authority. Look for manifest psychotic ideation, thought disorder, hallucinations, and delusional ideation; a history of social isolation; and identity and sexual concerns. May be severe suicide risk.

- Check: *ANX, FRS1, OBS, DEP1, DEP2, DEP3, DEP4, HEA1, HEA2, HEA3, BIZ1, BIZ2, ANG1* (low), *CYN2* (low), *TPA2* (low), *LSE1, LSE2, SOD1, WRK, AGG* (low), *PSY, NEN, D1, D2, D3, D4, D5, Hy1* (low), *Hy3, Hy4, Pd2* (low), *Pd4, Pd5, Pa1, Pa2, Sc1, Sc2, Sc3, Sc4, Sc5, Sc6, A, Es, MAC-R* (low), *Re, MDS*.

- Treatment: Rule out Bipolar Disorder, Depressed; Schizophrenia, Undifferentiated; Schizoaffective Disorder. Biological treatments more immediately effective than psychotherapy to improve symptomatic status and reduce suicide risk. Some risk of antidepressants precipitating mania. More accepting of structure and support, less well defended but less defensive, more access to insight, and more cognitively resourceful than *2-8/8-2*. Supportive and cognitive therapies are effective in the post-acute phase. Need direction as well as support. Better overall outcomes than *2-8/8-2*.

2-8/8-2

- Similar to *2-7-8/2-8-7/7-2-8/7-8-2/8-2-7/8-7-2*. Severe depression with suicidal ideation, anhedonia, apathy, blunted or inappropriate affect, anxiety, psychomotor retardation, pessimism, agitation, and fixed negative self-concept. Convictions of worthlessness, hopelessness, and helplessness. Severe impairment in concentration, memory, judgment, thinking, and decision making, and chronic feelings of inadequacy and inferiority. Thinking is ruminative, stereotyped, and unproductive, and efficiency is markedly reduced, often to the point of disability. Feelings of guilt may be accompanied by self-loathing. Vegetative signs of depression, somatic delusions, nihilistic delusions, derealization, and schizotypal features may be present. Socially withdrawn; actively avoids/discourages interaction; fears emotional closeness; is mistrustful, irritable, impatient, and resentful toward others. May be viewed as markedly incompetent (e.g., accident prone), and quick to give up. Acting out and problems with impulse control not uncommon. Look for manifest psychotic ideation, thought disorder, confusion, tangentiality, hallucinations, and delusions of persecution and control (especially with Scale *6* third highest), substance abuse, and history of academic underachievement, previous suicide attempts, and psychiatric hospitalizations. *2 > 8* more common in depression; *8 > 2* more common in schizophrenia.

- Check: *ANX, FRS1, OBS, DEP1, DEP2, DEP3, DEP4, HEA1, HEA2, HEA3, BIZ1, BIZ2, LSE1, LSE2, SOD1, WRK, AGG* (low), *PSY, D1, D2, D3, D4, D5, Hy3, Hy4, Pd4, Pd5, Pa1, Pa2, Sc1, Sc2, Sc3, Sc4, Sc5, Sc6, A, Es* (low), *MAC-R* (low), *MDS*.
- Treatment: Rule out Schizophrenia; Schizoaffective Disorder. Biological treatments more effective than psychotherapy to improve symptomatic status and reduce suicide risk. Supportive and cognitive therapies can be effective in the post-acute phase, but defenses and apathy reduce motivation to engage in therapy.

2-9/9-2

- Definition: A rare and unstable profile. It is found most commonly in patients with Bipolar Disorder who are in transition from a manic to a depressed state (manic defense) or vice versa. May be seen as so-called agitated depression.
- Emotional turbulence and instability with anxiety, tension, moodiness, agitation, restlessness, irritability, and disturbed sleep. Driven. Veers between excitability and upset or despondency. Distress tends to be generalized rather than differentiated into depression, anxiety, apprehensiveness, and so forth. Overactivity, when present, is pres-

sured and forced rather than natural and euphoric. Depression, when present, is manifested in anhedonia, vegetative signs, and pessimism and other depressive attitudes, rather than in sadness or (stable) dysphoria. Seeks stimulation as a distraction from subjective distress. Strong concerns and worries over declining health (feels stressed and sick) and inability to work. High-strung and irritable, impulsive, over-reactive to frustration and narcissistic injury, and quick to experience and express anger and hostility, sometimes explosively. Cynical and suspicious. Ego-dystonic dependency. Prone to passive-aggressive struggles. Extroverted but exaggerates self-confidence. Look for history of mood disorder, substance abuse, or both.

- Check: *ANX, DEP1, DEP2, DEP3, DEP4, HEA3, ANG1, ANG2, CYN1, CYN2, ASP1, TPA2, SOD2* (low), *D1, D2, D3, D4, D5, Hy3, Pa1, Pa3* (low), *Sc3, Sc4, Ma1, Ma2, Ma3, Ma4, MAC-R.*
- Treatment: Rule out Bipolar Disorder, Mixed; Major Depressive Episode with agitation; Cyclothymia. Risk of impulsive suicide. Consider retesting after an interval of observation and change in mental status as a guide to treatment. Consider neuropsychological evaluation.

2-0/0-2

- Definition: If the profile is coded *2-0-7-8* or *0-2-7-8,* consider interpretation under the *2-7-8* code.
- Mild to moderate depression, usually chronic, with anxiety, anergia, anhedonia, apathy, intropunitiveness, obsessiveness, low self-esteem, and social avoidance and withdrawal. Schizoid. May complain of insomnia. Feelings of inferiority and a lack of self-confidence; concerns about physical appearance; guilt and self-denigration. Inhibited, schizoid, socially awkward and fearful, timid and underaggressive, and self-defeating. Few or no friends and associates; poor social skills; avoids attention, prefers solitary activities. May be seen as odd. Ideas may seem odd or peculiar because of a lack of consensual validation. Low social visibility. Interpersonally shy, quiet, tense, meticulous, sensitive to criticism or disapproval, uptight, and fearful of emotional involvement. Lacks skills in heterosexual interaction; may be shy and uncomfortable even in marriage.

- Check: *ANX, DEP1, DEP2, DEP3, DEP4, HEA3, ANG2, CYN1, ASP2* (low), *TPA2* (low), *LSE1, LSE2, SOD1, SOD2, AGG* (low), *D1, D2, D3, D4, D5, Hy1* (low), *Hy2* (low), *Hy3, Pd3* (low), *Pd4, Sc1, Sc2, Sc3, Sc4, Ma3* (low), *Si1, Si2, Si3, A, R, MAC-R* (low).
- Treatment: Structured treatments that focus on social skills and assertiveness are more reliably beneficial than psychotherapy. Responsive to structure, support, and direction, but uneasy with reassurance or praise. Cognitive therapy, antidepressants, or both are helpful for relief of depression and anxiety.

Spike 3

- Conventional, outgoing, optimistic, and socially confident, but with some general concerns about health and physical functioning or narrowly focused symptoms (e.g., aphonia). May develop somatic symptoms under stress. Responsible, friendly, and trusting, but may be seen by others as immature, self-centered, shallow, and inhibited. Seeks to avoid conflict and unpleasantness; unaggressive. Refuses to recognize problems in self or others.
- Check: *HEA3, CYN1* (low), *CYN2* (low), *ASP1* (low), *SOD2* (low), *AGG* (low), *DIS* (low), *D3, Hy1, Hy2, Hy3, Hy4, Hy5, Pa3, Si1* (low), *Si3* (low), *A* (low), *R, O-H, Re, MAC-R* (low).
- Treatment: Treatment plan to focus on presenting problem.

3-2-1

- Weakness, fatigue, and stress-related gastrointestinal symptoms. Dysphoria. Prone to taking invalid role in family. Look for sexual inhibition, a history of gynecological complaints and surgery (e.g., hysterectomy), problems with weight, and insomnia. See *1-2/2-1, 1-3/3-1,* and *2-3/3-2.*

3-4/4-3

- Definition: *3-4* is associated with greater intropunitiveness, discomfort, immaturity, inhibition, passivity, mistrust of others, and somatic complaints and concerns. By contrast, *4-3* is associated with greater extropunitiveness, irritability, resentment, and personal and social comfort and skill.
- Emotional instability, immaturity, egocentricity, and irresponsibility,

with chronic problems in the control and expression of anger, and substance abuse. Moodiness and temper outbursts. Fragile and brittle emotional and behavioral controls. Temper may erupt in dangerous explosions; may be assaultive/combative when intoxicated. Health concerns and somatic complaints are common. Outwardly conforming but inwardly rebellious. Acts out conflicts but seeks to stay within the law. Disidentified with authority but tries to adhere to convention for the sake of appearances. Tends to pander to what others will approve. Prefers to express rebelliousness and hostility indirectly through covert and vicarious means. Chronically conflicted about dependency and self-control. Manipulative, seductive, dramatic, and controlling in interactions, but fearful of rejection. Socially smooth and poised; comfortable playing approved social roles. Seeks attention and approval, tending to become suddenly frustrated, irritable, or hostile when these are withheld. Strongly denying of anger, cynicism, hostility, mistrust, and resentment. Paranoid features not uncommon. Look for sexual promiscuity and substance abuse, a history of minor delinquencies and adult legal difficulties, instability in employment, marital conflict, fighting or assaults, and suicide attempts. Check *O-H*.

- Check: *ANX, DEP1, DEP2, HEA3, ANG1* (low), *ANG2* (low), *CYN1* (low), *CYN2* (low), *ASP1* (low), *ASP2, TPA1* (low), *TPA2* (low), *SOD1* (low), *SOD2* (low), *FAM1, FAM2, AGG* (low), *DIS* (low), *D1, D3, D4, Hy1, Hy2, Hy3, Hy4, Hy5, Pd1, Pd2, Pd3, Pd4, Pd5, Si1* (low), *Si2* (low), *A, R, O-H, MAC-R, APS, AAS, MDS.*

- Treatment: Rule out psychotic disorder, especially defensive paranoid schizophrenia. Nonintrospective, with denial and lack of insight. May benefit from assertiveness training or treatment of substance abuse, but course tends to be chronic.

3-4-6/3-6-4/4-3-6/4-6-3/6-3-4/6-4-3

- Rigid, rationalizing, resentful, and vindictive. Outwardly conforming but inwardly hostile; hypersensitive to criticism or rejection; unable to compromise; intolerant of any kind of challenge. Possessive. May collect evidence to prove others' bad faith. Look for severe marital conflict; pathological jealousy. See *3-4/4-3; 3-6/6-3; 4-6/6-4.* Check *O-H.*

3-4-9/3-9-4/4-3-9/4-9-3/9-3-4/9-4-3

- Better socialized than *4-9/9-4*, with strong needs for affection and approval, but with more stimulation seeking, irresponsibility, acting out, and easily threatened autonomy than *3-4/4-3*. Look for opportunism, expediency, promiscuity, and substance abuse.

3-5/5-3

- Defensive and grossly lacking in self-awareness. Men may be seen as somatically focused, sociable but superficial, possibly demanding. Women may be verbal, assertive, and concerned with physical appearance. Check third highest scale.

3-5-4

- Egocentric, passive-aggressive, articulate, and exploitive. Attention seeking. Anxious when not in control of situations. Soft exterior but hard interior. Sexually active but conflicted and insecure.

3-6/6-3

- Socially poised but controlling and hyperrational, with rigidity, overcontrol ("uptight"), egocentricity, paranoid defensiveness, projection, transfer of blame, and covert sadism. Generally tightly composed but subject to periods of anxiety, tension, and somatic symptoms such as headache and upset stomach. Socially skilled and polished but few friends. Oriented to power; extremely avoidant of criticism; can be cruel and ruthless. Inwardly mistrustful, suspicious, and hostile; seeks to control others through allure, manipulations through control of information ("keep 'em guessing"), and power. Expects approval based on appearance, attractiveness, intelligence, status, or some combination of these. Self-righteous; intolerant of others; unforgiving. Stimulates mistrust, dislike, and resentment in others. Rigidly deny mistrust and hostility. Look for marital and family conflict; conflict with coworkers, especially subordinates.
- Check: *ANX, DEP1, DEP2, HEA1, HEA2, BIZ1, BIZ2, ANG1, ANG2, CYN1* (low), *CYN2, ANT1* (low), *ANT2, TPA1, TPA2, SOD1, SOD2* (low), *AGG, PSY, DIS, D1, D3, D4, Hy1, Hy2, Hy3, Hy4, Hy5, Pd4, Pa1, Pa2, Pa3, Sc1, Sc2, Sc3, Sc4, Sc5, Sc6, Ma4, Si1* (low), *Si2, A, R, O-H, MDS.*

- Treatment: Rule out paranoid psychosis; paranoid personality. Usually unable to tolerate an inability to control the therapist and the feelings of vulnerability engendered in psychotherapy. Self-righteousness, hyperrationality, making others responsible for problems, and intolerance of the idea of having "mental problems" are all serious obstacles in therapy and predict early drop out. Treatments focused on the presenting problem and symptomatic relief may be successful.

3-7/7-3

- Anxiety, tension, fearfulness, and rumination, often with phobias or panic attacks. Moderate dysphoria with helplessness, problems in concentration, narrowing of interest, fatigue, and disturbed sleep. Depressed mood often secondary to anxiety. May feel helpless and threatened in the face of decisions and time pressures, and need advance approval, reassurance, and support for choices. Feels ill and in poor and declining health, and unable to meet responsibilities despite desire to do so. Accepts invalidism to avoid stresses. Behavioral control is adequate but emotional controls are tenuous and fragile. Impunitive. Credulous and psychologically naive. Passive and lacking in self-confidence in relations with others; avoids conflict. Often extremely dependent on others for affection, approval, and support; may be seen as clinging, helpless, or ingratiating. Sensitive, timid, and easily hurt; fends off aggression or criticism in others by appearing emotionally fragile and vulnerable. Tends to locate sources of distress outside the self, in symptoms and in the environment. Look for a history of underachievement, phobic anxiety, ingratiation, current invalidism within family.
- Check: *ANX, FRS1, FRS2, OBS, DEP1, DEP2, DEP3, DEP3, HEA3, ANG1* (low), *ANG2* (low), *ASP1* (low), *ASP2, TPA1, TPA2* (low), *LSE1, LSE2, AGG* (low), *DIS* (low), *NEN, D1, D2, D3, D4, D5, Hy1, Hy2, Hy3, Hy4, Hy5, Pd5, Pa2, Sc2, Sc3, Sc4, Sc5, Sc6, A, R, Re.*
- Treatment: Benefit from structure, support, and reassurance but reluctant to focus away from immediate symptoms and perceived sources of distress. Relief of anxiety and fears/phobias may enable other problems to be addressed.

3-8/8-3

- Multiple cognitive and neuropsychological symptoms, including unstable attention, forgetfulness, impaired judgment, losses of consciousness, intrusive and frightening thoughts, and cognitive disruption, as well as a variety of motor, sensory, and musculoskeletal symptoms. Meandering stream of thought; drifts off point. Symptoms may be bizarre and delusional. Anxious and depressed, with depression less evident in depressed mood than in apathy, affective blunting, anhedonia, agitation, vegetative symptoms (including sleep disturbance and fatigue), and depressive cognition and attitudes (pessimism, helplessness, hopelessness, worthlessness), including suicidal ideation. Hopelessness makes suicide a significant risk. Feels ill and in declining health. Prone to brief psychotic episodes of abrupt onset and subsequent amnesia; these may involve flamboyant bizarreness, sexual or religious themes, ideas of reference, delusions of persecution or control, somatic delusions, and visual hallucinations. Spends much time in fantasy and daydreaming. Fantasy may emphasize idiosyncratic, if not bizarre, violent, religious, or sexual themes, and may be frightening. Internally chaotic, with unstable controls and proneness to brief affective storms, with restlessness, demandingness, or angry outbursts. Not generally hostile. Adequate social skills but immature, dependent, and easily upset by conflict with others. Sexual and sexual-identity concerns. Family conflicts and resentments.
- Check: *ANX, FRS1, DEP1, DEP2, DEP3, DEP4, HEA1, HEA2, HEA3, BIZ1, BIZ2, ANG1, ANG2, LSE1, FAM1, FAM2, WRK, PSY, D1, D3, D4, D5, Hy3, Hy4, Pd4, Pd5, Sc1, Sc2, Sc3, Sc4, Sc5, Sc6, R, AAS, MDS.*
- Treatment: Rule out mood disorder and schizophrenia-spectrum disorder. Benefits from structure and support. Resistant to insight and psychological approaches, but may also have great difficulty focusing in therapy. Evaluate for neuropsychological impairment and biological treatments. Treatment plans initially focused on relief of psychotic symptoms, depression, anxiety, and problems such as disturbed sleep more effective than those targeting problems related to family, sexual identity, dependency, and so forth.

3-9/9-3

- Moderate emotional and behavioral undercontrol with overtalkative-ness, angry volatility, social aggressiveness and stimulation seeking, and strong avoidance of anxiety and internal discomfort. Affectively buoyant and excitable, but vulnerable to anxiety and panic attacks. May feel driven; especially to distract self from negative emotionality. Somatic complaints may include cardiac symptoms, chest pain, tachycardia, and the like. Socially skilled, smooth, and self-assured, with strong needs for recognition, approval, and admiration. Seeks social stimulation, but tends to be considered self-centered, demanding, overbearing, boastful, conceited, and insensitive. Unstable emotional and behavioral controls; may be verbally hostile or even assaultive when frustrated or slighted. Narcissistic. Holds others to high standards and may be critical with intimates. Rigidly denying; impervious to insight. Look for history of mood disorder and parental domination; current marital discord.
- Check: *ANX, HEA1, HEA2, HEA3, BIZ1, BIZ2, ANG1, ANG2, LSE1* (low), *LSE2* (low), *SOD1, SOD2* (low), *FAM1, FAM2, AGG, DIS, PSY, D4, Hy3, Hy4, Sc5, Sc6, Ma1, Ma2, Ma3, Ma4, Si1* (low), *Si2, R* (low), *MAC-R, AAS, MDS.*
- Treatment: Rule out mood disorder. Lack of distress and narcissism-based denial limits engagement with psychotherapy; diverts attention from problems to positive traits, acts, or achievements. Somatization may respond to reassurance. Focus on presenting problems and seek to provide symptomatic relief.

Spike 4

- Underdeveloped behavioral controls and emotional instability, with acting out, irresponsibility, social and interpersonal aggression, impulsivity, intolerance of frustration, and substance abuse. Judgment is often poor and sometimes reckless. Occult dysphoria and a lack of meaning and satisfaction in life are common. Good social skills, but selfish, self-centered, demanding, exploitive, and unreliable in relations with others. Appears unable to profit from punishing experience or to maintain progress toward long-term goals. Relationships evidence superficiality, absence of commitment, and high turnover. Intimidates with volatile temper. May be dependent in stable intimate relationships but often estranged from family. Rebellious toward rules, authority, and convention. Cynical; locates problems outside self. Sense of entitlement. Look for history of delinquency and adult antisocial conduct, job loss, fighting, substance abuse, and marital problems; recent loss of significant relationship.

- Check: *FRS* (low), *OBS* (low), *ANG1, ASP1, ASP2, LSE1* (low), *LSE2* (low), *SOD1, SOD2* (low), *FAM1, FAM2, AGG, DIS, Pd1, Pd3, Pd3, Pd4, Pd5, Ma1, Ma3, Si1* (low), *Si2, A, R, O-H, GF* (low), *MAC-R, AAS, MDS.*
- Treatment: Little or no motivation to change; sees problems as due to others. Treatment can sometimes be initiated around the issue of patient's judgment. May benefit from substance abuse treatment.

4-5/5-4

- Like Spike *4* but better socialized. Openly nonconformist; antiestablishment in dress and outlook. Angry disidentification with social convention; quick to view authorities as corrupt, and may defy and rebel against institutional authority through social protest, demonstration, and so forth. Ego-dystonic passivity and dependency. Often verbally fluent and articulate. May use idealistic posturing for rebellious, selfish, or exploitive ends. More exploitive than predatory. Look for self-centeredness, passive antisocial behavior (e.g., substance abuse), and sexual disturbance (including sex offenses; paraphilia) among men, and tendencies toward violence among women. Check third highest scale.

4-5-6

- Like *4-5/5-4,* but narcissistic, hypersensitive, and resentful. Fears domination and may become enraged when frustrated by others. See *4-5/5-4; 4-6/6-4; 5-6/6-5.*

4-5-7

- Sexually maladjusted and insecure. Self-centered and exploitive; behavior may antagonize others. May be compulsively promiscuous. See *4-5/5-4; 4-7/7-4; 5-7/7-5.*

4-5-8

- Sexual maladjustment and sexual identity concerns may be relatively severe. See *4-5/5-4; 4-8/8-4; 5-8/8-5.*

4-5-9

- Severe narcissism, exploitiveness, irresponsibility, expediency, hedonism. Psychopathic personality trends but often without extensive legal histories. May be charismatic. See *4-5/5-4; 4-9/9-4; 5-9/9-5.*

4-6/6-4

- Chronic resentment of family and authority. Tense, sullen, irritable, and hostile. Depression, when present, tends to be externalized. Chronic struggles over demands and expectations; quick tempered; demands much of others but resents reciprocal demands on self. Quick to see self as criticized, provoked, exploited, mistreated, or victimized by others (projections), but reluctant to admit to own provocativeness, exploitation, manipulativeness, and mistreatment of others. Hyperrational, stubborn, argumentative, unforgiving, resentful, oversensitive, and hypervigilant. Fearful of vulnerability. Men tend to be sullen and vengeful, women tend to be provocative and passive-aggressive. Craves affection but alienates those who would provide it. Shortsighted and self-defeating. Look for history of delinquency and scrapes with authority figures, job losses, and marital conflict or recent loss of significant relationship; rule out psychotic (paranoid) features.
- Check: *ANX, OBS, DEP1, DEP2, DEP3, DEP4, BIZ1, BIZ2, ANG1, ANG2, CYN1, CYN2, ASP1, ASP2, TPA2, SOD1, SOD2* (low), *FAM1, FAM2, AGG, PSY, DIS, D1, D4, D5, Hy3, Pd1, Pd2, Pd3, Pd4, Pd5, Pa1, Pa2, Pa3, Sc1, Sc2, Sc3, Ma1, Ma3, Si1* (low), *Si2, A, R, O-H, Re, MAC-R, AAS, MDS.*
- Treatment: Motivation for change is typically low, especially in younger patients who view lost relationships as easily replaced. Motivation is higher in older patients who have gained at least some insight into the destructiveness and self-defeating nature of their behavior patterns, although they are at a loss to know how to change them. In either case, the manipulativeness, provocativeness, and hostility of these patients, and their expectations of rejection, make their

treatment stressful for the therapist. Successful treatment tends to be long term.

4-6-8/4-8-6/6-4-8/6-8-4/8-4-6/8-6-4

- Alienated, suspicious, depressed, hopeless, and hostile. Thought disorder, with derailment, tangentiality, and circumstantiality; paranoid symptoms are common, as are anxiety and depression. Depression tends to be partially externalized and expressed in apathy, tension, and agitation; attitudes of hopelessness, worthlessness, and helplessness; and suicidal ideation. Thinking and behavior are often disorganized. May be unpredictably assaultive. See *4-6/6-4; 4-8/8-4; 6-8/8-6*. This codetype is discussed in Graham and colleagues (1999).

4-6-9/4-9-6/6-4-9/6-9-4/9-4-6/9-6-4

- Psychopathic and paranoid trends with brittle controls, rigidity, egocentricity, impulsiveness, hostility, hypersensitivity, resentment, suspiciousness, jealousy, and vindictiveness. Highly rationalized and externalizing. Hyperarousal may lead to sudden and explosive violence, but sufficiently organized to plan and coldly carry out dangerous violence on others. Look for homicidal ideation. See *4-6/6-4; 4-9/9-4; 6-9/9-6*.

4-7/7-4

- A recurrent cyclical pattern of impulsive acting out to relieve tension followed by periods of self-recrimination and self-control. Both phases characterized by compulsive elements (e.g., binge drinking followed by periods of sobriety enforced by compulsive means). Anxiety, tension, agitation, and turmoil, with dysphoria, guilt, remorse, and exaggerated self-criticism during periods of relative behavioral control. Impulse ridden. Low tolerance for frustration. Poorly consolidated conscience. Acts out in self-defeating ways; repeatedly sacrifices long-term goals for momentary tension reduction. Chronic dependency/independency conflicts; strong need for affection and security in relationships. Easily angered when frustrated or denied dependency gratifications. Cyclical pattern is also evident in relations with others, with periods of reckless disregard for the needs and feelings of others followed by abject efforts at reparation and reconciliation. Exploits others to gratify dependency needs; intermittently very fearful of the withdrawal of love and support. Look for a history of substance abuse, arrests for intoxication, compulsive gambling, sexual promiscuity/infidelity, employment instability, and marital conflict.

- Check: *ANX, OBS, DEP1, DEP2, DEP3, DEP4, Hea3, BIZ2, ANG1, ANG2, ASP1, ASP2, TPA1, LSE1, LSE2, FAM1, FAM2, WRK, DIS, NEN, D1, D4, D5, Hy3, Pd1, Pd2, Pd3, Pd4, Pd5, Pa2, Sc1, Sc2, Sc3, Sc4, Sc5, A, R, MAC-R, AAS, MDS.*

- Treatment: Rule out Major Depression; Anxiety Disorders. Motivation for therapy and behavior change may be initially strong but dissipate rapidly in treatment. Goals tend to devolve into short-term anxiety and tension reduction. May seek to manipulate therapists, family, or both around treatment. Group therapy, referral for substance abuse treatment, or both are usually more effective than individual psychotherapy.

4-7-8/4-8-7/7-4-8/7-8-4/8-4-7/8-7-4

- Graham and colleagues (1999) described their outpatients with this profile as manifesting symptoms of anxiety, including problems in concentration; agitation; phobias and obsessive-compulsive symptoms; and symptoms of psychosis, including disorientation, derailment, poor reality testing, hallucinations, and delusions. They also described patients as introverted, insecure, emotionally shallow, self-degrading and self-punishing, interpersonally sensitive and suspicious, and as having suicidal ideation.

4-8/8-4

- Severe alienation with pervasive distrust of others and fear of emotional involvement. Behavior pattern is impulsive, chaotic, and unpredictable. Depressed, anxious, tense, ruminative and worried, with moodiness, anhedonia, sleep disturbance, fatigue, hopelessness, and guilt, but also agitation/restlessness, irritability, intolerance of frustration, and hostility. Immature and self-defeating, with chronically poor judgment and feelings of inferiority. Thought disorder with hallucinations and ideas of reference is not common, but may be covered by withdrawal, mistrust, and acting out. Spend much time in fantasy and daydreaming, the themes of which are often morbid, involving physical and sexual violence. Poorly developed conscience. Interpersonally detached and cold; potentially sadistic. Rebellious toward authority figures; generally resentful and argumentative. Feels misunderstood and rejected. Craves affection but lacks empathy; fearful of rejection and intolerant of vulnerability. Expects mistreatment and questions others' motives. Prefers to reject others before others reject the patient (felt to be inevitable). Defends through acting out, projection, and rationalization. Sexual psychopathology common; tends to conflate sex with aggression. Borderline and/or antisocial trends. Look for a history of abuse (sexual abuse for women), family deprivation and neglect, or chronic exposure to conflict; children born out of wedlock and put up for adoption (women), multiple abortions (women); underachievement; employment and relationship instability; delinquency and criminality; sexual promiscuity/prostitution or paraphilias; family and marital conflict; self-mutilation and suicidal threats, gestures, and attempts; and substance abuse.

- Check: *ANX, DEP1, DEP2, DEP3, DEP4, HEA2, BIZ1, BIZ2, ANG1, ANG2, CYN1, CYN2, ASP1, ASP2, TPA1, TPA2, LSE1, FAM1, FAM2, AGG, PSY, DIS, D1, D2, D3, D4, D5, Hy3, Hy2* (low), *Hy5* (low), *Pd1, Pd2, Pd3, Pd4, Pd5, Pa1, Pa2, Pa3* (low), *Sc1, Sc2, Sc3, Sc4, Sc5, Sc6, Ma1, Ma4, Si3, A, R, Re, GF* (low), *MAC-R, AAS, MDS.*

- Treatment: Rule out psychosis/Schizotypal Personality Disorder; Borderline Personality Disorder; Paranoid Personality Disorder. Biological therapies only marginally effective but may provide limited symptomatic relief of anxiety and depression. Major difficulties establishing trusting relationship with therapist. Prognosis consistently better for women than for men, and for younger than older patients. Structured therapies such as dialectical behavior therapy and cognitive behavioral therapy are often effective.

4-8-9/4-9-8/8-4-9/8-9-4/9-4-8/9-8-4

- Like *4-6-9* but less organized and more charismatic, grandiose, exploitive, unstable, and chronically hostile. May be menacing, predatory, and sadistic. Severe disidentification with authority; empathy defects; may be cold, extremely manipulative, ruthless, and prone to violence. Unusual or bizarre dress and grooming may be used to attract attention or to keep others at an emotional or physical distance. May be psychotic and disorganized. Look for history of underachievement and poor socialization if not brutalization; criminality, assault, and substance abuse. See *4-8/8-4; 4-9/9-4; 8-9/9-8.*

4-9/9-4

- Stimulation seeking, intolerant of boredom and frustration; energetic and restless; disinhibited, undercontrolled, and emotionally unstable; rebellious and impulsive; socially skilled and aggressive; hedonistic, egocentric, and narcissistic. Irritable and hostile; overreactive to frustration, demands, and perceived threats/challenges to autonomy. Poorly developed conscience. Authority conflicts and disidentification with conventions, moral and ethical standards, rules, and regulations. Immature, irresponsible, and unreliable. Social skills, disinhibition (bold, brash, insouciant), and absence of anxiety may create an early impression of charm and attractiveness. Selfish, exploitive ("con artist"), entitled, and amoral in relations with others; manipulates goods, services, and gratifications from others through superficial charm. Defends through acting out and rationalization. Long-term risk of accidental death related to risk taking, or suicide. Look for a history of delinquency, adult antisocial behavior, and an overall failure to learn from punishing experience; underachievement, job losses, sexual promiscuity, fights, relationship instability, family and marital conflict, and substance abuse.
- Check: *FRS1* (low), *FRS2* (low), *BIZ2, ANG1, ANG2, CYN1, CYN2, ASP1, ASP2, TPA1, TPA2, LSE1* (low), *LSE2* (low), *SOD1* (low), *SOD2* (low), *FAM1, FAM2, AGG, PSY, DIS, Pd1, Pd2, Pd3, Pd4, Pd5, Pa1, Sc5, Ma1, Ma2, Ma3, Ma4, Si1* (low), *Si2* (low), *A, R* (low), *Re* (low), *GF* (low), *MAC-R, APS, AAS, MDS.*
- Treatment: Rule out Antisocial Personality Disorder; mania; and, rarely, paranoid syndromes. Lacks motivation for change but may seek to use therapy to manipulate others. Structured group therapy for antisocial behavior problems or substance abuse treatment may be helpful.

4-0/0-4
- Dysphoric, alienated, avoidant, resentful, and suspicious. Conflict with family. Substance abuse. Check third highest scale.

Spike 5
- Better adjusted than patients in general but with conflicts around aggression. Social aggression, self-confidence, decisiveness, insensitivity, competitiveness, narcissism, and low feminine identification in women. Neuroticism, passivity, introspectiveness, perceptiveness, dependency, low self-confidence, oversensitivity, disrupted thinking, mild suspiciousness, and low masculine identification in men. Check *Mf* subscales and *GM – GF*.

5-6/6-5
- Look for rigidity, intellectualization/hyperrationality, hypersensitivity, suspiciousness, guardedness, abrasiveness, overbearingness, irritability, and resentment. Rule out Schizophrenia. Check third highest scale.

5-7/7-5
- Look for anxiety, tension, worry, dysphoria, dependency, indecision, heterosexual relationship problems, and ruminative fears of failure. Check third highest scale.

5-8/8-5
- Look for sexual and sexual identity conflicts, alienation, rumination, disrupted thinking and subtle (if not overt) thought disorder. Check third highest scale.

5-9/9-5
- Conflicts about dependency, assertiveness in men. Competitiveness in women. Look for narcissism, cynicism, suspiciousness, social and hostile aggression, amorality, and antisocial impulses/conduct. Rule out mania; narcissistic, antisocial, and paranoid personality features. Check third highest scale.

5-0/0-5
- Cautious, inhibited, and overideational; and heterosexual discomfort in men.

Spike 6

- Overt paranoid trends, often with manifest well-organized and elaborate delusions of persecution, control, or both. Rigid, resentful, hypervigilant, and hyperrational. Denies suspiciousness, personal problems, and distress unrelated to primary delusion. Lack of insight usually severe. Look for history of seclusiveness, alienating others, hostile outbursts.
- Check: *OBS* (low), *CYN1* (low), *CYN2* (low), *ASP1* (low), *TPA1* (low), *TPA2* (low), *FAM1* (low), *Pa1, Pa2, Pa3, Sd.*
- Treatment: Rule out Delusional Disorder (paranoia vera). Partially responsive to antipsychotic medication and nonspecific milieu treatments. Interpersonal therapy is sometimes helpful following partial response to medication and restoration of affect.

6-7/7-6

- Severe anxiety, tension, and dysphoria but with concurrent anger and intropunitiveness. Feels isolated, trapped by feelings, and terrified of losing control. Mood is depressed and hopeless—often desperately so—with sleep disturbance and exhaustion. Distractibility and indecisiveness secondary to intensity of mood and sense of suffering. Obsesses and ruminates about guilt, misery, rage, current predicaments, and loss of control and ensuing catastrophe. May consider suicide as a way to relieve intense suffering. Fears criticism and disapproval; may be hypervigilant. Psychotic/paranoid symptoms not uncommon, especially hypersensitivity, intrusive thoughts, hyperreligiosity, ideas/delusions of reference, or a combination of these. Problem-solving approach is narrow, compulsive, and nonresourceful. Tends to be rigid and stubborn, with stress only increasing these trends. Tends to internalize criticism and slights but also develops resentment over them. Sensitive to perceived unfairness; quick to feel unfairly judged, criticized, and hurt. Lacks skills to state grievances and negotiate conflicts; is unassertive. May have severe but unreported and poorly recognized conflict with significant other. Risk of impulsive suicide. Look for marital conflict/dissatisfaction; history of head injury, seizures, or both; compulsive rituals; and substance abuse to relieve anxiety or insomnia.

- Check: *ANX, FRS1, OBS, DEP1, DEP2, DEP3, DEP4, BIZ1, ANG1, ANG2, TPA1, LSE1, LSE2, FAM1, AGG* (low), *PSY, NEN, D1, D4, D5, Hy3, Pd4, Pd5, Pa1, Pa2, Pa3, Sc1, Sc2, Sc3, Sc4, Sc5, Sc6, A, R, APS, MDS.*
- Treatment: Rule out Major Depression; seizure disorder. Biological therapies usually necessary to relieve severe discomfort and attenuate suicide risk. Individual and marital therapy are helpful and motivation is usually high. Consider neuropsychological evaluation.

6-7-8

- Like *6-8/8-6,* but with severe tension, hypervigilance, anger, and fears of loss of control. Fear and disorganization may combine with delusional ideation, leading to assault and violence against perceived enemies.

6-8/8-6

- Pervasive but poorly differentiated distress with severe cognitive and behavioral disorganization, regression, and disability. Anxiety expressed as dread or panic. Depression expressed in apathy; anhedonia; agitation; fatigue; moodiness; sleep disturbance; attitudes of helplessness, hopelessness, and worthlessness; and suicidal ideation, rather than in manifest dysphoric mood. Affect typically blunted or inappropriate. Chronic feelings of inadequacy and inferiority. Manifest psychotic symptoms include gross thought disorder, hallucinations, pervasive but loosely structured delusional ideation (reference, persecution, control), and bizarre preoccupations, as well as moderate to severe impairment of attention, concentration, memory, and judgment. Problem solving is unconventional, inadequate, incompetent, and often autistic. Severely alienated from both interpersonal and material worlds with suspiciousness and hostility, and bland but pervasive apprehensiveness and incomprehension, respectively. May spend majority of time in fantasy and daydreaming, often with sexual, violent, religious, or supernatural preoccupations. Feels misunderstood, despised, and mistreated by others and anticipates further unfriendliness, mistreatment, and rejection. Become angry for no apparent reason. Quick to feel threatened and attacked and may become unpredictably assaultive. Viewed by others as odd, peculiar, eccentric, or weird in dress and manner, and are interpersonally withdrawn. May use bizarreness to keep others at a distance, but feels lonely and isolated. Fears being seen as awkward and inept; easily embarrassed and humiliated. Disorganized by rejection. Severe lack of insight. Look for history of poor achievement, social isolation (never married [men]), spotty employment, prior hospitalizations, and substance abuse.

- Check: *ANX, FRS1, OBS, DEP1, DEP2, DEP3, DEP4, HEA1, HEA2, HEA3, BIZ1, BIZ2, LSE1, WRK, PSY, NEN, LPE, D1, D3, D4, D5, Hy3, Hy4, Pd4, Pd5, Pa1, Pa2, Pa3* (low), *Sc1, Sc2, Sc3, Sc4, Sc5, Sc6, A, R, AAS, MDS.*

- Treatment: Rule out Paranoid Schizophrenia; Disorganized Schizophrenia; Schizotypal Personality Disorder; Bipolar Disorder, Depressed (rare). Treatment with antipsychotic medications is most promptly and reliably (albeit incompletely) effective. Benefits from structure and support, including environmental manipulation, sheltered employment, and reliable assistance in managing daily affairs. Psychoeducational measures such as skills training, medication management, and relapse prevention are often helpful. Supportive psychotherapy is helpful in reducing sense of isolation and estrangement and in managing illness and its consequences, but requires long-term commitment. Ameliorative goals must be considered carefully because of the risk of distorted understandings secondary to autism and thought disorder. Treatments emphasizing insight tend to be stressful and disorganizing.

6-8-9/6-9-8/8-6-9/8-9-6/9-6-8/9-8-6

- See *6-9/9-6* and *8-9/9-8*. Scales *2* and *0* usually low. Manic hyperarousal with both persecutory and grandiose delusional ideation; and disorganization, agitation, and confusion. May be loud and hostile.

6-9/9-6

- Inflated, excited, loud, and circumstantial, grandiose, and possibly euphoric, but also tense, irritable, impatient, suspicious, and resentful. Emotional and especially behavioral controls are impaired and unstable. Speech is over-productive, and may show flight of ideas. Quick to become restless, agitated, overreactive, and hostile when feeling frustrated, threatened, or criticized. Shows multiple psychotic signs and symptoms including hallucinations; delusions of grandeur, persecution, conspiracy, reference, or control; hyperreligiosity, or religious delusions; but may show only minimal thought disorder. Most basic cognitive functions are intact except when aroused by threat, but judgment is impaired by delusional ideation, and problem solving is inflexible and stereotyped. Fears being controlled by others. Hypervigilant for criticism or attack. Spends much time in fantasy and daydreaming, and in ruminating on themes of persecution, mistreatment, vengeance, jealousy, and sexuality. Tense, rigid, and brittle, loss of behavioral control may result in violent acting out. Judges others harshly. Has strong needs for affection, loyalty, and to be sided with, but hyperrationality, suspiciousness, fear of emotional involvement, and lack of warmth keep others at a distance. Look for a history of prior hospitalization, substance abuse, and homicidal ideation.

- Check: *ANX, BIZ1, BIZ2, CYN2, SOD1* (low), *SOD2* (low), *AGG, PSY, DIS, D2* (low), *Hy2* (low), *Hy5* (low), *Pd4, Pa1, Pa2, Pa3, Sc1, Sc3, Sc5, Sc6, Ma1, Ma2, Ma3, Ma4, Si1* (low), *Si2* (low), *A, R, Re, MAC-R, AAS, MDS*.
- Treatment: Rule out Bipolar Disorder, Manic, with paranoid features. Severe lack of insight and resistance to psychological approaches. Biological therapies initially effective despite resistance to medication.

6-0/0-6
- Look for isolation, alienation, suspiciousness, guardedness, obsessiveness, and transfer of blame. Check third highest scale.

Spike 7
- Look for anxiety, obsessiveness, dependency, guilt, indecision, and inadequacy/inferiority. Check second highest scale.

7-8/8-7
- Ruminative, obsessive, and overideational. Intensely self-preoccupied, with convictions of severe impairment and vulnerability, dire expectations, and fears of "going crazy." Spends much time in fantasy and daydreaming, brooding on guilts and failures, identity concerns, and sexual and morbid themes, with intrusive and alien thoughts, often of violence. Periods of severe distress and panic. Experiences high levels

of internal struggle and turmoil with tension, worry, fearfulness, and anxiety; depression, agitation, irritability, and anhedonia. Affect may be flat and isolated. Severe problems with concentration, thinking, and decision making are characteristic. Thought process varies, remaining well organized in some patients, although perseveration and periods of confusion, derealization, and depersonalization can occur, and severely disorganized in others with neologisms, slang associations, echolalio, etc. Health concerns and widely distributed somatic complaints, including gastrointestinal, cardiovascular, cardiorespiratory, motor, and sensory symptoms are common. Longstanding feelings of inferiority, inadequacy, and insecurity; severe vulnerability to stress. Feels "stressed-out" and frightened by both internal and external events. Alienation, withdrawal, poor social skills, low self-esteem, and self-consciousness impair relations with others. Fears sudden rejection and losses of support. Interpersonally ambivalent; dependency, passivity, and loneliness are offset by mistrust and apprehensiveness. Look for obsessions and compulsions, psychotic features such as thought disorder, hallucinations, ideas/delusions of reference; suicidal ideation; history of underachievement, family conflict, prior hospitalization, and substance abuse.

- Check: *ANX, FRS1, OBS, DEP1, DEP2, DEP3, DEP4, HEA2, BIZ1, BIZ2, ANG1, ANG2, CYN1, CYN2, LSE1, LSE2, SOD1, SOD2, FAM1, FAM2, PSY, DIS, NEN, D1, D4, D5, Hy1* (low), *Hy2* (low), *Hy3, Hy4, Hy5* (low), *Pd1, Pd3* (low), *Pd4, Pd5, Pa1, Pa2, Pa3, Sc1, Sc2, Sc3, Sc4, Sc5, Sc6, Si1, Si2, A, R, Re* (low), *GM* (low), *AAS, MDS.*

- Treatment: Rule out Schizophrenia; mood disorder; Obsessive-Compulsive Disorder or other anxiety disorder; Schizotypal, Compulsive, or Dependent Personality Disorder. Risk of impulsive suicide. Biological treatments more effective than psychotherapy to improve symptomatic status and reduce suicide risk. Antidepressants may precipitate mania. Supportive and cognitive therapies are effective in the post-acute phase, as are social skills and assertiveness training. Motivated for symptomatic relief; introspective; insight often well preserved (except in Schizophrenia). Accepts and benefits from structure, support, and reassurance. Psychotherapy often helpful after initial difficulties in gaining rapport are overcome.

7-9/9-7

- Definition: An unusual and unstable profile. May be found in patients with Bipolar Disorder or patients who may be seeking to distract themselves from some kind of real or impending setback.
- Compulsive achievement strivings. Tense, apprehensive, and overreactive to security threats; very threatened by failure. Anxious, agitated, and obsessive, but driven, impulsive and excitable. Emotionally and behaviorally undercontrolled. Somatic complaints such as musculoskeletal symptoms, sexual problems, and disturbed sleep may represent effects of chronic tension and stress. May be at once fearful or panicky about impending failure or catastrophe, and unrealistically optimistic about success. May obsess about past failures and future triumphs, and shift from meticulousness to recklessness. Overactivity, when present, is pressured and forced rather than natural and euphoric, and is often closely focused on a specific project or issue. Concentration and memory are only mildly impaired, but judgment may be poor and dominated by impulse. Mild psychotic or schizotypal features such as intrusive and disruptive thoughts and suspiciousness may be present. Both intropunitive and extropunitive. Intolerant of boredom and others' demands. Seeks stimulation as a distraction from subjective distress. Conflicted about dependency. Threatened by disapproval and rejection. Egocentric and immature; may be thoughtless and unkind toward others, eventually driving them away. Look for history of mood disorder, substance abuse, or both; family conflict; and periods of impulsive and heedless action followed by periods of guilt, remorse, and self-condemnation.
- Check: *ANX, OBS, DEP1, DEP2, DEP3, BIZ1, BIZ2, ANG1, ANG2, CYN2, TPA1, TPA2, LSE1, LSE2, SOD1, SOD2, AGG, PSY, NEN, D1, D2* (low), *D4, D5, Hy2* (low), *Hy3, Hy5* (low), *Pd4, Pd5, Pa1, Pa2, Pa3* (low), *Sc1, Sc2, Sc3, Sc4, Sc5, Sc6, Ma1, Ma2, Ma3, Ma4, Si1, Si2* (low), *A, R* (low), *Re, MAC-R, APS, AAS, MDS.*
- Treatment: Rule out Bipolar Disorder, Mixed or Manic, Cyclothymia, and obsessive-compulsive features. Risk of impulsive suicide. May be amenable to a variety of treatments, including biological measures (e.g., mood stabilizers), behavioral and skills training procedures (e.g., assertiveness training and anger management) and conventional

psychotherapy. Consider retesting after an interval of observation and change in mental status as a guide to treatment.

7-0/0-7

- Anxiety and dysphoria with inhibition, indecision, inertia, severe self-consciousness, lack of self-confidence, and extreme interpersonal sensitivity. Overcontrolled. May be preoccupied about physical appearance or fears of unattractiveness. Check third highest scale.

Spike 8

- Look for eccentricity, apathy, and aloofness. See Chapter 6.

8-9/9-8

- Moderate to severe excitement, hyperactivity, hypertalkativeness, flight of ideas, loudness, impulsivity, anxiety, tension, agitation, restlessness, and vulnerability to panic. Severe emotional and behavioral undercontrol. Mood is inflated, even exalted, but labile and unstable, becoming quickly and often unpredictably irritable, hostile, and paranoid. Ruminative, obsessive, and overideational, with fantasizing or daydreaming, often on religious or sexual themes. Quick to disorganize under stress. Manifest psychosis and thought disorder are typical and often severe, with emotional inappropriacy; derailment, slang associations, echolalia, neologisms, circumstantiality, tangentiality, autism, and poor reality testing; behavioral disorganization, bizarreness, hallucinations, and delusions of grandeur, persecution, control, or a combination of these. Cognitive impairment is often severe, with problems in attention, concentration, memory, judgment, and lapses in consciousness. At the extreme, may be disoriented, confused, and perplexed, possibly leading to panic and potential assaultiveness. Identity and self-esteem are brittle and easily threatened, with underlying feelings of inferiority/inadequacy; failure or interpersonal rejection may lead to panic and collapse, and to a risk of impulsive suicide. Interpersonally suspicious and mistrustful, aloof, volatile, demanding, and entitled, with strong needs for attention and admiration. Hypersensitive to heterosexual rejection. Look for history of problems in school, previous hospitalization, substance abuse, interpersonal rejection, failures of achievement/aspiration or approval, or other stresses.

- Check: *ANX, DEP1, DEP3, DEP4, HEA2, BIZ1, BIZ2, ANG1, ANG2, CYN1, CYN2, ASP1, TPA2, FAM1, AGG, PSY, DIS, NEN, D1, D4, D5, Hy2* (low), *Hy3, Hy5* (low), *Pd1, Pd4, Pd5, Pa1, Pa2, Pa3* (low), *Sc1, Sc2, Sc3, Sc4, Sc5, Sc6, Ma1, Ma2, Ma3, Ma4, Si2* (low), *A, R* (low), *Re* (low), *MAC-R, AAS, MDS*.
- Treatment: Rule out Bipolar Disorder, Manic; Schizoaffective Disorder (excited); sympathomimetic toxicity; "homosexual panic" *(8-9-5/9-8-5)*. Severe lack of insight and resistance to psychological approaches. Biological therapies initially effective despite resistance to medication. Easily threatened by psychotherapy and prone to negativism and evasiveness. Needs high level of structure and support, with focus determined by patient.

8-0/0-8

- Dysphoria, inertia, anhedonia, impaired self-esteem, guilt; problems in concentration, memory, judgment, and decision making; autistic thinking; severe alienation, aloofness, social anxiety, and suspiciousness. Easily frightened. Avoids conflict and gives up in the face of difficulty. Check third highest scale.

Spike 9

- Inflated, expansive, and euphoric mood, with hyperactivity, hypertalkativeness, excitement, pressured speech, grandiosity, flight of ideas, impulsivity, jocularity, and fearlessness. Mood is relatively stable but may become quickly hostile when frustrated, thwarted, or rebuffed. Very intolerant of external controls and limitations. Thinking varies from fairly well organized though unrealistic (hypomania) to disorganized, fantastic, and bizarre (mania). Dress and grooming may be loud, conspicuous, and flamboyant. Tend to be involved in multiple projects and plans to which they attach messianic importance and to which they may devote themselves to the extent of going without sleep. Cognition is experienced as completely unfettered, with racing thoughts and effortless decision making, but may appear to others as circumstantial, prodigal, and impulsive. Grandiosity may have a religious complexion, with exaltation and "world-saving" or iconoclastic fantasies/delusions. Interpersonally promiscuous and outgoing but with poor empathy and suspicions/fears that others will not recognize, appreciate, or confirm patient's inflated identity; quick to feel invalidated. Look for family history of mood disorder, history of previous manic or depressive episodes requiring hospitalization, substance abuse, return to baseline functioning after previous episodes, interpersonal rejection, failures of achievement/ aspiration or approval, or other stresses.

- Check: *FRS1* (low), *FRS2* (low), *DEP1* (low), *DEP2* (low), *DEP3* (low), *DEP4* (low), *TPA1* (low), *LSE1* (low), *LSE2* (low), *SOD1* (low), *SOD2* (low), *AGG, PSY, DIS, LPE* (low), *D2, Sc2* (low), *Ma1, Ma2, Ma3, Ma4, Si1* (low), *Si2* (low), *A* (low), *R* (low), Re (low), *GF* (low), *MAC-R, AAS.*
- Treatment: Rule out Bipolar Disorder, Manic; substance abuse. Lack of insight and resistance to psychological approaches. Biological therapies initially effective. May fear depression. May accept supportive psychotherapy but require assistance to attend sessions.

9-0/0-9

- Anxiety, dysphoria, and inertia, with behavioral undercontrol, hostility, impulsiveness, fears of domination, and social discomfort. Check third highest scale.

Spike 0

- See Chapter 6.

TEST YOURSELF

1. **Although the well-defined codetyping strategy may blunt the influence of measurement error, it may not adequately control for the influence(s) of**
   - (a) response style.
   - (b) covariation among the clinical scales.
   - (c) item overlap.
   - (d) K-corrections.
   - (e) a and b.
   - (f) a and c.
   - (g) c and d.

(continued)

2. **Caldwell's A-B-C-D strategy emphasizes**

   (a) the basic scales.

   (b) the clinical scales.

3. **The A-B-C-D strategy should be employed only when codetypes are well defined.** True or False?

4. **In some instances, the sequence of steps proposed in the A-B-C-D strategy can and should be modified by scores on the content and other nonclinical scales.** True or False?

5. **When Scales 5 or 0 are highest or second-highest in the code,**

   (a) they should be interpreted only after the codetype based on the basic scales.

   (b) their interpretation should be supplemented by subsequent elevations (typically the third-highest scale).

   (c) the clinician should use only the well-defined strategy for codetyping.

Answers: 1. e; 2. a; 3. False; 4. True; 5. b.

Nine

STRENGTHS AND WEAKNESSES OF THE MMPI-2

The strengths and weaknesses of the MMPI-2, as with any test, must be judged, in part, against the standard of its intended applications and their extensions as these have emerged in practice and have received some degree of sanction in research. Although the MMPI/MMPI-2 grew out of the need for better psychodiagnostic methods for use with psychiatric inpatients, the accumulation of more than a half century of experience and research has tended to support the use of the MMPI-2 with a much wider range of populations than was originally envisioned. This range includes psychological and psychiatric outpatients; consumers of college mental health and vocational counseling services; screening and fitness for military service and general employment, especially for occupations involving issues of public safety, such as airline flight crews, nuclear power plant operators, and police; forensic and criminal justice populations; general medical populations; and a variety of normal range groups.

Detailed discussion of each of these diverse applications is beyond the scope of this book, but the reader should be aware that the particular strengths and weaknesses of the MMPI-2 may vary considerably with the particular application under consideration. The following discussion is intentionally limited to general issues with an emphasis on traditional in- and outpatient psychiatric populations. Rapid Reference 9.1 summarizes the MMPI-2's strengths and weaknesses.

DEVELOPMENT

Perhaps the greatest strength of the MMPI-2 is its substantial continuity with the MMPI. With only minor changes, the same empirically developed validity and clinical scales of the MMPI are available in the MMPI-2. Despite decades

Strengths and Weaknesses of the MMPI-2

Strengths	Weaknesses
Developed from methods emphasizing test validity; the statistical separation of criterion from reference groups.	The original criterion groups are now quite dated.
A vast literature on the empirical correlates of items, scales, and profile patterns.	The confounding of categorical and dimensional models of measurement, leading at times to inferential ambiguities regarding the probability versus the severity of disorder.
A large ethnically, geographically, and socioeconomically diverse contemporary normal standardization sample that is substantially in accord with recent U.S. census values.	Considerable item overlap between scales, thereby increasing their intercorrelations and attenuating their discriminant validity.
Ease of administration (usually 1–2 hours) with multiple administrative formats.	The high average educational and socioeconomic attainment of the restandardization sample may not adequately represent the lower education and economic status of most consumers of mental health services.
Objective scoring and high scorer reliability.	
The temporal stability of the standard clinical scales is in a range adequate to reflect both continuity and change in symptoms and personality.	The number of scales and the complexity of a few makes hand scoring inconvenient, cumbersome, and time-consuming.
Validity, especially convergent validity, has been shown to be high over thousands of studies of many different designs and samples. Incremental validity is modest but consistent.	For maximal accuracy and utility of results, the test requires a ninth-grade level of reading ability and at least a moderately cooperative attitude toward taking the test.
Assessment of a very broad range of attitudes, traits, and behaviors in both abnormal and normal populations.	The interpretive process and set of procedures and checks are considerably more subtle, complicated, and demanding than the appearance of the inventory suggests.
Availability of many measures that, in combination, enable a relatively precise specification of the examinee's test-taking attitude.	
Availability of several interpretive procedures that variously emphasize individual scales, profile patterns, and item content, each affording checks and potential elaborations on the others.	

of criticism, the empirical methods used to develop the basic clinical scales (e.g., carefully selected criterion cases, an emphasis on cross-validation, and an absence of preconceptions about which items belong on which scales) must be considered the chief strength of the MMPI-2. However, critics have recognized that the scale names (e.g., Hypochondriasis) refer to diagnostic conceptions that are no longer current (Helmes & Reddon, 1993), given the shifts in diagnostic practices and criteria that have taken place in the past 60 years. Although the significance of these changes could be—and has been—overstated, there is little doubt that for at least some scales, particularly *4, 7,* and *8,* the constructs that were operative when their criterion groups were formed have been superceded. At the same time, however, the constructs underlying the clinical scales have not remained static. They have shifted steadily away from their original diagnostic origins toward loose and open constructs defined by their empirical correlates as these have emerged in the course of research over the past half century. The practice of referring to scales by number (e.g., Scale *1*) rather than by name (e.g., Hypochondriasis) is largely a recognition of this trend.

The MMPI-2's continuity with the MMPI can also be considered a significant weakness. The restandardization was not a reconstruction. No new criterion groups were formed to modernize the original diagnostic constructs or to cross-validate the items originally selected for the basic clinical scales. The various structural problems of the MMPI, such as overlapping items between scales, continue in the MMPI-2. The reasons for not reconstructing the scales are not merely logistic. Whatever their defects, the properties of the basic scales have been thoroughly investigated and are widely known. The accumulation of empirical correlates has insulated them from interpretation based on their original diagnostic constructs. There was a nonnegligible risk that the constitution of a new set of basic scales would have severed the connection between the painstakingly gathered correlates of the original scales and thus scuttle 40 years of validity research. The design and logistics problems that would attend a contemporary reconstruction are not trivial. The diagnostic constructs codified within the successive editions of the American Psychiatric Association's *Diagnostic and Statistical Manual of Mental Disorders* are moving targets and also suffer from overlapping criteria. Their polythetic format is less than ideal for constituting homogeneous criterion groups because it allows patients to qualify for the same diagnosis on the basis of different criteria. Even if this obstacle could be overcome (or judged not to be an obstacle), formidable difficulties would remain. Consider Schizophrenia. Given Hathaway's reservations about the performance of his original Scale *8* and subsequent research documenting its limitations (e.g., Walters, 1983, 1988), a newer scale reflecting the advances made over the past half century in understanding this disorder would be desirable. But how to form a satisfactory criterion group? Should such a group favor acute patients or chronic ones? How acute/chronic? How many of each? How would the prior number of psychiatric hospitalizations be balanced against the total length of lifetime spent in hospital? Should patients be medicated? What kinds of medications and at what dosage ranges? Since this disorder is known to run in families, should a positive family history of mental disorder be required? What kinds of mental disorder in the family history and what degree of relation would qualify the history as positive for schizophrenia? For example, how would one choose between a putative schizophrenic with a second degree relative with schizoaffective disorder and one with a third degree relative with schizophrenia? How would comorbidity be handled? Should patients who abuse substances be excluded or limited in number? Which substances of abuse (if any) would disqualify one who was otherwise eligible? Although these problems are not insurmountable, they do illustrate some of the difficulties that would attend any effort to reconstruct the basic scales. Moreover, such efforts could not guarantee that a new scale would perform better than the original. Any reflection on diagnostic fashions since the inception of the MMPI reminds us that the current descriptive/biological approach in psychiatry was not always dominant. This approach can be seen as a return to the psychiatry of the nineteenth century, with its emphasis on careful description, course, and outcome. This approach was temporarily dislodged in this country by the influence of psychoanalytic and other theories emphasizing explanation over description, with this influence reaching its peak in the 1960s. In the late 1930s and early 1940s, when the MMPI was being developed, psychoanalysis had yet to make significant inroads to the psychiatry in practice at the University of Minnesota Hospitals. The influence of German psychiatry and the descriptive tradition, especially as transmitted through Adolf Meyer, remained dominant and largely governed conceptions of mental disorder that would have operated in the formation of Hathaway's criterion groups. In this sense, the original criterion groups may not be as conceptually antiquated as some have suggested.

In an important critical review of the MMPI and MMPI-2, Helmes and Reddon (1993) enumerated many theoretical and structural problems with the tests. The major theoretical shortcomings identified include the absence of an explicit theory of psychopathology to guide the construction of the MMPI/ MMPI-2, from the writing and preliminary keying of items to the assembly of criterion subjects. The absence of such theoretical guidance increases the risk that the scales may reflect outmoded conceptions of psychopathology and that the "blind" empirical selection of scale items may result in excessively heterogeneous item content and the inclusion of items because of covariation instead of genuine criterion variance. On the other hand, theories in psychopathology and the forces that move them in and out of currency can change rapidly, and the possibility should not be overlooked that the MMPI/MMPI-2's authors' mistrust of theory and their emphasis on establishing reliable and valid empirical relationships among test scores and patterns has enabled the MMPI/MMPI-2 to persist and flourish amidst the winds of a changing theoretical milieu. Helmes and Reddon (1993) criticized the exposure of the different criterion groups to a common item pool on the grounds that this practice invites excessive content heterogeneity for each scale, but this criticism overlooks the syndromal nature of the psychiatric maladies selected for scale construction.

A more significant criticism put forward by Helmes and Reddon (1993) concerns the ambiguities that grow out of the inadvertent mixing of categorical (e.g., diagnostic) and dimensional (e.g., single-trait) models of measurement. In the categorical model, the goal of measurement is the identification of group membership (or nonmembership), and this goal is traditionally met by psychometric signs, patterns, and cutting scores that rule the patient in or out of a particular group or category (e.g., Schizophrenia). The goal of the dimensional model is not to establish an either/or situation but to gain a more-than, less-than indication of the amount or strength of a trait. The clinical scales of the MMPI-2 tend to confound the issue of the *probability* of diagnostic class membership, given a particular score or elevation, with the *severity* of the disturbance/symptoms/disorder given that score. There can be little doubt that this ambiguity has at times given rise to erroneous if not harmful inferences and conclusions.

The structural problems identified by Helmes and Reddon (1993) include redundancy among the standard scales, a lack of cross-validation for the items comprising these scales, and the confounding of response style and social desirability with the substantive measurement of psychopathology. The redundancy among the clinical (and most other) scales of the MMPI/MMPI-2 is due to item overlap and to the boost that overlapping items force upon the correlations between scales. The extent of overlap is sufficient to impact the discriminant validity of the scales negatively and tends to impoverish the (scale level) factor structure of the test. Another effect of overlap, however, is to increase the sensitivity of the clinical (and other) scales, even if this is achieved at the cost of some loss in specificity.

Additional minor problems identified by Helmes and Reddon (1993) include (a) the imbalance between True- and False-keyed items on virtually all of the scales, which creates a vulnerability to the acquiescence response style (i.e., favoring True or False responses regardless of item content); (b) unequal scale lengths, which augment differences in their reliabilities; and (c) the continued uncertainty regarding the performance of the K-correction and the appropriateness of the weights routinely added to 5 of the 10 standard clinical scales since the mid-1940s. A minor problem not identified by Helmes and Reddon (1993) is the wide range of lexical values from scale to scale, which makes some items of some scales more difficult to read and comprehend than those of other scales.

ADMINISTRATION AND SCORING

The MMPI-2 is generally easy to administer and score. Both may be accomplished using trained nonprofessionals, thus saving professional time and costs to consumers. Administration is also efficient in that clinically relevant information on dozens of traits, attitudes, and symptomatic features can be obtained from the output of scores, codetypes, and configural features. Several administration formats are available, including the standard test booklet and answer sheet, audiotape, and computer. A 370-item short form is also available.

STANDARDIZATION

The MMPI-2 restandardization sample of 1,462 women and 1,138 men is thought to be of adequate size. It is geographically, ethnically, and socioeconomically diverse—sufficient to approximate modern United States census values in many respects, but tending to overrepresent the higher ranges of educational and socioeconomic attainment and to underrepresent the lower ranges of these dimensions. Although it is likely that the restandardization norms may be a good or even excellent reference for some clinical groups, such as private psychotherapy clients, they may disadvantage (overpathologize) some patients of limited educational attainment or lower socioeconomic backgrounds, such as patients treated in publically funded hospitals and mental health outpatient clinics.

The development of many new scales following the restandardization—including content and content component scales, the *PSY-5* personality scales, and the addiction acknowledgment and addiction potential scales—has strengthened and extended the range of the MMPI-2 in assessing psychopathology. Most of the scales developed in the MMPI environment can also be scored when their original item numbers are translated into MMPI-2 item numbers.

RELIABILITY AND VALIDITY

The MMPI-2 has acceptable temporal stability (test-retest reliability), with one-week estimates ranging from .58 to .92 for the basic clinical scales, .78 to .91 for the content scales, and .34 to .91 for the supplementary scales (Butcher et al., 1989). Although the optimal stability for personality scales is uncertain, these values appear to be in a range that would be expected for scales that should reflect both continuity and change in personality features over time. Internal consistency reliabilities (coefficients α) for the same groups of scales are .33 to .84, .68 to .86, and .24 to .91, respectively (Butcher et al., 1989). These values also tend to fall within the range of expectation, although the clinical scales have somewhat lower values for α, consistent with their syndromal origins, and the content scales have somewhat higher values, reflecting their derivation using means to maximize internal consistency.

Not only scales but also individuals and profiles vary along the dimension of reliability, with some being relatively stable over time and others being relatively unstable. Among individuals, the best known example is patients with Bipolar Disorder, some of whom may generate markedly different profiles within a few days. For example, a given patient may produce a Spike *9* code pattern on one occasion and a *2-7-8* profile on the next. By contrast, patients producing the classic *4-9* profile will often show the same code type months and years later. In the same vein, profiles with peak elevations on Scale *6* tend to be less stable than those with peak elevations on Scale *0*. For both individuals and profiles, the stability of scores can be ascertained only by retesting.

Substantial evidence for the validity of the MMPI-2 has accumulated over the past decade, adding to some 50 years of prior research on the MMPI. Investigations into the validity of the MMPI/MMPI-2 have included diverse experimental designs, including multivariate analyses; classification paradigms; incremental validity comparisons; and the identification of empirical correlates of items, scales, and profile patterns. These investigations have involved many different subject samples, including normal, psychiatric, medical, vocational, and forensic, as well as a variety of cultural and ethnic groups from around the world. The weight and diversity of this evidence must be counted as particular strengths of the test. In no study has the MMPI/MMPI-2 had the effect of degrading the accuracy of prediction when it was added to the clinical database, as has routinely been the case with projective tests (cf., Wiggins, 1973). Studies that have examined the empirical correlates of scale scores have repeatedly confirmed the main correlates found in previous research. Similar research focusing on the empirical correlates of profile patterns has likewise tended to support the results of previous investigations.

Evidence for the convergent validity of the MMPI/MMPI-2 is generally considered substantially better than that for its discriminant validity. Scores on the standard clinical scales have shown moderate convergence with scores on a variety of other self-report inventories and scales, rating scales, clinical judgments (including diagnostic status), and, to a more limited extent, even with projective devices such as the Rorschach (e.g., Hiller, Rosenthal, Bornstein, Berry, & Brunell-Neuleib, 1999; see also Garb, 1998, and Wood & Lilienfeld, 1999). It appears that the inclusion of overlapping items on the clinical scales has enhanced the test's convergent validity. The overlap of items between scales is a reflection of the overlap between the diagnostic constructs that the scales were designed to measure. The extent and nature of such construct overlap is codified in the *DSM-IV* in the form of overlapping diagnostic criteria for many mental disorders. Restricting this overlap would limit the assay of a given syndrome's features to only those exclusive to it, but at the cost of reducing the sensitivity of the clinical scales to those patients whose presentations include both distinctive and overlapping diagnostic features. Thus, there is a good rationale for allowing item overlap: It permits a clinical scale to reflect the syndrome's full range of symptoms and features, even when some of these symptoms are shared by other syndromes.

On the other hand, the item overlap between scales and the resulting enhanced correlations among them reduces their specificity and thereby compromises their discriminant validity. The reduction in discriminant validity caused by item overlap has important consequences in the clinic, chiefly in the context of differential diagnosis. Even such strong critics as Helmes and Reddon (1993) agreed that the MMPI/MMPI-2 discriminates "between adjustment and abnormality," and does so "very well" (p. 457). In hospital and outpatient settings, however, this strength counts for little because the abnormal status of the patient is not usually in question. In such settings a more precise formulation of the nature of the disorder that gives rise to the patient's symptoms and complaints is often needed. The MMPI-2 tends to perform reasonably well in identifying broad categories of patients, such as those with somatoform, anxiety, mood, psychotic, and personality disorders, but its validity for discriminating among disorders within these categories (e.g., unipolar versus bipolar depression) is much less established.

Moreover, although there is reason to believe that scales comprising items of similar content such as the Harris and Lingoes subscales and the MMPI-2 content scales extend the validity of the test in differential diagnosis, available research to support such confidence is at present modest. These scales, too, are not free of overlapping items; and the content scales, in particular, are often very highly correlated with one another, thereby limiting their own differential diagnostic efficiency.

Helmes and Reddon (1993) have stated that the K-correction exacerbates the problem of item overlap by increasing the correlation among those scales receiving this correction and thereby further decreasing their discriminant validity. In fact, however, the addition of the K-correction almost always acts to *decrease* the correlation among the clinical scales, and by a significant increment on the average (Greene, personal communication and unpublished data, July 18, 1999). Thus, the net effect of the K-correction appears to restore partially the loss of discriminant validity caused by overlapping items.

Finally, the validity of the MMPI-2 is significantly influenced by the pattern of motivations of those completing the inventory. Issues surrounding these various motives and their consequences for performance are discussed in greater detail in Chapters 2 and 5. From a psychometric standpoint, the MMPI-2's vulnerability to the distorting effects of various response styles, such as efforts to overreport or underreport psychopathology, must be considered a weakness. From a clinical standpoint, however, the availability of scales to detect and disentangle these motives and their operation in the completion of the test is a distinct strength. In clinical contexts, the distorting effects of response styles afford the clinician valuable access to the patient's motives, insight, willingness to cooperate, fears of adverse judgment, and a variety of other factors that may importantly influence diagnosis and treatment. The means to measure a disposition to distort test results may be of preeminent importance when the credibility of the examinee and his or her openness to the examination is part of the focus of assessment, which is often the case in civil and criminal forensic evaluations. Whatever the context of assessment, the validity of test findings is enhanced by the examinee's cooperativeness, openness, and engagement.

INTERPRETATION

The interpretation of the MMPI-2 is complicated by several factors, not least of which is the complexity of human personality and its organization and vulnerability to change over time. This complexity is reflected in the test's hundreds of scales and configural features. The process of interpretation takes advantage of this complexity in various ways. For those profiles that conform to previously studied code patterns, the empirical correlates derived from earlier research may be tentatively applied to the instant case. These correlates may be "tested" by evaluating their suitability for describing the patient with reference to subscales, content scales, and supplementary scales. For code patterns that are infrequent or novel, interpretation may proceed from the analysis of the high and low scores on the clinical scales on a scale-by-scale basis, with reference to the empirical correlates associated with each scale. Again, it is best to make reference to the subscales, content scales, and supplementary scales to assess the likelihood that the clinical scale correlates will be descriptive of the patient's personality and behavior. For those profiles that show very limited scatter or patterning, an approach that emphasizes item content, such as the MMPI-2 Structural Summary (Greene & Nichols, 1995; Nichols &

Greene, 1995), can provide a broad range of interpretive hypotheses as well as guidance for the selection of one or more pattern types under which a given profile might tentatively be subsumed.

An important strength of the MMPI-2 is the amount and quality of the literature available for education and training in understanding and using the test. This book serves as a comprehensive overview of clinical interpretations of the test. It can and should be supplemented by other guides and manuals of interpretation, such as those of Friedman and colleagues (2001) and Greene (2000); professional workshops; journal articles; and commercial software that focuses on MMPI-2 interpretation.

A counterbalancing weakness, however, is the complexity of the interpretive process. Because of the heterogeneity of most of the standard scales, equivalent scores may be obtained on the basis of markedly different patterns of item endorsement. For example, two patients may both achieve elevations of *T*-65 on Scale *4* despite their having endorsed no items in common. A related problem, especially when the clinician wishes to view the clinical scales as diagnostic constructs for the purpose of differential diagnosis, is that the items endorsed on a given scale may not be evenly distributed across the various components that enable the scale to model the syndrome that gives the scale its name, but may be largely confined to a single characteristic. For example, a patient with an average score on *K* (raw score 15) may achieve a score of *T*-81 on Scale *8* by endorsing 80% of the sensorimotor items from *Sc6* (16 items), but only 20% of the items from each of the remaining five subscales (e.g., 4 items from *Sc1*, 2 from *Sc2*, 2 from *Sc3*, 3 from *Sc4*, and 2 from *Sc5*). In such a case, the empirical correlates of the full Scale *8* may apply only narrowly (and, in the aggregate, poorly) to the patient in question, even though the correlates of *Sc6* might be seen to apply especially well.

For those scales that are less complex, such as Scales *1* and *7*, appropriate interpretation may require examination of other scales to determine the relative contributions of various symptoms to the level of distress signaled by their elevations. The interpreter may wish, for example, to examine the *Anxiety*

DON'T FORGET

Always refer to the subscales, content scales, and supplementary scales to assess the likelihood that the clinical scale correlates will be descriptive of the patient's personality and behavior.

(ANX), Fears and Phobias (FRS), Obsessiveness (OBS), and Depression (DEP) content scales and their components to better understand the symptoms underlying high scores on Scale 7 (or Scale 2), and the health concerns content component scales (HEA1, HEA2, HEA3) to better identify the symptoms giving rise to a high score on Scale 1. In some cases, however, these scales may not adequately specify such symptoms, and the interpreter may need to examine the specific items endorsed.

Although the norms gathered in the restandardization are undoubtedly more representative of the contemporary American population than those from the original MMPI, only about half of the time are they sufficiently different from the original norms to produce profile patterns (codetypes) familiar within the MMPI environment. Because so much of the interpretive corpus of the MMPI is linked to its familiar code patterns, the partial breakdown (and occasional incommensurability) of these patterns in the MMPI-2 environment can create formidable problems for the interpreter. Suppose, for example, that a given profile is coded 4-8 when plotted on the original MMPI norms, but 2-6 on the MMPI-2 norms. Should the interpreter rely on the MMPI code or the MMPI-2 code? Or attempt to meld them (in which case should either be considered "primary")? Caldwell (1997), Humphrey and Dahlstrom (1995), and others have recommended that MMPI-2 scores be plotted on both the old and new norms. The more conservative Caldwell recommends that the MMPI profile be given interpretive precedence because of its closer link with previous research, whereas Humphrey and Dahlstrom view either profile as a potentially valuable source of hypotheses and implicitly advocate that both be evaluated for areas of interpretive redundancy, allowing other patient information and clinician judgment to resolve differences in their interpretive implications. Double profiling may well be valuable, especially as an exercise to promote learning and increase familiarity with pattern types in general, but this practice is obviously cumbersome and time-consuming. It is recommended that double profiling be retained as an option to facilitate interpretation when needed, and that each user assess the value of this procedure in the context of his or her own population and practice.

TEST YOURSELF

1. **The clinical scales of the MMPI-2 are best understood in terms of their accumulated empirical correlates rather than in the light of the diagnostic constructs embodied in the original criterion groups.** True or False?

2. **The lack of an explicit theory of psychopathology underlying the MMPI-2 may be considered as much a strength as a weakness, given the pace of change in such theories.** True or False?

3. **A major advantage of the MMPI-2 is a model of measurement that prevents the confounding of categorical diagnostic assignment with the severity of psychopathology.** True or False?

4. **The restandardization of the MMPI on a diverse, contemporary, normal sample prevents the scores on the MMPI-2 from overpathologizing some groups while underpathologizing others.** True or False?

5. **The test-retest stabilities of most of the MMPI-2 scales appear to be in a range that allows them to retain sensitivity to both continuity and change in symptoms and personality.** True or False?

6. **The discriminant validity of the MMPI-2 is substantially better than its convergent validity.** True or False?

7. **The addition of the *K*-correction to five of the eight basic scales has which effects?**

   (a) It decreases their intercorrelation and probably enhances their discriminant validity.

   (b) It increases their intercorrelation and probably enhances their discriminant validity.

   (c) It decreases their intercorrelation and probably reduces their discriminant validity.

   (d) It increases their intercorrelation and probably reduces their discriminant validity.

Answers: 1. True; 2. True; 3. False; 4. False; 5. True; 6. False; 7. a

Ten

CLINICAL APPLICATIONS OF THE MMPI-2

The MMPI-2 has widespread applications for assessing personality and psychopathology in adult men and women. It is routinely used in the clinical assessment of psychiatric inpatients, consumers of psychiatric outpatient and psychotherapy services, and in college counseling centers. It is also commonly used in the course of psychological/psychiatric consultation to general medical services to detect previously undiagnosed mental disorders or identify problems in adjustment that may adversely influence treatment adherence, response, and recovery. It may be a component in test batteries assembled for the evaluation of neuropsychological function and status. As well, the MMPI-2 is used in screening and selecting personnel for employment, especially for positions involving high levels of stress and responsibility or occupations in which concern for public safety is a central consideration, such as law enforcement, airplane piloting, nuclear power-plant operation, and other employment contexts in which maturity and emotional adjustment may be considered likely to influence job performance. The MMPI-2 may often figure in criminal forensic proceedings for pretrial assessments of competence to stand trial, ability to aid and assist representative counsel, in sanity evaluations, and in the classification of adjudicated offenders. In civil forensic proceedings for determinations of eligibility for commitment, parental fitness and child custody; medical or psychological malpractice; evaluating stress, personal injury, disability, and related claims for compensation and damages, the results of the MMPI-2 may be used to assess the psychological adjustment and credibility of defendants or litigants in order to assist the trier of fact.

The primary focus of this book is on using the MMPI-2 to diagnose and plan treatment of persons being seen as patients in psychiatric inpatient or outpatient services and clinics and for clients receiving or being evaluated for psychotherapy by licensed mental health practitioners. Although the material contained herein may at times bear on questions of medical, neuropsychological, employment, or forensic interest, other publications contain more detailed treatments regarding accepted principles and practices for using the MMPI-2 outside traditional mental health settings.

This chapter identifies six clinical applications of the MMPI-2:

- Assessment of self-presentation
- Assessment of the severity and chronicity of disturbance
- Assessment of clinical syndromes
- Assessment of symptomatic status
- Assessment of personality and social functioning
- Assessment of personality change and suitability for psychotherapy

Having discussed the major symptoms of psychopathology in the context of individual scales in Chapter 6, in this section symptoms will be the starting point to highlight individual scales and patterns that are deemed relevant to the assessment of pathological syndromes, symptoms, and signs.

ASSESSMENT OF SELF-PRESENTATION

The MMPI-2 stands alone in the area of personality assessment in terms of the variety and usefulness of measures to assess a broad range of dimensions related to response styles, attitudes, and approaches to self-presentation. Nichols and Greene (1997) have described seven dimensions along which responses related to self-presentation on the MMPI-2 may vary: inconsistency versus inaccuracy, dissimulation versus simulation, generic versus specific deception, crude versus sophisticated deception, intentional versus nonintentional deception, self-deception versus impression management, and selectivity versus inclusiveness.

The first dimension, *inconsistency versus inaccuracy,* sets the basic condition for protocol interpretation, the requirement that an adequate level of consistency in responding to the test items is achieved. This condition is evaluated by scores on *VRIN* and *TRIN.* Meeting this condition permits the clinician to make inferences regarding the accuracy of self-report along the dimension of overreporting and underreporting. The presence and extent of overreporting is evaluated using scales F, F_B, F_P, Ds, and the $F - K$ Index; the presence and extent of underreporting is evaluated using scales L, K, S, Ss, Mp, and Sd.

The second dimension, *dissimulation versus simulation,* draws on the distinction between an approach to the test that seeks to mask actual traits, attitudes, and dispositions (dissimulation), and one that seeks to mimic such attributes when these are felt to be descriptively inaccurate (simulation). Scales F, F_B, F_P, Ds, and the $F - K$ Index may mask favorable traits and mimic unfavorable ones, whereas scales L, K, S, Ss, Mp, and Sd may mask unfavorable traits or mimic favorable ones.

The third dimension, *generic versus specific deception,* recognizes that examinees may mask and mimic favorable or psychopathological features generically or indiscriminately, or in terms of a set to claim or deny a specific set of traits or symptoms. For example, an examinee may seek to mask or mimic features of a particular disorder or class of disorder (somatization, anxiety, depressive, psychotic, etc.) or problem area (delinquency, anger, family enmity, etc.) in a highly selective manner, without concealing or simulating other symptoms or problem areas.

The fourth dimension, *crude versus sophisticated deception,* is fundamentally a dimension of competence in the execution of a strategy, whether implicit or deliberate, to mask or mimic self-favorable or self-negative traits. This dimension acknowledges that examinees bring varying levels of test-taking resources, including intelligence, test-taking experience, and even test-specific knowledge, to the assessment task. Crude approaches are suggested by a bias toward *True* ($T\% > 60$) or *False* ($T\% < 30$), or a preference for endorsing (or denying) psychopathology resulting in a mean elevation (ME) on the basic clinical scales (Scales *1* through *4* and *6* through *9*) of 85 or greater (or 45 or less). Scales L and R are also sensitive to this dimension when the approach favors the masking of negative features or the mimicking of positive ones, although they are not particularly sensitive to overreporting.

The fifth dimension, *intentional versus nonintentional deception,* recognizes the limits of ideation and self-awareness in test taking. Because the awareness of one's motives is virtually always incomplete and motives surrounding the communication of psychopathology and adjustment may be in conflict, the revelation and concealment of symptoms and problems are generally not entirely under conscious control. Thus, efforts at masking and mimicking psychopathology may fail to be in accord with the examinee's desire, with the result that such motives or the features on which these motives are focused may be unintentionally exposed. For example, scores on *MAC-R* and *O-H* with respect to their primary constructs are difficult if not impossible to manipulate. The same might be said of the subtle components of the clinical scales and some of the subscales. Similarly, such features as delusional ideation may be inadvertently exposed despite a desire to conceal it when the pathological implications of such a symptom fall outside conscious control (i.e., when such ideation is ego-syntonic). Long cherished self-attributions, whether positive or negative, may likewise infiltrate the response process in ways that affect test findings.

The sixth dimension, *self-deception versus impression management,* distinguishes between the tendency to bias test responses out of a belief that these responses are true and justified, and the self-conscious and deliberate attempt to tailor responses to mislead the clinician about the examinee's clinical status and functioning. This dimension grew out of studies of underreporting, but there is no prohibition in principle against applying it to overreporting (see, e.g., Fp, Ds). That is, overreporting, like underreporting, may result from unrealistically negative self-attitudes (self-deception) as well as from a calculated effort to malinger mental disorder (impression management). All of the validity scales have a role in assessing test-taking attitudes in terms of this dimension, as well as some of the others discussed here. Although F, F_B, F_p, Ds, and the $F - K$ Index are sensitive to broadly mimicked pathological features and broadly masked favorable attributes, F is differentially sensitive to psychotic features, F_B is differentially sensitive to negative emotionality, Ds is differentially sensitive to nonpsychotic disability (when F, F_B, and F_p are lower than Ds) and possibly to negative impression management, and F_p appears to be particularly sensitive to overreporting as a function of impression management (malingering). Similarly, although L, K, S, Ss, Mp, and Sd are sensitive to broadly mimicked favorable features and broadly masked pathological attributes, L is differentially sensitive to naively self-serving moral claims, K and S are differentially sensitive to favorable biases stemming from self-deception, Ss is differentially sensitive to ingrained (and usually justified) self-favorable attitudes, and Mp and Sd are differentially sensitive to intentionally deceptive self-favorable presentations (Mp by the denial of common flaws and failings, Sd by the assertion of unusually favorable traits and attitudes).

The seventh dimension, *selectivity versus inclusiveness,* concerns the range of items to be endorsed within particular symptomatic or personological domains, recognizing that some patients will endorse items reflecting a particular state or condition (e.g., depression) in a highly selective and discriminating fashion, whereas others will respond in a more inclusive, less discriminating way. For example, a patient's primarily depressive symptoms may become associated with items in adjacent symptomatic domains such as somatization, anxiety, alienation, hypersensitivity, social withdrawal, and so forth, thereby complicating and confounding the patient's self-report. Here again, the validity scales are useful in helping to specify the level of precision that the patient has tried to adopt in communicating symptoms and traits. Elevations on F, F_B, F_p, Ds, F–K, and ME, and high $T\%$ (or very low $T\%$ in the case of the over-inclusion of somatic symptoms) suggest a general bias toward overinclusion, and an overly inclusive approach to particular symptom domains may be identified by unusual elevations on many of the unidimensional scales, including Scales 1 and 7 and the content scales, among others. Conversely, elevations on L, K, S, Ss, Mp, and Sd may indicate an overly selective bias in reporting symptoms, especially when the scores on unidimensional scales are more or less uniformly suppressed. The ideal self-presentation in terms of this dimension is suggested by no more than moderate elevations on the validity scales, perhaps excepting Ss, and discrete and highly patterned elevations on the clinical and content scale profiles.

ASSESSMENT OF THE SEVERITY AND CHRONICITY OF DISTURBANCE

The concept of severity of disturbance in the MMPI-2 is inextricably linked to response style because of the latter's influence on scale and profile elevation and on the tendency to endorse the obvious versus the subtle items. It is impossible to arrive at hypotheses regarding severity apart from an adequate analysis of response style. It is also important to distinguish between the severity of distress and discomfort from the severity of dysfunction and disability. In general, A is a satisfactory marker for general maladjustment and subjective distress, but some patients with relatively low scores (e.g., some somatoform disorders) will show little apparent distress despite considerable disability, whereas others (e.g., anxiety disorders) will show much distress but little loss in day-to-day functioning. For both of these groups, Scale 2 may be a better index of severity. As a rule, disorders that differentially elevate the right half of the profile (positive slope) are more severe and disabling than disorders that differentially elevate the left half of the profile (negative slope), but here, too, there are many exceptions: Some negative slope hypochondriacal disorders are severely debilitating and all but intractable; some positive slope manic disorders respond to appropriate treatment promptly and recover completely. And then there are the personality disorders in which there may be little subjective distress but high severity in terms of the problems the patient's behavior creates for others.

Regardless of the severity of distress within episodes, some disorders will show a remitting course while others will show a prolonged one. There is some tendency for profiles in which Scales *1, 4,* and *8* exceed *2, 3,* and *7* to gravitate toward a more chronic course. Additionally, elevations on *F* and low scores on *K* and *Ss* suggest an acceptance of deviancy, misfortune, and a compromised or spoiled identity that can lead to a more ready acceptance of a marginalized social role (e.g., "mental patient") and hence a greater tolerance for a chronic status.

ASSESSMENT OF CLINICAL SYNDROMES

Despite its development in a psychiatric inpatient setting and the use of well-diagnosed criterion cases for scale development, there are very few MMPI-2 profile patterns or scores that are quasipathognomonic for specific mental disorders. MMPI-2 characteristics of several broad diagnostic groups are as follows.

Somatoform processes are reflected primarily on Scales *1* and *3* (especially *Hy4* and *Hy-O*), on subscales *D3* and *Sc6,* and on *HEA;* and secondarily on Scales *2, 7,* and *8,* and on *R, ANX,* and *DEP.* Representative codetypes include Spike *1, 1-2/2-1, 1-2-3/2-1-3, 1-7, 1-2-7/2-1-7* (somatization/hypochondriasis/chronic pain), *1-3/3-1, 1-3-2/3-1-2* (conversion/chronic pain), *1-8/8-1, 1-8-7/8-1-7/8-7-1* (somatization with psychosis; possible somatic delusions).

Anxiety disorders are reflected primarily on Scale *7* and *ANX;* and secondarily on Scales *1, 2, 3, 8,* and *0,* and on *GM* (low), *FRS, OBS, HEA, LSE,* and *SOD.* Scales *4* and *9, CYN, ASP, AGG,* and *DIS* tend to be low. Representative codetypes include *7-2/2-7, 3-2/2-3, 3-7/7-3* (with or without *1*), *7-8,* and *7-2-8/7-8-2.* Use *ANX > DEP* as an index to help distinguish anxiety from depressive disorders. Phobic patterns may emphasize Scales *7, 0,* and *SOD.* Obsessive patterns may emphasize Scales *7, 8,* and *OBS.*

Depressive and dysthymic disorders are reflected primarily on Scale *2* and *DEP,* and secondarily on Scales F_B, *1,* 3 (especially *Hy3*), *4* (especially *Pd5*), *6* (especially *Pa2*), *7, 8* (especially *Sc2* and *Sc4*), *9* (coded low), and *0*, and on *R, ANX, OBS, HEA, LSE, SOD, WRK,* and *TRT.* Scales *1* and *3*, and *HEA* and *9*, when not low, may mask depression. Representative codetypes include *2-7, 2-3, 2-4, 2-6, 2-8, 2-0, 2-7-3,* and *2-7-8/2-8-7.* Use *DEP > ANX* as an index to help distinguish depressive from anxiety disorders. There is a tendency for bipolar depressions to test as slightly more undercontrolled that unipolar depressions (look for Scale *9, MAC-R,* and *DIS* to be slightly higher in bipolar depression, *R* slightly lower).

Manic disorder is reflected primarily on Scales *9, 2,* and *0* (both coded low); and secondarily on Scales *4, 6,* and *8* (especially *Sc5* and *Sc6*), *DIS,* and *MAC-R;* and on *R, FRS, DEP, and LSE, SOD,* and *LPE* (all low). Scales *4* and *6* may especially implicate irritability. The pattern of *ANG1, ANG2, TPA1,* and *Sc5* high, along with *AGG* and *TPA2* is not uncommonly seen in mania when irritability is a major symptom. Representative manic codes are Spike *9* (euphoric mania), *9-6* (paranoid mania), *9-8* (disorganized mania), *9-4-8/9-8-4,* and *9-6-8* (all combinations).

Paranoid (delusional) disorders are reflected primarily on Scale *6*, and secondarily on Scales *4* (especially *Pd4*) and *8* (especially *Sc1*), and on *BIZ* (especially *BIZ1*) and *CYN.* Uncomplicated Delusional Disorder (pure paranoia/paranoia vera) is associated with Spike *6* (need not exceed *T*-65). In some defensive patterns, *L* may spike; in others *FRS* may be elevated while *CYN* is suppressed. Representative codetypes include Spike *6, 6-4/4-6, 6-5/5-6, 6-7/7-6.* False negative scores on Scale *6* are relatively common in paranoid disorders, but false positives are relatively rare.

Thought disorder is reflected primarily on Scales *6* (especially *Pa1*) and *8* (especially *Sc3*), *BIZ,* and *PSY;* and secondarily on Scales F, *2* (especially *D4*), *4* (especially *Pd1* and *Pd4*), *7,* and *0,* and on *ANX, DEP, OBS, FAM,* and *SOD.* Representative codetypes include *8-6/6-8,* especially with *2, 4, 7,* and *0* next highest in any order, *8-2, 8-2-4, 8-2-7/8-7-2,* and *8-7-4/7-8-4.*

Substance use disorders are reflected primarily on Scale *4* and on *MAC-R, AAS* and *APS;* and secondarily on Scales *1* and *3* (especially for the abuse of soporifics, hypnotics, and analgesics), *2, 7, 8,* and *9* (alcohol and street drugs), and *ASP* and *DIS.* Representative codetypes include *4-2, 3-4/4-3, 4-6/6-4, 4-8/8-4, 4-9/9-4, 2-4-7* (all combinations), *2-4-8* (all combinations), *2-4-9* (all combinations), and *4-7-8* (all combinations).

ASSESSMENT OF SYMPTOMATIC STATUS

Because the correspondence between MMPI-2 profile patterns or scores and formal psychiatric diagnostic categories cannot be taken for granted, the MMPI-2 clinician may approach the task of differential diagnosis more successfully by starting from the bottom up,—that is, by considering the MMPI-2 data as a source of signs and symptoms that may be evaluated for pattern and coherence in much the same way that the psychiatrist uses the data of history and mental status to arrive at a diagnosis. The assessment of disturbed mood is complex, requiring reference not only to matters related to mood and affect as narrowly construed, but also to aspects of thinking and behavior that may be affected by mood states. The remarks that follow borrow extensively from the MMPI-2 Structural Summary (Nichols & Greene, 1995).

Depression

Dysphoric mood is most directly assessed by *DEP2* and *D1,* with *D5* and *Pa2* providing additional information. Depressive ideation and attitudes, encompassing ideas of pessimism, helplessness, hopelessness, worthlessness, and dissatisfaction, may be assessed from *DEP* (especially *DEP1* and *DEP3*), *Sc2,* and *TRT1*. Anhedonia is suggested most directly by *LPE,* although various relevant aspects are contained in *Sc2* (loss of interest), *Sc4, DEP1,* and *TRT1* (apathy and amotivation), *D-S* and *D2* (inhibited aggression). Problems of memory, attention and concentration, and judgment, and of mental insufficiency and cognitive depletion are indicated by *D4* and *Sc3* and, secondarily, by *Sc4* and *D2*. *Sc2* and *Sc4* are sensitive to the affective deficits characteristic of schizophrenia as well as in depressive mood disturbance. Aspects of shame and social anxiety are indicated on *Si1, SOD2, Pd3* (low), and *Hy1* (low). Guilt, guilt-proneness, and negative self-esteem are suggested by *Pd5* and *DEP3,* and secondarily by *D5* and *LSE* (especially *LSE1*). The vegetative symptoms of depression such as anorexia, constipation, weight loss, anergia/fatigue, and sleep disturbance are reflected in *D3, Hy3, D2, HEA* (especially *HEA3*), and *Ma2* when low. The Lachar-Wrobel (1979) critical item list contains six items reflecting sleep disturbance: 5, 30, 39, 140F, 328, and 471. Suicidal ideation is directly indicated in items 150, 303, 506, 520, and 524, and by implication in items 75, 92, 234, 454, 505, 516, 526, 539, 546, and 554; see also *DEP4*.

Elation

There are no MMPI-2 measures of sufficient purity to be recommended for identifying elation in isolation. However, several scales and patterns are consistent with elated and euphoric mood. The most general is that of *Ma* higher than *D*, with elation being suggested at a difference of 20 *T* or greater and strongly implicated at differences of 30 *T* or greater especially when *Mo-S > Mo-D*. Low scores on Scale *0* (< *T*-40) and *LPE* are good secondary measures of elation when Scale *9* is at least moderately elevated. Several additional scales emphasize various facets of elation/euphoria, including *Ma4* (self-importance, grandiosity, control avoidance); *DEP2* and *LSE* (both low; grandiosity); *FRS* (low; fearlessness, recklessness); and Scale *2* and *DEP* (both low; freedom from normal cares and concerns).

Anxiety

ANX is the most specific measure of anxiety on the MMPI-2, but many other scales are sensitive to various aspects of anxiety, such as obsessive rumination (Scale *7*, especially when *7* is higher than *8* and both are elevated), anxious hypersensitivity *(Mf2)*, apprehensiveness *(FRS)*, indecision *(OBS)*, depression and lack of drive *(DEP, TRT)*, cardiorespiratory and other somatic manifestations of anxiety *(HEA)*, feelings of self-doubt and inadequacy *(LSE)*, and performance concerns *(WRK)*. These aspects are also reflected in Scales *1, 2, 3, 7,* and *8* and their various components. The relative success of somatization to reduce anxiety may be judged from $(1 + 3) - (2 + 7)$ and by the relationship between HEA and ANX, with large differences suggesting the successful binding of anxiety by somatic symptoms.

Anger/Irritability/Hostility/Resentment/Rage

Anger and related emotions vary in terms of their characteristic duration and cognitive accompaniments, with some appearing to be more directly mood-centered and state-like, and others being characteristically linked to cognitive patterns, beliefs, and attitudes that act to incite emotional response under certain conditions and to shape and direct its expression. *R* and *DIS* are broadly sensitive to emotional and behavioral control, respectively, influencing how emotions are experienced and expressed. Both *ANG* and *TPA* are sensitive to state and especially trait anger, with *ANG1* emphasizing the felt pressure to express and release angry affect, particularly as a response to frustration and deficits in control, and *ANG2* and *TPA1* emphasizing more trait-like features of an abnormally low threshold for anger arousal but better control over its expression. *TPA2* and *AGG* reflect chronically antagonistic trends with clearly vindictive and sadistic aims, making them sensitive to hostility as distinct from mere anger. Scale *8* is sensitive to a diffuse and alienated enmity toward others (especially *Sc1*) and to a sense of internal chaos and instability that may manifest itself in rage (especially *Sc5*), and these too may influence the intensity, occasion, and focus (or lack thereof) of angry or hostile expressions. Scale *6* is especially sensitive to resentment and therefore also tends to influence the threshold for angry or hostile expressions, usually in the context of rationalized responses to perceived provocations. It is useful to distinguish between the degree of focus that attends angry expression. When *ANG > TPA > Sc5,* angry expressions are likely to be focused on specific issues, perceived offenses, or persons. Conversely, when *Sc5 > TPA > ANG,* "blind" or diffuse expression may occur that are often seen as inappropriate and very poorly modulated, with the targets determined by opportunity and convenience. The component scales for *ANG* and *TPA* can provide additional interpretive guidance in these contexts. A second useful distinction is between "hot" expression, in which the release of crude affect is the primary goal, and "cool" expression, in which the goal is the infliction of emotional or physical injury to the target. *ANG1, ANG2, TPA1,* and *Sc5* are relatively hot scales, whereas *AGG* and *TPA2* suggest a calculated or even predatory desire to inflict harm on others, an orientation that may require patience and emotional and behavioral control if such a goal is to be achieved.

Assault

As a very low base rate event in most mental health settings, a rough gauge of assault risk is available in the following formulas: $(4 + 6 + 8 + 9) - (1 + 2 + 3 + 7)$, and $(AGG + DIS + [50 - R] + 8 + BIZ + PSY) - (D\text{-}S + GF + [50 - LPE] + Es + 2Ss)$, with high values suggesting impaired controls against the physical expression of hostility.

In addition to the preceding insights, a variety of cognitive and attitudinal features of psychopathology may be identified from MMPI-2 scales and indices as follows.

Unconventional Thought Processes

Sc2, Ma2, and *F,* as well as *BIZ2 > BIZ1,* are all sensitive to ways of thinking and thought content that may be infrequent and unconventional but not clearly bizarre or psychotic. Indeed, the number of items of frankly psychotic content is rather small. Elevations on these scales may alert the clinician to the presence of unusual ideation that may not be identified by scales such as *Pa1, BIZ1,* and *PSY,* which contain relatively high proportions of psychotic content.

Psychotic Thought Processes

There are several general indicators of psychosis, including the Goldberg Index (1965; $L + Pa + Sc - Hy - Pt > 45$; see also Goldberg, 1972, and Zalewski & Gottesman, 1991), for which the difference between Scales 8 and 7 contained most of the variance; and a newer but similar index: *PSY > NEN.* False positive decisions for $8 > 7$ and *PSY > NEN* may be reduced by requiring that differences between their components exceed $10T.$ *BIZ1* is the most sensitive indicator of bizarre and psychotic thought content, followed by *Pa1* and *PSY,* with psychosis being most strongly suggested when *BIZ1* is higher than *BIZ2.* *Sc3,* and to a much lesser extent *D4,* are sensitive to psychotic thought processes and, when both are elevated ($Sc3 > D4$) and the latter scales are accompanied by elevations on *BIZ* and *PSY,* psychosis is strongly suggested. Because *BIZ* is suppressed by low *T%, Ss, S, Es,* and *K,* raw scores of even 2 or 3 are a cause for concern, as these items may have been endorsed on an ego-syntonic basis.

Grandiosity

See discussion under *Elation.*

Paranoid Thought Processes

Pa1 is the most sensitive indicator of paranoid ideation, although such content is shared with *BIZ, PSY, CYN* (especially *CYN2*) and, to a lesser extent, with *Pd4, Sc1,* and *Pa3* (when *low*). Items reflecting delusional ideation are concentrated on *Pa1*, *BIZ*, and *PSY*, whereas the items on *CYN*, *Pd4*, *Sc1*, and *Pa3* (low) emphasize features of mistrust, suspiciousness, and severe alienation from others (when *Sc1* is higher than *Pd4*).

Obsessions/Ruminations/Compulsions

Scale *7* and the difference between Scales *7* and *8* (when both are elevated and *7* is higher than *8* by at least 10*T*) remain the most sensitive measures of obsessional processes. Scale *7* is limited in this regard by its saturation with First Factor variance. It is likely to function best for identifying obsessional processes when required to exceed *A* and *NEN* by at least 10*T*. *OBS* is especially sensitive to indecision, and *HEA* may be elevated by an obsessional focus on infection, germs, and the like. These considerations are likely to apply to ego-dystonic obsessive symptoms rather than to compulsive personality traits, which are characteristically ego-syntonic.

Cynicism

Items related to cynicism are widely dispersed throughout the MMPI-2. Misanthropic beliefs and attitudes are reflected in *CYN1* and *Pa3* (low), and *Hy2* (low) reflects the view that the self is no better than others. The pattern created by scores on *Hy2* and *Pa3* (both low, *Hy2* high but *Pa3* low, etc.) can be informative. For example, high *Hy2* with low *Pa3* may suggest cynical attitudes that emphasize competitiveness, narcissism, suspiciousness, or a combination of these. *ASP*, especially *ASP1*, suggests considerably less fearfulness, including social fearfulness, than *CYN* and *CYN1*, and implies a more corrosive and predatory form of cynicism, with willingness to implement cynical attitudes by cheating and exploiting others.

Memory, Attention, Concentration, and Judgment

Experienced problems in these areas are most specifically addressed by *D4*, with its emphasis on thinking as effortful, taxing, and prone to error and failure, and *Sc3*, with its emphasis on thinking as subject to intrusion and disruption.

Psychomotor Abnormality

Sc6 and *HEA2* are both sensitive to motor and sensory concerns and experienced malfunction.

ASSESSMENT OF PERSONALITY AND SOCIAL FUNCTIONING

Introversion/Extroversion

Scale *0* and *SOD* are both sensitive to this dimension, with *Si1* and *SOD2* emphasizing shyness, self-consciousness, social anxiety and discomfort, awkwardness, and ease of embarrassment, and *Si2* and *SOD1* emphasizing the avoidance of groups, crowds, and interaction. *Hy1* emphasizes the seeking of attention, approval, support, and affection, and *Pd3* emphasizes social aggressiveness, insouciance, and fearlessness.

Internalization/Externalization

As a personality style variable, this dimension may be expressed as a ratio between the sum of Scales *2 + 5 + 0 (2 – 5 + 0* for women) over the sum of *3 + 4 + 9.* This ratio provides a rough index of the tendency to cope with distressing or unwanted emotionality by acting out that is relatively free of pathological implications. An alternative ratio of greater significance for the assessment of psychopathology, *2 + 7 + 0* over the sum of *4 + 6 + 9,* suggests a coping style marked by emotional constriction and the internalization of stress and of responsibility for deficits and failures when values are greater than 1. Values of less than 1 suggest an externalizing coping style, one marked by the export of distress to others through anger, blaming, avoiding responsibility, and acting out.

Control/Impulsivity

(See *Internalization/Externalization*) Various qualities of emotional and behavioral control are suggested in most of the MMPI-2 scales. Emotional control (inhibition, constriction) is best indicated by *R,* with *D2, D-S, ANG* (low), *TPA* (low), and *Hy5* having various implications for inhibited angry/hostile emotionality. Behavioral control is best indicated by *DIS* (low), *Pd2* (low), *Re, GF, MAC-R* (low), *ASP* (low), *Pd-O* (low), and *O-H* having implications for how behavioral control is motivated and manifested. Hathaway and Monachesi (1963) found that Scales *2, 5,* and *0* acted as suppressors of delinquency, whereas Scales *4, 8,* and *9* acted as "excitors" for these trends. In general, Scales *2, 5* (low scores in women), and *0* do appear to inhibit or soften some of the more socially offensive characteristics of the other clinical scales, with Scales *4, 8,* and *9* making the latter characteristics more visible, problematic, or even dangerous. In particular, see the description of the *3-4/4-3* and *4-9/9-4* codetypes.

Social Alienation

Feelings of estrangement, emotional distance, and isolation from others are reflected in *Pd4* and *Sc1,* as well as in their parent scales, albeit in more diffuse form. *Pd4* has a relatively greater emphasis on emotional deprivation, and a sense of not being treated fairly or well, with residual sadness and longing. *Sc1* reflects a sense of interpersonal aversiveness and a more hardened and resolved preference for distance from and noninvolvement with others.

Self-Criticism/Negative Self-Esteem

See discussion for *Depression.*

Aggression

There are many MMPI-2 scales and patterns that have implications for one or another form of aggression. Benign social aggression is suggested in Scale *0, SOD* and their components (all low scores), and *Hy1.* *Pd3* connotes a somewhat more clearly aggressive sociability with overbearingness. Scale *4* likewise connotes more intrusive and visibly predatory social aggression, especially when accompanied by Scale *9* and not contradicted by scores on Scale *0* and *SOD.* Such social aggression takes on a more clearly hostile quality as Scales *6* and/or *8* enter the code; for example, *4-6, 4-8, 4-6-9, 4-8-9.* Primary predatory aggression is best marked by *AGG.*

Dependency/Passivity/Submissiveness versus Confidence/Assertiveness/Dominance

Although few or none of the MMPI-2 scales were intended as explicit measures of these dimensions, several are related to them on an approximate basis. Dependency is related to *Si3, LSE, WRK, GM* (low), *Hy1* (low), and *Pd3* (low), primarily through implications of inadequacy and incompetence, and therefore needs for approval and assistance. Passivity and submissiveness are variously suggested in *Hy2* (going along to get along), *D2* (avoiding risk or offense), *Ma4* (low; tolerance of domination), *Pd2* (low; submitting to rules), and *LSE* (self-doubt; submissiveness). These trends are contrasted in scores on *Do* (charismatic dominance), *LSE* (low; self-confidence), *Pd3* (no fear of disapproval), *Si1* (low; freedom from self-consciousness; social confidence), *Si* (low; extroversion), and *GM* (strength and composure). Conflicts, passive-aggressive struggles, or both in this area are suggested by *Sc4* (evading compliance by pleading extenuating circumstances) and *Ma4* (rebellious counter-submissiveness or counterdependency). See also Scale *5*.

Masculinity/Femininity

The assessment of masculinity-femininity encompasses aspects of identity, role, and interests. Scale *5* and subscales, along with *GM* and *GF*, may be used together as a basis for inferences in this area. Recall that scores on Scale *5* are an unreliable basis for inferences about stereotypical interests; the subscales *must* be consulted. Scores on both *GM* and *GF* are strongly suppressed by psychopathology and should be interpreted with caution when either *A* or *DIS* exceeds *T*-60.

Strengths/Social Adequacy/Positive Mental Health

The assessment of positive traits and dispositions with the MMPI-2 is complex, encompassing aspects of social functioning, self-control, self-esteem, and tolerance for stress, among others. Candor in test-taking attitude, and scores on scales like *Do* (high), *LPE* (low), *R* (average), *DIS* (average), *LSE* (average to low), *Es* (high), *GM* (average to high), *GF* (average to high), and *WRK* (average to low) may all indicate strengths, even in profiles with a few significant clinical scale elevations.

ASSESSMENT OF PERSONALITY CHANGE AND SUITABILITY FOR PSYCHOTHERAPY

The MMPI-2 is suitable for the assessment of the effects of clinical interventions, including psychotherapy, chemotherapy, and milieu-based measures to effect therapeutic change, as well as for normal personality changes that may occur over time. The interpretation of changes between a protocol obtained at Time 1 and another obtained at Time 2 is somewhat complex, as observed changes cannot always be attributed to changes in clinical status as a consequence of response to treatment. Shifts due to the imperfect reliability of scales and patterns and to regression (toward the mean) effects should not be overlooked as potential sources of observed changes in test scores and profiles. Given the potential for these factors to act as noise, obscuring true treatment effects ("signal"), merely examining baseline and subsequently gathered protocols to observe what aspects have changed over the time separating them is not recommended. However, when used in connection with a hypothesis-testing approach that specifies antecedently the particular scales or aspects of pattern expected to change in response to targeted interventions, the MMPI-2 is sensitive to treatment influences, and informative about their efficacy. For example, the success of interventions directed toward the amelioration of depression may be evaluated with reference to scores on those scales or patterns known to reflect aspects of depressed mood and ideation (Scale *2, D1-5, Hy3, Pa2, Sc2, Sc4, DEP, DEP1* and *2, LSE,* etc.). The clinician should also bear in mind that different symptoms are likely to respond to treatment at different rates, even when the interventions selected are highly effective. Thus, one would expect abnormal mood to respond to effective treatment more promptly than somatization, which, in turn, would be expected to respond more rapidly than personality traits such as dependency. At times, the clinician may wish to assess the source and consequences of changes observed independently of treatment. For example, the adequate assessment of clinical changes that may be a function of course of illness such as the transition from a manic to a depressed phase may also justify periodic retesting (see, e.g., Nichols, 1988, pp. 82–87).

A variety of treatment issues have been discussed in relation to the clinical scales (Chapter 6). Although much remains to be learned about the MMPI-2 and prognosis for psychotherapy, factors such as ego-strength *(Es),* better resources *(Ss)*, less alienation *(Pd4, Sc1)* and cognitive disorganization (Scale *8*), and the ability to contain impulse *(DIS)* and experience feelings *(R)* appear likely to be related to retention and successful outcomes. A rough general index of trends favorable to persistence and change in psychotherapy is $(2 + 7 + 0) - (3 + 4 + 9)$, with positive scores suggesting motivating distress; a capacity for self-awareness, reflection, introspection, and doubt; a sense of agency and responsibility; and a capacity for restraint, leading to better prognosis.

🖎 TEST YOURSELF 🖎

1. **Establishing an adequate level of response consistency is a desirable but not a necessary precondition for proceeding with MMPI-2 interpretation.** True or False?

2. **Although the distinction between self-deception and impression management emerged from studies of underreporting, it may be applied to overreporting as well, at least in principle.** True or False?

3. **The concept of severity in MMPI-2 scores is largely a function of elevation and relatively independent of response style.** True or False?

4. **False negative scores on Scale 6 are relatively common in paranoid disorders, but false positives are relatively rare.** True or False?

5. **Among the clinical scales of the MMPI-2, substance abuse is most reliably associated with**

   (a) Scale 2.

   (b) Scale 4.

   (c) Scale 8.

   (d) Scale 9.

6. **Distinguishing between psychotic and nonpsychotic conditions may be aided by which of the following?**

   (a) 8 minus 6

   (b) 8 minus 7

   (c) 8 minus F

   (d) PSY minus NEN

   (e) a and c

   (f) b and c

   (g) b and d

   (h) c and d

7. **The pattern of masculine versus feminine interests may be adequately assessed with reference to Scale 5, but only in the context of scores on *GM* and *GF*.** True or False?

Answers: 1. False; 2. True; 3. False; 4. True; 5. b; 6. g; 7. False.

Eleven

ILLUSTRATIVE CASE REPORT

L ike the results of any psychological test, those of the MMPI-2 may be interpreted "blind," in isolation from information that specifies the setting and circumstances of testing, the examinee's demographic position, legal status, presenting problems, reason for referral, history, and mental status. Without such information, interpretation must emphasize those actuarial features of the test that derive from research and clinical lore, the empirical correlates of scales, and the patterns they create as the basis for clinical prediction and personality description. In many situations a test-centered approach may be preferable, particularly when test results may figure in a current or future legal proceeding. In most routine clinical situations, however, the goals of assessment include an enhanced understanding of the patient within the context of his or her unique set of life circumstances, which requires blending test data with extra-test information that will enable the former to be construed in terms of the latter. The person-centered approach is especially apropos when test results are intended to serve as a source of feedback to the patient to enhance self-understanding, to select appropriate treatment measures and methods, or to enlarge the shared understandings between patient and clinician to strengthen the treatment contract and its focus.

BACKGROUND INFORMATION

Demographic information should include age, gender, marital status, educational attainment, usual occupation, and employment status. It is also helpful to have information regarding the patient's sexual and religious preference, socioeconomic status/social class, and racial or ethnic group membership. Note if the patient's native language is other than English, and list that language along with information about the patient's instruction in/exposure to English and whether the assessment was conducted in the native language with a translated version of the MMPI-2. Information regarding the setting or context of testing may specify private psychotherapy or assessment practice; psychiatric, neurological, or general medical setting; and whether the examinee is an inpatient or outpatient. Assessments conducted in other settings should identify the type of setting or auspices and the purpose of the assessment: occupational (vocational or career counseling, vocational rehabilitation, employment screening/discipline/termination/promotion/sensitive occupations), domestic relations (conciliation, child custody), correctional (pretrial, presentence, prison classification), or disability (assessment of, eligibility for compensation, litigation/liability).

In some cases, information bearing on the patient's legal status may be important, whether the patient is voluntary and whether self-referred or other-referred and, if non-voluntary, whether the assessment is court mandated (e.g., for commitment, emergency care, police hold, including whether criminal charges are pending). The patient's legal status regarding competency, such as whether he or she is under conservatorship or guardianship, may also be relevant.

REASON FOR REFERRAL, PRESENTING PROBLEM, HISTORY, AND MENTAL STATUS

The presenting problem should be identified in both subjective (direct quote) and objective terms. If the reason for referral is different from the presenting problem (e.g., differential diagnosis, disposition or placement, recommendations for treatment), this should be noted. Personal history may include physical development including birth and complications, if any; normal milestones; and maturation. Social development may include information regarding family environment, the marital situation of the parents, the primary caretakers if not the parents, the patient's birth order, siblings and their ages, family atmosphere, methods of discipline, family and peer relationships, and delinquency. Information about educational and sexual development may cover motivation, school interest and comportment, as well as achievement, favorite subjects, school problems, puberty, dating patterns, sexual information and initiation, and adjustment. Information about adult development may include selection of an occupation, employment history (job changes, termination), occupational adjustment (responsibility, promotion, relations with coworkers, acceptance of supervision), marital history and adjustment, children, current living situation (apartment, house, renting vs. buying), current family and extrafamilial social supports, physical health status, and leisure activities and interests (hobbies, pastimes, etc.). Where indicated, history should include information about mental disorder: age and circumstances of onset, prior treatment and hospitalization, major life stresses, and response to treatment. When a personal history of mental disorder is present, family history should include information about mental illness and hospitalization of first-, second-, and third-degree relatives, treatment and response to treatment, physical illness, addiction, criminality, and causes of death. Finally, as in all psychodiagnostic reports, detailed observations on mental status should be available.

The format of an MMPI-2 interpretive report may vary somewhat with the needs of the referrer and the preferences of the clinician preparing it, but a characteristic and flexible format includes, in order: a description of issues related to test validity, consistency, and test taking attitude or accuracy; a general description of the profile, including its position in terms of the basic scale-level factor structure of the MMPI-2; a description of symptoms, complaints, attitudes, traits, dispositions, and other personality characteristics, including the patient's interpersonal/interactional style; a summary of the diagnostic implications of test findings; and a section elaborating on the implications of these findings for patient treatment or disposition. Within the main interpretive section of the report, some have found it convenient to present a brief introductory summary of the major implications of the profile and to subdivide test findings into categories of mood, cognition, interpersonal relations, and special problems (e.g., Nichols & Greene, 1995). A number of report formats with examples are available in Friedman, Lewak, Nichols, and Webb (2001) and in Greene (2000).

Once the report format is selected, it is necessary to decide among various presentation styles. At one extreme is a style limited to the replicated empirical correlates of scale patterns (e.g., codetypes) and scores, at the other one may limit the interpretation to the actual content of endorsed items (e.g., Greene & Nichols, 1995, Nichols & Greene, 1995). Both of these extremes have advantages and disadvantages, and either may be preferred for some circumstances and not for others. Moreover, for most codetypes, empirically derived profile correlates for the MMPI-2 are not yet available. Most commercial reports therefore reflect a combination of actuarial/empirical information with information from item content and blended with varying amounts of clinical lore. The Minnesota Report seeks to present findings that are maximally reliable by combining content and empirically supported relationships and is relatively conservative in exploiting scale patterning details. The Caldwell Report emphasizes empirically supported correlates and is much more exhaustive in exploiting interscale relationships, but it places less emphasis on item content. Regular users of the MMPI-2 should have experience with both reports, and samples for identical cases are available in Friedman, Lewak, Nichols, and Webb (2001) and in Greene (2000).

The interpretive example that follows is formatted according to the outline given in Rapid Reference 11.1 and represents a hybrid of empirical and content-based approaches.

≡ Rapid Reference 11.1

Outline for Sample MMPI-2 Report

I. Protocol validity
  A. Response omissions
  B. Response consistency
  C. Response accuracy
  D. Test taking attitude
II. General description of profile
  A. Profile code
  B. Characteristics in terms of MMPI-2 factor structure
III. Symptoms, problems, and complaints
  A. Major interpretive implications (summary)
  B. Mood
  C. Cognition
  D. Interpersonal relations
  E. Other problems or issues
IV. Diagnostic considerations
V. Treatment considerations

THE CASE OF ANDREW M.

Reason for Referral

The patient is a 22-year-old, never-married Caucasian male high-school graduate with a Christian religious preference. He entered the hospital from another county on court commitment status as dangerous to self and others after refusing to eat, believing that his food was being poisoned, leading to a weight loss of more than 25% in 6 months and an assault on staff at another psychiatric facility. On admission to this hospital, he reported not knowing why he was hospitalized but suggested that staff in the previous facility thought he was not as "normal" as he should be. He was referred for assessment for differential diagnosis and treatment planning.

Background Information

The patient is the youngest of four siblings with three sisters 7, 8, and 10 years older, and was born into an intact family of college-educated, middle-class parents, the father an electrical engineer and the mother a staff writer for a newspaper. Delivery was normal and milestones were achieved on time, but the patient was hospitalized at 16 months for a severe bacterial infection. His parents divorced when the patient was age 2 and the mother remarried when the patient was 5. The mother retained primary custody but visitations with his father were frequent until age 8 when the mother and her new husband relocated to another state. The patient got along well with both parents and siblings, had several peer friends, and enjoyed sports while growing up. Discipline in the home was relaxed. Comportment and achievement in school were average to above average, and the patient maintained a B average through the tenth grade when he began to experiment with alcohol, marijuana, and later hallucinogenic mushrooms, ecstacy, and LSD. His grades deteriorated thereafter, but he was nevertheless able to graduate from high school on time. Sexual orientation is given as heterosexual but inactive. He had heterosexual friendships in high school and some thereafter but has never dated or been involved romantically. He has no occupation but has worked for brief periods at unskilled labor and in fast food service. Family history is negative for mental disorder but the patient describes his biological father as "alcoholic."

Onset of illness dates to age 16 with increased isolation, fear, suspiciousness, irritability, and beliefs that some of his peers wished to harm him, leading to fist fights on a few occasions. Substance abuse that had started with alcohol and marijuana gave way to hallucinogens in late high school, accompanied by ideas of reference and the belief that Eric Clapton was having his guitar-playing skills transferred to the patient. He was first hospitalized at age 18 after feeling his face "melting" following LSD use and was diagnosed with depression with psychotic features at that time. The etiologic significance of his substance abuse for the onset and persistence of illness was uncertain.

Admission mental status indicated the patient was oriented, alert, hypervigilant, and somewhat guarded. He exhibited mild psychomotor slowing with reduced movement and gesture and increased response latencies. Mood was moderately to severely depressed with suicidal ideation but no plan; mood was attributed to being in hospital. Affect was full range. Facies were typically serious, fearful, unhappy, or depressed. Thought was mildly to moderately disorganized with tangentiality and loss of track, especially when questions were not concrete. He reported being unsure whether he was hallucinating but thought he might be. Thought content was positive for somatic delusions, delusions of poisoning, and vague persecutory ideation about being mugged on the street and having a gun pointed at him. (The patient was badly beaten in a street fight two years earlier.) Memory and judgment were fair to good, but concentration was impaired. Insight was impaired to poor. He was considered to be at significant risk for suicide.

Initially he spent most of his time in his room and actively avoided interaction with staff. He was often seen in his bathroom staring at his face in the mirror. Sleep was undisturbed; energy appeared to be within normal limits. While out on the ward the patient appeared profusely hallucinated, apparently seeing things unseen by others, including faces in his room, was often seen staring or glaring at nothing in particular, and spoke of reading others' lips and speaking in a foreign language. Responses to questions were vague and mildly perplexed, with frequent losses of place in his stream of thought. He described his mood as depressed and fatigued and voiced concerns that others were confusing him with his father or stealing from his father. Worries that he had cancer of the genitals and a stricture in his throat were incorrigible to medical reassurance.

≡ *Rapid Reference 11.2*

Validity Scale Scores and Indices for Andrew M.

(All scores are in *T*-scores unless otherwise noted.)

Omissions:	**Consistency:**
Cannot Say (?) = 3 (raw)	VRIN = 54
	TRIN = 50

Accuracy:

F	= 79	S	= 47
F_B	= 87	S1	= 60
F_P	= 63	S2	= 50
Ds	= 65	S3	= 35
F − K = 1 (raw)		S4	= 35
L	= 56	S5	= 43
K	= 45	Mp	= 58
Ss	= 30	Sd	= 59

Percent True (*T%*) = 47
Mean Elevation (Scales *1, 2, 3, 4, 6, 7, 8,* and *9*) = 76

Test Findings

Andrew initially refused to participate in psychodiagnostic assessment, but after a period of modest improvement on rispiridone agreed to cooperate with testing and was administered the MMPI-2 6 months after admission.

In the interpretive sections that follow, the scales and patterns deemed to warrant most of the inferences are given at the end of sentences in parentheses. The scales and patterns referenced are illustrative and selective rather than definitive and exhaustive. Rapid Reference 11.2 presents the patient's scores for validity scales and indices; Rapid Reference 11.3 presents the patient's scores for all other scales and subscales.

Protocol Validity

The patient's profile of approved validity scales is presented in Figure 11.1 The obtained profile was valid. The patient responded to the items at an average

≋Rapid Reference 11.3

Clinical, Subscale, Content, *PSY-5* and Supplementary Scales and Indices for Andrew M.

Clinical Scales and Subscales

Scale 1 = 66	Hy4 = 62	Mf5 = 60	Sc4 = 60
Scale 2 = 89	Hy5 = 55	Mf6 = 2	Sc5 = 75
D-O = 88	Scale 4 = 79	Mf7 = 63	Sc6 = 95
D-S = 63	Pd-O = 82	Mf10 = 17	Scale 9 = 53
D1 = 82	Pd-S = 56	Scale 6 = 97	Ma-O = 54
D2 = 59	Pd1 = 58	Pa-O = 84	Ma-S = 54
D3 = 91	Pd2 = 60	Pa-S = 73	Ma1 = 58
D4 = 82	Pd3 = 33	Pa1 = 82	Ma2 = 49
D5 = 74	Pd4 = 66	Pa2 = 62	Ma3 = 35
Scale 3 = 57	Pd5 = 67	Pa3 = 65	Ma4 = 43
Hy-O = 73	Scale 5 = 50	Scale 7 = 87	Scale 0 = 67
Hy-S = 38	Mf1 = 23	Scale 8 = 79	Si1 = 71
Hy1 = 30	Mf2 = 50	Sc1 = 59	Si2 = 49
Hy2 = 47	Mf3 = 42	Sc2 = 69	Si3 = 53
Hy3 = 75	Mf4 = 39	Sc3 = 84	

Content and Content Component Scales

ANX = 70	HEA1 = 44	CYN2 = 43	SOD = 60
FRS = 80	HEA2 = 80	ASP = 53	SOD1 = 56
FRS1 = 98	HEA3 = 81	ASP1 = 46	SOD2 = 63
FRS2 = 61	BIZ = 77	ASP2 = 74	FAM = 60
OBS = 63	BIZ1 = 67	TPA = 48	FAM1 = 60
DEP = 71	BIZ2 = 73	TPA1 = 63	FAM2 = 49
DEP1 = 57	ANG = 56	TPA2 = 40	WRK = 67
DEP2 = 76	ANG1 = 52	LSE = 77	TRT = 66
DEP3 = 83	ANG2 = 61	LSE1 = 80	TRT1 = 66
DEP4 = 62	CYN = 44	LSE2 = 55	TRT2 = 60
HEA = 70	CYN1 = 44		

(continued)

PSY-5 Scales

AGG = 46
PSY = 81
DIS = 53
NEN = 73
LPE = 66

Supplementary Scales

A = 71	Do = 38	PS = 76	MAC-R = 60
R = 50	Re = 37	GM = 30	APS = 65
Es = 30	Mt = 71	GF = 44	AAS = 60
O-H = 52	PK = 68		

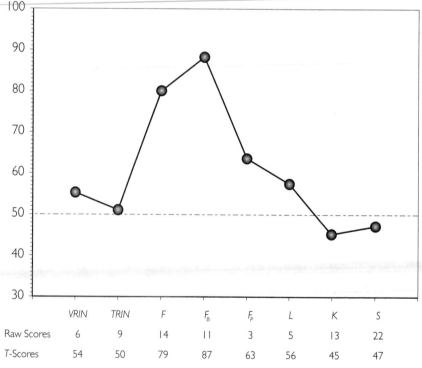

	VRIN	TRIN	F	F_B	F_P	L	K	S
Raw Scores	6	9	14	11	3	5	13	22
T-Scores	54	50	79	87	63	56	45	47

Figure 11.1 Validity Scales Profile for Andrew M.

Source: Minnesota Multiphasic Personality Inventory-2 Validity/Clinical Scales. Form for use with the MMPI-2™ test as published and copyrighted by the Regents of the University of Minnesota. All rights reserved. Distributed exclusively by National Computer Systems, Inc. under license from the University of Minnesota. "MMPI-2" and "Minnesota Multiphasic Personality Inventory-2" are trademarks owned by the University of Minnesota.

level of consistency *(VRIN, TRIN)* for normals, suggesting that he read the items carefully and was attentive to and understood their semantic characteristics. Responses to three items were omitted (96, 281, and 473). He presents himself as being in considerable distress *(F, F_B)*, and such distress appears to be predominantly affective and akin to panic, with distress due to psychotic mentation being secondary *($F_B > F$)*. There are no indications of an effort to exaggerate psychopathology *(F_p, Ds)*. In fact the patient made a conscious effort to deny minor failings *(L, Mp)* and to project a somewhat inflated social image *(Sd)*. His efforts to minimize abnormal adjustment appear to be focused on denying cynical, suspicious, and resentful attitudes toward others *(S1)*; however, he readily admits dissatisfaction with his basic life circumstances and current situation, and to anger, irritability, or impatience with others, especially when he feels provoked *(S3, S4)*. In spite of his efforts to deny problems in a number of areas, his coping capacity and emotional stability appear to be significantly reduced *(K)*, and self-concept and self-esteem are generally inferior and impaired *(Ss)*. The overall pattern of scores in this area suggest a severely compromised emotional equilibrium against which his usual defensive operations are inadequate to contain or reduce distress, or to preserve his ability to cope (e.g., *F − K, K > Es*).

Clinical Profile

The MMPI-2 profile shown in Figure 11.2 is markedly elevated, with 7 of the 10 clinical scales exceeding *T*-65. The profile code is 6*27″48′01+-395/F′-L/K. In terms of the basic factor structure of the MMPI-2, the pattern of scores emphasizes distress, discomfort and negative emotionality (First Factor: *A* = 71). He scores in the middle range on the control dimension (Second Factor: *R* = 50, *DIS* = 53).

Symptoms, Problems, and Complaints

The profile suggests a severe personality disturbance with mixed features of mood and thinking disorder (2, 6, 8) and high levels of anxiety and tension that appear to center on extreme fearfulness, persecutory ideation and possibly resentment, and fears of loss of control *(7, ANX, FRS, FRS1, NEN; 6, Pa1; Sc5)*. A psychotic disorder is probable *(PSY > NEN)*.

Mood and affect are marked by depression, brooding, emotional with-

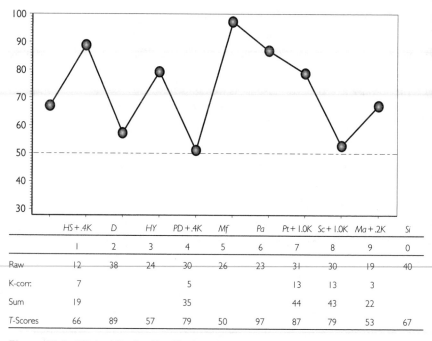

	HS + .4K	D	HY	PD + .4K	Mf	Pa	Pt + 1.0K	Sc + 1.0K	Ma + .2K	Si
	1	2	3	4	5	6	7	8	9	0
Raw	12	38	24	30	26	23	31	30	19	40
K-corr.	7			5			13	13	3	
Sum	19			35			44	43	22	
T-Scores	66	89	57	79	50	97	87	79	53	67

Figure 11.2 Clinical Scales Profile for Andrew M.

Source: Minnesota Multiphasic Personality Inventory-2 Validity/Clinical Scales. Form for use with the MMPI-2™ test as published and copyrighted by the Regents of the University of Minnesota. All rights reserved. Distributed exclusively by National Computer Systems, Inc. under license from the University of Minnesota. "MMPI-2" and "Minnesota Multiphasic Personality Inventory-2" are trademarks owned by the University of Minnesota.

drawal, and anhedonia; feelings of helplessness and hopelessness; mental insufficiency; and guilt *(2, D-O, D1, D5, Sc2, DEP, DEP2; Pd5)*. The level of depression is relatively severe, with probable psychomotor slowing *(2, 9* [relatively low], *D2, D4)* , limited affective expression *(Sc4)*, stereotypically depressed ideation *(DEP)*, loss of interest *(Sc2)*, withdrawal from his usual activities *(D2, D4, D5)*, and preoccupation with ill and declining health *(D3, Hy3)*. Some patients with similar profiles seemed at times to blame their depression on others or particular circumstances, giving the impression of being "depressed at" someone or something *(2-6)*. His level of anxiety is such as to suggest that he feels overwhelmed *(2-7, A, ANX, NEN)*. He experiences doubt and uncertainty when faced with decisions or in determining a course of action, with a tendency to obsess and ruminate about dire consequences for the choices he may make *(7, ANX, OBS)*. At times, the stress of worry and doubt may become so great that he may overreact to minor stresses with agitation and irritability *(ANG2, TPA1)* or lose control and react impulsively or aggressively as a means of resolving tension *(4, NEN)*. To the extent that anger is present, he tends to feel anger at both himself and others, which may leave him feeling tense and "trapped" *(6-7, ANG2, TPA1, NEN)*. Others would tend to see him as more angry and resentful than he sees himself *(6, ANG2, TPA1, NEN vs. Pa3, ANG1, CYN1, CYN2, TPA2)*. He may develop obsessions or compulsive rituals and symptoms as a means of controlling his anxiety *(7, OBS)*. He complains of light and easily disturbed sleep, nightmares, and being frightened at night (items 5, 30, 471).

Cognition is positive for disordered and inefficient thought processes, with significant problems in memory, attention, concentration, and judgment *(8, Sc3, D4)*; complaints of intrusive and disruptive thoughts, feelings, and impulses *(Sc3, Sc5)*; and doubt and indecision *(7, OBS)*. At times, his level of detachment interferes with his ability to distinguish between internal and external reality *(6-8, PSY)*, leading to the development of delusional beliefs *(6, Pa1, BIZ1, PSY)*. His thought content appears disturbed *(BIZ, BIZ1, BIZ2, PSY)*, with an emphasis on persecutory ideation *(6, Pa-O, Pa1, BIZ1, PSY)*. Such ideation may also include chronic feelings of mistreatment, and resentment of being unfairly blamed and punished *(6-4, Pa-O, Pd4, 8, PSY)*.

To at least some extent his detachment and withdrawal from the interpersonal *(Sc1, Pa-O, DEP)* and material *(Sc2, Sc4, DEP1)* worlds coincides with increased health concern *(HEA3)*, feelings of a changed perception of body image, and unusual motor and sensory experiences *(D3, Hy3, Sc6, HEA2, BIZ2)*; these may well also involve delusional elements. Self-esteem is very low *(7-8, LSE, LSE1)*, with themes of self-devaluation and a tendency toward self-criticism *(2-7, 2-8, 7-8, Pd5, Sc1, DEP, DEP3)*; at times these dominate his ideational production. He tends to internalize stresses ($[2 + 5 + 0] - [3 + 4 + 9] = 16$; $[2 + 7 + 0] - [4 + 6 + 9] = 13$) and to feel an exaggerated sense of responsibility for his problems and failings *(Pd5)*. Characteristic defenses include projection *(6, Pa-O, Pa1, Pd4)*, somatization *(D3, Hy-O, Sc6, HEA, HEA2, HEA3)*, and rationalization/intellectualization *(4, 5, 6, 7)*.

He feels that others do not understand him and may have great difficulty in communicating his thoughts and feelings to others in a coherent and organized fashion *(6-8, Sc3, BIZ2)*. For the time being at least, he may prefer fantasy and daydreaming to interpersonal interaction *(6-8, 2-8, 7-8, BIZ2)*. Although his relations with others are severely strained by his problems in thinking and communication, these are not entirely rejected *(Pd4 > Sc1)*. In fact, he may wish for closer relationships but not know how to achieve them and is fearful that others may not be able or inclined to accept him *(8, LSE)*. He is severely lacking in self-confidence *(LSE1)* and feels awkward, inept, and easily embarrassed in social situations *(0, Si1, LPE)*. Current interactions would be marked by rigidity, suspiciousness, and mistrust, and an inability to comply, or to comply only grudgingly or resentfully, with reasonable requests because of these *(6-4, Pa1, Pa1 > Pd4)* and the sense of fear that they engender *(FRS, FRS1, Sc1, Si3)*. He is highly sensitive to any form of criticism or rejection and quick to interpret malevolent intent to situations that others would see as innocent and benign *(6-2, 6-4, 6-8)*. He is also quick to resent demands made on him at this time because of his feelings of vulnerability to others' hostility toward him *(6-4, 6-8, Pa1)* and his fears of losing control of negative impulses *(6-7, FRS)*. In general, however, his conflicts with others are primarily an outgrowth of his current symptomatic status rather than characterological or passive-aggressive trends *(Sc4, Ma4, TPA, TPA2, AGG)*, despite some degree of chronicity in his alienation and resentment *(8, Pd4, Pa1)*. It is possible that his somatic concerns and preoccupations reflect, at least in part, an effort to obtain dependency gratifications and maintain a sense of ongoing relatedness with others that he feels unable to pursue through conventional means of communication because of his current impairments in mood and cognition. Mild to moderate family discord is reported *(Pd1, Sc1, FAM, FAM1)*, but he continues to feel generally connected to and supported by his immediate family *(FAM2)*.

His pattern of social behavior is currently regarded as predominantly introversive *(Hy-S, Hy1, Pd3, 0, Si1, SOD, SOD2)* due to his fears and feelings of incompetence in social interaction rather than out of avoidance of social gatherings as such *(Si2, SOD1)*. When interaction cannot be avoided, he tends to appear passive and unassertive *(Pd3, 5, Mf7, Ma4, Si1, Do, GM, TPA2, LSE1)* except when the demands of others impinge on areas of delusional conviction.

He admits to a history of delinquency *(Pd2, ASP2)* but generally denies antisocial attitudes *(ASP1)*. His basic orientation to others appears to be fundamentally trusting *(CYN, CYN1, CYN2)*, even in his relations with authority figures *(Ma4, CYN2, ASP1)*. In particular, hostile and aggressive attitudes toward others are denied *(D-S, ANG, ANG1, TPA, TPA2)*, although he does admit to moderate impatience and irritability *(ANG2, TPA1)*. He also admits to substance use and to problems secondary to such abuse *(AAS)*, and appears to remain at some risk for substance abuse in the future *(MAC-R, APS)*.

His pattern of masculine and feminine interests is consistent with masculine gender identity *(Mf6, Mf10)*. He tends to enjoy vigorous, outdoor, stereotypically masculine activities and pastimes *(Mf1)* and admits aesthetic or intellectual interests *(Mf5)* but denies stereotypically feminine interests *(Mf3)*.

Diagnostic Considerations

The profile reflects a severe thought disorder that may at times be masked by depression, fear, and anxiety. A diagnosis of Schizophrenia, Paranoid Type, should be considered. Diagnoses to be ruled out would include Major Depression with Psychotic Features and Bipolar Disorder, Depressed Type. On balance, the profile is somewhat more consistent with thought disorder than mood disorder, although both thought disorder and depression appear to require treatment. It is suggested that his current depressed mood and its concomitants are secondary to schizophrenic disorganization and its consequences as perceived by the patient for current and anticipated failures and frustrations, reduced satisfactions in interpersonal relationships, and impairment in aspirations for achievement in work and in life more generally. A secondary diagnosis of Substance Use Disorder also appears warranted, by history. Diagnosis on Axis II is deferred pending the resolution of Axis I disorder, as his current level of symptomatology is such as would obscure any stable pattern of traits and attitudes related to personality disorder. At such time as the Axis I disorder becomes resolved, however, Dependent, Paranoid, and Schizotypal Personality Disorders might be considered on Axis II.

Treatment Considerations

Both the current profile and the patient's symptomatology appear less than usually stable, and retesting should be considered upon any significant change in mental status. Although the pattern of his symptoms and problems is unstable, the chronicity of severe disturbance would suggest a guarded prognosis, even considering his recent modest improvement. Positive prognostic factors would include the patient's age, the absence of a strong family history of mental disorder, his willingness to complete the MMPI-2 after initial refusals, his current emotional discomfort, his bias toward the internalization of stresses, and his basic desire for relatedness, however fearful and apprehensive.

Current suicide risk appears only somewhat reduced from that on admission, and continued vigilance and precautions to manage this risk are recommended. Staff should be especially alert for any sudden change in mood or comportment, including positive change, and rapidly assess the implications of such change for suicide risk.

Given his prior assault and current unstable mental status, the possibility of future assault on peers or staff should not be overlooked. A buildup of frustrations or an increase in his conflicts with others could increase risk of violent acting out toward either self or others.

Standard chemotherapeutic approaches to the treatment of thought and mood disorder appear appropriate, but with the caveat that excessive sedation may interfere with the patient's self-protective hypervigilance, thereby increasing his feelings of vulnerability to perceived threats, and risking panic or overreaction.

Psychotherapeutic measures are unlikely to be effective until symptoms come under better control and the patient has experienced sufficient relief that he no longer feels under near-constant external and internal threat. Similar patients have responded well to a therapeutic style that is conducive to the patient feeling in control of interaction. At this time the patient should probably not be pressed to interact with caregivers, but nondemanding inquiries into his comforts and satisfactions and how these might be enhanced may be well tolerated when the patient initiates interaction. In particular, efforts to socialize him into accepting the patient role or to have him acknowledge having a "mental illness" are to be avoided, as such efforts are likely to be construed as criticism if not rejection. Both clinician and staff should guard against reacting to the patient's rigidity and stubbornness, while providing a level of support that he can perceive as concerned but not controlling.

Upon further improvement in mental status and an observed increase in the patient's tolerance for interaction, efforts to engage the patient in psychotherapy may be tentatively recommended. Short-term behavioral interventions directed toward problems and concerns the patient raises may provide the best initial focus of treatment, pending the establishment of a therapeutic alliance. The alliance with similar patients tends to be highly fragile and easily undermined by the patient's suspiciousness and hypersensitivity and a tendency to see the therapist as unsympathetic, critical, blaming, or even treacherous. Such patients tend to feel vulnerable to the therapist and commonly resort to intellectualization, rationalization, hyperrationality, and even belligerence as a means of self-protection and to prevent premature incursions into more tender emotional areas in which the patient feels least able to cope and confide. These include feelings of hurt and shame, loneliness and isolation, rejection, and emotional vulnerability to the therapist, among others. The clinician should be alert to the possibility of elements of delusional ascriptions or attributions involving him or her, and to avoid overreactions should these occur.

Issues of constancy, dependency, and trust tend to be persistant and require adroit handling by the therapist to avoid premature termination. The patient may experience a cognitive-behavioral approach to depressive cognition as helpful and as neutral and safe, providing him both a degree of symptomatic relief and insulation from deeper emotional issues and fears, especially as these may become incited in the therapeutic relationship. Supplemental concurrent training in assertiveness and social skills have been helpful to similar patients in increasing their ability to confront emotional issues less fearfully, especially when framed to address "common, practical problems in living." With increasing patient confidence and comfort, a focus on patterns of interaction that leave the patient feeling coerced, helpless, uncared for, or rejected is usually appropriate, including the feelings of anger and resentment that such feelings may engender, in turn. A concurrent focus on achieving a greater balance between self- and other-interest in his day-to-day choices, on the resolution of feelings about past "wrongs" and rejections, and increasing insight into how he may provoke others would lead to a greater ability to place his interactions with others in a more benign perspective, even when these are stressful. A decreased reliance on the need to deny, rationalize, or justify feelings of anger and resentment will signal significant improvement, especially when accompanied by an increased ability to take a more generous and forgiving stance toward the failings of both self and others.

References

Baer, R. A., Wetter, M. W., & Berry, D. T. R. (1992). Detection of underreporting of psychopathology on the MMPI: A meta-analysis. *Clinical Psychology Review, 12,* 509–525.

Baer, R. A., Wetter, M. W., Nichols, D. S., Greene, R. L., & Berry, D. T. R. (1995). Sensitivity of MMPI-2 validity scales to underreporting of symptoms. *Psychological Assessment: A Journal of Consulting and Clinical Psychology, 7,* 419–423.

Bagby, R. M., Nicholson, R. A., Buis, T., Radovanovic, H., & Fidler, B. J. (1999). Defensive responding on the MMPI-2 in family custody and access evaluations. *Psychological Assessment: A Journal of Consulting and Clinical Psychology, 11,* 24–28.

Barron, F. (1980). An ego-strength scale which predicts response to psychotherapy. In W. G. Dahlstrom & L. E. Dahlstrom (Eds.), *Basic readings on the MMPI* (pp. 267-285). Minneapolis: University of Minnesota Press. (Original work published 1953)

Ben-Porath, Y. S., & Butcher, J. N. (1989). Psychometric stability of rewritten MMPI items. *Journal of Personality Assessment, 53,* 645–653.

Ben-Porath, Y. S., Hostetler, K., Butcher, J. N., & Graham, J. R. (1989). New subscales for the MMPI-2 social introversion scale. *Psychological Assessment, 1,* 169–174.

Ben-Porath, Y. S., & Sherwood, N. E. (1993). *The MMPI-2 content component scales: Development, psychometric characteristics and clinical application.* Minneapolis: University of Minnesota Press.

Bernreuter, R. G. (1933). The theory and construction of the personality inventory. *Journal of Social Psychology, 4,* 387–405.

Berrios, G. E. (1985). Obsessional disorders during the nineteenth century: Terminological and classificatory issues. In W. F. Bynum, R. Porter, & M. Shepherd (Eds.), *The anatomy of madness: Essays in the history of psychiatry: Vol. I. People and ideas* (pp. 166–187). London: Tavistock.

Boerger, A. R., Graham, J. R., & Lilly, R. S. (1974). Behavioral correlates of single-scale MMPI code types. *Journal of Consulting and Clinical Psychology, 42,* 398–402.

Burkhart, B. R., Christian, W. L., & Gynther, M. D. (1978). Item subtlety and faking on the MMPI: A paradoxical relationship. *Journal of Personality Assessment, 42,* 76–80.

Butcher, J. N. (Ed.). (2000). *Basic sources on the MMPI-2.* Minneapolis: University of Minnesota Press.

Butcher, J. N., Dahlstrom, W. G., Graham, J. R., Tellegen, A., & Kaemmer, B. (1989). *MMPI-2: Manual of administration and scoring.* Minneapolis: University of Minnesota Press.

Butcher, J. N., Graham, J. R., Williams, C. L., & Ben-Porath, Y. S. (1990). *Development and use of the MMPI-2 content scales.* Minneapolis: University of Minnesota Press.

Butcher, J. N., & Han, K. (1995). Development of an MMPI-2 scale to assess the presentation of self in a superlative manner: The S scale. In J. N. Butcher & C. D. Spielberger (Eds.), *Advances in personality assessment* (Vol. 10, pp. 25–50). Hillsdale, NJ: Erlbaum.

Butcher, J. N., & Williams, C. L. (1992). *Essentials of MMPI-2 and MMPI-A interpretation.* Minneapolis: University of Minnesota Press.

Caldwell, A. B. (1988). *MMPI supplemental scale manual.* Los Angeles: Caldwell Report.

Caldwell, A. B. (1997). Whither goest our redoubtable mentor, the MMPI/MMPI-2? *Journal of Personality Assessment, 68,* 47–68.

Caldwell, A. B. (1998). *Advanced MMPI/MMPI-2 theory and interpretation seminar.* (Unpublished materials.)

Carson, R. C. (1969). Interpretive manual to the MMPI. In J. N. Butcher (Ed.), *MMPI research developments and clinical applications* (pp. 279–296). New York: McGraw-Hill.

Chang, A. F., Caldwell, A. B., & Moss, T. (1973). *Stability of personality traits in alcoholics during and after treatment as measured by the MMPI: A one-year follow-up study.* Proceedings of the American Psychological Association, 8, 387–388.

Cleckley, H. M. (1941). *The mask of sanity.* St. Louis, MO: Mosby.

Cofer, C. N., Chance, J. E., & Judson, A. J. (1949). A study of malingering on the MMPI. *Journal of Psychology, 27,* 491–499.

Cohen, M. B., Baker, G., Cohen, R. A., Fromm-Reichmann, F., & Weigert, E. V. (1954). An intensive study of twelve cases of manic-depressive psychosis. *Psychiatry: Journal for the Study of Interpersonal Processes, 17,* 103–137.

Colligan, R. C., Osborne, D., Swenson, W. M., & Offord, K. P. (1983). *The MMPI: A contemporary normative study.* New York: Praeger.

Constantinople, A. (1973). Masculinity-femininity: An exception to a famous dictum? *Psychological Bulletin, 80,* 389–407.

Cook, W. W., & Medley, D. M. (1954). Proposed hostility and Pharisaic-virtue scales for the MMPI. *Journal of Applied Psychology, 38,* 414–418.

Dahlstrom, W. G., Archer, R. P., Hopkins, D. G., Jackson, E., & Dahlstrom, L. E. (1994). *Assessing the readability of the Minnesota Multiphasic Inventory Instruments—the MMPI, MMPI-2, MMPI-A.* Minneapolis: University of Minnesota Press.

Dahlstrom, W. G., Welsh, G. S., & Dahlstrom, L. E. (1972). *An MMPI handbook: Vol. I. Clinical interpretation* (rev. ed.). Minneapolis: University of Minnesota Press.

Dahlstrom, W. G., Welsh, G. S., & Dahlstrom, L. E. (1975). *An MMPI handbook: Vol. II. Research applications* (rev. ed.). Minneapolis: University of Minnesota Press.

DiLalla, D. L., Carey, G., Gottesman, I. I., & Bouchard, T. J., Jr. (1996). Heritability of MMPI personality indicators of psychopathology in twins reared apart. *Journal of Abnormal Psychology, 105,* 491–499.

DiLalla, D. L., Gottesman, I. I., Carey, G., & Bouchard, T. J., Jr. (1999). Heritability of MMPI Harris-Lingoes and Subtle-Obvious subscales in twins reared apart. *Assessment, 6,* 353–366.

Drake, L. E. (1946). A social I.E. Scale for the Minnesota Multiphasic Personality Inventory. *Journal of Applied Psychology, 30,* 51–54.

Dubinsky, S., Gamble, D. J., & Rogers, M. L. (1985). A literature review of subtle-obvious items on the MMPI. *Journal of Personality Assessment, 49,* 62–68.

Duckworth, J. C., & Anderson, W. (1986). *MMPI interpretation manual for counselors and clinicians* (3rd ed.). Muncie, IN: Accelerated Development.

Evans, C., & McConnell, T. R. (1941). A new measure of introversion-extroversion. *Journal of Psychology, 12,* 111–124.

Finn, S. E. (1995). *Using the MMPI-2 as a therapeutic intervention.* Minneapolis: University of Minnesota Press.

Fowler, R. D. (1975). *A method for the evaluation of the abuse prone patient.* Paper presented at the meeting of the American Academy of Family Physicians, Chicago.

Friedman, A. F., Lewak, R., Nichols, D. S., & Webb, J. T. (2001). *Psychological assessment with the MMPI-2.* Mahwah, NJ: Erlbaum.

Gallucci, N. T., Kay, D. C., & Thornby, J. I. (1989). The sensitivity of 11 substance abuse scales from the MMPI to change in clinical status. *Psychology of Addictive Behaviors, 3,* 29–33.

Garb, H. N. (1998). *Studying the clinician: Judgment research and psychological assessment.* Washington, DC: American Psychological Association.

Gibson, R. W., Cohen, M. B., & Cohen, R. A. (1959). On the dynamics of the manic-depressive personality. *American Journal of Psychiatry, 115,* 1101–1107.

Gilberstadt, H., & Duker, J. (1965). *A handbook for clinical and actuarial MMPI interpretation.* Philadelphia: Saunders.

Goldberg, L. R. (1965). Diagnosticians vs. diagnostic signs: The diagnosis of psychosis vs. neurosis from the MMPI. *Psychological Monographs, 79* (9, Whole No. 602).

Goldberg, L. R. (1971). A historical survey of personality scales and inventories. In P. McReynolds (Ed.), *Advances in psychological assessment* (Vol 2, pp. 293–336). Palo Alto: Science and Behavior Books.

Goldberg, L. R. (1972). Man versus mean: The exploitation of group profiles for the construction of diagnostic classification systems. *Journal of Abnormal Psychology, 79,* 121–131.

Goodwin, F. K., & Jamison, K. R. (1990). *Manic-depressive illness.* New York: Oxford University Press.

Gottesman, I. I. (1959). More construct validation of the Ego Strength scale. *Journal of Consulting Psychology, 23,* 342–346.

Gottesman, I. I. (1991). *Schizophrenia genesis.* San Francisco: Freeman.

Gottesman, I. I., & Prescott, C. A. (1989). Abuses of the MacAndrew MMPI Alcoholism Scale: A critical review. *Clinical Psychology Review, 9,* 223–242.

Gottesman, I. I., & Shields, J. (1972). *Schizophrenia and genetics: A twin study vantage point.* New York: Academic Press.

Gough, H. G. (1947). Simulated patterns on the Minnesota Multiphasic Personality Inventory. *Journal of Abnormal and Social Psychology, 42,* 215–225.

Gough, H. G. (1948a). A new dimension of status: I. Development of a personality scale. *American Sociological Review, 13,* 401–409.

Gough, H. G. (1948b). A new dimension of status: II. Relationship of the St scale to other variables. *American Sociological Review, 13,* 534–537.

Gough, H. G. (1950). The F minus K dissimulation index for the Minnesota Multiphasic Personality Inventory. *Journal of Consulting Psychology, 14,* 408–413.

Gough, H. G. (1954). Some common misconceptions about neuroticism. *Journal of Consulting Psychology, 18,* 287–292.

Gough, H. G., McClosky, H., & Meehl, P. E. (1951). A personality scale for dominance. *Journal of Abnormal and Social Psychology, 46,* 360–366.

Gough, H. G., McClosky, H., & Meehl, P. E. (1952). A personality scale for social responsibility. *Journal of Abnormal and Social Psychology, 47,* 73–80.

Graham, J. R. (1977). Review of Minnesota Multiphasic Personality Inventory Special scales. In P. McReynolds (Ed.), *Advances in psychological assessment* (Vol. 4, pp. 11–55). San Francisco: Jossey-Bass.

Graham, J. R. (1978, March). *MMPI characteristics of alcoholics, drug abusers, and pathological gamblers.* Paper given at the 13th Annual Symposium on Recent Developments in the Use of the MMPI, University of the Americas, Puebla, Mexico.

Graham, J. R., Ben-Porath, Y. S., & McNulty, J. L. (1999). *MMPI-2 correlates for outpatient mental health settings.* Minneapolis: University of Minnesota Press.

Graham, J. R., Schroeder, H. E., & Lilly, R. S. (1971). Factor analysis of items on the social introversion and masculinity-femininity scales of the MMPI. *Journal of Clinical Psychology, 27,* 367–370.

Graham, J. R., & Strenger, V. E. (1988). MMPI characteristics of alcoholics: A review. *Journal of Consulting and Clinical Psychology, 56,* 197–205.

Graham, J. R., & Tisdale, M. J. (1983, April). *Interpretation of low Scale 5 scores for women of high educational levels.* Paper presented at the 18th Annual Symposium on Recent Developments in the Use of the MMPI, Minneapolis, MN.

Greene, R. L. (1994). Relationships among MMPI codetype, gender, and setting and the MacAndrew Alcoholism Scale. *Assessment, 1,* 39–46.

Greene, R. L. (2000). *The MMPI-2: An interpretive manual* (2nd ed.). Boston: Allyn & Bacon.

Greene, R. L., & Garvin, R. D. (1988). Substance abuse/dependence. In R. L. Greene (Ed.), *The MMPI: Use with specific populations* (pp. 159–197). San Antonio: Grune & Stratton.

Greene, R. L., & Nichols, D. S. (1995). *MMPI-2 Structural Summary* [Computer software]. Odessa, FL: Psychological Assessment Resources.

Gynther, M. D., Altman, H., & Sletten, I. W. (1973). Replicated correlates of MMPI two-point code types: The Missouri actuarial system. *Journal of Clinical Psychology, 29,* 263–289.

Hare, R. (1991). *Manual for the Revised Psychopathy Checklist.* Toronto: Multi-Health Systems.

Harkness, A. R., McNulty, J. L., & Ben-Porath, Y. S. (1995). The Personality Psychopathology Five (PSY-5): Constructs and MMPI-2 scales. *Psychological Assessment, 7,* 104–114.

Harris, R. E., & Lingoes, J. C. (1955). *Subscales for the Minnesota Multiphasic Personality Inventory: An aid to profile interpretation.* Mimeographed materials. University of California, Langley Porter Neuropsychiatric Institute, San Francisco.

Harris, R. E., & Lingoes, J. C. (1968). *Subscales for the Minnesota Multiphasic Personality Inventory: An aid to profile interpretation* (rev. ed.). Mimeographed materials. University of California, Langley Porter Neuropsychiatric Institute, San Francisco.

Hartshorne, H., & May, M. A. (1928). *Studies in deceit.* New York: Macmillan.

Hathaway, S. R. (1939). The personality inventory as an aid in the diagnosis of psychopathic inferiors. *Journal of Consulting Psychology, 3,* 112–117.

Hathaway, S. R. (1965). Personality inventories. In B. B. Wolman (Ed.), *Handbook of clinical psychology* (pp. 451–476). New York: McGraw-Hill.

Hathaway, S. R. (1980). Scales *5* (Masculinity-Femininity), *6* (Paranoia), and *8* (Schizophrenia). In W. G. Dahlstrom & L. E. Dahlstrom (Eds.), *Basic readings on the MMPI* (pp. 65–75). Minneapolis: University of Minnesota Press. (Original work published 1956)

Hathaway, S. R., & McKinley, J. C. (1943). *Minnesota Multiphasic Personality Inventory Manual*. New York: Psychological Corp.

Hathaway, S. R., & McKinley, J. C. (1980). A multiphasic personality schedule (Minnesota): I. Construction of the schedule. In W. G. Dahlstrom & L. E. Dahlstrom (Eds.), *Basic readings on the MMPI* (pp. 65–75). Minneapolis: University of Minnesota Press. (Original work published 1940)

Hathaway, S. R., & McKinley, J. C. (1980). A multiphasic personality schedule (Minnesota): III. The measurement of symptomatic depression. In W. G. Dahlstrom & L. E. Dahlstrom (Eds.), *Basic readings on the MMPI* (pp. 24–33). Minneapolis: University of Minnesota Press. (Original work published 1942)

Hathaway, S. R., & Monachesi, E. D. (1963). *Adolescent personality and behavior: MMPI patterns of normal, delinquent, dropout, and other outcomes*. Minneapolis: University of Minnesota Press.

Helmes, E., & Reddon, J. R. (1993). A perspective on developments in assessing psychopathology: A critical review of the MMPI and MMPI-2. *Psychological Bulletin, 113,* 453–471.

Henderson, D. K. (1939). *Psychopathic states*. New York: Norton.

Hiller, J. B., Rosenthal, R., Bornstein, R. F., Berry, D. T. R., & Brunell-Neuleib, S. (1999). A comparative meta-analysis of Rorschach and MMPI validity. *Psychological Assessment, 11,* 278–296.

Hjemboe, S., Almagor, M., & Butcher, J. N. (1992). Empirical assessment of marital distress: The Marital Distress Scale (MDS) for the MMPI-2. In C. D. Spielberger & J. N. Butcher (Eds.), *Advances in personality assessment* (Vol. 9, pp. 141–152). Hillsdale, NJ: Erlbaum.

Hoffmann, H., Loper, R. G., & Kammeier, M. L. (1974). Identifying future alcoholics with MMPI alcoholism scales. *Quarterly Journal of Studies on Alcohol, 35,* 490–498.

Hollrah, J. L., Schlottmann, R. S., Scott, A. B., & Brunetti, D. G. (1995). Validity of the MMPI subtle items. *Journal of Personality Assessment, 65,* 278–299.

Holmes, T. H., & Rahe, R. H. (1967). The Social Readjustment Rating Scale. *Journal of Psychosomatic Research, 11,* 213–218.

Huber, N. A., & Danahy, S. (1975). Use of the MMPI in predicting completion and evaluating changes in a long-term alcoholism treatment program. *Journal of Studies on Alcohol, 36,* 1230–1237.

Humm, D. G., & Wadsworth, G. W., Jr. (1935). The Humm-Wadsworth Temperament Survey. *American Journal of Psychiatry, 92,* 163–200.

Humphrey, D. H., & Dahlstrom, W. G. (1995). The impact of changing from the MMPI to the MMPI-2 of profile configurations. *Journal of Personality Assessment, 64,* 428–439.

Jenkins, C. D., Rosenman, R. H., & Friedman, M. (1967). Development of an objective psychological test for the determination of the coronary-prone behavior pattern in employed men. *Journal of Chronic Disease, 20,* 371–379.

Katz, M. M. (1968). A phenomenological typology of schizophrenia. In M. M. Katz, J. O. Cole, & W. E. Barton (Eds.), *The role and methodology of classification in psychiatry and psychopathology* (pp. 300–320). Public Health Service Publication No. 1584. Washington, D.C.: U.S. Government Printing Office.

Keane, T. M., Malloy, P. F., & Fairbank, J. A. (1984). Empirical development of an MMPI subscale for the assessment of combat-related posttraumatic stress disorder. *Journal of Consulting and Clinical Psychology, 52,* 888–891.

Kellner, R. (1991). *Psychosomatic syndromes and somatic symptoms.* Washington, D.C.: American Psychiatric Press.

Kleinmuntz, B. (1960). Identification of maladjusted college students. *Journal of Counseling Psychology, 7,* 209–211.

Kleinmuntz, B. (1961a). The college maladjustment scale (Mt): Norms and predictive validity. *Educational and Psychological Measurement, 21,* 1029–1033.

Kleinmuntz, B. (1961b). Screening: Identification or prediction? *Journal of Counseling Psychology, 8,* 279–280.

Kranitz, L. (1972). Alcoholics, heroin addicts and nonaddicts: Comparisons on the MacAndrew Alcoholism Scale of the MMPI. *Quarterly Journal of Studies on Alcohol, 33,* 807–809.

Lachar, D., Berman, W., Grisell, J. L., & Schoof, K. (1976). The MacAndrew Alcoholism Scale as a general measure of substance abuse. *Journal of Studies on Alcohol, 37,* 1609–1615.

Lachar, D., & Wrobel, T. A. (1979). Validating clinicians' hunches: Construction of a new MMPI critical item set. *Journal of Consulting and Clinical Psychology, 47,* 1349–1356.

Landis, C., & Katz, S. E. (1934). The validity of certain questions which purport to measure neurotic tendencies. *Journal of Applied Psychology, 18,* 343–356.

Leary, T. (1956). *Multilevel measurement of interpersonal behavior.* Berkeley, CA: Psychological Consultation Service.

Leary, T. (1957). *Interpersonal diagnosis of personality.* New York: Ronald Press.

Levitt, E. E. (1989). *The clinical application of MMPI special scales.* Hillsdale, NJ: Erlbaum.

Lewak, R. W., Marks, P. A., & Nelson, G. E. (1990). *Therapist guide to the MMPI and MMPI-2: Providing feedback and treatment.* Muncie, IN: Accelerated Development.

Litz, B. T., Orsillo, S. M., Friedman, M., Ehlich, P., & Batres, A. (1997). Posttraumatic stress disorder associated with peacekeeping duty in Somalia for U.S. military personnel. *American Journal of Psychiatry, 154,* 178–184.

MacAndrew, C. (1965). The differentiation of male alcoholic outpatients from nonalcoholic psychiatric patients by means of the MMPI. *Quarterly Journal of Studies on Alcohol, 26,* 238–246.

MacAndrew, C. (1981). What the MAC scale tells us about men alcoholics: An interpretive review. *Journal of Studies on Alcohol, 42,* 604–625.

Manosevitz, M. (1971). Education and MMPI *Mf* scores in homosexual and heterosexual males. *Journal of Consulting and Clinical Psychology, 36,* 395–399.

Marks, P. A., & Seeman, W. (1963). *The actuarial description of abnormal personality: An atlas for use with the MMPI.* Baltimore: Williams & Wilkins.

Martin, E. H. (1993). *Masculinity-femininity and the MMPI-2.* Unpublished doctoral dissertation, University of Texas, Austin.

Martin, E. H., & Finn, S. E. (1992). *Masculinity-femininity and the MMPI-2.* (Unpublished manuscript.)

McKenna, T., & Butcher, J. N. (1987, March). *Continuity of the MMPI with alcoholics.* Paper presented at the 23rd Annual Symposium on Recent Developments in the Use of the MMPI, Seattle, WA.

McKinley, J. C. (Ed.). (1944). *Outline of Neuropsychiatry* (4th ed.). St. Louis: Swift.

McKinley, J. C., & Hathaway, S. R. (1980). A multiphasic personality schedule (Minnesota): II. A differential study of hypochondriasis. In W. G. Dahlstrom & L. E. Dahlstrom (Eds.), *Basic readings on the MMPI* (pp. 12–33). Minneapolis: University of Minnesota Press. (Original work published 1940)

McKinley, J. C., & Hathaway, S. R. (1980). A multiphasic personality schedule (Minnesota): IV. Psychasthenia. In W. G. Dahlstrom & L. E. Dahlstrom (Eds.), *Basic readings on the MMPI* (pp. 34–41). Minneapolis: University of Minnesota Press. (Original work published 1942)

McKinley, J. C., & Hathaway, S. R. (1980). The MMPI: V. Hysteria, hypomania, and psychopathic deviate. In W. G. Dahlstrom & L. E. Dahlstrom (Eds.), *Basic readings on the MMPI* (pp. 42–64). Minneapolis: University of Minnesota Press. (Original work published 1944)

McKinley, J. C., Hathaway, S. R., & Meehl, P. E. (1948–1980). The MMPI: VI. The K scale. In W. G. Dahlstrom & L. E. Dahlstrom (Eds.), *Basic readings on the MMPI* (pp. 122–138). Minneapolis: University of Minnesota Press. (Original work published 1948)

Meehl, P. E. (1945). The dynamics of "structured" personality tests. *Journal of Clinical Psychology, 1,* 296–304.

Meehl, P. E. (1962). Schizotaxia, schizotypy, schizophrenia. *American Psychologist, 17,* 827–838.

Meehl, P. E. (1972). Reactions, reflections, projections. In J. N. Butcher (Ed.), *Objective personality assessment* (pp. 131–189). New York: Academic Press.

Meehl, P. E., & Hathaway, S. R. (1980). The K factor as a suppressor variable in the MMPI. In W. G. Dahlstrom & L. E. Dahlstrom (Eds.), *Basic readings on the MMPI* (pp. 83–121). Minneapolis: University of Minnesota Press. (Original work published 1946)

Megargee, E. I., Cook, P. E., & Mendelsohn, G. A. (1967). Development and validation of an MMPI scale of assaultiveness in overcontrolled individuals. *Journal of Abnormal Psychology, 72,* 519–528.

Merskey, H. (1995). *The analysis of hysteria: Understanding conversion and dissociation* (2nd ed.). London, England: Gaskell/Royal College of Psychiatrists.

Nelson, S. E. (1952). The development of an indirect, objective measure of social status and its relationship to certain psychiatric syndromes (Doctoral dissertation, University of Minnesota, 1952). *Dissertation Abstracts, 12,* 782.

Newmark, C. S. (1985). The MMPI. In C. S. Newmark (Ed.), *Major psychological assessment instruments* (pp. 11–64). Boston: Allyn & Bacon.

Nichols, D. S. (1988). Mood disorders. In R. L. Greene (Ed.), *The MMPI: Use with specific populations* (pp. 74–109). San Antonio, TX: Grune & Stratton.

Nichols, D. S., & Greene, R. L. (1988, March). *Adaptive or defensive: An evaluation of Paulhus' two-factor model of social desirability responding in the MMPI with non-college samples.* Paper presented at the 23rd Annual Symposium on Recent Developments in the Use of the MMPI, St. Petersburg Beach, FL.

Nichols, D. S., & Greene, R. L. (1995). *MMPI-2 Structural Summary: Interpretive manual.* Odessa, FL: Psychological Assessment Resources.

Nichols, D. S., & Greene, R. L. (1997). Dimensions of deception in personality assessment: The example of the MMPI-2. *Journal of Personality Assessment, 68,* 251–266.

Pancoast, David L., & Archer, R. P. (1989). Original adult MMPI norms in normal samples: A review with implications for future developments. *Journal of Personality Assessment, 53,* 376–395.

Paulhus, D. L. (1984). Two-component models of socially desirable responding. *Journal of Personality and Social Psychology, 46,* 598–609.

Paulhus, D. L. (1986). Self-deception and impression management in test responses. In A. Angleitner & J. S. Wiggins (Eds.), *Personality assessment via questionnaires: Current issues in theory and measurement* (pp. 143–165). Berlin: Springer.

Peterson, C. D. (1991). *Masculinity and femininity as independent dimensions on the MMPI.* Unpublished doctoral dissertation, University of North Carolina, Chapel Hill.

Peterson, C. D., & Dahlstrom, W. G. (1992). The derivation of gender-role scales GM and GF for the MMPI-2 and their relationship to scale 5 (Mf). *Journal of Personality Assessment, 59,* 486–499.

Pope, H. G., & Lipinski, J. F. (1978). Diagnosis in schizophrenia and manic-depressive illness: A reassessment of the specificity of schizophrenic symptoms in the light of current research. *Archives of General Psychiatry, 35,* 811–828.

Quinsey, V. L., Maguire, A., & Varney, G. W. (1983). Assertion and overcontrolled hostility among mentally disordered offenders. *Journal of Consulting and Clinical Psychology, 51,* 550–556.

Rhodes, R. J., & Chang, A. F. (1978). A further look at the institutionalized chronic alcoholic scale. *Journal of Clinical Psychology, 34,* 779–780.

Rohan, W. P. (1972). MMPI changes in hospitalized alcoholics: A second study. *Quarterly Journal of Studies on Alcohol, 33,* 65–76.

Rohan, W. P., Tatro, R. L., & Rotman, S. R. (1969). MMPI changes in alcoholics during hospitalization. *Quarterly Journal of Studies on Alcohol, 30,* 389–400.

Rothke, S. E., Friedman, A. F., Dahlstrom, W. G., Greene, R. L., Arredondo, R., & Mann, A. W. (1994). MMPI-2 normative data for the F – K index: Implications for clinical, neuropsychological, and forensic practice. *Assessment, 1,* 1–15.

Schinka, J. A., & LaLone, L. (1997). MMPI-2 norms: Comparisons with a census-matched subsample. *Psychological Assessment, 9,* 307–311.

Schlenger, W. E., & Kulka, R. A. (1987, August). *Performance of the Keane-Fairbank MMPI scale and other self-report measures in identifying post-traumatic stress disorder.* Paper presented at the annual meeting of the American Psychological Association, New York.

Schlenger, W. E., Kulka, R. A., Fairbank, J. A., Hough, R. L., Jordan, B. K., Marmar, C. R., & Weiss, D. S. (1989). *The prevalence of post-traumatic stress disorder in the Vietnam generation: Findings from the National Vietnam Veterans Readjustment Study.* Report from Research Triangle Institute, Research Triangle Park, NC.

Schneider, K. (1959). *Clinical psychopathology.* New York: Grune & Stratton.

Serkownek, K. (1975). *Subscales for Scales 5 and 0 of the MMPI.* Unpublished manuscript.

Sheehan, N. (1989). *A bright shining lie: John Paul Vann and America in Vietnam.* New York: Vintage.

Southwick, S. M., Morgan, C. A., III, Nicolaou, A. C., & Charney, D. S. (1997). Consistency of memory for combat-related traumatic events in veterans of Operation Desert Storm. *American Journal of Psychiatry, 154,* 173–177.

Spanier, G. B. (1976). Measuring dyadic adjustment: New scales for assessing the quality of marriage and similar dyads. *Journal of Marriage & the Family, 38,* 15–28.

Strong, E. K. (1927). Vocational interest test. *Educational Record, 8,* 107–121.

Sutker, P. B., Archer, R. P., Brantley, P. J., & Kilpatrick, D. G. (1979). Alcoholics and opiate addicts, comparison of personality characteristics. *Journal of Studies on Alcohol, 40,* 635–644.

Tellegen, A., & Ben-Porath, Y. S. (1992). The new uniform T scores for the MMPI-2: Rationale, derivation, and appraisal. *Psychological Assessment, 4,* 145–155.

Terman, L. M., & Miles, C. C. (1936). *Sex and personality: Studies in masculinity and femininity.* New York: McGraw-Hill.

Terman, L. M., & Miles, C. C. (1938). *Manual of information and directions for use of Attitude-Interest Analysis Test.* New York: McGraw-Hill.

Trimboli, R., & Kilgore, R. (1983). A psychodynamic approach to MMPI interpretation. *Journal of Personality Assessment, 47,* 614–626.

Voelker, T. L., & Nichols, D. S. (1999, March). *Can the MMPI-2 predict Psychopathy Checklist-Revised (PCL-R) scores?* Paper presented at the annual midwinter meeting of the Society for Personality Assessment, New Orleans.

Walters, G. D. (1983). The MMPI and schizophrenia: A review. *Schizophrenia Bulletin, 9,* 226–246.

Walters, G. D. (1988). Schizophrenia. In R. L. Greene (Ed.), *The MMPI: Use in specific populations* (pp. 50–73). Philadelphia: Grune & Stratton.

Warner, W. L., Meeker, M., & Eells, K. (1949). *Social class in America.* Chicago: Science Research Associates.

Weed, N. C., Butcher, J. N., McKenna, T., & Ben-Porath, Y. S. (1992). New measures for assessing alcohol and drug abuse with the MMPI-2: The APS and AAS. *Journal of Personality Assessment, 58,* 389–404.

Welsh, G. S. (1956). Factor dimensions A and R. In G. S. Welsh & W. G. Dahlstrom (Eds.), *Basic readings on the MMPI in psychology and medicine* (pp. 264–281). Minneapolis: University of Minnesota Press.

Wiener, D. N. (1948). Subtle and obvious keys for the MMPI. *Journal of Consulting Psychology, 12,* 164–170.

Wiener, D. N., & Harmon, L. R. (1946). *Subtle and obvious keys for the MMPI: Their development.* (Advisement Bulletin No. 16). Minneapolis: Regional Veterans Administration Office.

Wiggins, J. S. (1959). Interrelationships among MMPI measures of dissimulation under standard and social desirability instructions. *Journal of Consulting Psychology, 23,* 419–427.

Wiggins, J. S. (1964). Convergences among stylistic response measures from objective personality tests. *Educational and Psychological Measurement, 24,* 551–562.

Wiggins, J. S. (1966). Substantive dimensions of self-report in the MMPI item pool. *Psychological Monographs, 80* (22, Whole No. 630), 1–42.

Wiggins, J. S. (1973). *Personality and prediction: Principles of personality assessment.* Reading, MA: Addison-Wesley.

Wong, M. R. (1984). MMPI Scale Five: Its meaning, or lack thereof. *Journal of Personality Assessment, 48,* 279–284.

Wood, J. M., & Lilienfeld, S. O. (1999). The Rorschach Inkblot Test: A case of overstatement? *Assessment, 6,* 341–351.

Woodworth, R. S. (1920). *Personal Data Sheet.* Chicago: Stoelting.

Yehuda, R., & McFarlane, A. C. (1995). Conflict between current knowledge about post-traumatic stress disorder and its original conceptual basis. *American Journal of Psychiatry, 152,* 1705–1713.

Young, A. (1995). *The harmony of illusions: Inventing post-traumatic stress disorder.* Princeton, NJ: Princeton University Press.

Zalewski, C. E., & Gottesman, I. I. (1991). (Hu)man versus mean revisited: MMPI group data and psychiatric diagnosis. *Journal of Abnormal Psychology, 100,* 562–568.

Annotated Bibliography

MANUAL AND RELATED DOCUMENTS

Butcher, J. N., Dahlstrom, W. G., Graham, J. R., Tellegen, A., & Kaemmer, B. (1989). *MMPI-2: Manual of administration and scoring.* Minneapolis: University of Minnesota Press.

The most basic reference for the MMPI-2, the Manual *introduces the test and its uses and provides information on development and standardization, norms, item characteristics, reliability and validity, and interpretation. It provides a description of most scales discussed in this book, including item composition and scoring criteria. Extensive tables are given, including tables for translating MMPI into MMPI-2 item numbers, and vice versa. A new edition is expected to be published in 2001.*

Butcher, J. N., Graham, J. R., Williams, C. L., & Ben-Porath, Y. S. (1990). *Development and use of the MMPI-2 content scales.* Minneapolis: University of Minnesota Press.

Ben-Porath, Y. S., & Sherwood, N. E. (1993). *The MMPI-2 content component scales: Development, psychometric characteristics and clinical application.* Minneapolis: University of Minnesota Press.

These references are essentially supplements to the Manual *and provide extensive information about the content and content component scales, including interpretive examples.*

Harkness, A. R., & McNulty, J. L. (1994). The personality psychopathology Five (PSY-5): Issue from the pages of a diagnostic manual instead of a dictionary. In S. Strack & M. Lorr (Eds.), *Differentiating normal and abnormal personality.* New York: Springer.

Harkness, A. R., McNulty, J. L., & Ben-Porath, Y. S. (1995). The Personality Psychopathology Five (PSY-5): Constructs and MMPI-2 scales. *Psychological Assessment, 7,* 104–114.

Basic references on the PSY-5 scales, now somewhat dated, including a new and promising method for scale development, replicated rational selection.

FUNDAMENTAL ARCHIVAL SOURCES

Butcher, J. N. (Ed.). (2000). *Basic sources on the MMPI-2.* Minneapolis: University of Minnesota Press.

Dahlstrom, W. G., & Dahlstrom, L. E. (Eds.). (1980). *Basic readings on the MMPI*. Minneapolis: University of Minnesota Press.

Dahlstrom, W. G., Welsh, G. S., & Dahlstrom, L. E. (1972). *An MMPI handbook: Vol. I. Clinical interpretation* (rev. ed.). Minneapolis: University of Minnesota Press.

Dahlstrom, W. G., Welsh, G. S., & Dahlstrom, L. E. (1975). *An MMPI handbook: Vol. II. Research applications* (rev. ed.). Minneapolis: University of Minnesota Press.

Welsh, G. S., & Dahlstrom, W. G. (Eds.). (1956). *Basic readings on the MMPI in psychology and medicine*. Minneapolis: University of Minnesota Press.

The most important of the archival documents for the MMPI/MMPI-2, written or edited from the standpoint of Dahlstrom's encyclopedic knowledge of the MMPI. Dahlstrom and Dahlstrom (1980) partially overlaps and updates Welsh and Dahlstrom (1956), and these have now in turn been updated by Butcher (2000). All three contain all of the standard validity and clinical scale development articles of Hathaway, McKinley, and Meehl. Welsh and Dahlstrom (1956) contains numerous examples of scale development. Volume II of the Handbook *contains extensive appendices detailing issues not covered in the MMPI-2* Manual, *including item structure and ambiguity, scoring criteria for 454 research scales, and an exhaustive list of more than 6,000 references.*

Hathaway, S. R., & Meehl, P. E. (1951). *An atlas for the clinical use of the MMPI*. Minneapolis: University of Minnesota Press.

Invaluable. "The Atlas was compiled to provide a reference book that might serve to recall similar cases from the user's own experience by a kind of 'consultive' looking up of cases with MMPI patterns similar to the one being considered" (p. iii). Contains more than 900 case histories, arranged by code pattern and cross-indexed. Out of print but used copies may still be found.

Marks, P. A., & Seeman, W. (1963). *The actuarial description of abnormal personality: An atlas for use with the MMPI*. Baltimore: Williams & Wilkins.

Gilberstadt, H., & Duker, J. (1965). *A handbook for clinical and actuarial MMPI interpretation*. Philadelphia: Saunders.

These actuarial "cookbooks" are longer out of print than they are out of date. Both remain excellent sources for acquiring a feel for MMPI/MMPI-2 profile patterns.

Meehl, P. E. (1945). The dynamics of "structured" personality tests. *Journal of Clinical Psychology, 1,* 296–304.

Butcher, J. N. (2000). Dynamics of personality test responses: The empiricist's manifesto revisited. *Journal of Clinical Psychology, 56,* 375–386.

Meehl's spirited defense of the empirical approach to personality test construction remains a true classic. In the years since its publication, Meehl's regard for this approach has declined to the point that he now views his manifesto as "half-right, half-wrong." Butcher places Meehl's manifesto in the context of subsequent developments in objective personality assessment, highlighting the role of test item content, item subtlety, protocol validity, and the depth or "dynamic" attributes of objective assessment. He points out the continuing influence of the empirical approach but indicates that it may have overreached in neglecting the importance of test item content, and shows that Meehl's current view of inventory construction is in greater accord with the positions of Loevinger and Jackson. Butcher's critique of the subtle items is weakened by neglecting the distinction between convergent and discriminant validity, and by the lack of data attesting to the heritability of the subtle items at the time his appraisal was written (see DiLalla, Gottesman, Carey, & Bouchard, 1999).

CONTEMPORARY INTERPRETIVE RESOURCES

Caldwell, A. B. (1988). *MMPI supplemental scale manual.* Los Angeles: Caldwell Report.

A very efficient and perceptive discussion of supplementary scales, including the Harris and Lingoes and Obvious-Subtle subscales. Now somewhat dated, scales developed since the release of the MMPI-2 are not covered. However, a number of the scales described here but not yet approved by the publisher of the MMPI-2 (e.g., Ds, Ss, Mp, Sd) are covered.

Carson, R. C. (1969). Interpretive manual to the MMPI. In J. N. Butcher (Ed.), *MMPI research developments and clinical applications* (pp. 279–296). New York: McGraw-Hill.

One of the earlier of the informal brief interpretive guides to scale and profile interpretation, written from a Sullivanian point of view. It remains one of the best.

Graham, J. R., Ben-Porath, Y. S., & McNulty, J. L. (1999). *MMPI-2 correlates for outpatient mental health settings.* Minneapolis: University of Minnesota Press.

The newest of the actuarial guidebooks provides empirical correlates for almost all of the approved scales (excluding validity scales) as well as for many two- and three-point codetypes. The text comprises only a sixth of the whole, and the remaining tabular appendices, the most clinically useful since Marks and Seeman (1963), will keep treasure hunters busy for years.

Greene, R. L. (Ed.). (1988). *The MMPI: Use with specific populations.* San Antonio: Grune & Stratton.

A dated but still useful set of detailed reviews of the MMPI and chronic pain, schizophrenia, mood disorders, personality disorders, substance abuse, and other groups.

Greene, R. L., & Nichols, D. S. (1995). *MMPI-2 structural summary* [Computer software]. Odessa, FL: Psychological Assessment Resources.

Nichols, D. S., & Greene, R. L. (1995). *MMPI-2 structural summary: Interpretive manual.* Odessa, FL: Psychological Assessment Resources.

The MMPI-2 Structural Summary is a content-driven approach to the organization and interpretation of MMPI-2 data. Scales from all groups (e.g., clinical, content, supplementary, subscales, etc.) are rearranged and gathered under standard clinical rubrics of mood, cognition, defenses, and interpersonal relations. The ability to view under a given symptom or trait the scores of scales having overlapping clinical implications for describing it may lead to more precise description and prediction.

Greene, R. L. (2000). *The MMPI-2: An interpretive manual* (2nd ed.). Boston: Allyn & Bacon.

Friedman, A. F., Lewak, R., Nichols, D. S., & Webb, J. T. (2001). *Psychological assessment with the MMPI-2.* Mahwah, NJ: Erlbaum.

The most comprehensive of the general guides and manuals for using the MMPI-2. The two contrasting approaches complement each other well. Both are clinically sophisticated. Greene (2000) is scholarly and reliable, with profuse and informative tabular material. Friedman and colleagues (2001) is less formal but more clinically focused, and contains scoring information for all of the scales discussed in this book.

Nichols, D. S., & Greene, R. L. (1997). Dimensions of deception in personality assessment: The example of the MMPI-2. *Journal of Personality Assessment, 68,* 251–266.

An exhaustive, conceptually based treatment of various response styles and strategies and the means for their detection in the MMPI-2; highlights important distinctions in the assessment of protocol validity and accuracy.

THE MMPI/MMPI-2 AND TREATMENT

Lewak, R. W., Marks, P. A., & Nelson, G. E. (1990). *Therapist guide to the MMPI and MMPI-2: Providing feedback and treatment.* Muncie, IN: Accelerated Development.

Butcher, J. N. (1990). *Use of the MMPI-2 in treatment planning.* New York: Oxford University Press.

Finn, S. E. (1995). *Using the MMPI-2 as a therapeutic intervention.* Minneapolis: University of Minnesota Press.

These books address the use of the MMPI-2 in feedback and treatment. Lewak and colleagues (1990) is the most optimistic and extensive with respect to profile patterns, and draws extensively from Caldwell's interpretive approach; it is also the most speculative. Butcher (1990) is more cautious and relies more heavily on the empirical literature. Finn (1995) outlines a novel approach to using test feedback to achieve therapeutic goals.

CRITIQUES AND CONTROVERSIAL ISSUES

Caldwell, A. B. (1997). Whither goest our redoubtable mentor, the MMPI/MMPI-2? *Journal of Personality Assessment, 68,* 47–68.

A sophisticated discussion of several controversial issues raised by the transition from the MMPI to the MMPI-2, and an anticipation of future trends and applications.

Gottesman, I. I., & Prescott, C. A. (1989). Abuses of the MacAndrew MMPI Alcoholism Scale: A critical review. *Clinical Psychology Review, 9,* 223–242.

Focusing on the effects of differences in base rates on the validity of predictions from MacAndrew scores, the lessons of this article should be widely applied to interpretive strategy and practices.

Helmes, E., & Reddon, J. R. (1993). A perspective on developments in assessing psychopathology: A critical review of the MMPI and MMPI-2. *Psychological Bulletin, 113,* 453–471.

A flawed but serious and sophisticated critique of the MMPI/MMPI-2 by students of Douglas N. Jackson. The MMPI/MMPI-2 is implicitly and invidiously contrasted with the substantive approach to personality inventory construction championed by Jackson. Some of their criticisms are important and telling; others are simply mistaken. However, this remains the best available critical review of the inventory.

Hollrah, J. L., Schlottmann, R. S., Scott, A. B., & Brunetti, D. G. (1995). Validity of the MMPI subtle items. *Journal of Personality Assessment, 65,* 278–299.

Easily the most competent and well organized review of this controversial topic in the literature.

Index

Acknowledgments

This book owes much to my mentors in the MMPI/MMPI-2 over the past 30 years, including Jim Butcher, Alex Caldwell, Bob Carson, Bob Colligan, Grant and Leona Dahlstrom, Joe Finney, Irv Gottesman, Jack Graham, Roger Greene, Phil Marks, Paul Meehl, George Ritz, and Auke Tellegen. All have enriched my view of this instrument, and none will be fully pleased with the presentation I give here. Nevertheless, they all have my sincere gratitude for their efforts in trying to educate me. I am even more indebted to those I cannot acknowledge by name, the patients whose lives touched mine in the course of my work at Oregon State Hospital, who completed the MMPI/MMPI-2 and sat with me and taught me, about themselves and about this test. I gratefully acknowledge the specific contributions of Roger Greene, my research partner of twenty years, who provided the zero-order correlations that occur throughout the book, and of Alex Caldwell, who provided the data from 52,543 psychiatric patients on which these correlations are drawn. Whatever elements of this book will be lucky enough to stand the test of time can be traced to the labor and devotion of these two dear friends.

Early drafts of Chapters 1 and 6 benefited greatly from both stylistic and substantive review by Jane Rosen who, beset by a crush of obligations to family, graduate school, and work, nevertheless undertook this generous act of friendship.

My heartfelt thanks are also due to Tracey Belmont, my terrific editor at John Wiley & Sons. Her soft touch, encouragement, flexibility, and patience kept me going when my will and confidence flagged, and her dedication to improving my prose at every turn made this a far better book than it would otherwise have been. Both I and the reader are much in her debt.

About the Author

David S. Nichols, PhD, is recently retired from Oregon State Hospital—Portland (formerly Dammasch State Hospital), where he worked as a staff clinical psychologist for 27 years. He continues as Adjunct Professor at the School of Professional Psychology at Pacific University, in Forest Grove, Oregon. He is a Diplomate of the American Board of Assessment Psychology and a Fellow of the Society for Personality Assessment. He serves as a consulting editor for *Assessment*, and for the *Journal of Personality As-*

sessment. He is a self-described MMPI/MMPI-2 hobbyist and has done research and writing on this topic for the past 25 years. The author of some 30 reviews, articles, chapters, and monographs, he has presented numerous lectures and workshops on introductory and advanced interpretation around the country and internationally. He is co-author, with Roger L. Greene, of the *MMPI-2 Structural Summary* (1995) and, with Alan F. Friedman, Richard Lewak, and James T. Webb, of *Psychological Assessment with the MMPI-2* (2001).